The Evaluation of Instruction

Symposium Participants

Chairman, M. C. Wittrock

Presenting Major Papers	*Presenting Discussants' Papers*	*Discussants*
Marvin Alkin	Richard Anderson	Alexander Astin
Benjamin Bloom	Paul Blommers	Norma Feshbach
Robert Gagné	John Bormuth	John Goodlad
Robert Glaser	Leonard Cahen	Margaret Harris
Dan Lortie	N. L. Gage	Margaret H. Jones
Samuel Messick	Gene Glass	Evan Keislar
Martin Trow	C. Wayne Gordon	Erick Lindman
David E. Wiley	J. P. Guilford	Fred McDonald
	Chester Harris	John McNeil
	Marvin Hoffenberg	C. Robert Pace
	Theodore Husek	W. James Popham
	Eugene Litwak	Richard Schutz
	Arthur Lumsdaine	Rodney Skager
	David Nasatir	Louise Tyler
	Leo Postman	
	Michael Scriven	
	Robert Stake	

The Evaluation of Instruction

Issues and Problems

Edited by

M. C. WITTROCK
University of Illinois

and

DAVID E. WILEY
University of Chicago

HOLT, RINEHART AND WINSTON, INC.
New York   Chicago   San Francisco   Atlanta   Dallas
Montreal   Toronto   London   Sydney

All materials in Chapter 2 through and including Chapter 9, except
the open discussions, were sponsored in part by funds from the U.S. Office of
Education, and are in the public domain and not subject to the above copyright.

The preparation of this entire volume was also sponsored by
The Ford Foundation's Fund for the Advancement of Education.

To Nancy Wittrock and Marty Wiley

Preface

The symposium reported in this book brings new approaches to old problems and issues of evaluating instruction. For many years evaluation studies have produced data useful for making decisions about curricula and instruction. However, comprehensive new conceptual approaches to problems of evaluating curricula and instruction are needed to understand better the complexities of instruction and teaching.

The book also offers a new role in educational research for evaluation studies. In the past, evaluation studies have not often been part of instructional research designed to contribute to knowledge and judgments about teaching and learning. If evaluational studies are to contribute further knowledge about instruction, we believe that new research approaches and designs are needed.

This book is dedicated to producing these new conceptual and research approaches to evaluation. The papers and discussions reported in this volume are not the first recent attempts to bring new approaches to the study of evaluation. In the 1950s massive curriculum projects arose after the dramatic Soviet achievements in space. With the creation of new curricula, it became clear that new and more comprehensive ways had to be found to judge and to understand curricula and instruction and their effects upon individuals.

Many of the people who designed new curricula felt that the way to make judgments and decisions about curricula and instruction was to evaluate the adequacy and scope of their content. People with experience in programmed instruction often felt that evaluation must be behavioral, comparative, and must show evidence of student learning. People from a measurement tradition were usually concerned with the psychometric adequacy of the achievement instruments for measuring individual differences in achievement.

More recently others began to emphasize more comprehensive approaches appropriate to the complexity of the problems and purposes of evaluation. The earliest products of this rethinking were Cronbach's (1963) paper, the original draft of Scriven's (1967) paper, and several of Bloom's papers. Later, we began to emphasize the role evaluation studies could play in instructional research, where naturalistic data have not often contributed to theory and to knowledge about teaching and learning. We began to pursue new research approaches to evaluation.

With those events in mind, M. C. Wittrock arranged the symposium whose proceedings are reported in this volume. The symposium, sponsored by the UCLA Research and Development Center for the Study of Evaluation and by The Ford Foundation's Fund for the Advancement of Education, was held on the UCLA campus December 13–15, 1967.

Eight individuals were invited to give papers in the five areas we felt were the fundamental components of a comprehensive approach to evaluation: theory of evaluation, instructional variables, contextual variables, criteria of instruction, and methodology of evaluation. Two or more people gave prepared reactions after each of the eight papers. A general discussion concluded each of the eight sessions.

All of these components mentioned above are reported in this volume. In addition, a conference dinner was held on the second evening of the three-day conference and the discussion that followed it is reported at the end of the book, prior to the appendix. Along with the conference proceedings, several additional papers and prepared discussions are reported here to complete the conceptual theme of the volume. The rationales for these and for the organization of the conference are given in the first chapter, prepared by M. C. Wittrock, which also presents his conceptualization of evaluation.

We wish to acknowledge the help of all the people who worked with us to prepare this volume. Space permits mentioning only a few of them. Benjamin Bloom gave us ideas about the conference and the volume. The staff of the Center for Advanced Study in the Behavioral Sciences at Stanford, California, and the staff of the UCLA Research and Development Center on Evaluation contributed their time and effort extensively to the conference and to the preparation of the manuscript.

Elizabeth Holstein Delgass helped with the editing of the manuscripts, and Nancy Wittrock proofread manuscripts in all phases of their development.

We are grateful to The Ford Foundation and to its staff, especially Marjorie Martus and Ed Meade, for their help and support in the preparation of this volume.

We have voluntarily decided not to accept any royalties from the publication of this book, and we thank our publishers, Holt, Rinehart and Winston, for agreeing to reduce the purchase price in lieu of remitting royalties to us. We hope this decision of ours furthers distribution of *The Evaluation of Instruction* and results in communicating ideas to many people and in reconceptualizing issues in evaluation.

M. C. Wittrock
David E. Wiley

June 1970

Contents

PART I

Introduction

CHAPTER 1

The Evaluation of Instruction: Cause-and-Effect Relations in Naturalistic Data

M. C. WITTROCK

The evaluation of instruction has unique purposes and problems. They differ from the purposes and problems of evaluating environments of learning, learners, or learning.

The purposes of evaluating instruction are to make judgments and decisions about instruction and instructional programs. To make these judgments and decisions from the data of empirical evaluation studies involves new and comprehensive problems.

One of these problems is that the data of evaluation studies and our quantitative methods for analyzing them should enable us to measure the cause-and-effect relations existing among individuals, instructional environments, and learning. We need data and procedures to estimate the relationships between the naturalistic environments of learning and the learner's intellectual and social processes, on the causal side, and the learning, on the effect side. That is, in evaluating instruction we are usually trying to estimate cause-and-effect relations in nonexperimental data to make judgments and decisions about the instruction. This problem in educational evaluation warrants new conceptual approaches towards its understanding and solution.

This volume is devoted to developing new approaches to problems of evaluating instruction. In this introductory chapter I will outline one such approach. It is the approach to evaluating instruction that underlies the organization of this volume, the organization of the symposium from which this volume grew, and the organization of the UCLA Center for the Study of Evaluation, as I conceived it in the original proposal that established the Center.

In the approach described below I maintain that to evaluate instruction one must first measure at least three parts of instruction: (1) the environments of learning, (2) the intellectual and social processes of learners, and (3) the learning. Second, to evaluate instruction the relationships among these three parts of instruction must then be quantitatively estimated. New quantitative methods developed in statistics, econometrics, sociology, political science, and psychology are described for estimating cause-and-effect relations in nonexperimental data, although more conventional techniques of multiple regression might also serve our purposes.

In the approach described below I have also tried to show how differential and experimental psychologies can contribute to evaluating instruction. The approach is an example, I believe, of a rapprochement between differential and experimental psychologies, which Lee Cronbach has been advocating for years (Cronbach, 1957).

If it proves successful, the emerging rapprochement would diminish some venerable dichotomies we overlearned in graduate school. Theory could be tested in natural settings, not only in laboratories. Cause-and-effect relations could be estimated in the nonexperimental data of evaluation studies, not only in experimental data. Differential and experimental psychologies could complement each other, not combat each other.

The next part of this chapter introduces the approach underlying the organization of this volume and, consequently, many of the major issues discussed in greater detail in the following chapters. I will begin with the purposes of evaluation, then turn to the approach itself, and conclude the chapter with an introduction to the remaining chapters of this volume.

PURPOSES AND PROBLEMS OF EVALUATING INSTRUCTION

One purpose of evaluating instruction is to make decisions about it. Teachers, administrators, and evaluators make decisions about instruction and about the causes of learning. Their decisions involve the following types of questions. "What were the important effects of the assignments, curricula, and experiences upon learners of different abilities and interests? In the future, what are the results of similar instructional experiences for different learners likely to be?" To answer these types of questions, data about the cause-and-effect relations existing among learners, their environments, and learning are needed by teachers, administrators, and evaluators.

A second purpose for evaluating instruction is to make judgments about it. Educational researchers try to understand instruction, to make generalizations about it and about the cause-and-effect relations within it. Experiments and descriptive research studies are two commonly used methods for understanding instruction; but evaluation studies could also contribute to the purpose of understanding and judging instruction, if we could put together the proper conceptual and methodological tools.

Unfortunately, with the difficult decisions and judgments to be made about instruction, teachers, administrators, evaluators, and researchers have been only modestly helped by the data and methods of many evaluation studies. One reason for this lack of help is that these data and methods were designed to evaluate learners, learning, or learning environments, but not for the more comprehensive problems of relating the learner's interactions with his environment to his learning.

A second reason why some of the previous approaches to evaluation have been only modestly helpful when applied to the comprehensive problems of evaluating instruction is that they have been extrapolated far from their origins in differential psychology or experimental psychology. In these areas there has been experience with only parts of the problems of evaluating instruction.

In differential psychology the central problem is the measurement of individual differences including the writing of tests that, above all, measure differences among people. When these methods are applied to evaluating instruction the central concern remains the measurement of individual differences among learners, not the measurement of the cause-and-effect relations among learners, instructional environments, and learning.

As a result, when teachers and administrators try to evaluate instruction with standardized tests of student achievement, they find themselves struggling with the properties of the normal curve. They find themselves unable to state what their students know or what they have learned, in an absolute sense. Although they can tell how their students perform relative to other students, the teachers and administrators are not helped very much by data about differences in students' achievement to know how their students' behavior has been changed, much less to know what causal role instruction has played in determining student learning.

The methods of experimental psychology were also designed for somewhat different problems. Although experimentation is designed to determine probable causes of learning, it is not often realistic to use experiments in evaluation studies. An experiment involves treatments each applied uniformly to two or more students. It is obviously not often useful to solve the common problems of teachers and administrators, who want to evaluate the day-to-day teaching and instruction occurring in the natural contexts of their schools without resorting to techniques of random assignments and manipulated treatments.

From the above discussion, I conclude that teachers, administrators, evaluators, and researchers are interested, albeit for different reasons, in evaluating the cause-and-effect relations in instruction occurring in non-experimental settings to make decisions and judgments about the instruction. For years, sociologists, political scientists, econometricians, and statisticians have been developing quantitative methods for estimating cause-and-effect relations in nonexperimental data. Now that these methods are being used with some success in these fields, it seems time to apply them to educational problems such as evaluation of instruction, which involves estimating these types of relations in naturalistic data.

AN APPROACH TOWARD EVALUATING INSTRUCTION: CAUSE-AND-EFFECT RELATIONS IN EVALUATION

The next part of this chapter is devoted to synthesizing the elements of one approach towards evaluating instruction. This approach incorporates three earlier approaches to evaluation and a quantitative viewpoint useful in estimating cause-and-effect relations. The last four articles of this volume are reprints from statistics, sociology, and psychology which will help to provide some of the details of this approach too complex to treat in this chapter.

To introduce my approach to empirical evaluation studies, which I will call "cause-and-effect evaluation," I must first make a distinction among conceptual approaches to evaluation by the variables and behavior they make explicit. Although explicitness is not the only basis for differentiating among approaches to evaluation, it is the best one for my purposes. Explicitness of the variables and behavior distinguishes formal from informal evaluation, and it distinguishes my approach from the other approaches discussed in this chapter.

Informal Evaluations

We informally evaluate when we judge the worth of our own surroundings, our behavior, change in our behavior, and events in our lives. Informal evaluations are judgments that do not necessarily involve an explicit statement of their bases, values, experiences, variables, and data.

For example, in our daily lives we informally evaluate our environment when we say that something, such as a course in mathematics, is good. We informally evaluate our behavior when we say that we are proficient at something, for example, differential calculus; and we informally evaluate learning when we say that we are more proficient at differential calculus today than we were yesterday. Finally, we informally evaluate instruction when we say that listening to a lecture about limits and functions helped us to become more proficient at calculus than we were yesterday.

These four examples are evaluations in the informal sense of the word. They are statements only of our decisions and our judgments, not of our values, experiences, nor the data basic to these decisions or judgments. In informal evaluations, our bases for making evaluation—our values, data, experience, theory, and knowledge—need not be made explicit. It is enough that the judgment is made explicit. We assume that careful and intelligent, informal evaluations will be based upon experience, values, and knowledge.

Formal Evaluations

In a formal evaluation, the judgments and decisions are again made explicit. However, we also require explicit statements and objective measures of the bases of the evaluations. In an evaluation study, the selection and objective measurement of the bases of the judgments and the decisions are the focus of most of our time and effort. Making explicit and measuring the bases of our judgments are central to the empirical study of evaluation of instruction.

THE EVALUATION OF ENVIRONMENTS, LEARNERS, AND LEARNING

Now I want to discuss three of the four fundamental parts of my conceptualization of evaluation of instruction. Each of these three parts has served as a conceptualization of evaluation in its own right, and I will refer to the three components as separate conceptual approaches to evaluation. A comprehensive evaluation of instruction involves relating all three components to one another to obtain cause-and-effect relations from non-experimental data.

First, if one wishes to evaluate a given course of instruction he might look at characteristics of the instructional environment provided in the course, for example, the amount of time devoted to learning or the textbook used in the course. He might look also at the sequence of instruction, characteristics of the curriculum, of the classroom, of the school library, and of the training of the teacher of the course. In short, he would focus the study upon qualities of the student's environment; he would make them explicit and he would make decisions about them. This type of formal evaluation, which I will call *evaluation of environments,* is still commonly used in schools by teachers and administrators. It will be discussed in more detail, after other types of formal evaluations are introduced.

A second way to evaluate instruction is to make explicit the students' abilities, interests, and achievements to determine their performance at the end of the instruction, usually by determining their relative standing in a group. I will call this type of study *evaluation of learners.* It is usually accomplished by measuring individual differences among students. It is a popular way for professional evaluators to evaluate curricula.

Third, one might make explicit the changes in students' behavior to try to determine what had been learned during instruction. I will call this type of study *evaluation of learning* or evaluation of relatively permanent change in behavior occurring as a result of experience. This is a relatively new approach to evaluation that is a by-product of research in learning.

Fourth and last, one might measure learning (as in the third approach mentioned above), quantify several of the learners' intellectual and social characteristics (as in two above), and also measure several of the environmental characteristics (as in the first approach above), and then try to relate the interactions of these learner and environmental characteristics to student learning. This new, uncommon, and complicated type of evaluation, I will call *evaluation of instruction.* Now that multivariate statistical procedures are becoming available for estimating the cause-and-effect relations in evaluation studies, this approach is feasible.

Fundamental to the above distinction among approaches to evaluation is the making explicit and quantifying of the bases for decisions and judgments about instruction. The act of judging or of deciding the merits of instruction is also part of evaluation, but it is not the focus of our interests here.

In elaborating the conceptual approach mentioned above, I will deliberately avoid giving examples of evaluation studies that fall into each category. My purpose in omitting examples of past work is to focus upon a new approach and to avoid implying criticism of evaluation studies quite adequately designed for their intended purposes.

The Evaluation of Environments

When our evaluation study concentrates on making explicit the physical and the human characteristics of the learners' environments, we are evaluating environments. Counting the number of books in libraries, hours spent in instruction in the classroom, school budget per pupil, intellectual merit of the teachers, college credits of a teacher in his major, or even the number of homework problems assigned to the class are examples that measure environmental characteristics commonly used by teachers and administrators to index learning.

That there may be more meaningful environmental characteristics is not the issue here. Library books and dollars invested in pupils are important to learning; but the nature and extent of the relationships among the environments, learners, and learning cannot be studied by making explicit and measuring only environmental characteristics. Obviously, measures of environmental characteristics alone are not sufficient to enable one to make objective inferences about their effects upon learners. Measures of intellectual and social processes in learners, which greatly influence the outcomes of learning, are needed, as are measures of learning.

The evaluation of student environments alone, as described above, would be a futile approach toward the evaluation of instruction. It is not well regarded among researchers in evaluation as an approach toward evaluation.

However, characteristics of instructional environments should be made explicit in evaluation studies. The teacher's primary function is to provide environments best suited to the learner to enhance his learning and development as an individual. To do this a teacher obviously must make decisions and inferences about the educational value of environments and their probable effects upon individuals. He needs to characterize and describe those crucial qualities of environments he can manipulate; but he also needs to be able to relate them objectively to individual learners and to change in the behavior of learners. The first element of my approach to evaluating instruction has now been identified.

The Evaluation of Learners

When an evaluation study focuses upon making explicit the behavior and characteristics of learners, the term *evaluation of learners,* usually of individual differences among students, describes the procedure adequately. Many recent evaluation studies fit well into this group. Achievement tests and sometimes ability tests are the instruments often used to evaluate individual differences in student behavior for selection and placement of learners.

This prevalent approach to evaluation has grown from the study of individual differences and its psychometric problems rather than from experimentation in human learning. For a long time some of the best work in educational evaluation has come from the study of individual differences. Probability theory, psychometrics, and differential psychology have had a substantial effect upon thinking about educational evaluation and about what should be made explicit in an evaluation study.

The student's scores on standardized tests of interests, abilities, and achievements are useful for measuring individual differences in learning to select students for more advanced study and to place them in different treatments. With these scores we can compare a student's performance to that of other students, and we can select or place students with some success in predicting their relative standing in groups. But these tests, designed to discriminate individual differences in behavior among students, do not enable us to make rigorous inferences about what the students have learned nor about the role of environments and intellectual processes in producing the learning. In short, data on the relative achievement status of children do not tell us what, how, or why students have learned, nor what the roles of antecedent learner and environmental factors are in learning.

To measure what the students have learned we need to measure changes in their behavior. To answer the questions of how and why students learn we need to quantify the salient characteristics of environments and we need to measure their relationships to intellectual and social processes, as well as to student achievement.

As a conceptualization of evaluation, the evaluation of learners is adequate for its intended purpose of obtaining data on the relative state of students' achievements, abilities, and preferences. Evaluating learners is the second essential part of my approach to evaluating instruction and its interactions with students. However, measures of individual differences among learners is only one way to measure the abilities, interests, and achievements relevant to designing and evaluating instruction for individuals. For example, to evaluate the effects of instruction designed to teach people to read French, we need to measure proactive variables, for example, how well they read French at the beginning of instruction. If all of them read no French, that is, if there are no individual differences in a test of ability to read French, we are still highly interested in their scores on this test. The basic issues are the relationships between the learner's aptitudes, achievements, and interests and the instruction, not only whether there are individual differences among the learners.

The Evaluation of Learning

One difference between measuring individual differences and evaluating the learning of individuals is that regardless of what or how well students learn, the writing of test items to discriminate among individuals does not evidence their progress directly. Common techniques of test construction and interpretation require that, regardless of how much or how little students learn, half of them are below average in achievement, most of them receive C grades, and as many of them receive D and F grades as receive B and A grades, respectively. By concentrating upon measuring differences among students, we tend to forget about the learning by individuals—that all or many of them might learn to a mastery level, an A level—if we went about our teaching discriminatively and differently for different students. Bloom (1968) has made this point quite well.

It is ironic that our quest for individual differences has led us away from individualized instruction. We would do well to design different types of instruction for each individual or for each group of individuals rather than to persist in our hunt for individual differences in achievement resulting from treatments designed for all students collectively. It would be better to vary our instruction with individuals to help them learn rather than to change the criteria until we find some, perhaps trivial, differences among their achievements. Changing the criteria of learning until, sure enough, we find some differences among individuals is an easy out. It avoids the basic issue of tailoring the instruction to the individual. In evaluating learning, the focus is upon individuals, not upon differences among individuals.

By retaining in our achievement test only the test items that on the average discriminate among students, we may be omitting content-valid items that all or nearly all students have learned to answer correctly as a result of instruction. Our prevalent habits of discarding valid but nondiscriminating items to find some ways, perhaps irrelevant, in which individuals differ in achievement skirts the main issue: What instruction is best for each individual to help him learn defined objectives and content?

These habits, involving use of the normal curve, have had a deleterious effect upon instruction and have retarded the search for improved instruction. Measures of individual differences among students' achievements are useful for evaluating instruction, but their measurement must not become the overriding objective of a study designed to evaluate learning or instruction.

Measuring change in student behavior toward behaviorally defined objectives is a relatively new approach to evaluation, involving psychometric procedures that may ignore classical wisdom. This newer approach is commonly used in the study of human learning. For example, researchers with experimental backgrounds who study instruction and curriculum usually want to evaluate the effects of instruction by using criteria and test items chosen for their content validity. These researchers are not likely to discard content-valid test items to improve the ability of the test to discriminate differences among students. Their *Zeitgeist* emphasizes selecting criteria and items first, and looking for individual differences later. To experimental researchers, to alter the criteria of learning deliberately to produce a test that will discriminate among learners is unseemly at best if one is trying to evaluate the learning.

During the last several years curriculum evaluation has increasingly become viewed as the evaluation of change in behavior toward behaviorally defined goals, as described above. Unlike the evaluation of learners, learning is evaluated by taking *two* or more measures, either one measure upon each of several different people or two or more measures upon the same people obtained at two or more different times, usually before and after instruction. We need not compute change in scores to evaluate learning.

Let us discuss this two-step process of measuring students' performance. With this model we begin our evaluation by making explicit those changes in behavior of interest to us. Other less relevant areas of behavioral change are ignored, at least for the moment.

These interesting changes of behavior must next be made explicit and defined as observable student behavior. If a student in a sixth-grade mathematics class is to learn the meaning of the Pythagorean theorem, or an appreciation of mathematics, the desired changes in his behavior are defined by writing specific behavioral objectives and then by preparing tests to measure changes in his behavior.

Next, a student's change in behavior is indexed, often by measuring the difference in his behavior on a pretest and a posttest. These before and after measures are obtained to help insure that his behavior has changed during the instruction, that is, that he did not know the meaning of the Pythagorean theorem before the instruction began but that he does know its meaning after the instruction is completed. We still cannot be certain that the instruction has been involved in his learning, but we have increased the probability that our instruction and his learning are related to each other.

Some distinctive psychometric characteristics of evaluating learning, as different from measuring individual differences, will become more apparent by discussing them a little further. The ways of choosing items differ if we want to compare learners rather than to measure changes in their behavior. To measure individual differences, test items are chosen largely by their average ability to discriminate among individuals. If nearly all or almost none of the students answer a particular item correctly, that item is not very useful for measuring individual differences among students. Its difficulty level would not be appropriate to the job of discriminating among students, the level being either too low or too high.

On the other hand, when we measure change in behavior produced by instruction, the choice of items is determined largely by their relevance to the instruction, not only by their ability to discriminate among students. To measure whether a student learned in a history class that Lincoln was President in 1861, an item that sampled that information would be included in a test of behavioral change. The fact that all or none of the students gave the right answer to it is not nearly as relevant to the measuring of learning as is the validity of the content of the item. Given a group of items, all of which met the criterion of content validity, we could, of course, then select among them those items which best discriminate differences among learners. The criteria of content validity and discrimination are not mutually exclusive.

If all the students got a valid and reliable item wrong on a posttest, the instruction, not the test, would be changed. This kind of thinking comes hard for some evaluators trained in the psychometrics of measuring individual differences.

Evaluating learning has distinctive characteristics other than its psychometric procedure. One of the more important of these characteristics is an emphasis on making explicit the behavioral objectives of the instruction. A general objective, such as "to appreciate mathematics," is an anathema. Refinement and iteration are needed to produce precisely defined, observable behaviors of students to evidence that they appreciate mathematics. Even the time limits and other conditions for the behavior need to be specified to apply this approach properly. The essence of this approach is to make explicit the changes in behavior accruing through instruction, beginning with the writing of behavioral objectives for student learning and followed by measuring changes in behavior toward these objectives.

For evaluating learning this approach has obvious advantages over the two approaches discussed above. The most important one is not the popular notion of writing behaviorally defined objectives before beginning to instruct learners; instead, it is a logical result of writing these objectives—the use of an absolute rather than a relative standard for measuring learning. The objectives lead to test items written for their content validity, not for their ability to discriminate among learners. As a result our interest shifts from individual differences to individuals. As a result of the focus on content validity, evaluators are becoming less concerned about discriminating among learners and more concerned about the individual student and his changes in behavior—his learning; and teachers are freed to conceive of mastery learning for any number of students.

Although this approach does not include explicit descriptions of educational environments or of learners, it has produced a fundamental change in our thinking about evaluation. We now think of the learning of each student, and we are less concerned about comparing him with other students.

The evaluation of learning helps us to determine what people have learned. It is the third element of my approach to evaluating instruction, and I wish to include in it changes in behavior occurring in students, teachers, and other people.

THE EVALUATION OF INSTRUCTION: CAUSE-AND-EFFECT EVALUATION

Critics of the evaluation of learning are quick to find faults in it. Some of these criticisms are justified; others are not.

If one measures only behavioral changes toward objectives, he will ignore other significant changes in students resulting from instruction. Perhaps students learn the Pythagorean theorem but in the process also learn to dislike mathematics. Since dislike for mathematics was not an objective of instruction, according to the above approach, evaluation of learning, we would not measure it. Not all important dimensions of change in student behavior can be foreseen. We should not ignore important criteria because they were not apparent nor desired before instruction began.

Changes in behavior of people other than students—teachers, parents, and so forth—are also important and should not be omitted from evaluation studies because they are different from student learning. These changes ought somehow to be incorporated into our thinking about evaluation.

Another commonly mentioned and, I believe, valid criticism is that precisely worded behavioral objectives easily tend to become narrow and trivial and to lose the essence of the instruction. In time this narrowness could be overcome by writing hierarchical sets of more specific objectives to sample more general, imprecisely worded, but significant objectives.

The three criticisms mentioned above apply to the current use of the approach called evaluation of learning, not to the approach itself, which requires neither prespecified objectives nor a limited number of narrowly defined criteria of learning. These criticisms notwithstanding, this approach is well designed to evaluate learning, and it is a significant concept in the evaluation of instruction.

A telling criticism of evaluation of learning is that it requires one to make explicit only the behaviors learned, not the characteristics of the environment of instruction, nor the intellectual and social characteristics of learners interacting with this environment, nor the characteristics of the school as a social system. The environment of instruction is made explicit only in gross and vague terms. The instructional package is viewed as an entity—a box marked "contents unknown." We call it a program, a curriculum, or a course of instruction; and we color the box black.

Explicitness is also lacking in the definition of the crucially important, antecedent intellectual and social processes of the learners and of the social characteristics of the school. The model is therefore not adequate for obtaining cause-and-effect relations about instruction from the data of evaluation studies. If one wants to evaluate instruction, a more comprehensive approach is logically more appropriate than the one described above for evaluating learning.

A comprehensive approach to evaluating instruction would require us to make explicit and to relate to each other the salient characteristics of: (1) individual learners, (2) their instructional environments, and (3) their learning, as these three exist in naturalistic settings. The concept of explicitness would then be extended to include learning, antecedent student behavior, and environmental characteristics of instruction. With the appropriate multivariate statistical tools for this approach we could estimate "cause-and-effect relations" in the naturalistic data of evaluation studies.

The remaining element of such an approach can now be sketched very briefly because three of its four components have already been introduced and discussed. The approach is based upon the assumption discussed above that formal evaluation includes making explicit the bases for decisions and judgments about relationships between learners and their environments— the same assumptions responsible for the progress attributable to evaluating learning. To evaluate instruction rather than environments, behavior, or learning involves a comprehensive approach, which makes explicit the salient characteristics of all three of the above. By making all three of these explicit, and given the multivariate statistical procedures, we should be able to relate them to each other to make conclusions and judgments about instruction not possible before.

The question is, "Do we have the fourth element to complete the approach—the methodological knowledge to estimate the cause-and-effect relations in naturalistic situations such as instruction in schools?" In 1967–1968, I was one of a group of Fellows at the Center of Advanced Study in the Behavioral Sciences at Stanford, California, that met regularly to study this question. This group found in the literature of sociology, econometrics, statistics, political science, and in the recent literature of psychology, much interest and research on this problem, ranging from attempts by political scientists to explain the causes of role-call votes of legislators to explanations by sociologists of the causes of IQ. Some of the better papers on this subject are cited below.

An excellent discussion of the general problem of obtaining causal inferences in nonexperimental research is in a book by Blalock (1964) and, from a different point of view, in one by Simon (1957). Hayward Alker, a political scientist, has many papers on causal relationships in analyses of nonexperimental data, but two are of special interest to evaluators (Alker, 1966; and Alker, 1967).

Because the methodology of obtaining causal relations from nonexperimental data is of obvious relevance to evaluating instruction, four articles on this subject are reprinted in the appendix of this volume. The first two articles (Wold, 1956, and Wold, 1963) introduce the basic concepts and limitations of these approaches; the third paper (Duncan, 1966) discusses path analysis as used in sociology; and of the currently available articles the fourth paper (Yee and Gage, 1968) is most relevant to the problems of evaluating instruction. Space permits reprinting only those four references. Also of interest are papers by Boudon (1965), Goldberg (1966), Simon and Rescher (1966), and the earlier work by Lazarsfeld (1954), Kempthorne (1954) and, of course, by Sewall Wright (1934).

The above mentioned approaches to causal explanations from nonexperimental data are too complex to discuss in detail in this chapter. The article by Duncan (1966), reproduced in the appendix, explains one approach, path analysis, pioneered by Sewall Wright with potential for educational evaluation and for educational research. By using path analysis one can compute path coefficients for each chain or network of variables that he hypothesizes to be influencing one another in a causal way. The path coefficients, each representing a different prediction from a different theory, provide one empirical way to compare theoretical predictions about causation in nonexperimental data. Path coefficients do not "prove" causation (neither does anything else), but they can help to reduce the error variance in our statements about causes and effects.

These comments about methodological analyses complete my introduction of an approach to the evaluation of instruction. If the approach proves useful in evaluation research, we should be able to relate learning to the environments and individuals "causing" it. We should be able to evaluate instruction rather than learners or learning. It may become possible to learn how social and other characteristics of the environments of instruction interact with students to mediate changes in their behavior. At the

UCLA Research and Development Center on Evaluation work is currently in progress on applying this approach to evaluating instruction.

In summary, I view the study of evaluation of instruction to be the study of the relationships between naturalistic learning environments and learners, on the one hand, and the criteria of learning on the other. From my point of view, evaluation studies should contribute not only to decisions about the specific instruction measured in each study but also to judgments, knowledge, and understanding of teaching and instruction. For too long we have compartmentalized theory and laboratory research from practice and naturalistic research. Because we now have useful methodological tools, in evaluation studies we should try to examine the cause-and-effect relations in instruction in schools, and we should try to obtain estimates of the probability of our explanations being wrong. My approach brings together experimental psychologists, differential psychologists, sociologists, and statisticians to work on a significant problem of common interest—the evaluation of instruction.

Cause-and-effect evaluation is obviously in its infancy. It is too early to know its usefulness and its limitations. It does offer the hope of reducing the error variance in quantifying and explicating some of the relations that exist in instruction. This approach should enable us to analyze teaching and instruction, to study theoretical and practical issues in naturalistic settings, and to evaluate instruction.

If it does none of these things well, I hope it will yet have emphasized the underlying purpose for developing it. That purpose is to find new and comprehensive approaches to studying problems of education. These approaches must go beyond our habits of routinely applying disciplines or methods to problems of education when intellectual effort at the conceptual level is needed before these applications and extrapolations can have much meaning. Without implying that education is a discipline, we can be disciplined in our study of its problems; and we need to devise comprehensive research approaches appropriate to studying its complex problems.

AN OUTLINE OF THE VOLUME

Following the conceptual approach sketched above, the symposium and this volume are divided into five major sections to include respectively: (1) theories of evaluation, (2) instructional (environmental) variables, (3) individual and social (learner) variables, (4) criteria in evaluation studies, and (5) methodology of evaluation. Speakers and discussants were invited to the symposium to talk about the fundamental problems of each respective area. Consistent with the approach described above, these people represented different theoretical interests and intellectual backgrounds, including experimental psychology, differential psychology, sociology, and measurement and statistics.

In outline form, the five sections of the symposium were composed as follows. In the first area, theory of evaluation, the two speakers, Benjamin Bloom and Robert Glaser, provide new perspectives on evaluation.

Bloom develops a creative synthesis of measurement, evaluation, and assessment, which changes former perspectives of evaluation. He begins with the problems and approaches characteristic of studies in evaluation, measurement, and assessment. From these he builds a comprehensive, theoretical approach to evaluation, which is not dependent upon any one model of human learning. His paper deserves careful study. Reading it is a rewarding experience for someone interested in evaluation and willing to consider the problems of evaluation in relation to the problems of measurement and assessment.

In a subtle way, Bloom's paper influences all of the open discussions of the conference. He and David Wiley, later in the symposium, raise the basic issue of the importance of developing theory of evaluation from its problems. Not all the symposiasts are inclined to think with Bloom, Wiley, Stake, and myself that theory should be developed from the data of evaluation studies. Gene Glass, Michael Scriven, and J. P. Guilford discuss Bloom's paper.

Robert Glaser shows that a model of learning has direct implications for evaluation and that one can use a theory of learning to devise his methods of evaluation. With this approach one need not develop a theory of evaluation; ways of evaluating students follow from learning theory. He demonstrates that psychometric approaches commonly used in studies of evaluation are not always appropriate for the problems of evaluating the effects of programs of instruction. The psychometric procedures, popular in studies of evaluation, are better adapted to their original purpose of differentiating among students, regardless of the content validity of the items and tests used to quantify student interest and achievement. Robert Stake and Arthur Lumsdaine discuss Glaser's paper.

In the second section of the volume, instructional variables, Robert Gagné articulately shows how the evaluation of learning involves procedures uncommon among psychometricians and evaluators who have for many years emphasized measuring individual differences among students. Evaluation is different from the selection of test items that will discriminate among individuals. Gagné convincingly argues that evaluation of learning involves the quantification of behavioral change on items selected because they measure knowledge important to the teacher, not because they discriminate among the learners. He argues that a two-step process of measuring learning is necessary to provide evidence that the learning occurred in the environment designed to produce it and that the learner possessed the knowledge and skill prerequisite to the learning task. Leo Postman, Richard Anderson, and John Bormuth are the discussants of Gagné's paper.

The variables of learners and the social processes of schools are discussed in the third section of the volume. Dan Lortie's paper and the interesting discussions by N. L. Gage, C. Wayne Gordon, and the conferees tie the symposium's discussions of research on evaluation closely to the practical problems of schools.

Individual differences among learners and criteria for studies of evaluation are discussed in the next paper. Samuel Messick discusses cognitive style and its value as a measure in an evaluation study. His paper is relevant to both section three (learner variables) and section four (criteria). He raises the salient issue of whether, in evaluation studies, we should measure the effects of instruction upon personality variables such as cognitive style. He also raises the question of how we might use information about individuals' cognitive styles best to tailor instructional treatments to different types of individuals. The issues of the heated discussion that follow his paper continue to recur sporadically throughout the remainder of the discussions of the symposium.

The open discussions of the conference become increasingly interesting as the participants become aware of each other's positions and arguments. Paul Blommers and Leonard Cahen, the two discussants, raise issues above the threshold, and the open discussions elaborate them. The issues include whether there are interactions between instructional treatments and cognitive styles, as well as whether one should try to use measures of individual differences either as moderator variables or as criteria in an evaluation study.

Marvin Alkin's paper on cost effectiveness continues the discussion of criteria for evaluation studies. Participants were not asked to speak on commonly accepted criteria of evaluation, such as student achievement, because it seemed more productive to explore controversial yet useful criteria such as cognitive style and cost effectiveness. Alkin, and his discussants, Hoffenberg and Bormuth, add a new dimension to the symposium.

The fifth and final section of the symposium, methodology of evaluation, consists of papers by Martin Trow and David Wiley. Their papers offer different approaches to methodological problems of evaluating instruction. Trow, whose paper follows Wiley's paper, discusses problems of evaluating innovations and of putting evaluative research to the service of innovative enterprise. His paper also merits a careful reading. Litwak and Nasatir discuss Trow's paper.

Wiley holds that a model of evaluation must precede any methodology of evaluation, and that it should be logically developed from the problems of evaluation rather than from the problems of learning or those of sociologists or psychologists. He develops a model that leads to deductions related to the units to be evaluated rather than to morals and methodology. He also discusses methodological inferences of his model. His position is too complex and too pervasive to discuss adequately here; however, a few comments will help introduce his approach and several of his deductions.

Wiley makes the classroom of students, not the individual student, the unit of evaluation. This drastically alters the methods and procedures of conducting an evaluation study. Individual differences are viewed as differences among classrooms of students in specific environments. If, in a certain classroom, boys and girls differ in their ability to learn to read after they have been taught by a given method of instruction, this difference is considered a situationally bound characteristic, not necessarily a sex difference. If the sexes had been taught separately or by another method of instruction, the same group differences would not necessarily be expected to occur. The differences in reading achievement, then, are not simply of sex but are also situational. At least tentatively, one must consider the difference in ability to read to be a function of both the situation and the sex of the individual. Chester Harris and Ted Husek discuss Wiley's paper.

The volume concludes with an open discussion of evaluation that concentrates on several issues: objectives and criteria for evaluation studies, interactions between instruction and types of individuals, and theory of evaluation.

In these following chapters, the discussants express different approaches to evaluation. To some of the members of the symposium, measurement of individual differences (evaluation of learners) is the essence of evaluation. To other discussants, evaluation means writing behavioral objectives, then measuring change in students toward these precisely defined, measurable goals (evaluation of learning). To still others of us, it seems time to reconceptualize evaluation, its units, and problems, and to measure environments and individual differences as precisely as student learning. That position (evaluation of instruction) is difficult to communicate. Evaluation is "something-more-than" change toward goals. It is a way to relate characteristics of environments and people interacting with each other to build knowledge about education as well as to make decisions about curricula and learners.

As I mentioned earlier in this chapter, the underlying purpose of this volume and the symposium leading to it is to stimulate new ways to study education that emphasize conceptualizations of its basic problems and issues. If we are to make fundamental progress in education, I believe we must go beyond our habits of routinely applying disciplines and methods to the study of problems of education. These problems, such as evaluating instruction, involve intellectual effort at the conceptual level to devise comprehensive research approaches and paradigms to do justice to their complexity.

REFERENCES

Alker, H. R., Jr. Causal inference and political analysis. In J. Bernel (Ed.), *Mathematical applications in political science,* II. Dallas, Tex.: The Arnold Foundation, Southern Methodist University, 1966.

Alker, H. R., Jr. Statistics and politics: The need for causal data analysis. Paper presented at the annual meeting of the American Political Science Association, Chicago, September 1967.

Blalock, H. M., Jr. *Causal inferences in nonexperimental research.* Chapel Hill, N.C.: University of North Carolina Press, 1964.

Bloom, B. S. Learning for mastery. *Evaluation Comment,* 1968, *1,* No. 2.

Boudon, R. Methodes l'analyse causale. *Revue Francaise de Sociologie,* 1965, *6,* 24–43.

Cronbach, L. J. The two disciplines of scientific psychology. *American Psychologist,* 1957, *12,* 671–684.

Duncan, O. D. Path analysis: Sociological examples. *The American Journal of Sociology,* 1966, *72,* (1) 1–16.

Goldberg, A. S. Discerning a causal pattern among data on voting behavior. *The American Political Science Review,* 1966, *60,* 913–922.

Kempthorne, O., Bancroft, T. A., Gowen, J. M., & Lush, J. L. (Eds.) *Statistics and mathematics in biology.* Ames, Iowa: Iowa State University Press, 1954.

Lazarsfeld, P. F. (Ed.) *Mathematical thinking in the social sciences.* New York: The Free Press, 1954.

Simon, H. A. *Models of man: Social and rational.* New York: John Wiley & Sons, Inc., 1957.

Simon, H. A., & Rescher, N. Cause and counterfactual. *Philosophy of Science,* 1966, *33,* No. 4.

Wold, H. O. Causal inference from observational data: A review of ends and means. *Journal of the Royal Statistical Society (London).* Series A. (General) 1956, *119,* 28–50.

Wold, H. O. The approach of model building and the possibilities of its utilization in the human sciences. Manuscript, for Entretiens de Monaco en Sciences Humaines. (1963).

Wright, S. The method of path coefficients. *Annals of Mathematical Statistics,* 1934, *5,* 161–215.

Yee, A. H., & Gage, N. L. Techniques for estimating the source and direction of causal influence in panel data. *Psychological Bulletin,* 1968, *70,* 115–126.

PART II

Theory of Evaluation of Instruction

CHAPTER 2

Toward a Theory of Testing Which Includes Measurement-Evaluation-Assessment

BENJAMIN S. BLOOM

In the sixty years since Binet first introduced his intelligence test, testing has become the pride and despair of psychology and education. Testing runs like a powerful minor theme through most of the research and the applied work in these fields. We take pride in testing because it is the one area that has shown clearest development and most widespread use in these two fields. Our sophistication has grown rapidly in testing, and we know what we know and we know what we don't know in such clear ways that we can take advantage of the former while we attempt to reduce the latter.

But, our despair arises from the overuse of testing, its tendency to dominate both psychology and education, and the negative effect it sometimes has on human relations. Especially in education, testing is a two-edged sword that can do incalculable good as well as great harm to the individual. The recent reaction against intelligence testing in the large city schools, although emotional and in many ways misguided, brings home to us that children are judged in terms of test results and that faith in one child's ability to learn or rationalizations of a teacher's inability to teach another child are both related to test scores.

To control the matriculation examinations of a country is to control its educational system; to develop tests that are widely used for selection and prediction purposes is to determine which human qualities are prized and which are neglected; to develop instruments that are frequently used to classify and describe human beings is to alter human relations and to affect a person's view of himself.

It is no great exaggeration to compare the power of testing on human affairs with the power of atomic energy. Both are capable of great positive benefit to all of mankind and both contain equally great potential for destroying mankind. If mankind is to survive, we must continually search for the former and seek ways of controlling or limiting the latter. What is needed in testing is a clearer understanding of what we have been doing and a new synthesis of our disparate methods and concepts in testing. Perhaps I can describe a few terms necessary for such a synthesis.

What I propose to do is to describe briefly three very different approaches to the field of testing, indicate why a new synthesis of these is in order at this time, and suggest some of the directions such a new synthesis could take. I do hope that I can impress you with the great need for such a synthesis even though you may be reluctant to accept my suggestions for the synthesis.

THREE APPROACHES TO TESTING

If we view testing as a systematic method of sampling one or more human characteristics and the representation of these results for an individual in the form of a descriptive statement or classification, we can discern three very different approaches to this problem. For purposes of convenience, I will refer to these approaches as Measurement, Evaluation, and Assessment. I am sure that some of you will use other terms to describe these approaches. However, the problem is not the accuracy or meaningfulness of the terms, but how to discern the very basic differences underlying these approaches and the contrast among them in the assumptions they make about the world, about man, and about the nature of evidence.

Measurement[1]

Perhaps the first approach (historically) to testing human characteristics began with the work of Galton and Binet. Although they differed in many respects, what they had in common was the development of standard stimuli, tasks, and questions. The subject's responses to these standard situations were to be appraised in terms of speed and/or accuracy—where accuracy was to be judged in a standard way—by all trained testers. The results for each examinee were translated into some quantitative form

[1] Some illustrations of the measurement approach are Terman and Merrill (1959), Thurstone (1938), Strong (1943), Gulliksen (1950), and Hathaway and McKinley (1951).

(IQ, raw score, time of response, and so forth), which was then given further meaning by relating it to the normative data for a given sample of individuals.

Since testing under this approach usually involves a sample of the individual's responses at a particular point in time (and at a particular point in the individual's career) there has been a great concern for determining the error of the sample by means of methods for estimating the reliability and objectivity of the score assigned the examinee. The meaningfulness of the results has been usually determined by some form of concurrent or predictive validity. That is, the validity of a measurement instrument is usually approached in terms of its relation with another measurement or appraisal.

Although the measurement view has not entirely ignored the environment in which the individual has developed, the environment is generally ignored at the time of making the measurements. What a measurement specialist does is to attempt to take into consideration the environment as an error term, since he assumes that his measurements are accurate to the extent to which the examinees have had "equal opportunity" to develop the characteristics being sampled. However, the measurement approach does seek characteristics which are "in the individual." That is, the individual is the possessor of IQ, ability, creativity, and so forth, and he is to be measured to determine the amount of each characteristic he possesses.

In measurement there is an assumption that the same characteristics (IQ, memory, and so forth) can be measured in all men—no matter what their background—and that the characteristics can be measured in an analogous way at different times and at different places. IQ is very similar in 1967 and in 1917 in the United States, France, or India.

The use of the tests under the measurement view is largely for classification, prediction, and experimentation. The major quest in measurement is for a small number of dimensions or measures which will completely account for the variance of a criterion when put together in some additive or summative combination. The problems that are most alive in measurement today are the search for better units (hopefully with properties akin to physical measurement units), the search for a parsimonious measurement system that will account for the variance of a large number of variables or measures, and the search for improved methods of sampling characteristics and individuals.

The great power of measurement is in its great efficiency. Given a dimension or a criterion, psychometric procedures enable measurement to secure parsimonious procedures for measuring it and for describing it in terms of a small number of dimensions.

Evaluation[2]

Starting in the 1930s, Ralph Tyler (1934) proposed that educational testing be concerned with the changes in students produced by educational means. He used the term *evaluation* to refer to a set of procedures for appraising changes in students.

The stress on appraisal of change meant that, theoretically at least, testing had to be done at two or more points in time on each individual to determine the extent of change. Since it was necessary to limit the types of changes to be tested, Tyler suggested that tests be constructed to sample the changes in students specified by the objectives of instruction—that is, the changes that were intended by the instructors, instruction, or the curriculum.

While the evaluation approach is concerned with the reliability, objectivity, and efficiency of the tests used, these are secondary questions. Its primary concern is with the *content* validity of the instruments developed. That is, there must be an adequate definition of the objectives or characteristics to be appraised and a search for ways of testing these characteristics which appropriate experts can agree are sampling the desired behaviors. Once it has been possible to construct a valid test of the objective, it is possible to use concurrent validity to determine more efficient and parsimonious instruments to test the same objective (using the valid test as the criterion). Reliability and objectivity can then be improved until they reach the desired standard.

It should be pointed out that evaluation is concerned with securing evidence on the attainment of specific objectives of instruction. As the objectives becomes more varied in nature, it is to be expected that a greater variety of types of evidence may be appropriate. Thus evaluation evidence may include products developed by students, processes in which they engage, and behaviors they manifest in a great variety of situations. The evidence may be qualitative as well as quantitative. This is a far cry from the standard stimulus-standard response evidence gathering in measurement.

Evaluation follows the objectives of instruction. Therefore, to the extent that objectives differ from teacher to teacher, school to school, or curriculum to curriculum, it is necessary to devise evaluation procedures appropriate to the specific situations. A single standard test may not be equally appropriate to all situations.

Although evaluation is primarily concerned with changes in individuals, it may be applied to evaluating the effects of a curriculum, a course, a

[2] Some illustrations of the evaluation approach are Smith and Tyler (1942), Furst (1958), Bloom (1956), Dressel and Mayhew (1954).

teacher, a method of instruction, and so forth. For such problems where the concern may be with group changes rather than individual changes, it is possible to utilize student-test sampling methods that will yield evidence about the group rather than the individuals.

Since evaluation attempts to appraise the changes in students, it is necessary to find methods to judge the extent to which the objectives have been met. The standard against which the evidence is appraised may be the usual type of normative data on particular samples, it may also include absolute criterion-referenced standards, and it may even include the student as his own standard—for example, the change in the student over one period of time as contrasted with the change in that student over another period of time.

Evaluation need not be confined to a summative combination of items or scores. Various patterns of responses may be interpreted to determine the types of changes taking place in the student, the types of errors he makes, and the reasons underlying his attainment or lack of attainment of the objectives specified for instruction.

In measurement, the environment is a source of error in the scores or attainments of the individuals being measured. In evaluation, the environment (instruction, class, school, and so forth) is assumed to be the major source of the changes. Ideally, evaluation is as much concerned with the characteristics of the environment that produces the change as it is with the appraisal of the changes in the individuals who are interacting with the environment. In practice, the evaluator frequently limits himself to a description of the environment while he appraises in detail the changes taking place in the individuals.

One major use of evaluation has been to classify individuals for purposes of grading, certification, and placement or promotion. Perhaps of equal importance is the use of evaluation to determine the effectiveness of a method of instruction, a specific course, curriculum or program, or a specific instructor. Evaluation may be used in educational experimentation, and it can be used as a method for maintaining quality control in education.

Perhaps a major difference between measurement and evaluation is the recognition (and utilization) of the effects of testing on the persons involved. Characteristically, measurement strives to limit or control the effects of testing on the student performance. Measurement's concern with "equal opportunity" usually is directed to limiting or equalizing the opportunity students have to learn about the sample of problems on which they will be tested. In contrast, in evaluation there is a more explicit concern with student growth or change and with the *utilization* of the effects of testing to promote such change. Thus, it is recognized that both teachers and students can be motivated to teach and learn by the nature of the tests they anticipate will be used; this effect can be maximized or minimized as desired. Furthermore, the translation of objectives into testing situations has the effect of giving operational definition to the desired characteristics, and, in turn, such operational definition can focus and intensify the development by teacher and students of these desired characteristics. Also, the frequency of testing and its use for feedback purposes can do much to enhance the development of the desired characteristics in students.

The major quest in evaluation is for the identification of learning experiences and educative environments that produce significant changes in individuals and for the creation of instruments and methods of testing that will best reveal these changes. The problems that are most alive in evaluation today are the search for better appraisal methods for a great variety of changes (cognitive, affective, psychomotor, and so forth); the search for ways of determining the types of changes that are of greatest significance in contemporary societies; the search for more accurate ways of determining change indices; and the search for ways in which evaluation may be best utilized in the promotion of the desired changes (that is, the use of formative in contrast with summative evaluation).

The great power of evaluation is in its concern for human betterment through a systematic process of relating testing to the development of desirable characteristics in individuals. Used properly, it does much to lead educators to a quest for desirable changes and the means for attaining them. Its means-ends approach has considerable implications for the growth of institutions as well as the growth of individuals.

Assessment[3]

While the term assessment is a very old one, its use, in the sense in which this paper is concerned, may be attributed to the work of Henry Murray (1938) in the book, *Explorations in Personality,* and the book *Assessment of Men,* by the O.S.S. Assessment Staff (1948) in World War II. As used here, it refers to the attempts to assess the characteristics of individuals in relation to a particular environment, task, or criterion situation.

Assessment in this sense is as much concerned with the environment as it is with the individuals who interact with the environment. The need-press scheme of Murray has been useful in analyzing the individual and the environment in analogous terms. The use of role theory has been effective

[3] Some illustrations of the assessment approach are Murray (1938), O.S.S. Assessment Staff (1948), Barron (1963), Stern, Stein, and Bloom (1956), Sanford (1956).

in relating the roles demanded or emphasized by the environment with the roles that the individual is able to "play."

Assessment characteristically begins with an analysis of the criterion and the environment in which the individual lives, learns, and works. It attempts to determine the psychological pressures the environment creates, the roles expected, and the demands and pressures—their hierarchical arrangement, consistency, as well as conflict. It then proceeds to the determination of the kinds of evidence that are appropriate about the individuals who are to be placed in this environment, such as their relevant strengths and weaknesses, their needs and personality characteristics, their skills and abilities.

The evidence collected about the individual in assessment is multiform in that many types of qualitative and quantitative evidence may be collected, some of it highly structured and some of a more projective or unstructured form. The assessor may use evidence from self-reports, observations by others, interviews, projective situations, situational tests, role playing, free association, and so forth. Relevant evidence on a particular characteristic may be secured from several instruments or methods. The assessor attempts to determine the congruence of the different evidence in respect to selected human characteristics.

Through the analysis of the possible relations between evidence on both the individual and the environment, the assessor attempts to determine the kinds of transactions or interactions likely to take place between the two. In order to put all this evidence together, he may attempt to create a model of the environment and a model of the functioning individual.

The task of the assessor in studying the congruence or lack of congruence of the different types of evidence on the individual is dependent on the availability of a *construct* or model that relates otherwise disparate pieces of evidence. Similarly, the interaction between the individual and the environment can be understood only if there is a construct, theory, or model that enables the assessor to infer relations between characteristics of the individual and characteristics of the environment. Thus, the primary type of validation for assessment is *construct validity,* that is, the extent to which evidence for specific characteristics in individual and environment or the interactions between the two are explained or explainable in terms of a theory or construct. Assessment may also make use of *predictive* validity in that particular interactions between an individual and an environment are to be predicted from a knowledge of the characteristics of each.

Assessment has been used for prediction (and selection), for experimentation, and for classification. However, during the past decade assessment has been used to analyze the characteristics of the environment or criterion situation in order to better understand how environments or situations differ and the kinds of demands they create or the ways in which they influence human characteristics. It is safe to say that, with a few exceptions, in the last fifteen years there have been few contributions of assessment to new instruments or methods of testing individuals, while there have been major contributions to analyzing and testing the environment (Dave, 1963; Wolf, 1964; Hess and Shipman, 1965; Stodolsky, 1965; Pace and Stern, 1958; Pace, 1963).

The major strength of assessment is in the search for evidence on both individual and environment. The attempt to relate the two types of evidence has contributed more to the understanding of phenomena than it has to the prediction or control of such phenomena, although the first does give a basis for the second. The problems that are most alive in assessment today are the search for more effective and efficient instruments to understand both the individual and the environment, the improvement of methods of processing evidence from a variety of instruments, and the development of more adequate ways of securing evidence on the criteria to be predicted.

CONDITIONS THAT MAKE A SYNTHESIS
POSSIBLE AND NECESSARY

It is the writer's opinion that a synthesis of these three approaches to testing is more possible at this time than ever before. Until recently, many of us were so concerned with the distinctive characteristics of each approach that we tended to overemphasize the differences. We suggested that each of these approaches had its own value and that each could make a useful approach to those problems for which it was best fitted.

Each of these approaches can be considered to be a partial view of the nature of man, the world, and the nature and use of evidence. If this is so, then we must seek a more complete view of man, the world, and evidence that can best utilize what each of these approaches offers at present. It is the writer's belief that we are in desperate need of such a synthesis, if we are to avoid further narrowing of the field of testing. Further, that any attempt to bring these approaches together is likely to bring about a period of "hybrid vigor" in which new problems and new techniques will give the field of testing a period of unprecedented challenge and growth.

What are some of the conditions that make this synthesis possible or necessary at this time?

Experience

We now have had approximately sixty years of experience with measurement, about thirty years of experience with evaluation, and almost the same amount of experience with assessment. There is an extensive literature already available and it is possible to use this literature as the basis for building on the foundation already available. Furthermore, the limits and the uses of each approach are recorded so that one can start where these leave off.

The length of the history of each of these approaches suggests that the pioneers who helped to create and develop each approach are now replaced by new generations of workers and students who are less committed to the differences (and the emotional involvement of the pioneers) and who may take a more dispassionate view of the problems and opportunities for which various combinations of the three approaches may be useful and even necessary.

Linked to this history is the development of a large number of instruments and techniques that have been used under a variety of conditions. This means that the original ideas of the pioneers have been given an operational meaning and illustration and that one is no longer left to deal with the original verbal formulations—but can deal with the operational consequences of these formulations. Furthermore, the instruments and techniques yield a reservoir of procedures that can be built on as new problems are identified. Of special value in this connection are the reviews, bibliographies, and collections of information represented by the *Buros' Mental Measurement Yearbooks,* the reviews of educational research, the yearbooks, and the journals, such as *Educational and Psychological Measurements, Psychometrika,* and *Measurements Used in Education.* The point is that much of the information about tests and testing is now in a codified form that is easily located.

Sophistication in Statistics and Data Processing

During the past twenty years there has been an unprecedented development in the sophistication of statistical methods and data processing. In part this growth has been responsive to developments in testing, but in large part it has been quite independent of this field.

Factor analysis, multivariate procedures, canonical correlation, path coefficients, sampling methodology, and so forth, have moved very far during this period such that problems which were difficult or impossible to attack before are now amenable to an efficient and effective solution.

Factor analysis as a method of reducing the detail and dealing with a smaller number of variables (or tests) has been effectively used in testing. Other statistical procedures are increasingly becoming available which are likely to enable testers to deal with more complex problems than have been possible up to the present.

It is, however, the computer that is likely to make the greatest difference in the work of testers. The enormous amount of data that can be stored, the ease with which data can be analyzed and summarized in a great range of ways, and the storage of longitudinal as well as cross-sectional data should enable the tester to attack problems that have hitherto been out of his reach.

A synthetic theory or approach to testing can give direction and meaning to this increased sophistication and ease in data collection and analysis. Problems that were impractical to attack in 1960 are relatively easy to attack in 1968. Furthermore, the facility with which complex theoretical ideas can be dealt with in the day-to-day data processing of test constructors and test users make a synthetic theory of testing a highly practical concern, where hitherto it might have seemed to have a set of ideas that could be dealt with only by a few highly skilled persons in the field.

Development of Educational Methods and Learning Theory

Testing is most powerfully related to education and to learning, instruction, and research in the schools. This is not to say that it does not have great value for industry, human development, and psychology. However, the advances in education have been such in recent years as to create new needs in testing.

Some of the advances in education that create the need for advances in testing have to do with new curriculum developments, new problems in education arising from new tasks being assumed by the school, and basic changes in instruction and instructional technology.

The new curriculum developments in mathematics, science, languages, and social sciences have been of a magnitude not dreamed of previously. Large teams of experts and specialists have been involved in a systematic approach to new curricula in which basic changes in the content and structure of the subject matter have been accompanied by a variety of instructional materials and methods. In addition, many teachers have been provided with in-service training on the new content and instructional material. These changes in curricula have not always been supported by changes in testing procedures at the level required for evaluation of the cognitive and affective consequences. There is a need for a theory of testing that will be appropriate to the new curricula and the problems they pose for testing.

The schools are very rapidly taking on many tasks that have hitherto been assumed by the home, social welfare agencies, employers, and so forth. For example, preschool programs are being devised for the culturally disadvantaged children to compensate for presumed inadequacies in the home's preparation of these children for education by the schools. Problems of integration of ethnic and racial groups are being thrust on the schools as are some of the problems of providing food, medical care, and special instruction (and day care) for children of poverty groups. The special problems of youth in need of employable skills (aside from the regular academic instruction in the schools) are being assumed by schools and other educative agencies. As the schools assume tasks that represent a departure from previous practices, there is an especially urgent requirement that testing and related methods of gathering evidence be appropriate to insure that the task is well done and that the consequences of performing the new task are positive and desirable rather than negative and harmful to the individual, the schools, and the community. New tasks require the appropriate development of new testing procedures as well as new conceptions of the nature of testing.

There have been some major changes in instructional methodology, such as programmed instruction, TV, and videotape, computer-assisted instruction, and even the widespread use of tutors. These, the development of discovery and inquiry methods of teaching, and the use of nongraded school programs raise many new problems for testing and related activities. In general, the development of approaches to individualized learning make it necessary to develop more effective ways of gathering and using relevant evidence.

Testing must serve not only to determine the effectiveness of these new procedures and programs, it must also serve to help us understand the nature of the phenomena involved in order that educational policy and practice may increasingly be based on such understanding. Furthermore, testing must serve to predict consequences of particular educational decisions as well as to provide quality controls on the implementation of these decisions in practice. Such tasks require a larger and more complex theory of testing than is presently available.

Effect of Testing on the Phenomena

During the past few years there has been a great deal of criticism directed against testing. These criticisms should remind us that testing cannot be completely separated from the phenomena it attempts to record and study. The act of testing in the social sciences affects the humans who are involved. Especially in education, what is tested influences the perception of students, teachers, parents, and others in the society. To measure intelligence, specific attitudes, and achievement is to influence the values of the society, the ways in which people value themselves and others, the nature of educational policy and practice, and the very ends of education. External examinations do much to influence the curriculum, the ways in which students view school, and the things students study and learn.

Try as we will to control the effects of testing, we find that the nature of the tests used may under some conditions do more to influence student learning and teacher practice than the other educational procedures that we regard as the substance of education.

A full awareness of the consequences of our ways of testing must be an intrinsic part of our use of tests to understand, predict, or control human behavior. We must, in the development of test theory, give full recognition to the range of effects the tests may have on the society as well as on the schools, the students, and teachers.

THE INTERPLAY OF THE DIFFERENT APPROACHES

One way of relating the different approaches to testing is to recognize the special qualities of each and to have them support each other in attacking specific problems.

Thus, we may approach a problem of prediction by making an assessment approach to the individual, the environment, and the criteria. Using a great variety of evidence-gathering instruments and a theoretical framework, we may complete a very comprehensive assessment approach to our prediction problem. Such an approach is very costly in terms of resources and personnel required and makes use of complex human judgments—frequently requiring rare clinical skills and a team of experts not only to collect the data but to make the clinical appraisals of the data and their implications. If such an approach is relatively effective, the insights, instruments, and criteria can then be systematically reduced to a more efficient and parsimonious set of procedures by the use of measurement methodology. And, with computer analysis of very complex patterns of data, it is quite likely that the measurements and their processing can yield results not significantly inferior to that secured by the most costly assessment approach.

Or, the situation can be reversed. Through measurement approaches it is possible to efficiently measure and predict certain behavior. Quite frequently, the measurement includes symptoms and behaviors that yield satisfactory levels of prediction, but which are not "understood" in terms of why the relations are what they are. Assessment may be used to probe more deeply into the underlying relationships and into the reasons that would help to explain the results. Thus measurement, sometimes blind to causation, can be supplemented by assessment to probe into the theory and underlying behavior to account for the measurement results.

Evaluation seeks to determine the extent to which change has taken place in students as the result of particular learning experiences. Once the learning experiences have been defined and described, evaluation attempts to account for the changes in students in terms of the effectiveness of these learning experiences.

Measurement may be used in relation to evaluation in finding more parsimonious procedures for describing and testing the changes made. Are there multiple changes or are the changes accountable for in terms of a single factor or very few factors? Measurement can do much to improve the techniques for determining the amount of change and for determining the characteristics in the students and/or selected characteristics in the environment which "account" for the changes. Measurement can be used to make the evaluation instruments more efficient.

Assessment, with its concern for the individual and the environment, can be used to determine why some individuals are responsive to particular aspects of the learning environment while others are not, or what in the personality and other characteristics of the individual leads to certain changes (in relation to the environmental press) and what in the individual leads to other changes.

Furthermore, if there are appropriate theoretical models, assessment can be used to "explain" and "understand" what has taken place in the curriculum-evaluation situation. In short, assessment can be used to help understand the evaluation results.

Evaluation can also make use of assessment methodology to appraise changes made in very complex affective objectives—values, attitudes, and personality. In turn, evaluation can seek more economical methods of appraising such changes after the criterion measures have been assessed by clinical procedures.

TOWARD A SYNTHETIC THEORY OF TESTING

The fact that each method of testing can make a contribution to the other methods is not very new. Each tester would insist that this is precisely what he has been doing as he approaches a complex new problem. That it could be done more systematically would be agreed to by all. What is at issue is that each method has its own ways of proceeding and that it is rare that all of the test approaches are fully used in attacking a new problem; especially when each approach requires highly specialized talents, instruments, and data processing and interpretative skills. It is exceedingly rare that a measurement problem is attacked after a full-scale assessment and/or evaluation approach has been used. Nor is it likely that assessment would be used to probe more deeply into a problem that has first been attacked from the measurement or evaluation point of view.

What is needed is a more comprehensive approach to testing that fully utilizes what we have already learned and can do with each of the distinct approaches to testing. What is needed is a comprehensive theory of testing that will give direction to the training of testers in the future and will show the testing tactics required in attacking any given problem. Such a theory should help us determine the kinds of specialized personnel, team efforts, instrumentation, and data processing relevant for any given problem. This paper does not attempt to provide a quick solution to theory building of this type.

What will be done in the remainder of this paper is to suggest some of the ways in which such testing terms as *validity, reliability,* and *norms* might be altered to take care of some of the problems posed by measurement, evaluation, and assessment. The expansion and redefinition of these terms could serve to enlarge the range of ideas and methods available to testers and as a result carry us one step toward a synthesis of these approaches to testing.

In addition, two problems in testing have been selected, the determination of *stability* and the *appraisal* of change. For each of these problems, the writer has suggested some of the ways in which the problem would be altered if the three testing approaches were used simultaneously.

It is to be hoped that further work along these lines will pose the issues and underlying assumptions more clearly. Hopefully, out of such work will come theoretical developments that can effectively synthesize what at the moment appear to be very distinct and different approaches to testing.

We might begin with a brief definition of testing that encompasses all present theories of testing. *Testing may be defined as the act of gathering and processing evidence about human behavior under given conditions for purposes of understanding, predicting, and controlling future human behavior.* While such a definition leaves much to be further defined, it does help us delimit the phenomena for which a theory must account.

Validity

Perhaps the key problem in testing is to establish the validity of the instruments and techniques developed. While this is the most difficult problem to solve in actual operation, the place of validity in relation to measurement, evaluation, and assessment has largely been solved by the work of The American Educational Research Association (1955) and the American Psychological Association (1954) in their attempts to delineate the different types of validity. In these reports, the committees described four types of validity:

Content validity
Construct validity
Concurrent validity
Predictive validity

Any testing instrument may be validated by one or more of these types of validation. It would, of course, be the rare test that would be validated by all four types. As we review these different types of validity, it is striking that each of the testing approaches has emphasized particular types of validity and has developed techniques and procedures for utilizing the preferred types of validation.

Thus, evaluation has stressed *content validity* and has developed the techniques of defining objectives and content in behavioral terms such that competent judges can determine the appropriateness of particular test problems and situations for the defined specifications. While evaluation does make use of concurrent validation when it seeks to make more efficient instruments that will yield results relating to the original and more direct instrument (validated by content validity), it is clear that the emphasis in evaluation is on content validity.

Assessment has characteristically emphasized *construct validity,* since it goes to more elaborate lengths to use theories or models to guide it in particular assessment situations. It is these theories or models that make it possible to use construct validity, and it is the very complexity of the data collection and analysis required in assessment that make it necessary to have a theory or model to guide the workers through the intricacies of an assessment process.

Measurement has characteristically employed *predictive* and *concurrent validity.* And, as was pointed out earlier, given a criterion, measurement has very powerful methods of developing instruments that will yield maximum predictive and concurrent validity.

The suggestion that emerges from the work to date on validation is that an approach to validation that makes use of the best features of the particular test approaches leads to an inclusive approach rather than to any new concepts of validity. Thus, for our purposes, validity may be defined by four terms:

$$\text{Validity} = \frac{\text{CONTENT}}{\text{Validity}} : \frac{\text{CONSTRUCT}}{\text{Validity}} : \frac{\text{CONCURRENT}}{\text{Validity}} : \frac{\text{PREDICTIVE}}{\text{Validity}}$$

It is the task of the tester to determine which types of validity are germane to the problem at hand and to determine when he has exhausted the validation possibilities for the particular test problem. Hopefully, the tester who is carefully trained in the different approaches to testing can be more ingenious and creative than those of his predecessors who tended to rely on a single type of validation. Hopefully, also, content and construct validity would become more central in the initial approach to a testing problem, while concurrent and predictive validity would become more central to the development of more efficient testing procedures *after* criterion measures with high content and construct validity have been created.

Reliability

Reliability has been the one testing concept that has been most fully developed, although primarily from the measurement point of view. If reliability is to more adequately deal with the problems posed by each of the testing approaches, several additional terms and operations might be added to the more traditional approach to this concept. Perhaps a more comprehensive view of reliability might include the following:

$$\text{Reliability} = \frac{\text{READER}}{\text{Reliability}} : \frac{\text{INTERNAL}}{\text{CONSISTENCY}} : \frac{\text{INSTRUMENT}}{\text{STABILITY}} : \frac{\text{EXAMINEE}}{\text{Reliability}} : \frac{\text{SAMPLING}}{\text{Reliability}} :$$

$$\frac{\text{CONGRUENCE}}{\text{Reliability}}$$

Reader Reliability. The agreement of competent judges on the *meaning* or *value* of a particular product, response, or process, presents few difficulties. This type of reliability or objectivity was one of the first problems attacked by testers. However, the definition of a *competent judge* would vary for each of the testing approaches. For measurement, this could vary considerably depending on the human characteristics being measured; for evaluation, especially in education, this is likely to be a person with considerable competence in the subject matter and learning processes under consideration, while in assessment this is most likely to be someone with considerable training and experience in the use of dynamic theories of personality or clinical psychology. However, the main point is that the specific testing problem must determine the qualifications needed by the judges for reader reliability.

Internal Consistency. This type of reliability is based on estimates of the extent to which a scale or test contains items that are getting at a common characteristic, trait, or factor. This type of reliability has been widely used in both measurement and evaluation. It must be recognized that internal consistency is both a function of the items in the test and a function of the subjects being tested. Thus, from the evaluation point of view it is quite likely that the internal consistency of a set of items may be higher after the subjects have had the relevant learning experiences than prior to these learning experiences. It is necessary in stating the level of internal consistency to give some indication of the nature of the subjects used in determining this form of reliability.

Instrument Stability. These indices are attempts to determine the error likely to be attached to a particular score as a result of fluctuations in the performance of the examinee from sample to sample. As the time intervals between samples increase, there is a shift from the usual concept of test reliability to the stability of the instrument or characteristic under consideration. There is increasing evidence (Bloom, 1964) that particular characteristics become more stable at some ages or stages of development than at others and that under some conditions the reliability of the test results over a five-year span may be as great as it is over a five-day span of time. This type of reliability is needed for problems encountered in each of the testing approaches. It is important that the tester be able to indicate the stability of the test results, especially when major decisions are being made on the test results (for example, admission to a special school for the mentally retarded, admission to a particular educational program, guidance with regard to a vocational career). This is developed more fully on pages 45 to 47. Here, it may be pointed out that a stability index would serve to caution the user of test results against long-term decisions where the stability is low, and it would caution the psychologist or educator against overoptimism with regard to changes in an individual (for example, intelligence, values, problem-solving ability) where the stability of test results is very high.

Examinee Reliability. While reliability is generally attached to an instrument in relation to a particular group of subjects, the tester is finally interested in the reliability with which he has measured a particular individual examinee. The error attached to the test results for a group of examinees may not apply equally well to each of the examinees who has taken the test. It is likely to be most accurate for the individuals who have passed 50 percent of the items and who have failed the other 50 percent. However, for the individuals who have passed only 5–10 percent of the items or 90–95 percent of the items, it is likely that the error term is less appropriate. There is some value in having an error term for each score or examinee.

If testing procedures could be devised so that each individual passes 50 percent of the items and fails 50 percent, the reliability for each individual is likely to be maximal. This might require a somewhat different sample of items for each individual to be tested. (The Stanford-Binet testing procedures approach this.) While this type of reliability is most appropriate to the measurement approach, it is likely to be useful for both evaluation and assessment, especially if an approach can be used which reduces the length of testing time for each examinee without reducing the reliability.

Sampling Reliability. This could be considered as another form of content validity. By sampling reliability we mean that a test should reliably sample the different types of content and behaviors stressed in the specifications for a test. This requires some description of the population of content and behaviors and some index of the extent to which the sample in the test is an adequate representation of the population of tasks or problems from which it is drawn. If two equivalent forms of a test are *independently* developed from the same set of specifications, then the relationship between performance on the two tests would form a type of sampling reliability.

This type of reliability is especially useful when one is attempting to extrapolate from the performance on the sample to the population being sampled. An illustration of this is Terman and Merrill's (1959) attempt to estimate the size of an individual's vocabulary from his performance on the vocabulary sample in the Stanford-Binet Intelligence Test. They selected a random sample of words in a particular dictionary and then attempted to generalize from performance on the sample to the total set of words in the dictionary. While it is probable that this form of reliability would be appropriate to all three test approaches, it would be most useful in describing test results from the evaluation point of view where the tester is trying to give meaning to the individual's score as representing performance over the entire set of content and behaviors being sampled.

Congruence Reliability. This is a difficult concept to explain. It arises especially in assessment where a variety of evidence is used to assess a particular individual or group. Thus, evidence on leadership qualities may come from self-reports, projective techniques, observations in special situations, and from reports of superiors or subordinates. Finally, the assessor must put all this evidence together in a descriptive statement or in a rating. What he needs is some way of estimating the congruence of all the pieces of evidence. With what certainty can a particular statement or rating be made? While it may be straining a point to call this reliability, this seems to me to be the most appropriate place to put this problem. Another illustration is the college admissions officer's problem in determining the admissibility of an applicant on the basis of previous grades, test scores, interviews, and letters of recommendation by secondary school personnel. When all the evidence is positive or negative, he has little difficulty; the results are congruent. When the evidence yields conflicting pictures of the candidate, the admissions officer has difficulty in reaching a sound decision.

The determination of congruence may require great insight on the part of the interpreter of the evidence, since it is quite possible for what on the face of it appears to be contradictory evidence to really be highly consistent in the light of a particular theory of personality or human behavior. Thus, contradictory projective test results and self-reports may be perfectly congruent for particular characteristics such as aggressiveness, anxiety, attitudes toward persons in authority, and so forth.

One may draw an analogy between the attempt to determine congruence in testing with medical diagnosis on the basis of a great variety of symptoms and evidence. The medical practitioner begins with the assumption that there is a medical explanation for the different symptoms; that is, he assumes that the evidence will be congruent, if he can find the appropriate ailment, cause, or condition. I have no clear suggestions for the form that a *congruent-reliability* index might take, since it is both a qualitative as well as a quantitative problem. However, I suspect that we may find leads to it in one or more error terms based on multivariate methods, which relate a variety of predictive indices to a variety of criterion indices.

Here again, it is the task of the tester to determine which types of reliability are relevant to the problem at hand. Relatively simple types of reliability are required for many measurement problems, while more complex forms of reliability may be required for some assessment problems. However, it is the use to which the evidence is to be put which will be the primary determinant of the form of reliability that is appropriate.

Norms

Test results are usually given meaning in relation to normative data of some sort. Especially for aptitude and educational achievement tests, test makers have devoted a great deal of time and resources to the securing of normative data. Quite frequently more resources are expended on the development of norms than on the construction of the instruments themselves. Several types of norms are suggested for the problems encountered in three approaches to testing. A more comprehensive approach to the development of norms for tests might include the following:

$$\text{Norms} = \frac{\text{DISTRIBUTION}}{\text{Norms}} : \frac{\text{INTRA-PERSON}}{\text{Norms}} : \frac{\text{CHANGE}}{\text{Norms}} : \frac{\text{CRITERION REFERENCED}}{\text{Norms}} : \frac{\text{SEQUENTIAL}}{\text{Norms}}$$

Distribution Norms. These are the usual type of norms in which a well defined sample of individuals take a given test and the results for individuals and groups are related to the appropriate distributions. Such norms are indispensable to the measurement approach, while they are useful to the other test approaches.

Intra-person Norms. For some test problems where there are several scores (for example, *Differential Aptitude Tests, Kuder Preference Record*), it is useful to have norms on the differences between pairs of scores as an additional basis for interpreting scores. This type of norm would appear to be most vital for evaluation and assessment problems. However, there are many problems of interpreting measurement test results for guidance purposes that could make use of this type of norm.

Change Norms. Especially for evaluation of change as a result of therapy or education, it would be useful to have norms on change scores. Such norms could indicate the statistical significance of particular measures of change, and they could also indicate the frequency with which a particular change is found under given conditions. Thus, a measure of change in vocabulary or other language measures under various preschool programs, reading and language programs in the elementary school years, and so forth, could do much to help in the evaluation of the changes produced by a given curriculum or learning strategy. It is likely that this type of norm would be most useful for the evaluation approach.

Criterion-Referenced Norms. Glaser (1963) has advocated norms that indicate the attainment of a particular level of skill or competence. These are not norms in the sense of distributions. Instead, they make use of definitions of a task attainment or expert judgment to determine particular standards of performance. While Glaser was recommending this type of norm from the evaluation point of view, it is likely that procedures for determining such norms would be most valuable for the assessment approach.

Sequential Norms. A somewhat different type of norm is suggested by the problem of evaluation. Given a set of scores at two or more points in time, what are the expectancies for a third or later point in time? This type of norm would be especially useful in longitudinal studies of school achievement. Thus, Payne (1963) finds that achievement at Grade 6 can be highly predicted from achievement in Grades 1 and 2. Such predictions, put in the form of normative data, would help to determine the long term consequences of the changes taking place over shorter time intervals. The great value of such sequential norms is that they could alert educators, therapists, medical practitioners, and others to the consequences of present procedures. Such norms would make it possible to use the time interval between the prediction and the consequences to take those steps that may prevent consequences that are regarded as undesirable or to maximize consequences regarded as desirable.

It is quite likely that other types of norms would be useful, in addition to these named in the foregoing. The major point is that an expanded view of the scope of testing requires the development of a variety of terms and operations to deal with the changing nature of the problems in this field.

SOME APPLICATIONS OF A SYNTHETIC THEORY

Perhaps some ideas of the value of a synthetic theory of testing may be seen in the consequences it could have for several problems. The reader is invited to consider other problems in the special fields with which he is concerned. Here, we will limit ourselves to the consideration of two rather general problems: stability of human characteristics and the appraisal of change.

Stability

We have already referred to stability as one form of test reliability. However, the problem of determining stability of a human characteristic is one that goes beyond the long-term reliability of an instrument. Given a human characteristic that can be measured by one or more tests at a particular age or development, what will be the most probable state of that human characteristic at some point of time in the future? Thus, if we measure height, general intelligence, language competence, anxiety, and so forth, at age 6, what can we expect on similar measurements at age 7? age 10? age 18?

It is suggested that some basic terms in the determination of stability might be the following:

$$\text{Stability}_{X_1 \text{ to } X_2} = \text{INSTRUMENT Stability}_{X_1 \text{ to } X_2}$$
$$+ \text{DEVELOPMENT}_{X_1} + \text{ENVIRONMENT}_{0 \text{ to } X_1}$$
$$+ \text{ENVIRONMENT Future (Likely)}_{X_1 \text{ to } X_2} + \text{ENVIRONMENT (Future Ideal)}_{X_1 \text{ to } X_2}$$

Each of these terms is briefly described or explained in the following.

INSTRUMENT Stability$_{X_1 \text{ to } X_2}$. This is merely the long term reliability of the instrument over the period of time X_1 to X_2. This term was explained briefly on page 41. Thus, it might be the stability of the Stanford-Binet Intelligence Test for ages 6 to 10 or the stability of the Stanford Reading Comprehension score Grades 2 to 5.

DEVELOPMENT$_{X_1}$. This would be some index of the level of development in the particular age or grade. Ideally, this should be on some scale of absolute development.

ENVIRONMENT$_{0 \text{ to } X_1}$. This would be some index of the relevant environmental characteristics (for the particular human characteristic) over the time interval birth to X_1. However, an approximation to this may be secured by an estimation of the environment at time X_1. (See Wolf, 1964, for the home environment index for general intelligence; Stodolsky, 1965, for maternal behavior influencing language development.)

ENVIRONMENT$_{Future (Likely) X_1 \text{ to } X_2}$. This can only be an estimation of what is likely to take place between times X_1 and X_2. While we need to know a great deal about the stability of environments over periods of time, it is possible to make some estimates of this for those age periods in which the home and the school are the dominant environments. There is some likelihood that, barring major crises, the home environment is not likely to be fundamentally altered over a three-year period with respect to those characteristics in it which influence general intelligence or language development. Also, it is likely that a particular school environment will not be fundamentally altered over a three- to five-year period insofar as it affects language development or reading, if studies of the school as a bureaucracy can be relied upon. In any case, an environmental study of the school over the previous three or four years gives some indication of what may be expected in the next few years.

$ENVIRONMENT_{Future\ (Ideal)\ X_1\ to\ X_2}$.   This is an estimation of what is possible if the environment approximated some ideal: (a) if the home environment during period X_1 to X_2 approximated the best home environment for these characteristics (for example, general intelligence, language development), (b) and/or if the school environment during this period approximated the best school environment for these characteristics.

Where the *ideal* environment is similar to the *likely* environment and the *past* environment, stability of the characteristic is likely to be greatest. Where the ideal environment is very different from both the likely and past environments, stability of the characteristic could be considerably decreased if some intervention measures are successful in the attempt to produce such an environment. The point is that the use of these different terms in the estimation of stability provides a basis for determining the conditions under which stability is likely to be maximal or minimal and thus serve as a basis for intervention if this is regarded to be in the best interests of the individual.

In a problem of this type, the distinction between measurement, evaluation, and assessment are no longer as clear as they were in the consideration of validity, reliability, and norms. Techniques based on all three approaches to testing would be used in the determination of stability. Each of the terms suggested for stability would profit from a synthetic approach to testing.

Change

Another problem to which a synthetic theory of testing might be applied is the appraisal of change, a problem to which the evaluation approach to testing has been applied in the past. Some of the possible terms for the appraisal of change might be the following:

$$\text{Change} = \frac{\text{FINAL}}{\text{Status}} - \frac{\text{INITIAL}}{\text{Status}} + \frac{\text{STRATEGY}}{\text{Employed}} + \frac{\text{EFFECT OF}}{\text{Instrument}} + \frac{\text{RELATED}}{\text{Changes}}$$

Final Status.   This represents the post measurements for each of the characteristics under consideration. Ideally, these instruments are parallel in content and form to those used in the initial status tests, with high validity and reliability. Both the initial and final status measurements should have high content and construct validity based on the specifications desired in the change.

Initial Status. This represents the initial measurements for each of the characteristics under consideration. Presumably each of these characteristics is tested with instruments that have high validity and reliability.

Strategy Employed. The specific learning experiences, therapeutic techniques, environmental intervention, or other strategy used must be described in sufficient detail to delineate it from other strategies and, if possible, the context in which the strategy is used must be included in this description. In the past, it has been common to label two or more instructional strategies, which quite frequently turned out to be very similar in major respects.

Effect of Instrument. It is possible for the instruments used to appraise initial and final status to be as powerful as the instructional strategy in producing the changes. There must be some way of distinguishing the effects of the strategy from the effect of the instruments used. Research design procedures represent one approach to this problem.

Related Changes. It is likely that other changes take place in addition to those specifically sought and appraised by the initial and final-status instruments. Some of these related changes may be regarded as desirable while others may be regarded as undesirable. It is possible that the constructs of the assessment approach may be useful in hypothesizing what related changes are likely to be produced in relation to the strategy employed, the instruments used, or in relation to the changes showing up in the comparison of initial and final status measurements. The basic problem here is one of limiting the number of related changes that are to be investigated to those which are most probable.

Here again, it is likely that a problem of the type suggested above could only be attacked by a combination of the resources and techniques of all three of the existing test approaches.

CONCLUSION

The main thesis of this paper is that testing is now ready for a major effort to create a synthesis out of what has hitherto been a series of unrelated approaches to testing. Such a synthesis is necessary if testing is to adequately deal with the very complex problems of describing, explaining, and predicting human characteristics. The attempt in this paper is to indicate the ways in which some of the powerful aspects of each testing approach may be brought together into a more complex way of handling test problems.

Perhaps the major weakness of this paper is that it approaches a synthesis of testing methods by adding terms to the more traditional ones. Hopefully this is only one step toward a more effective synthesis that creates an entirely new view of testing with fewer terms and clearer operational procedures than can now be described.

The value of work toward a new synthesis would be in its effect on the training of a new generation of specialists in this field as well as in opening up to a greater variety of attack those problems that have hitherto been regarded as the special province of a single approach—whether it be measurement, evaluation, or assessment.

REFERENCES

American Educational Research Association. *Technical recommendations for achievement tests.* Washington, D.C.: AERA, 1955.

American Psychological Association. *Technical recommendations for psychological tests and diagnostic techniques.* Washington, D.C.: APA, 1954.

Barron, F. *Creative and psychological health.* Princeton, N.J.: D. Van Nostrand Company, Inc., 1963.

Bloom, B. S. (Ed.) *Taxonomy of educational objectives: Handbook I: Cognitive domain.* New York: David McKay, Inc., 1956.

Bloom, B. S. *Stability and change in human characteristics.* New York: John Wiley & Sons, Inc., 1964.

Dave, R. H. The identification and measurement of environmental process variables that are related to educational achievement. Unpublished doctoral dissertation, University of Chicago, 1963.

Dressel, P. L., & Mayhew, L. B. *General education: Exploration in evaluation.* Washington, D.C.: American Council on Education, 1954.

Furst, E. J. *Constructing evaluation instruments.* New York: David McKay Company, Inc., 1958.

Glaser, R. Instructional technology and the measurement of learning outcomes: Some questions. *American Psychologist,* 1963, *17*, 519–521.

Gulliksen, H. *Theory of mental tests.* New York: John Wiley & Sons, Inc., 1950.

Hathaway, S. R., & McKinley, J. C. *Minnesota multiphasic personality inventory.* New York: Psychological Corporation, 1951.

Hess, R. D., & Shipman, V. Early experience and socialization of cognitive modes in children. *Child Development,* 1965, *36*, 869–886.

Murray, H. A. *Explorations in personality.* New York: Oxford University Press, 1938.

OSS Assessment Staff. *Assessment of men.* New York: Holt, Rinehart and Winston, Inc., 1948.

Pace, C. R. *College and university environment scales: Technical manual.* Princeton: Educational Testing Service, 1963.

Pace, C. R., & Stern, G. G. An approach to the measurement of psychological characteristics of college environments. *Journal of Educational Psychology,* 1958, *49,* 269–277.

Payne, A. The selection and treatment of data for certain curriculum decision problems: A methodological study. Unpublished doctoral dissertation, University of Chicago, 1963.

Sanford, N. (Ed.) Personality development during the college years. *Journal of Social Issues,* 1956, *12,* 1–71.

Smith, E. R., Tyler, R. W., & others. *Appraising and recording student progress.* New York: Harper & Row, Publishers, 1942.

Stern, G. G., Stein, M. I., & Bloom, B. S. *Methods in personality assessment.* New York: The Free Press of Glencoe, 1956.

Stodolsky, S. Maternal behavior and language and concept formation in Negro pre-school children. Unpublished doctoral dissertation, University of Chicago, 1965.

Strong, E. K., Jr. *Vocational interests of men and women.* Stanford, Calif.: Stanford University Press, 1943.

Terman, L. M., & Merrill, M. A. *Measuring intelligence.* Boston: Houghton Mifflin Company, 1959.

Thurstone, L. L. *Primary mental abilities.* Psychometric Monographs, 1938.

Tyler, R. W. *Constructing achievement tests.* Columbus, Ohio: The Ohio State University Press, 1934.

Wolf, R. M. The identification and measurement of environmental process variables related to intelligence. Unpublished doctoral dissertation, University of Chicago, 1964.

Science and Evaluation: Reflections on Professor Bloom's Paper

MICHAEL SCRIVEN

INTRODUCTION

The distinctions proposed by Professor Bloom are not entirely clear to me, but it is clear that an immense variety of tasks falls under each of his headings. He calls for a synthesis; I am more struck by the need for recognizing the right to autonomy. But a debate at this level of generality is unlikely to be fruitful, so let me be more specific. I think the simplifying urge in all scientists, appropriate though it is in certain areas where Occam's razor is needed to clear the jungle, is often extended into regions where we need, instead, to be tenderly nurturing new growth. Running amuck with Occam's razor can happen at the metalevel, too. In particular, an arid emphasis on the descriptive aim of science has weakened our efforts in other equally legitimate directions.

THE NARROW VIEW OF SCIENCE

A common view among empiricists is that science has only one legitimate aim—to "tell it like it is," to describe the universe in terms of general laws and particular facts. The idea that understanding involves more than description is regarded as naïve psychologism; prediction is regarded as simply instantiation of descriptive laws and, hence, not significantly distinct; control is the business of engineers and politicians who may or may not use science, but whose administrative decisions are certainly not its affair; and evaluation is pretty close to an obscenity, symptomatic of failure to achieve the value-free ideal of science.

I want to express, though I cannot defend in detail, a strongly different view that I hope will allow a broader perspective of Professor Bloom's interesting paper. Curiously enough, methodological reductionists of the value-free school have been exceptionally careless in their analysis of what is for them the fundamental process, that of description. They have overlooked the highly sophisticated taxonomical developments that are presupposed by good scientific description, the differences between observation, identification, classification and description, and many other points that make scientific description of particular facts a very sophisticated process. When we turn to "general description," that is, laws, the failure to analyze is truly astonishing. It is still common to think that *the* logical form of scientific law is "All A's are B's."

THE FULL SCOPE OF SCIENCE

Science is an activity as well as a body of knowledge. It can be subdivided topically (into astronomy, biology, chemistry . . . zoology) or methodologically. The latter subdivisions, with which we are concerned, will be worth noting if they reflect substantial differences in training, practical procedures, assumptions, or instrumentation, even if there is some philosophical sense in which some of them can be reduced to others, or all to one.

Some proposed methodological subdivisions of the scientific process are: explanation, prediction, control, description, evaluation, experimentation, observation, measurement, classification, identification, diagnosis, retrodiction, analysis, generalization, deduction, induction, intuition, understanding, reflection, speculation, checking, construction of artifacts, and training. In these terms, I see the scientific aspects of the educational enterprise, for example, as (a) observation of student and other behavior (including attitudes, capacities, and so forth) in putative learning situations; (b) development and application of new scales, taxonomies, generalizations, and theories to describe this behavior; (c) experimentation and theorizing to identify and distinguish the environmental and subject variables (genetic and learned) that produce the behavior; (d) evaluation of the student, his performance and the effect of the environment (including both contrived and natural features, for example, textbooks and weather) with respect to various educational criteria [using (a) through (c)]; (e) prediction/ retrodiction of later/earlier behavior, and so forth [using (a) through (c)]; (f) creation of new materials to achieve desired effects [using (a) through (c)].

This account does not, I think, involve any new and potentially confusing senses of old terms like "assessment," or distinctions, which seem artificial, between it and "evaluation." It does involve a good many more distinctions than his primary three, but they are ones with which we are familiar enough in practice and seem to have more simplicity of reference. "Testing," for example is to be seen as sometimes measurement leading to description, sometimes as checking the consequences of a theory and sometimes as the key element in evaluation. I prefer not to define it in the totally comprehensive way that Bloom does, where it includes all data-gathering; surely field-study observation is not usefully described as testing.

In the end, Bloom has far more distinctions than I do, but mine are already in the language and do not have to be learned. That is no excuse for not learning his if they really pull their weight, but there I confess that the point of many of them eludes me. So I am proposing a more conservative and less technical taxonomy than his for the scientific investigation of education, but still one that considerably expands the commonly used range of distinctions.

SCIENTIFIC EVALUATION

The main aim of this note, however, is to argue for a more honest and powerful conception of evaluation. "Telling it like it is," that is, meaningful description, must involve evaluation. Owing to rather widespread methodological sloppiness and a degree of understandable cowardice by social scientists, including those in the educational field, we have diluted the threatening notion of evaluation until it has become almost as harmless as instruction or observation and hard to distinguish from testing. Not many people feel they are beyond reproach, and not very many like to administer reproach; so we have an almost united front of negative motivation about evaluation. But evaluation is an obligation that cannot be avoided by wishing it would go away.

The simple fact is that evaluation is one of the absolutely fundamental tasks and obligations of science, both pure and applied, whether or not one accepts the view that it is part of effective description. Not only is the goal of a value-free science unattainable in practice, it is absurd in principle. The aim of pure science is to produce good or better explanations, principles, and classifications (for example), and the use of the valuational terms "good" and "better" in that claim is essential. Nor can they be translated into other terms in any general way. What counts as good is different in the three cases mentioned, just as the practical criteria for a good FM tuner are different from those for a good skinning knife; but what is common is the process of evaluation and the production of value judgments, and a scientist who is not skilled in this process and production cannot be a good scientist. Even if a wholly general but still usefully applicable translation could be given for the value vocabulary, this would not banish evaluation; it would only rechristen it. There remain to be discussed three evasive moves and modifications in the methodological game of decontaminating science from value judgments.

DECONTAMINATING ATTEMPTS

First, it is sometimes argued that this kind of evaluation is "only instrumental (or derived) evaluation," using criteria that are not established by science: the forbidden enterprise is "fundamental (or basic) evaluation," the setting up of the ultimate values. Second, it is argued that these methodological value judgments are not at issue; it is only moral value judgments that science cannot make. Third, it may be said that in certain applied areas, like education, the relevant value criteria in fact and properly come from outside science.

It is worth summarizing the major objections to these moves, because evaluators need a philosophical platform if they are to withstand the slings and arrows of outraged peers, parents, and pupils.

It is true there is a difference between instrumental and fundamental evaluation. Judging the merits of scientific contributions, for example, Bloom's work, is indeed different from deciding what criteria for merit are to be (should be) applied. But I would argue that the scientific enterprise embraces both.

The search for new paradigms of theory in science often involves decisions on the criteria for a good theory; for example, is it essential that it be prediction-generating or deterministic? Surely scientists, with some help and hindrance from philosophers of science, do discuss and answer these questions in a rational manner. The conceptual analysis of the nature of science involved is a metascientific rather than an intrascientific task, but it is not a field where only arbitrary choices are possible. It seems entirely appropriate that metascience, especially since its results crucially affect specific sciences, should be regarded as a legitimate branch of science just as the foundations of math is regarded as a branch of math. Even if some kind of distinction of degree is made, it is certainly part of the province of the empirical and logical analysis of scientific activity, not a mere matter of taste.

Suppose someone said: in an important sense, what we define as "science" is still an arbitrary decision, and it is only that decision which makes possible the derived value judgments about the merits of theories, and so forth, which do admittedly occur within science. For we might just say that "science" includes theology and astrology and Christian Science, in which case the aspects of scientific theories that are to count as meritorious would also have to be redefined. So the judgments of merit depend on a lexicographical decision, which is of course arbitrary. And arbitrary decisions are not the business of science. Then one can reply that in this sense of "arbitrary," it is arbitrary that truth is not falsehood, one is not two, heat is not temperature, and so forth. Conversely, there is nothing less arbitrary than definitional truths, and it is a definitional truth that scientific theories should imply truths about the world. It is such definitional truths that provide the basis for methodological value judgments. The only grain of truth in the value-free line is the fact that the basic value judgments might be said to be part of the logic of science rather than of particular sciences. The fact remains that they are securely established and provide the foundation for all standards of quality in science.

The second move concedes the role of methodological value judgments in science and excludes only moral ones. In this case, we may take moral value judgments as those made about human behavior, attitudes, and so forth, with respect to their effects on other humans, judged from the point of view that treats humans as having prima facie equal rights. The toughest countermove here consists in saying that ethics itself *is* a (social) science and that *it* certainly involves moral value judgments. One cannot argue against this by invoking the normative/descriptive distinction because of the previous arguments. Nor do I think it can be defeated by the usual antiutilitarian arguments about morality being an end in itself and not a matter of calculating consequences for people, since these can be met (see "Morality" in *Primary Philosophy,* McGraw-Hill, 1966).

An independent but weaker counterargument suggests that in certain applied sciences moral considerations enter essentially. For example, in psychotherapy, the definition of improvement in the patient or client cannot legitimately exclude considerations of his effects on the welfare of others. This is a more powerful claim than the general observation that a scientist's output, whether bombs or banana bread, can be used for good or ill; the latter point shows only that he cannot as a person avoid some responsibility for foreseeable applications of his work. The present point suggests that his work as a scientist necessarily involves moral value judgments. The best counter is to attempt to separate the moral from the medical criteria; it is not a promising one. Even psychoanalytical theory, for all the moral relativism espoused by many of its practitioners, embodies an account of the good life and of obligations and duties. The same is true of most personality theory and approaches to educational psychology, abnormal psychology, the psychology of sex, and so forth. At the very least, there are moral obligations on the scientist in these areas which intermingle with scientific considerations in his work.

The final skirmish particularly concerns "service" fields like educational evaluation. Now it is true that an applied scientist in principle can evaluate almost anything with respect to almost any set of criteria. But his task as a scientist is not confined to such factual inquiries, though the exigencies of his employment situation may require it. A good research man helps in the development of evaluation criteria at both the abstract and the operational levels, whether he is concerned with detergents, hoppickers or Headstart. He is usually not the only source of, though he may well be the chief assessor of, considerations relevant to criterion-picking, since there is usually a market involved in one sense or another. In education this is the population of parents, prospective employers, citizens, and especially the students themselves. Their needs and wants are indeed relevant, but none of these groups has absolute priority over the others; nor are any of them well-equipped to identify their unfelt needs, to translate their felt needs into educationally usable criteria, or to give an intelligent weighting to possible side-effects. For this we need the skills of social science. So the educational evaluator has a double task: determining appropriate criteria and applying them. It is a task in the best tradition of the most abstract theoretical science as well as the most practical applied science.

Comments on Professor Bloom's Paper

GENE V GLASS

First, I want to suggest that syntheses of the concepts Bloom identifies under *reliability* and *norms* do exist. Second, I want to offer an answer to the question of whether we *ought* to synthesize measurement, evaluation, and assessment into a theory of testing.

Cronbach, Gleser, and Rajaratnam's liberalization of reliability theory known as "generalizability theory" has, to my mind, synthesized diverse concepts and methods of reliability assessment. Variability in performance arising from any universe of influences (whether "readers," "time," "types of instrument," or "content") can be estimated in a factorially designed *G*-study (*generalizability*-study) and used to determine the generalizability of measures taken in some practical application (a decision-study). In a *G*-study, lack of generalizability from an observed score to a universe score is conceived of as the interaction (in the Fisherian sense) of examinees with the factors over which generalization is sought. It is possible with present techniques to determine, for example, a lower bound to the correlation of an observed "neuroticism" score derived by averaging the ratings of two psychiatrists (*reader reliability*)[1], on three occasions (*instrument stability*) over six symptoms (*sampling or congruence reliability*) with a universe "neuroticism" score defined to be the average score for an examinee over universes of the psychiatrists, occasions, and symptoms sampled (Gleser, Cronbach, & Rajaratnam, 1965). I don't think we need to look far beyond generalizability theory for a synthesis of reliability notions.

Though I can suggest no conceptual synthesis of the five types of norms

[1] The terms in parentheses are Bloom's.

Bloom identifies, there is, I believe, a technological synthesis worth pursuing. We have long acknowledged that the validity of a test is always for a particular purpose. However, we have been slower to acknowledge that one always has a particular purpose in mind when referring a test score to a set of norms. Seldom is this purpose to determine the status of a person in an anonymous and ill-defined norm group. For example, in counseling an eighteen-year-old Negro dropout on making a vocational choice, it may be irrelevant to determine the status of his mechanical aptitude score with respect to the general population in getting a job, labor unions being what they presently are.

Instead of publishing test norms as is presently done, perhaps we should record on magnetic-tape test performance, on more than one occasion, along with extensive biographical, social, and psychological data for a large sample of persons. Anyone seeking normative information would need only to specify the composition of the norm group that suits his purpose. For example, one might request the norms on the Bennett Test of Mechanical Comprehension for Negro males between the ages of sixteen and thirty-five without a high school diploma and living in cities of over 500,000 population. The problems of programming a computer to search the available data and produce norms for such a group seem insignificant.

A practical synthesis of the four types of validity Bloom lists seems less imminent, although Rozeboom (1966) has recently examined these issues and exposed greater unity in our diverse notions of validity than we might have imagined existed.

A synthesis of the terms Bloom lists seems clearly possible. However, the primary question he has posed in his paper is, "How do we synthesize three separate data-gathering activities into one theory of testing?" To seek an answer begs the question that they ought to be synthesized, a question we should examine carefully.

Should one attempt to synthesize measurement, evaluation, and assessment into a theory of testing, a theory of "gathering and processing evidence about human behavior . . . for purposes of understanding, predicting, and controlling future human behavior?" I think not. Achieving the synthesis would misdirect the development of one of the constituents, namely, evaluation, and further subvert the already abused goal of that activity. A synthesis would redirect the development of measurement and assessment as well; but in the context of Bloom's paper and this symposium, I wish to deal only with what such a merger would mean to evolving strategies of evaluation.

Bloom and I have roughly the same thing in mind when we think of evaluation. It deals with gathering evidence about the effects of instruction; it has to do with whether a curriculum is doing its job, and so forth. But we define evaluation differently; we ascribe different roles to it; and we see it developing along different lines. To Bloom, evaluation is the appraisal of change in students due to instruction, and its major quest is the "identification of learning experiences . . . which produce significant changes in individuals. . . ." I am more sympathetic with Scriven's declaration that it "consists . . . of the gathering and combining of performance data with a weighted set of goal scales to yield either comparative or numerical ratings, and in the justification of (a) the data-gathering instruments, (b) the weightings, and (c) the selection of goals" (Scriven, 1966a, p. 40). Tyler has defined evaluation similarly: " 'Evaluation' designates a process of appraisal which involves the acceptance of specific values and the use of a variety of instruments of observation, including measurement, as bases for value-judgments" (Tyler, 1951, p. 48).

The current meaning of the term "evaluation" in several recent writings and in federal legislation is that it is the gathering of empirical evidence for decision-making and the justification of the decision-making policies and the values upon which they are based. (See Stake, 1967b, and Stufflebeam, 1966.) Evaluation can contribute to the construction of a curriculum, the prediction of academic success, or the improvement of an existing course. But these are roles it can play and not its goal. The goal of evaluation must be to answer questions of selection, adoption, support, and worth of educational materials and activities. It must be directed toward answering questions like, "Are the benefits of this curriculum worth its cost?" or, "Is this textbook superior to its competitors?"

The contrast between the view of evaluation as gathering test data about how well a curriculum accomplishes its objectives and the above view is the contrast between the first and second dictionary definitions of "evaluation": "to find the amount or numerical value of something $\lfloor$ for example, evaluate $f(x) = log\ (x)$ at $x = 2\,\rfloor$" versus "to appraise the worth or value of something." The latter function corresponds to the goal of educational evaluation; the former function corresponds to one of many roles it can play. In the past, we have avoided the goal of evaluation with its inherent threat to teachers, administrators, and curriculum developers and have concentrated on one or more of the nonthreatening roles evaluation can play. We have measured performance without questioning merit. Scriven claimed that "if we do *not* know that (and usually how) . . . performance bears on merit, it is a travesty to refer to the measurement of it as evaluation: and exactly this travesty is involved in a great deal of curriculum evaluation where no defensible conclusions about merit can be drawn from the kind of data that is so earnestly gathered" (Scriven, 1966b, pp. 6–7).

"Evaluation," which is no more than the measurement of whether a curriculum attains its stated objectives, is guilty of *values-relativism,* that is, the acceptance of the idea that any objective is as valuable as any other.

Are not empirical facts irrelevant to questions of value? The answer to the last question is *no.* We cannot force knowledge into a facts-values dichotomy. "Our image of value and our image of fact are symbiotic. They are part of a single knowledge structure, and it is naïve in the extreme to suppose that they are independent" (Boulding, 1967, p. 886). In view of what cultural anthropologists and physiologists have learned about man, it is no longer possible rationally to value the "pure Aryan race." In education there would exist no basis for valuing recall of isolated facts about history if it could be demonstrated empirically that such recall is unrelated to scholarship in history of intelligent citizenship.

Now what part do our empirical methodologies have to play in a theory of *evaluation* that assesses *value?* What do testing, psychometrics, experimental design, survey research, and so forth, have to do with questions of merit or worth? First, the objectives of instruction need justification. Evaluation should seek to determine their comparative merit or worth empirically while philosophy seeks logical justification. Occasionally, both empirical science and rational thought will have to seek justification for the very values upon which course objectives are based. Second, if we are to approach rationality in decision-making, we must be able to measure the values of the decision-makers and the value-weights they ascribe to the outcomes of instruction. It is here that psychometric methods of scaling and factor analysis can make a contribution (Taylor, 1967; Maguire, 1967). Third, once the objectives of instruction and value-weights for criteria are determined and justified, comparative experimentation will arbitrate questions of relative merit and worth.

It may seem that too much is being made of an idiosyncratic definition of "evaluation," especially since Bloom expressed little interest in the "accuracy or the meaningfulness of the terms measurement, evaluation, and assessment." I cannot help being greatly concerned with the meanings of words and, more importantly, with how they influence action. I frequently come into contact with educationists whose most energetic efforts are victimized by a semantic confusion. By happenstance, habit, or methodological bias, they may, say, label the trial and investigation of a new curriculum or organizational plan with the epithet "experiment" instead of "evaluation." I am convinced that the inquiry they conduct is different for their having chosen to call it an "experiment" and not an "evaluation." Their choice predisposes the literature they read (it will deal with *experimental* design), the consultants they call in (only acknowledge experts in designing *experiments*), and how they report the results (always in the best tradition of the *Journal of Experimental Psychology*). In some instances, none of these paths will lead to relevant data or promote rational decision-making. The crucial data may be "soft" instead of "hard"; they may deal with the instructional materials or parents' reactions to them instead of students' behavioral outcomes.

To be sure, many psychometricians, measurement specialists, and methodologists will want to have nothing to do with evaluation as depicted here. Some will dismiss it because it attempts to deal with "philosophical questions" and questions of value (Carroll, 1965, p. 253), as indeed it does. Others will maintain that they are free to investigate whatever they please and that broadening the definition of evaluation to include telling Congress how to spend money or administrators how to choose curricula does not please them. For them, evaluation will stop with the attribution of behavioral change to instructional experience.

Others will want to consider seriously whether we can afford to go on merely playing one of the roles of evaluation instead of trying to fulfill its goals. The curriculum movement, the entry of industry into the production of educational materials, the development of new organizational plans, and so forth, are confronting educationists with choices, with decisions. The entire rapidly changing nature of education is pressing the *goal* of evaluation upon us. Of course, we are free not to play any part at all in this revolution. We who identify with "measurement" and "psychometrics" seem to feel (with poorly disguised satisfaction) that we stand among the angels. But my own self-satisfaction has been disturbed by my perception that increasingly educationists see us as standing among the Philistines. We react with conventional solutions (regression analysis, reliability and validity estimation, factor analysis, item analysis, and so forth) to their earnest requests for help in facing unprecedented problems in decision-making; and we are even rather smug about how we think we have helped them. I know of an instance of a corporation contracting with a curriculum development project for a handsome sum to perform an "evaluation" which eventuated in nothing more than an item analysis of an achievement test.

Should we attempt to synthesize measurement, evaluation, and assessment into a theory of testing? It would seem preferable to allow evaluation (with its emphasis upon judging the overall merit of an educational enterprise) to develop along its own lines independent of the development of testing (with its emphasis on measuring and predicting human characteristics). Instead of thinking of measurement, evaluation, and assessment as elements of some unitary, higher-order theory, we might profit more from thinking of them as existing and growing individually in a relationship of mutual assistance and support. Evaluation will *borrow* from measurement and assessment to suit its needs as it will borrow from all the social sciences (Stake, 1967a); the other disciplines can be expected to do likewise. It has been a struggle to establish educational evaluation with an identity apart from educational testing; it would be a shame to see it engulfed again by the more mature discipline of testing.

REFERENCES

Boulding, K. E. Dare we take the social sciences seriously? *American Psychologist,* 1967, *22,* 879–887.

Carroll, J. B. School learning over the long haul. In J. D. Krumboltz (Ed.), *Learning and the educational process.* Skokie, Ill.: Rand McNally & Company, 1965.

Cronbach, L. J., Rajaratnam, N., & Gleser, G. C. Theory of generalizability: A liberalization of reliability theory. *British Journal of Statistical Psychology,* 1963, *16,* 137–163.

Gleser, G. C., Cronbach, L. J., & Rajaratnam, N. Generalizability of scores influenced by multiple sources of variance. *Psychometrika,* 1965, *30,* 395–418.

Maguire, T. O. Value components of teachers' judgments of educational objectives. Unpublished doctoral dissertation. University of Illinois, 1967.

Rajaratnam, N., Cronbach, L. J., & Gleser, G. C. Generalizability of stratified-parallel tests. *Psychometrika,* 1965, *30,* 39–56.

Rozeboom, W. W. *Foundations of the theory of prediction.* Homewood, Ill.: Dorsey Press, 1966.

Scriven, M. The methodology of evaluation. In R. E. Stake (Ed.), *AERA monograph series on curriculum evaluation.* Skokie, Ill.: Rand McNally & Company, 1966a.

Scriven, M. Value claims in the social sciences. Publication No. 123. Lafayette, Indiana: Social Sciences Education Consortium, 1966b.

Stake, R. E. An emerging theory of evaluation—borrowings from many methodologies. Paper presented at the Annual Meeting of the American Educational Research Association, New York, February, 1967a.

Stake, R. E. The countenance of educational evaluation. *Teachers College Record,* 1967b, *68,* 523–540.

Stufflebeam, D. L. Evaluation under Title I of the Elementary and Secondary Act of 1965. Paper read at the Evaluation Conference sponsored by the Michigan State Department of Education, East Lansing, Michigan, January 1966.

Taylor, P. A. The mapping of concepts. Unpublished doctoral dissertation, University of Illinois, 1967.

Tyler, R. W. The functions of measurement in improving instruction. Chapter 2 in E. F. Lindquist (Ed.), *Educational measurement.* Washington, D.C.: American Council on Education, 1951.

Comments on Professor Bloom's Paper

J. P. GUILFORD

Professor Bloom's paper reflects considerable thought on problems of measurement in education. In saying this, I am using the term "measurement" in my familiar broad sense and not in the limited sense in which Bloom chooses to apply it, namely, to those concerned with basic psychological traits. The paper considers the broad range of places at which measurements are needed in education and the reasons for those needs. Types of techniques are mentioned and where they apply. Varieties of reliability, validity, and norms are discussed as well as the purposes that they serve.

The paper is not so much about a synthesis of methods of measurement as it is a systematic survey, with comparisons and assignment of roles. Since psychological tests of basic traits and achievement examinations have had common use for many years and the assessment procedures (in the narrow sense) have not, it might be said that he is making a plea for the addition of those techniques. He more clearly makes a plea for more attention to the environment of the student. This means quantitative descriptions of environments on the one hand, and taking environmental conditions somehow into account in measuring traits of individuals, on the other. Just how the latter is to be achieved is not made clear. There is also a plea for more theory, which includes psychological theory, in connection with the question of what is being measured. He contrasts the apparent wealth of theory on the part of those who deal in assessment procedures and the apparent poverty of theory on the part of the testers, or what he calls the "measurement" approach. The contrast actually seems exaggerated, however, for some testers have been very much concerned about theory, and they possess and they use more rigorous methods for testing their theories.

There are many excellent points made in the paper to which one can agree. Again we see a warning against the misuse of testing. All of us probably know instances in which some very bad decisions have been made, based on rigid interpretations of IQ's and other scores. Those making such decisions are functioning like technicians rather than as sophisticated, professional psychologists. The wrong use of tests can do much harm, but I should hesitate to go as far as Bloom, when he speaks of the potential of tests for destroying mankind as being equal to that of atomic energy. I sometimes wonder, however, what effect the widespread use of answer-sheet tests may have had on our population. Our extensive experiences in the Aptitudes Research Project at the University of Southern California has demonstrated many times over that one cannot measure abilities for productive thinking, divergent or convergent, with one or two possible exceptions, by means of answer-sheet tests. There are even a few cognition abilities (where cognition is defined in the restricted sense of the structure of intellect) that require completion items, not multiple-choice.

It is easy to agree with Bloom that "evaluation" or measurement of achievement in education should be in terms of the objectives that have been set up for education in an area of instruction. This principle is often given lip service, but not so often observed in practice. A corollary to this principle, a very important one, is that the objectives should be so clearly spelled out that examination items can be written for each one of them. The objectives should often be as specific as the items themselves. Another corollary, which Bloom mentions, is that where objectives differ, examinations should differ. This calls into question the overemphasis on national testing programs and national norms.

It is very true, as Bloom says, that the kinds of tests that we apply influence the learner in his learning and the teacher in his teaching. They both work toward the end that the student shall do well in the tests. Tests also determine certain educational values, which, in turn, determine social values. For years, the IQ has helped to set educational goals. We have tried to see to it that each student shall perform educationally at a level consistent with his IQ. Now the IQ test is weighted heavily with cognition abilities (cognition in the structure-of-intellect sense), which represent only one-fifth of all known or expected intellectual abilities. The student can achieve in this respect just by understanding and absorbing information; there is little or no premium in also learning how to use that information in productive thinking.

I cannot agree with Bloom when he says that the psychological testers (whom he calls measurement people) assume that individuals who take their tests have had equal environmental opportunities. There may have been a day when developers of tests of abilities thought that what they wanted to measure is entirely determined by heredity. Although test theorists, following Spearman, have recognized that every test score has an error component, I cannot recall anyone saying that he regarded that error to be completely contributed by the environment of the individual. I think it is safe to say that most testers regard any individual's score as being a function of both the person's heredity and his environment, and the true component is not necessarily attributed entirely to his heredity. The individual's score, allowing for its error component, tells us how the person stood on a certain scale at a certain time, without telling us how he got that way. It would take information from different sources to tell us how he got that way.

What I have just said applies more strictly to cognition tests. If I may refer to the structure of intellect again as a frame of reference, I can point out some exceptions. Cognition tests tell us how much information of a certain kind the examinee has in his possession. We do not know how or when he obtained it. In tests of memory abilities, however, we must ensure that examinees have had equal opportunity to learn the information on which we are going to test them. We therefore apply experimental controls, exposing them for a constant period of time to the same stimulus material. As a further control, in order to minimize or exclude cognition variance, the selected information to which they are exposed is made so easy to cognize that on a cognition test of it, they would all make perfect scores. For the measurement of production abilities, divergent or convergent, and evaluative abilities, we also apply the latter control, staying well within the range of common experience for all individuals tested. We do not always succeed in this, but we try. Factor analysis tells us when we have not succeeded.

As I read the section regarding evaluation, I had the impression that the interest in gain scores is overemphasized at the expense of status scores. The measurement of change offers numerous problems, which Chester Harris is well prepared to tell us about. There are problems of scaling so that numerical differences on one part of a scale are equivalent to those on other parts of the same scale. Some kind of absolute scaling seems called for. Furthermore, reliabilities of gain scores, in the form of differences between status scores, are notoriously unreliable. Rarely would they be sufficiently reliable for the purpose of individual measurement and there would be little use for norms. They would be sufficiently reliable for research on groups.

I agree with Bloom's concern about gaining information concerning the student's environment, past and present. In general, psychologists have paid too little attention to human environments. We need very much to know what relevant features and variables should be made known and should be measured in relation to behavioral variables. But I am puzzled by the insistence that information about the environment should somehow enter into the measurement of psychological and educational variables. Nor are we told how this can or should be done. Information regarding the environment is often very useful in understanding an individual's scores, but why should we combine that information with measures of the individual? I hope that I have not misinterpreted Bloom's intention.

A survey of available techniques for quantitative descriptions of students is useful, but I think that Bloom would agree that this is not the best place to start in planning a comprehensive program in education. The first question to ask is for what aspects of personal development are the schools responsible? In this connection, what information do we need or want about individuals? No technique should be used just because it is available. If there are aspects of development for which no techniques of evaluation exist, we should see that those techniques are developed. There are other considerations. Is the method efficient and economical? Is what it has to tell us worth the effort? Will it arouse student or parental resistance? Will someone use the information that the method provides, and use it wisely?

There is one aspect of measurement in the form of evaluation that Bloom touched upon but which deserves greater emphasis. This is the aspect of continual feedback information, which measurement provides to the student as well as to the teacher, administrator, and counselor. The teacher should want to know how well the educational objectives are being fulfilled in the class that he teaches. Where are the weak spots and what kind of weakness exists? The serious student, like all motivated humans, wants to know, "How well am I doing?" He may be satisfied to know the answer in terms of a general quantity, such as a score or a grade. What he may not know, and we as psychologists do know, from the laws of learning, is that he would profit even more by having specific feedback information. It would be wise to arrange matters so that there is prompt and specific feedback to the student at every step of his learning.

At one time I knew a professor of chemistry who proposed a procedure and a kind of device that I am sure would be a big step forward in education. It would provide for individual testing of students during a lecture. After making a particular point in lecturing, the teacher would give the class a multiple-choice test item on that point. Each student would press one of several buttons on his chair, which has a wired connection with a device on the lecturer's table. On a screen visible to teacher and students would flash the correct answer, also the number of correct answers. In the device on the table each student's score would be cumulated.

We are approaching this kind of operation, of course, in computerized learning. But I am sure that you will agree that we are far from realizing all the potential that our electronic age has made possible. My plea is that we give much more time to evaluation than we do and that it also be made an integral part of the teaching process, taking advantage of the best learning principles that we know.

As to broader aspects of educational evaluation, I should like to propose a general approach to which I have given some thought, without coming to any concrete procedural decisions. So far as the intellectual aspects of school learning are concerned, we have a two-fold obligation to the student: (a) to see that he acquires the desirable items of specific information, and (b) to see that he develops general, intellectual skills for dealing with that information. Together, these aspects make up what should be included in the individual's total intelligence. The first of these is now fairly well evaluated in terms of standard achievement examinations. The second is measured by tests of intellectual abilities. By this I do not mean that we be content with present IQ tests and academic-aptitude tests, for they do not go nearly so far as they should and are limited to one or two scores. We are learning a great deal concerning the numerous unique intellectual abilities, which can be regarded as being equivalent to the generalized intellectual skills just mentioned. I do not contend that all of them would be of interest to the educator at all age levels or for all school subjects, but I am sure that many of them should be of serious educational interest in relevant places; and their periodic measurement should provide valuable information about the development of individuals. A program that involves such assessments should include sophisticated personnel who know how to use such information.

Open Discussion of Bloom's Paper and of Scriven's, Guilford's and Glass's Comments

BLOOM: With regard to Guilford's paper, I am not now suggesting that one has to test every individual with the whole range of error terms. Testing has been very powerful in classifying, predicting, and in controlling human behavior. It has not contributed as much to the understanding of human behavior and human institutions as I believe many of us would desire; and it is my feeling that only as we learn to combine these different views will we move in on this particular problem of understanding. We do not have the resources to do a full-scale test on every individual in every environment. I plead only for the attempt to move more toward the understanding of human behavior, human characteristics, and human environment.

I am very glad that Gene Glass emphasized evaluation. I think that was my wife. I am not quite sure we were talking about the same girl there.

The other thing I am concerned about, and it is the basic problem, is whether one should move into the more complex view or whether one should keep these views working side-by-side and relate them as one finds necessary.

There might be a new generation of people in this field, who would think very differently from the way we would if we had a way of synthesizing these areas. We do develop a particular view among our students and some disdain for all the other approaches.

LUMSDAINE: Gene expressed the purpose of evaluation as decision making. This is fine. He also identified some overall kinds of decisions, adoption, support, and so on, of curricula or programs. However, there is also a more humble but equally important form of "fine-grained" evaluation that can contribute, not to an overall acceptance-rejection decision but to specific guidance for the teacher or programmer in revising a curriculum, lesson, or program. I would stress the importance of evaluation, not just for deciding whether to throw something out or embrace it with open arms, but for deciding how to improve it, use it, supplement it. This is a "diagnostic" evaluation, as compared with "overall" evaluation. (The distinction here is similar to Scriven's distinction between, respectively, formative and summative evaluation.)

My second response to Gene Glass's remarks is closely related to my first one. I am referring to his statement that we have done the safe thing and have avoided asking dangerous or embarrassing questions. We have avoided asking some embarrassing questions, but not only because we have ignored value questions and concentrated on measurement aspects. It is also important to notice that we have evaluated students but not teachers or programs; obviously, for these two, quite different kinds of assessment procedures are required.

GLASS: I acknowledge the roles that evaluation can play in improving instruction: namely, to avoid the threat to certain persons inherent in any question of support or adoption; but I think there is a strong motive to turn toward the role you discussed and away from the goal of truly *evaluating*, which involves the ultimate questions of support and adoption. We must continually emphasize what ultimately we want to do with evaluation.

What presently is infecting our efforts to evaluate education is a rampant relativism of values, where any goal, any objective of instruction is considered acceptable and worth striving for. We no longer question whether it is worth achieving but just how we can get there faster and better. I think we have to face the question of whether we ought to attempt to achieve the goal, whether it's worthwhile and meritorious.

PACE: If one takes a broad definition of evaluation, such as Gene Glass suggested, having to do with judging the overall merit of an educational enterprise, you will not be interested only in the overall merit of something. Instead, you will first want to know some of the very specific things about which Art Lumsdaine was talking.

I might make one comment about the role of objectives in evaluation. If you want to judge the overall merit of an educational enterprise, objectives may be of secondary importance. The College Entrance Examination Board has a Commission on Tests to make an overall appraisal of the College Board testing program. At no point in the discussions of this Commission have we ever asked, "What are the objectives of the College Board testing program?" Instead, we have asked, "What are some of the effects of testing in our society?"

If you start off with a client orientation, that is, if you ask for the objectives of the Board, you may never look for information in relation to the question, "What are the effects of testing in society? What are the social consequences of the fact that College Board exists?" The information you look for obviously depends on the questions you ask. When you are dealing with large-scale problems, it may not be sufficient or even wise, to have all your inquiry determined by the client, in the sense of "What is the client trying to achieve?"

C. HARRIS: I would like to say two things. First of all, in response to Bloom's paper, I would define both evaluation and assessment as enterprises in which a number of technical measurement problems are embedded; and I would not set the three on the same level and compare them. I would deal with measurement embedded only within these two. In that sense I would disagree very much with your view, Mr. Bloom, of this whole area.

I would also like to disagree with Mr. Glass, because I think he is forcing us into a kind of decision theoretic model. Mr. Wiley and I will have more to say about this when we present our papers on the methodology of evaluation.

BLOOM: Chet, may I ask whether you enlarge the meaning of measurement beyond that which I was using?

C. HARRIS: I would like measurement to mean some very specific sets of technical problems associated with our concepts of reliability, validity, and so forth. Measurement problems are embedded in assessment; they are embedded in evaluation; they are embedded in research.

GAGNÉ: I think what Ben tried to do is extremely commendable and important; and I think we ought to be grateful to him for getting it started. I don't know that anybody has tried to do it in as orderly a fashion until now; but I think he handicapped himself by using these old terms, with all the connotations that surround them. The names that Ben mentioned conjure up in our minds all sorts of enterprises and approaches and techniques—O.S.S., Tyler and the Eight-Year Study, and so forth.

As an old taxonomist, Ben and others would do better if, instead of burdening themselves with these three historic terms, they liberated themselves from them. They could then proceed to be logical and rigorous without the excess connotative baggage of these three sets of terms.

CHAPTER 3

Evaluation of Instruction and Changing Educational Models[1]

ROBERT GLASER

Social institutions, whether educational, medical, religious, economic, or political must constantly prove their effectiveness to insure society's support. Acceptable proof of an institution's effectiveness depends largely upon the public attitude toward that institution, an attitude based both upon a respect for authority and tradition and a desire for demonstrated objective proof (Suchman, 1967). To some extent, the field of educational measurement and evaluation has developed in response to the requirement for objective proof of the effectiveness of the educational enterprise. Furthermore, the demand for evaluation is related to the growing alliance between educational practice and behavioral science and to the pressures that arise from the necessity to make competing social investments. These increasing pressures upon educators, in all parts of the field, to evaluate their activities are one aspect of a growing maturity of the profession and of the commitment of modern society to the belief that its educational problems can be met most effectively through development planned in conjunction with advancing knowledge. However, the main point I wish to make is that the form which evaluation procedures take is influenced by changes and advances in a given field.

It is reasonable for evaluation practices and procedures to change as the nature of education changes. This is not to imply that educational inno-

[1] Preparation of this chapter was supported under Contract No. Ponr-624(18) with the Personnel and Training Branch, Psychological Sciences Division, Office of Naval Research.

vation can completely ignore current standards and procedures of evaluation—a concept that could lead to chaos—but change in educational practice should influence the need for evaluation and the form it takes. Suchman (1967) has pointed out that in the field of public health, evaluation techniques require change as the nature of disease changes. His discussion is pertinent to the theme of this paper. In recent years, acute communicable diseases have been displaced as major causes of death and disability by chronic degenerative diseases. The new diseases are not amenable to the traditional proven methods of environmental sanitation and immunization. The degenerative disease programs, unlike communicable disease programs, cannot depend on either legislative fiat or mass immunization drives but require a greater degree of voluntary public cooperation and long-term programs of prevention and treatment. Evaluation of the control of the new major diseases requires new objectives and the development of new criteria of effectiveness. A heart disease control program, for example, in contrast to a smallpox or diphtheria control program, cannot be evaluated solely in terms of decreasing mortality. Early detection and treatment become new objectives, replacing prevention; accomplishment is evaluated and measured in terms of such immediate goals as case finding and the continuity of medical care.

The objectives and evaluation practices of a field are influenced not only by changes in the nature of the field itself but also by changes in the organization and operation of the field. For example, in public health, there is a trend toward broader responsibility for community health; and the dividing line between prevention and treatment is less distinct. Earlier public health services that concentrated on the poor and medically indigent now begin to encompass much larger segments of society. This broad emphasis enlarges the scope of a program's planning, implementation, and evaluation.

As the nature and organization of the field change, so do the attitudes and behaviors of the public, who are both targets of the social enterprise and ultimate determiners of its support. In the early days of the public health movement, the need for environmental sanitation and compulsory immunization did not require proof because the threats from disastrous epidemics were obvious. The feedback and consequences were relatively immediate. Today, the delayed effects of smoking or diet are much less immediate, and evaluation procedures require greater information and proof of the effectiveness of their measures. Today, motivation is a key problem in public health, and one of the primary conditions of motivation is the individual's belief in the effectiveness of the action he is being asked to undertake.

The field of public health provides an apt analogy to the situation that seems to be coming about in educational practice. Consider the three aspects mentioned above: the nature of the field, its organization, and expectations from its user and target groups. Several forces are changing the nature of educational practice, and of these I shall mention three. One is the increased focus on the cultivation of skill, understanding, and intellectual power in the basic disciplines. Witness the introduction of the massive curriculum development programs in physics, mathematics, English, history, and so forth. A second force is the growing conception that education does not have a fixed beginning or end point with neat packages of elementary, secondary, and higher education. The stress is less upon third-grade arithmetic or freshman English and more upon the continuity from grade to grade and from age to age and upon a commitment to a transmission of the ability to teach people to teach themselves. The third force is that as we learn more about the psychological and technological foundations of education, the individualization of instruction is being viewed less as an ideal and more as a practical enterprise.

Concurrent with the change in the nature of educational activities is the change in the structure, organization, and functioning of these activities and the agencies involved. The trend is toward larger schools, more pervasive educational philosophies, and the integration of social classes in one educational environment. This larger organization and integration deemphasizes local norms and introduces more widely accepted standards of accomplishment and competence. Coupled with this is the necessity for taking account of the increasing heterogeneity of a school by adapting to individual requirements. Another organizational factor that profoundly changes the nature of educational practice is the continued development of the educational profession and the accruing knowledge in the behavioral sciences.

There is a growing similarity between the public health field and education. Whereas the older diseases had immediately contingent effects that shaped the behavior of the public, the consequences of the newer diseases are more delayed. Perhaps the educational field generally produces effects that have not had immediate consequences mandating immediate action. In this regard, evaluation procedures might provide more immediate feedback of educational outcomes.

A GENERAL INSTRUCTIONAL MODEL

Since the nature of educational practice and its organization influences evaluation procedures, it is necessary to present a model of educational practice that can be assumed to underlie any general discussion of the evaluation of instruction. The model I shall describe is one that I believe is likely to come about as a result of the trends I have indicated—the emphasis on cognitive development in the disciplines, the continuity of education over the span of life, the ability to know how to learn and to teach oneself, and the adaptation of instruction to individual requirements. The accomplishment of these objectives suggests an instructional model with the following properties presented as a sequence of operations:

1. Outcomes of learning are specified in terms of the behavioral manifestations of competence and the conditions under which it is to be exercised. This is the platitudinous assertion of the fundamental necessity of describing the foreseeable outcomes of instruction in terms of certain measurable products and assessable student performance.

2. Detailed diagnosis is made of the initial state of a learner coming into a particular instructional situation. This careful workup of student performance characteristics relevant to the instruction at hand is necessary to pursue further education. Without the assessment of initial learner characteristics, carrying out an educational procedure is a presumption. It is like prescribing medication for an illness without first describing the symptoms. In the early stages of a particular educational period, instructional procedures will adapt to the findings of the initial assessment, generally reflecting the accumulated performance capabilities resulting from the long-term behavior history and activity of the learner. The history that is specifically measured is relevant to the next immediate educational step that is to be taken.

3. This immediate instructional step consists of educational alternatives adaptive to the classifications resulting from the initial student educational profiles. These alternative instructional procedures will be selectively assigned to the student or made available to him for his selection.

4. As the student learns, his performance will be monitored and continuously assessed at longer or shorter intervals appropriate to what is being taught. In early skill learning, assessment is quite continuous. Later on, as competence grows, problems grow larger; as the student becomes increasingly self-sustaining, assessment occurs more infrequently. This monitoring serves several purposes: providing a basis for knowledge of results and appropriate reinforcement contingencies to the learner and a basis for adaptation to learner demands. This learning history accumulated in the course of instruction is called "short-term history" and, together with information from the long-term history, provides information for assignment of the next instructional unit. The short-term history also provides information about the effectiveness of the instructional material itself.

5. Instruction and learning proceed in a kind of servomechanism, cyber-

netic fashion, tracking the performance and selections of the student. Assessment and performance are interlinked, one determining the nature and requirement for the other. Instruction proceeds as a function of the relationship among measures of student performance, available instructional alternatives, and learning criteria that are chosen to be optimized. The question of which criteria are to be optimized becomes critical. Is it retention, transfer, the magnitude of difference between pre- and posttest scores, motivation to continue learning including the ability to do so with minimal instructional guidance, or is it all of these? If tracking of the instructional process permits instruction to become precise enough, then a good job can be done to optimize some gains and minimize others unless the presence of the latter gains is desired, expressed, and assessed. The outcomes of learning measured at any point in instruction are referenced to and evaluated in terms of competence criteria and the values to be optimized; provision is always made for the ability of humans to surpass expectations.

6. Inherent in the system's design is its capability for improving itself. Perhaps a major defect in the implementation of educational innovations, especially in the area of individualization, has been the lack of the cumulative attainment of knowledge—on the basis of which the next innovation is better than the one that preceded it.

Given that the changing trends in education will lead to an instructional model somewhat like that just described, the main question to which this paper is addressed is "What are the implications for the nature of evaluation procedures?" I shall examine this question by some elaboration of each of the points just listed.

THE SPECIFICATION OF LEARNING OUTCOMES

In a system designed to maximize the attainment of certain objectives, the specification of learning outcomes in terms of observable student performance determines how the instructional components are used. Vague specification of desired outcomes leaves little concrete information for the evaluator about what to look for and what to help the system strive to attain. However, interaction between specification of outcomes and instructional procedure provides the basis for redefining objectives. The need for constant revision of objectives is as inherent in the system as is the initial need for defining them. There is a sustained process of clarifying goals, working toward them, evaluating progress, reexamining the objectives, modifying instructional procedures, and clarifying the objectives in the light of evaluated experience. This process should indicate the inadequacies and omissions in a curriculum. The fear of many educators that detailed specification of objectives limits them to simple behaviors only—those which can be forced into measurable and observable terms—is an incorrect notion if one thinks of them as amendable approximations to our ideals. If complex reasoning and open-endedness are desirable aspects of human behavior, then they need to be recognized and assessable goals. Overly general objectives may force us to settle for what can be easily expressed and measured.

A helpful distinction can be made between the evaluation of procedure and the evaluation of accomplishment. It is possible to evaluate a procedure, such as a difficult surgical operation, and to show that it is being done properly; it is another matter to evaluate its beneficial result. Evaluation of technique may be meaningless without evaluation of its effect, although it is often necessary to show that a new procedure in educational research in the schools is indeed being carried out appropriately. When one neglects the evaluation of technique and moves directly to the evaluation of accomplishment, the effective implementation of the procedure is assumed. One moves from procedural objectives to accomplishment objectives at many points in an instructional sequence. Attaining a procedural objective represents progress toward the accomplishment objective. Even though the two interact and accomplishment objectives are initially established, evaluation designed for the development of an operating instructional system should work from the evaluation of technique to the evaluation of accomplishment objectives, not the other way around as often seems to be the case. In succinct terms, it is necessary to make sure that the independent variable is in effect before measuring the dependent variable. Of course, in developmental or formative evaluation, assessment of each may suggest changes in the other.

A final point with respect to the specification of objectives relates to the distinction between criterion-referenced and norm-referenced measurement. The measurement of learning outcomes involves the assessment of criterion behavior; implicit in this process is the determination of the characteristics of student performance with respect to specified standards. It can be assumed that regardless of the way a subject matter is structured, some existing hierarchy of subobjectives indicates that certain performances must be attained as a basis for learning subsequent performance. An individual's competence level falls at some point on this hierarchy of increasing subject-matter competence. The degree to which the individual's measured performance resembles the desired performance at any specified competence level is assessed by referencing his performance to the criterion by some criterion-referenced measure. Criterion levels can be established at any point in instruction where it is necessary to obtain information concerning the adequacy of the learner's performance. The specific behaviors identified at each level of proficiency describe the tasks a student is capable of performing when he achieves this level of knowledge. Performance measured in this way provides explicit information concerning what the individual can and cannot do. Such criterion-referenced measures indicate the content of his behavior and the correspondence between his performance and the continuum of educational objectives. Measures that assess learner performance in terms of such criterion-referenced standards thus provide information about the competence of a student, independently of reference to the performance of others. In contrast to this procedure, as has been pointed out by Glaser (1963), the general practice in education is to measure achievement by norm referencing rather than by criterion referencing. Norm-referenced measures evaluate the learner's performance in terms of a comparison with the performance of others. Such measures need provide little or no information about the degree of competence exhibited by tested behaviors; they tell that one student is more or less proficient than the other but do not tell how proficient either of them is with respect to the desired learning outcomes. Evaluation in terms of criterion-referenced measures requires that we specify at least minimum levels of performance that the student is expected to attain or that he needs to attain in order to go on to the next step in an instructional sequence.

DIAGNOSIS OF INITIAL STATE (ENTERING BEHAVIOR)

The second item in the description of the model refers to the measurement and diagnosis of the initial state or entering behavior with which the learner comes into an instructional situation. Here we appear to be entering the domain of much of the work in the general field of psychological testing and evaluation. It seems obvious, however, that in order to follow through with the model I describe, we must go in the direction pointed to by Cronbach (1957) and by Cronbach and Gleser (1965), that is, to depart from the standard practices of test theory based upon the basic data of correlations between tests and static criterion variables, and to move toward decision-making procedures based upon the relationships between entering behavior and instructionally manipulated variables. The ultimate purpose of testing in this context is to arrive at decisions with respect to assignment to the instructional treatments defined by these instructional variables.

Evaluation of initial entering behavior involves measuring the products of the long-term history of the learner, which includes what we generally have called aptitudes. These aptitudes have attained importance as fundamental characteristics in the measurement of human behavior because they are useful in predicting long-range criteria such as school and college success. However, the model I describe demands that an additional task for measures of initial behavior be the prediction of very immediate success, that is, success in immediate learning. It can be postulated that if the criteria for aptitude test validation had been immediate learning success rather than some long-range criteria, the nature of today's generally accepted aptitude batteries would be quite different. This postulation seems likely since factorial studies of the changing composition of abilities over the course of learning (Fleishman, 1965) show different abilities involved at the beginning and end of the course of learning. Thus, while it is useful to forecast over the long range, our instructional model also requires measures that are closely related to more immediate learning criteria, that is, success in initial instructional steps. Current types of measured aptitude may be limited in that they are operationally designed to predict over the long period, given reasonably nonadaptive forms of educational treatment.

Aptitude tests or general psychometric reference tests resulting from factor analyses of aptitude tests would not be expected to correlate very highly with individual differences in learning and thereby would not be useful for the placement of individuals in alternate instructional treatments. As Jensen (1967) has pointed out, the predictive power of tests like the Primary Mental Abilities test is due to the fact that they sample learned behavior and therefore reflect something about the rate of learning in a given environment. They also measure the acquisition of broad verbal or symbolic capabilities (mediational systems), which play an important role in enabling an individual to generalize and solve problems. However, such standard psychometrically developed tests, as a result of the way in which they have been validated and evaluated, are more closely related to the products of learning that they predict, such as ability in school subjects, than they are to the kinds of variables generally dealt with in the learning laboratory; these are the variables relevant to instructional manipulation and educational alternatives. Evidence for this lack of utility of general psychometric measures with respect to instructional decisions comes from the line of studies dealing with correlations between psychometric variables and learning measures that was begun in 1946 by Woodrow's classic article. Woodrow showed data from laboratory and classroom experiments that indicated that the correlations between intelligence measures and ability to learn, in the sense of ability to improve with practice, were generally insignificant and often close to zero. More recently, this work has been followed up by Gulliksen and his students, for example, Stake (1961) and Duncanson (1964); but the results obtained are not clear-cut, and Woodrow's basic point has not been clearly disclaimed.

It seems that approximately five categories of entering behavior would require measurement for instructional decision-making (Travers, 1963): (a) the extent to which the individual has already learned the behavior to be acquired in instruction, that is, previously attained achievement in the skills and knowledge to be taught, (b) the extent to which the individual possesses the prerequisites for learning the behavior to be acquired, for example, knowing how to add before learning to multiply, (c) learning set variables, that consist of acquired ways of learning that facilitate or interfere with new learning procedures under certain instructional conditions, for example, prior success when acting impulsively or being cautious and reflective, (d) specific ability to make discriminations necessary in subsequent instruction, for example, musical aptitude or spatial visualization, and (e) general mediating abilities as measured by general tests of verbal or symbolic intelligence.

INSTRUCTIONAL ALTERNATIVES

On the basis of the initial measurement, instructional alternatives are available to the student. But what are these instructional alternatives, where do they come from, and how are they developed? In other words, on what basis do different instructional treatments differ so as to be adaptive to individual requirements? This is a significant problem fundamental to psychologically-based instructional design but which, in this paper emphasizing evaluation, can only be mentioned. Some alternatives seem easy to implement, such as adapting to the student's present level of accomplishment, his mastery of prerequisites, the speed at which he learns including the amount of practice he requires, and his ability to learn independent of highly structured situations. Adaptation to treatments differing in these respects, which are shown to be related to measured aspects of entering behavior, might be able to provide a significant beginning for effective adaptation to individual differences. However, in designing instructional alternatives, it is difficult to know how to use other variables that come out of learning theory (such as requirements for reinforcement, distribution of practice, the use of mediation and coding mechanisms, and stimulus and modality variables, for example, verbal, spatial, auditory, and visual presentation); and more needs to be known about their interaction with individual differences.

If one assumes that measures of entering behavior and instructional treatments are both available, then at our present state of knowledge, empirical work must take place to determine those measures most efficient for assigning individuals to treatment classes. The task is to determine those measures that have the highest discriminating potential for allocating between treatments and then determine their intercorrelations so that they can be combined in some way and all of them need not be used. This task seems to be a reasonably typical multivariate problem. As a result of the initial diagnostic or placement decision, the universe or sample of students involved is reduced to subsets, allocable to the various available instructional treatments. These initial decisions will be corrected by further assignments as learning proceeds so that the allocation procedure becomes a multistage decision process which defines an individualized instructional path.

CONTINUOUS ASSESSMENT

The next item in the model indicates that as a student proceeds to learn his performance will be monitored, and at appropriate intervals, measures of this performance will be summarized and indexed. In contrast to the long-term history used for initial placement, the measures obtained in learning are called the short-term history, even though prolonged use of the model may fuse the two items to some extent. Here again, the problem of what instructional alternatives are made available is of major concern. Of equal importance are the kinds of measures to be obtained in the course of learning.

The kinds of measures of learning progress one usually obtains, and on which instructional decisions are made, consist of test-score information that measures the frequency of correct responses, errors in relation to some performance standard, and the speed of performance. Less frequently, measures of transfer and generalization are specifically employed. Perhaps, to some extent, this is done when one selects a set of test items that are derived from the same universe of subject-matter content but are not the same sample as was used in initial learning.

Of special interest in the assessment of short-term history are measures that are being suggested by experimental work on learning; these are measures that can be obtained in the course of learning and may be predictive of future learning requirements. Two examples may give the flavor of this. One comes from the work of Zeaman and House (1967) on a theory of discrimination learning accounting for the performance of retarded children learning to solve two-choice visual discrimination problems, such as may be involved in letter or numeral discrimination. The theory postulates a chain of two responses for problem solution: the first, paying attention to the relevant stimulus dimensions, and the second, the correct selection of the positive cue of the relevant dimensions. They ask whether individual differences in empirical learning curves are attributable to differences in the speed of acquisition or to some underlying process such as attention. The data they obtain show wide individual differences in learning curves, with higher IQ subjects doing better than the lower; however, the important differences in the curves between the brighter and duller subjects is not the slope of the curve, that is, the rate of learning, but the length of the initial plateau. Thus, it is not the rate of improvement, once it starts, that distinguishes bright and dull but how long it takes for improvement to begin. The length of time for improvement to begin is considered an attentional variable and suggests, at least with respect to the concerns of this paper, that the measurement of plateau length rather than rate of improvement is a sensitive measure of discrimination learning.

The second example is a study performed in my own laboratory by Wilson Judd (1969) on paired-associate learning. The interest here was on response latency, that is, the interval between the onset of a stimulus and the occurrence of a response, as an index of learning. Hull, in his theory and experimental work, strongly suggested latency as a measure of habit strength. Our study investigated changes in the latency measure over the course of learning, from initial learning through a criterion of nearly perfect performance, and then through overlearning. Throughout this course, frequency of correct response increased to criterion and then continued at asymptote through overlearning. In contrast, latency showed no change and remained constant as correct response probability increased from chance to near 1.0; however, during the overlearning period, while response probability remained constant, latency showed a significant and sustained decrease, presumably related to the consolidation of learning during the overlearning period. The suggestion from this work is that the latency measure, as a short-term learning history variable, seems to detect aspects of learning not detectable from response frequency and may be related to and predictive of future retention. With the talk about the possibility of computer-assisted instruction, latency measures would be easy to obtain and be available for instructional decision-making.

The work of Jensen (1967) on individual differences in learning variables is also relevant here. His factor analyses of learning tasks of the kind used in the learning laboratory showed interesting results. For example, two types of learning that on the surface look very much alike, serial learning and paired-associate learning, were not found to be significantly intercorrelated, even when the stimulus materials were the same in both tasks. In addition there was little transfer between the two tasks. On the other hand, serial learning was found to have much in common with memory span. Jensen also found that in serial learning, individual differences in original learning are not highly correlated with individual differences in subsequent learning. The reliability of measures of learning variables for individual difference work posed problems for Jensen. This raises the point that the psychometrics of learning measures poses itself as a new evaluation task.

ADAPTATION AND OPTIMIZATION

The fifth item in the instructional model indicates that reassessment of behavior during learning and instructional assignment are interlinked in a series of adaptive stages. Two points are appropriate here. First, information about learning relevant to this kind of instructional model should come primarily from the interaction effects generally neglected in studies of learning. As Cronbach and Gleser (1965) have pointed out, the learning experimentalist assumes a fixed population and hunts for the treatment with the highest average and least variability. The correlational psychologist has, by and large, assumed a fixed treatment and hunted for aptitude that maximizes the slope of the function relating outcome to measured aptitude. The present instructional model assumes that there are strong interactions between individual measurements and treatment variables; and unless one treatment is clearly the best for everyone, as may rarely be the case, then treatments or instructional alternatives should be differentiated in a way to maximize their interaction with performance variables. If this assumption is correct, then individual performance measures that have high interactions with learning variables and their associated instructional alternatives are of greater importance than measures that do not show these interactions. This forces us to break out the error term in learning experiments so that the subject by independent-variable interaction can be evaluated. When this interaction is shown to be negligible, the learning variable can then be used in instruction without correcting its values with respect to individual differences. It seems that the model I have described will require major experimental research to determine the extent to which instructional treatments need to be qualified by individual difference interactions. The search for such interactions has been a major effort in the field of medical diagnosis and treatment and seems to be so in education (Lubin, 1961).

Second, the continuous pattern of assessment and instructional prescription, and assessment and instructional prescription again, can be represented as a multistage decision process where decisions are made sequentially and decisions made early in the process affect decisions made subsequently. The task of instruction is to prescribe the most effective sequence. Problems of this kind in other fields, such as electrical engineering, economics, and operations research, have been tackled by mathematical procedures applied to optimization problems. Essentially, optimization procedures involve a method of making decisions by choosing a quantitative measure of effectiveness and determining the best solution according to this criterion with appropriate constraints. A quantitative model is then developed into which values can be placed to indicate the outcome that is produced when various values are introduced.

An article by Groen and Atkinson (1966) has pointed out that the kind of instructional model I have described is set up for this kind of analysis. There is a multistage process that can be considered as a discrete N-stage process. At any given time, the state of the system, that is, the learner, can be characterized. This state, which is probably multivariate and described by a state vector, is determined by a decision which also may be multivariate; the state is transformed into the new updated state. The process consists of N successive stages where at each of the $N - 1$ stages a decision is made. The last stage, the end of a lesson unit, is a terminal stage where no decision is made other than whether the terminal criteria have been attained. The optimization problem of major concern in this process is finding a decision procedure for deciding which instructional alternatives to present at each stage, given the instructional alternatives available, the set of possible student responses to the previous lesson unit, and specification of the criteria to be optimized at the terminal stage. This decision procedure defines an instructional strategy and is determined by the functional relationship between (a) long- and short-range history and (b) student performance at each stage and at the terminal stage.

Groen and Atkinson (1966) point out that one way to find an optimal strategy is to enumerate every path of the decision tree generated by the multistage process. Obviously, this can be improved upon by the use of adequate learning models that can reduce the number of possible paths that can be considered. In order to reduce these paths still further, Bellman (1957) and Bellman and Dreyfus (1962), refer to dynamic programming procedures as useful for discovering optimal strategies and hence for providing a set of techniques for reducing the portion of the tree that must be searched. I am intrigued by this and suggest that it is an interesting approach for evaluation theory to consider, although some initial experimentation has not been overwhelmingly successful and, perhaps, slightly discouraging.

In order to carry out such an approach, we need only to do two trivial things: first, obtain quantitative knowledge of how the system variables interact, and second, obtain agreed upon measures of system effectiveness. Upon the completion of these two simple steps requiring, respectively, knowledge and value judgment, optimization procedures can be carried out. It has been shown that relative to the total effort needed to achieve a rational decision, the optimization procedure itself often requires little work when the first two steps are properly done (Wilde and Beightler, 1967). We are thrown back to the tasks we have always known that we must confront: (a) knowledge and description of the instructional process and (b) the development of evaluation measures.

In the first task the question is what kinds of experimental tactics and learning theory are most useful for discovering individual-difference-learning-variable relationships required to develop an instructional system. Fortunately, there is a growing commitment in learning theory to the individual case—recognized but not incorporated to any extent by Hull, certainly urged upon us by Skinner and associates, and well recognized in the recent information-processing computer simulation models of human behavior. There seems little doubt that one major test of the adequacy of competing learning theories will be the extent to which they incorporate individual differences.

The second task refers to the fact that in the educational model described, criterion measures and what is to be optimized become critical. If tracking the instructional process permits instruction to become precise enough, a good job can be done to maximize some gains and minimize others but some criteria may be minimized inadvertently unless the presence of the latter are desired, expressed, and assessed. In this regard, it seems almost inescapable that we abandon only norm-referenced measurement and develop more fully criterion-referenced measures, measures that assess performance on a continuum of competence and growth in the area under consideration. In addition, serious attempts must be made to measure what has been heretofore so difficult; such aspects as transfer of knowledge to new situations, problem solving, and self-direction—those aspects of learning and knowledge that are basic to an individual's capability for continuous growth and development.

EVOLUTIONARY OPERATION

The final item in my model refers to the capability of an instructional system to gather information and accumulate knowledge from which it can improve its own functioning and come closer to its expressed goals. I think the current notion of "formative" evaluation inherent in programmed instruction and presently being discussed more generally in curriculum evaluation is a major step along these lines (Cronbach, 1963). The industrial concept of "evolutionary operation" is relevant here (Box, 1957). The underlying rationale of this concept states it is seldom efficient to run an industrial process to produce a product alone; the process should produce the product plus information about how to improve it.

In closing the remarks in this paper, I can think of nothing better than to quote the end of Cronbach's 1963 article entitled "Evaluation for Course Improvement." He writes:

> Old habits of thought and long-established techniques are poor guides to the evaluation required for course improvement. Traditionally, educational measurement has been chiefly concerned with producing fair and precise scores for comparing individuals. Educational experimentation has been concerned with comparing score averages of competing courses. But course evaluation calls for description of outcomes. This description should be made on the broadest possible scale, even at the sacrifice of superficial fairness and precision.
>
> Course evaluation should ascertain what changes a course produces and should identify aspects of the course that need revision.
>
> . . . Evaluation is a fundamental part of curriculum development, not an appendage. Its job is to collect facts the course developer can and will use to do a better job, and facts from which a deeper understanding of the educational process will emerge.

CONCLUSION

I have stated the thesis that changing educational practices require changes in our theories and techniques of evaluation. In a general model of an emerging instructional process, I have itemized six educational practices and suggested the considerations for evaluation and measurement that each raises. They are the following:

1. With respect to the specification of learning outcomes, the following are required: (a) behavioral definition of goals, evaluating progress toward these goals, and clarifying these goals in the light of evaluated experience, (b) prior evaluation of educational procedures, insuring they are in effect before assessing educational accomplishment, and (c) development of techniques for criterion-referenced measurement.

2. For the diagnosis of initial state, what is required is determination of

long-term individual differences that are related to adaptive educational alternatives.

3. For the design of instructional alternatives, a key task is to determine measures that have the highest discriminating potential for allocating between instructional treatments.

4. For continuous assessment, discovery of measurements of ongoing learning that facilitate prediction of the next instructional step is required.

5. For adaptation and optimization, the instructional model requires: (a) the detailed analysis of individual-difference by instructional-treatment interactions and (b) the development of procedures like the optimizing methods so far used in fields other than education.

6. For evolutionary operation, we require a systematic theory or model of instruction into which accumulated knowledge can be placed and then empirically tested and improved.

REFERENCES

Bellman, R. *Dynamic programming*. Princeton, N.J.: Princeton University Press, 1957.

Bellman, R., & Dreyfus, S. E. *Applied dynamic programming*. Princeton, N.J.: Princeton University Press, 1962.

Box, G. E. P. Evolutionary operation: A method for increasing industrial productivity. *Applied Statistics*, 1957, *6*, 81–101.

Cronbach, L. J. The two disciplines of scientific psychology. *American Psychologist*, 1957, *12*, 671–684.

Cronbach, L. J. Evaluation for course improvement. *Teachers College Record*, 1963, *64*, 672–683.

Cronbach, L. J., & Gleser, G. C. *Psychological tests and personnel decisions*. Urbana: Ill.: University of Illinois Press, 1965.

Duncanson, J. P. *Intelligence and the ability to learn*. Princeton, N.J.: Educational Testing Service, 1964.

Fleishman, E. A. The description and prediction of perceptual-motor skill learning. In R. Glaser (Ed.), *Training research and education*. New York: John Wiley & Sons, Inc., 1965. Pp. 137–176.

Glaser, R. Instructional technology and the measurement of learning outcomes. *American Psychologist*, 1963, *18*, 519–521.

Groen, G. J., & Atkinson, R. C. Models for optimizing the learning process. *Psychological Bulletin*, 1966, *66*, 309–320.

Jensen, A. R. Varieties of individual differences in learning. In R. Gagné (Ed.), *Learning and individual differences*. Columbus, Ohio: Charles E. Merrill Books, Inc., 1967, 117–135.

Judd, W. A., & Glaser, R. Response latency as a function of training method, information level, acquisition, and overlearning. *Journal of Educational Psychology Monograph,* 1969, *60* (Part 2).

Lubin, A. The interpretation of significant interaction. *Educational and Psychological Measurement,* 1961, *21,* 807–817.

Stake, R. E. Learning parameters, aptitudes, and achievements. *Psychometric Monographs,* 1961, No. 9.

Suchman, E. A. Principles and practice of evaluative research. In J. T. Doby (Ed.), *An introduction to social research.* New York: Appleton-Century-Crofts, 1967. Pp. 327–351.

Travers, R. M. W. *Essentials of learning: An overview for students of education.* New York: Crowell-Collier and Macmillan, Inc., 1963.

Wilde, D. J., & Beightler, C. S. *Foundations of optimization.* Englewood Cliffs, N.J.: Prentice-Hall, Inc., 1967.

Woodrow, H. A. The ability to learn. *Psychological Review,* 1946, *53,* 147–158.

Zeaman, D., & House, B. J. The relation of IQ and learning. In R. Gagné (Ed.), *Learning and individual differences.* Columbus, Ohio: Charles E. Merrill Books, Inc., 1967. Pp. 192–212.

Comments on Professor Glaser's Paper

ROBERT STAKE

I received a draft of Bob Glaser's paper several weeks ago. There was postage due. Bob had missed the mark by a factor of .64. On payment of the additional 28 cents, I reflected on the possibility of this being an omen: Was he going to miss the mark on his theory of the evaluation of instruction as well?

I think he did.

Let me refresh your memories. He presented six components of a model of instruction. As I understand them, they were the specification of objectives, the diagnosis of entry behavior, the selection of instructional procedures, the surveillance of instruction, the modification of instruction, and the modification of the system. He spotted needs for measurement and evaluation within each of the six. He claimed that the needs for measurement and evaluation were fluid, subject today particularly to three forces: increased emphasis on cultivation of skill and understanding of the basic discipline, increased emphasis on the continuity of education through the life span, and increased emphasis on individual instruction, passing it from the ideal to reality.

Bob presented a model of instruction and discussed some of the implications for evaluation. He did not develop a model or a theory for the evaluation of instruction. Earlier Ben Bloom talked about evaluation within a theory of testing; Bob Glaser talked about evaluation within a theory of instruction, not a theory of evaluation. Perhaps if Merl Wittrock had given them behavioral specifications, we would have covered by now a theory of evaluation. I am not claiming that he should have. I am just saying that in spite of the original titles of the morning's paper, we have not yet considered a model or theory of evaluation in the sense that either Ben Bloom or Gene Glass define it.

Bob Glaser indicated six functions that require extensive measurement. There are many responsibilities for student testing: there are observations to be made, descriptions to be recorded, judgments to be set, decisions to be made. Instruction requires all of these. Evaluation of instruction, as separate from evaluation within instruction, requires them, also. Bob Glaser has not told us how the descriptions and judgments of the instructional process might be fitted together to provide us with the information we need to make educational decisions.

Repeatedly Bob referred to his system, or the phenomenon or the task, as one of individual student learning. This is an important focus. With Maurie Lindvall and other colleagues at the University of Pittsburgh Oakleaf School, Bob has helped us to realize how, in this day of large student bodies, we can individualize instruction; but our concern is the evaluation of instructional systems.

This evaluation is considerably more than the aggregate of assessment of progress for all children at all levels. Here the unit of analysis is not the child but the classroom, the school system, or the nation. The satisfaction we get from its operation is the focus. The changes we can make to increase our satisfaction with the system are our focus. It is a different focus.

Where we might have expected him to discuss evaluation *of the system* (in his sixth section), we found only a mention of the need for evaluation, plus an inspirational quote from Lee Cronbach. Bob did not consider any of the more recent literature on evaluation. What of Mike Scriven? What of Michaels and Metfessel? What of the writings that have attempted to apply operations analysis, cost-benefit analysis, and decision theory to the instructional system?

Perhaps I am wrong in expecting Bob Glaser (and many of my colleagues specializing in measurement) to expand the concept of evaluation beyond ascertainment of how well objectives have been accomplished. Perhaps it would be more useful to postpone the call for a broader definition until we are doing a satisfactory job of a more limited kind. But I think not. It is important to help today's educator discover the worth of instruction. *Now* is the time for the technologist to come to the aid of his colleagues.

There are many points in the paper with which I enthusiastically agree. I warmed with satisfaction on hearing Bob's declaration that it is worthwhile trying to learn the nature and judge the quality of the teaching, whether or not we can measure the extent and judge the quality of the resulting student content. I was pleased to hear his emphasis on the need for continuous, automatic correcting and system-wide correcting techniques for evaluation.

Bob's concern for interaction is well placed. Although I am not encouraged by the research results from Larry Stolurow, Jacob Beard, and others, I believe that we should continue to anticipate interaction between instructional methods and student characteristics. If there are important accommodations of instruction to children, in addition to those in the area of pacing and step size, we should learn the additional real and indirect cost of individualization.

There are many important bits and pieces of the paper that I would like to discuss at length. But I feel I should use the remaining time on just one.

Bob Glaser spoke of the "now platitudinous assertion" of the necessity for behavioral objectives. "Platitudinous" means "dull" and "insipid," and I wouldn't have been so uncharitable as to call the assertion that. It also means "commonplace." That it is. It does not mean "no longer needing validation." I challenge the validity of the role that he gives to behavioral objectives.

I object to his statement that the first responsibility in evaluation is the specification of objectives. Much of what he said in the paper conveys the conviction that student-outcome behavior should be specified—that is, committed early to formal language, English language. He supports those who say that all human accomplishment can be objectively, operationally described. So do I. He also says, as a regular initial step in instructional evaluation, objectives should be formally stated. For some large-scale instructional projects, I agree. For classroom evaluation, I do not. I claim that it is impractical, unnecessary, and distractive to develop and evaluate curricula with high reliance on behavioral objectives. Analysis does not necessarily aid performance. A designer of "paint by numbers" kits might point out, as I believe information theorist Claude Shannon has, that any painting is essentially a collection of areas of discernably different solid colors. It does not follow that painting by numbers is the best way to paint a Mona Lisa.

Few of you in the audience, in your creative, scholarly work, operate from a table of specified objectives. The quality of painting or researching or instruction we are getting from today's best specifications is greatly inferior, as I see it, to what we can get from the best craftsmen. Professional education does not have the talent for specifying objectives. It does not make sense to me to base evaluation plans on a talent we do not have, nor can afford. The price of gaining and using this talent, I claim, is one hundred times the price of the instruction itself. Impractical, I say.

I am not saying behavioral specification will not work because teaching is an art rather than a science. I am saying behavioral specification will not work because teachers are artists and artisans, not linguists and philosophers; and it costs too much for us technologists to talk to them in a language they do not understand.

It is right for us to continue to develop a technology of education. Our plans for a technology should be practical. The technology we build should not require a revolution but should be realistic, designed with an eye to the cost of institutionalization. As much as possible, we should capitalize on present teaching skills and commitments. To insist on behavioral specifications is to ask for new evaluation skills and commitments. I believe that a high quality of instruction and a high quality of evaluation can be developed without this specification.

There are other ways of representing objectives. Obviously, we can use examples. An educator, by a nod of the head, can indicate which representation of behaviors is close to his ideals. We can film behaviors. We can describe them in anecdotal form. We can use test items to represent goals. There are alternate ways of specifying objectives, further, perhaps, from some true intent that lies within the mind or heart of an educator; but these are specifications that are within our budget of talent and patience. With them we can get along without formal goal statements.

Some of these are not popular notions with some of you, I know. It may be only your politeness and pity that quiets your irritation. Obviously I criticize not only Bob Glaser, but the Learning Research Center, the Center for the Study of Evaluation of Instructional Programs, the Southwest Regional Laboratory, the National Society for Programmed Instruction, and all those Camelots of behavioral linguistics.

My first two points are that behavioral specification, as we usually define it, is often impractical and unnecessary. I will now challenge the placement of goal specification as a *first logical* step. Bob and others have agreed that you do not do all your goal specification first. You modify as you go along. So, we agree on that. The point I want to make is that there is a still prior logical step that Bob did not mention. Gene Glass has already referred to it. We need to consider the vital question of goal competition and goal selection. Goal selection is an integral part of instruction. We psychologists are not without qualification for dealing with preferences and priorities. Yet we have, I believe, avoided incorporating goal selection into our evaluation technology so far.

The other day I refreshed my impressions of the difference between the goal domain of the programmer and the goal domain of the classroom teacher. I looked over the programmed text on population genetics that Dick Anderson and his lab workers wrote for the BSCS biology project. I also visited a biology class at the University High School in Urbana. Worlds apart!

Both were smooth, provocative, response-oriented operations but were seeking quite different responses. The program writers knew what specific responses they wanted. The teacher did not. The aim of the classroom teacher was to provide opportunity for reflection and reaction that she could use in an operant conditioning paradigm. She was willing to pick up, reinforce, and build upon many kinds of responses. More generally, may I say that our qualified classroom teachers seek a response with potential for development. They scan hundreds of actual responses to find any one of many desired responses. Sometimes the ideal responses can be elicited directly; many times not. Some responses are suspect when *directly* elicited. The skilled teacher has learned to recognize a set of desired behaviors and to reinforce them and to shape them when they occur. The context is deemed very important. What is the classroom situation? What is the student's situation? The presence of these responses in terms of a problem context, in an affective context, is very important.

Bob Glaser made the point that there can be important interactions between student type and teaching method. These teachers show me that there can be important interaction between student readiness and teaching method. We need more research on that. The skilled teacher has many objectives to work from. She is not very concerned about getting them all done. She says, "There's another teacher coming along next year, or next hour." Each one will seize an opportunity to do particular objectives well. They will reassign priorities to goals on the spot. This reconsideration of priorities is the important purchase that we make when we choose skilled teachers rather than programmed material.

The educational evaluator must deal with priorities. To give priorities to goals, he must know what those goals are. But the goals of educators increase and grow. The evaluator cannot avoid early definition of general goals, but he cannot ignore changing goals and changing goal priorities. As a first logical step, the instructional specialist may consider how to define and operationalize objectives. As a prior logical step, the curriculum and evaluation specialists should consider how to define and give priorities to objectives.

Selection of goals and revision of priorities are important components of instruction. They belong in a model of instruction; they belong also in a model of evaluation. Our technology should not ignore the fact that educators need more rational and objective procedures for specifying the competing priorities of different instructional goals.

The mark of evaluation is information for decision-making. It is more than a by-product of good instruction. I think Bob owes us another 28 cents worth.

Comments on Professor Glaser's Paper

ARTHUR A. LUMSDAINE

In relation to the controversy between Glaser and Stake, I want to say that I am on Glaser's side with respect to the importance of behavioral objectives. It is impossible for me to imagine how we are going to make progress in evaluation unless we do a better job of providing a rationale, a logical foundation for what we are measuring. I think that the most important contribution of programmed instruction to date has been less the improvement of instruction per se as a process of teaching than as an engineering effort emphasizing what is required to derive reasonable, measurable, usable instructional objectives from general statements.

I would enter one caveat here. In seeking what outcomes to assess in the process of evaluation, we can concentrate too fully on stated objectives and fail to include an assessment of the extent to which unexpected outcomes may eventuate. That is, the ultimate criterion of whether an educational program is a good program is what it accomplishes. It may have had some unintended bad effects that need to be ascertained, if possible, though they certainly were not among the objectives of the educational planner. A program also may have some unexpected good effects. Thus, if we confine our assessment of the outcomes of an educational program to its effects on its specified objectives, we may be overlooking some extremely important effects.

There are several points on which I would like to comment briefly: One problem of prime importance, in addition to improving the technology of evaluation (conceived as the means of ascertaining the outcomes of educational programs), is to try to create a better market for assessment data. As it now stands, there is not much demand for evidence about the effectiveness of specific programs. Educational products are still sold on the basis of unsubstantiated advertising. Those who have tried to change this situation have sometimes become quite discouraged by the realization of this. It seems rather futile to create data about an educational product and its effectiveness if there is little inclination on the part of those responsible for the purchase or selection of such products to look at the data. There is need for an educational job for the educational administrator or the curriculum supervisor, the person that makes the purchase decisions, to teach him about the usefulness of data and the demonstrable effectiveness of programs in making educational decisions. This important problem of long-range education is not necessarily going to be accomplished by those who are concerned with the technology of evaluation as such.

I also ought to mention my conviction related to the work of the American Psychological Association and the National Education Association joint committee (Lumsdaine, 1965), on which several of us here participated—as part of a viable technology of assessment of program measurements we also need standards for the adequacy of such data. The reason for the standards derives from the following sequence of events. First, you have programs with no evidence of output. Then you say, "Let's have evidence or data about the effectiveness of the programs." But then, in absence of standards, you get cheap, fallacious kinds of evidence, statistically reported in an impressive manner, perhaps, but technically unsound, that is, with respect to methods of control. There emerges a sort of Gresham's Law of data, in which bad data, being easier to obtain and more impressive to report than good data, tend to drive out good data. So, some kinds of standards are needed, such as those that have come to be taken for granted and which will be observed in papers reported in, say, *Journal of Experimental Psychology*—but which are far from being safely assumed in the data being reported by evaluations of educational programs and materials.

I would also like to emphasize a point on which Marvin Alkin will probably comment further: namely, that if we are going to try to use cost-effectiveness criteria, we have to be able to measure output in cost translatable terms. Lack of this is the big hang up, as I see it, in any cost-effectiveness program at the present time. It is very hard to say what the economic significance is of the difference between an achievement score of 128 and one of 212, even if these are translated into normative standard scores. The dependent variables that we characteristically use for measuring the outcomes of education are not easily translated into cost terms.

This may be, however, a fortunate accident, because I think that such measures as test scores are probably not what we really ought to use as measures of educational output, anyway. That remark could be easily misunderstood. Let me see if I can clarify it.

Often we need to know that the most important competence is not that achieved through an educational procedure immediately after instruction. Rather, what we need to know (and this will become increasingly important as knowledge multiplies) is how well the effects of education enable a person to relearn something that he has forgotten, or to get quickly up to current operational proficiency from a background of prior training. There is just too much for everyone to know to expect that people will have a complete repertoire of competences on tap at all time.

What we need can be described in part as a problem of transfer. It is to begin to assess proficiency in terms not of what the person *can* do now or at the end of instruction or what he retains a week or a month or a semester later; but, rather, in terms of the amount of educational effort that is required to bring him up to proficiency from where his education to date has left him (or to bring him *back* up to it after he has forgotten).

This implies something like a "savings" measure. Although there are many problems in developing and using such measures, they are attractive as measures of the effects of education that have promise of being translatable into cost terms. This is also true, of course, of the measure of instructional time needed to reach a criterion (as opposed to difference in scores after a fixed time of instruction).

Let me turn briefly to a different point. One thing that is very important to recognize clearly is that there are great differences in the procedures needed for different purposes of evaluation.

The needs of program evaluation (particularly for such purposes as program improvement) are quite different from testing to evaluate the potentialities or achievement level of *individuals*. To take one example: when we are concerned with the evaluation of programs, we have quite a different sampling task than when we are dealing with the evaluation of individuals. For the evaluation of individuals, to oversimplify a little, we need a small sample of items about a large sample of people. We want to give each person a score but are willing to base each person's figure of merit on a relatively small sample of items. But in the problem of program evaluation, the opposite is true. We now want evidence from a relatively small, adequate but relatively small, number of individuals on *all* relevant items. This is because we are assessing the program for the purpose of product improvement; so, it is very important for us to have this fine-grain differential knowledge of the successes and the failures of the program on each point it covers to detect its very specific failures and successes.

I have tried hard to think of something about which to disagree with Bob Glaser. One point of partial dissent concerns the alleged lack of relation between intelligence and program effects. There are, in fact, numerous instances in which successful attempts have been made to relate measures of ability to differences in programs. I can think of examples because I have been involved in collecting, analyzing, and reporting such data, in studies in which effects of instructional devices, such as films, were analyzed with concern for differential effects on individuals of greater and lesser ability, as measured by standard tests of intelligence. Great differences, in fact, were found between the effectiveness of programs as a function of such ability-test scores and educational level of adults (Hovland, Lumsdaine, and Sheffield, 1949).

These differential effects as a function of stratifying variables, such as educational level, IQ, or other measures of ability, are of the form of interactions talked about as significant effects in our statistical tests. However, there are two kinds of interactions. One kind is as follows: The effects of Program A are greater for Group X than they are for Group Y. Here the difference in the relative effectiveness of two programs, A and B (for example, color versus black and white films, overt versus implicit response procedures, and so forth) is greater for a segment or subgroup of the population, X, than it is for some other segment, Y. There are many instances where this is the case—where a particular instructional variable demonstrably makes more or less difference for, let's say, brighter students than for less bright students (see Hovland, Lumsdaine, and Sheffield, 1949, chapters 8 and 9).

However, the argument for the individualization of instruction rests in part on the assumption that there is a more powerful kind of interaction at work than the kind just described. This would be where not only is the difference between A and B greater for Group X than for Group Y, but A is superior for Group X while B is superior for Group Y. This is a "reversal" kind of interaction that demonstrates, as a function of some population characteristic, that one program is better for certain persons, whereas other programs are better for other persons.

Now, if you search the literature, both on formal instruction and on attitudes, you will find very few such instances of reversible interactions documented by solid evidence. There are a few of them, and modesty forbids mention of the first that come to mind. But it is interesting that with all our talk about the importance of tailoring instruction to individual characteristics, we find so few instances of differential effects of this kind, permitting us to conclude that a program tailored for a particular subgroup of individuals will be differentially more effective for them, while a different program will be more effective for some other subgroup of individuals.

REFERENCES

Hovland, C. I., Lumsdaine, A. A., & Sheffield, F. D. *Experiments on mass communication*. Princeton, N.J.: Princeton University Press, 1949.
Lumsdaine, A. A. Assessing the effectiveness of instructional programs. In R. Glaser (Ed.), *Teaching machines and programmed learning, II: Data and directions*. Washington, D.C.: National Education Association, 1965.

Open Discussion of Glaser's Paper and of Stake's and Lumsdaine's Comments

GLASER: I would have given Bob Stake the money beforehand if I had known he was going to do that! I want to thank him for pushing closer to the threshold all those little nagging doubts I had about what I was saying, and also for making me realize that complacency is the real enemy.

He said I really didn't propose a theory, and he's right. I don't believe that there is a theory of evaluation. There is a theory in a science, a science descriptive of events around us. Evaluation has a model. It has techniques. I don't know if it has a theory. You may use evaluation procedures to substantiate theories of behavior or theories in biology; but I don't know if there's a theory of evaluation, so that is not a strong criticism.

He indicated that I didn't say how Atkinson constructs his decisions. This is true in the sense that a procedure is suggested but not implemented. I thought I said that what is suggested is to measure long-range history, measure short-range history, state what you want to optimize, and put all three of those together in a relevant functional relationship. This is a very large order, I know.

He said the unit of analysis is not always the child. That confuses me! Education refers to a change in behavior in an individual student. Stake seems to be looking for some more global focus that I found difficult to interpret. I think the unit of analysis is the child and the change in his behavior.

He indicated that the recent literature contains a lot of work on cost benefit analysis, and so forth. Again, I don't think those things are relevant to changes in individual behavior. They are more relevant to administrative functions of a school. He indicated I didn't tell you how to do all those things. I supposed my job was to ask the questions. I think the answers may be around in many ways, but I was trying to pose some good questions so the answers could be found.

He said that he thinks classes are becoming larger and larger, and that individualization really wasn't becoming more and more of a practical ideal. I think individualization takes many forms, depending upon the subject matter with which it is used. Individualization in social study might be game-playing for groups, and so forth, but it is inconceivable that individualization, or some adaptation to individual differences, is not going to happen in the future, even though current educational pressures for very practical purposes may be pushing people into larger classrooms.

He indicated that behavioral specifications were not possible. He fell into the error of saying that to describe things carefully is degrading and ungodlike. I don't agree with that. To my way of thinking, the specification of the goals of instruction has been the single most important factor in educational improvement of the last ten years, even more important than instructional manipulations. The identification of where we are going, working toward where we're going, and identifying the behavior of the child in terms of our goals have been important factors contributing to improvement in education.

He said we shouldn't do this because the teacher finds it hard to understand, and we have a lot of trouble communicating with the technicians. It's the technicians' job to write things understandable to the practitioner.

He indicated that there is a behavioral linguistics and that people always have to use language to describe objectives. I don't think we have ever said that you have to use language all the time. You can use any kind of communication you want to communicate an objective. You can use movies or you can point to something or, since you can get much more power and communication from discrimination than from identifying an absolute, you could show teachers how to discriminate between when they have something and when they don't have it.

Goal selection? I don't know whether I'm prepared to operate as a value maker and scientist both. My job in terms of values is to provide the methodology to help decide upon values; and maybe to point out the relationship between present values and future behavior.

Finally, he talked about operating conditions and I didn't catch his point; but, in terms of behavioral specifications, if operating conditions do indeed shape, they shape toward something, even though what they shape toward might change. Every time teachers reinforce a particular response, they have something in their heads that they are shaping toward. Again, it is hard to see how they shape in the abstract.

GUILFORD: I want to make several responses to Glaser's paper. I was very happy to hear Bob Glaser recite research which showed that there is independence between ability to learn paired-associate and serial learning. The paired-associate learning is primarily a learning of what I call implications; and serial learning is a learning of a system that is an order or sequence.

I would like to remind you that there are four other kinds of products, and you will find such an independence between types of learning when these other kinds of products are involved also. Not only that, but if you include the four kinds of content, there are twenty-four kinds of learning and memory to be concerned about. We have demonstrated twelve of these already, and by next year we shall have probably demonstrated six more. But the more important point has to do with the relation of intellectual abilities to learning new tasks or new information.

During the last two or three years, we have engaged in a major study of concept learning in relation to certain of the primary mental abilities. The learning was of class ideas, three different kinds of tasks (one in semantic information, one in figural, and one in symbolic) and four concepts to be learned in each of these categories, the learning to be done by successive exposures of exemplars of the class with immediate feedback and correction, if necessary, between students' responses.

The Princeton studies, which you briefly mentioned, I think are defective in several ways. One is that they did not have any good basis of theory of intellectual ability. There are two technical flaws in their approach, which I think we corrected in our own study. One is not to analyze the learning scores along with the test scores, but to establish the factor structure from the tests only and then project the learning scores into the factor structure. There is quite a different result when you analyze the learning scores along with the test scores.

We selected from theory the kinds of abilities we expected to be important or relevant in these different concept learning tasks. We were limited, of course, by time, in the number of abilities we could survey. We concentrated heavily upon abilities concerned with memory for classes, cognition of classes, and so on.

We had one or two surprises in the results. First, in general, we did find that certain abilities were significantly related to the learning scores and some were not. Secondly, those that were related showed systematic changes from the beginning of the first trial score to the twelfth trial score.

The most strongly related abilities were those in the category of memory. We didn't expect this, but I think it is reasonable when you consider operationally the kind of test we used to measure the memory abilities, which involves learning a certain set of information. A memory test is pretty close in kind to the typical learning task.

Another surprise was the fact that the cognition abilities, those for cognition of these kinds of classes, tended to have negative relationships to the learning scores during the first few trials and then shifted over onto the positive side and kept climbing toward the end of the learning task. The cognition abilities had their greatest loadings at the end of learning.

The learning did not go far enough for everybody to have mastered the task completely, of course. There was still some variance among individuals; but it seems to me that this kind of thing needs to be done for every kind of learning that a child happens to encounter. The teacher can then perform like an engineer, knowing what abilities are relevant at what stages of learning, and he can instruct children on strategies that they might employ. In the case of the negative relationship, he can instruct the child on what strategies to avoid or what dangers to look out for.

It will, of course, take mountains of research to be able to find specifications for all kinds of things that have to be learned; but it seems to me that, if we are going to be quite knowledgeable about how we proceed in helping people learn, we badly need this kind of information.

ANDERSON: I would like to speak to the point raised by Bob Stake. We have a profound issue here, and I want to make sure that it isn't lost in the polemics and the counter-polemics. Bob Stake didn't commit the heresy of saying that he was against behavioral objectives. We could generally concur—Bob might not go this far—that this has been one of the most salutary effects of the educational technology movement. A model which entails operationally specified objectives allows us in a systematic, rational way to upgrade instruction.

There are other models—Bob suggested one of these—which apply to the teacher who presumably has in mind, although these are not explicitly inventoried, a broad range of objectives. The teacher capitalizes upon the opportunities within the classroom to make some progress with respect to one objective at one time, even if this involves throwing away the plan based on the preplanned objectives for a lesson or series of lessons. If we want to view education broadly, we have to consider alternative kinds of models.

The second point Bob made is not a trivial logistic question. It is hard to train teachers to use behavioral language. Some of the major curriculum reform projects have had a big impact; generally the Zachariases and Beber-mans are not comfortable with our stated objectives. It would be wrong to conclude that their enterprises are without merit because they don't fall into our forms. I want to hastily add that I still hold the orthodox position myself.

POPHAM: I would be more sympathetic with what Bob Stake said if I shared his estimate of the skill of teachers in the public schools. Teachers are not carefully responding to the action of the pupils nor capitalizing on what they see them doing in classes. The teachers are simply responding. They are not thinking very rationally about what they are doing.

Instead of having teachers generate their own precise goals, I propose that we set up agencies that have the responsibility for constructing precise objectives, and then let the teachers be the selectors, rather than the generators, of objectives.

STAKE: I think that's an attractive alternative. For any particular evaluation of instruction, the evaluator has to decide whether to define outcome behaviors and goals a priori or as the instruction goes along—in either case he can have people "abstract" the goals or select from representations that the evaluator has authored.

GLASS: Art's point about assessing the outcomes of a curriculum in terms only of the behavioral objectives partially indicts his own position on what role such objectives would play in creating a curriculum. If so many unexpected secondary and tertiary outcomes result from the curriculum, think how much is overlooked when one lets the behavioral objectives dictate what he puts into the curriculum.

LUMSDAINE: Two points: would it clarify things if we talked about behavioral specification of *outcomes* and made a serious attempt to anticipate the foreseeable outcomes, including the four categories: good and bad outcomes not sought, as well as outcomes sought (objectives)?

Second, I don't see how you cannot have a plan. If you are going to assess the extent to which your plans or objectives were attained, you must translate objectives of the plan into broad classes of behavior and then into more specific terms that you will accept as evidence that the plan was realized. But of course one should also look for outcomes that weren't planned, also revealed only in behavior of some sort.

TYLER: Several times, Bob Stake, you have described statements of behavioral goals as being unnecessary. I am not sure that I understand what you mean by unnecessary. I need some elaboration on that. Do you feel that verbal statements of behavior goals are unnecessary?

STAKE: Goals are necessary. Verbal statements are not. I tried to say that people like Bob Glaser were claiming that you had to use formal English language and had to state goals in advance. Those seem to me to be the demands of the instructional technology people who deal with curriculum development. They act as behavioral linguists, I said, forcing the discussion of the impact of instruction into a sometimes awkward language.

To evaluate a program we do want to talk about goals. It's unnecessary to use the formal English language; it's unnecessary for the educator to declare a list of fifteen goal statements; it's unnecessary to use Bob Gagné's approach, to formalize a chain or hierarchy of general specifics on down to specific specifics—sometimes these will work, sometimes they will not. Luckily, informal-language specifications can be substituted for formal-language specifications. Mike Scriven says, "Let the item pool be your statement of behavioral objectives." Another person will say, "Let the goals be no more than action manifestations of behaviors as opposed to verbal manifestations."

TYLER: It seems to me now what you are saying is that we do want behavioral specifications but not put in verbal statements.

STAKE: For evaluation, some form of specification is essential. I differ with some people here on the language we should use. Not all goals should be stated behaviorally because behavioral change is not the goal some people have. It is not the evaluator's privilege to tell people what their goals are or to tell them how they should be expressed.

BLOOM: If I may change the subject slightly, the problem of interaction between the children, I think, is a very special one. We find that very, very good tutors seem to be able to get children up to certain levels of mastery by what appear to be very different routes. I guess I would make the plea only that we keep searching for these crossovers that we have been talking about here and eventually try to find the technology that would do what a good tutor does.

I think I still have a faith that there may be something that we might call individualization of learning, having to do with children who vary enormously and instructional materials, approaches, call it what you will, that also vary enormously.

C. HARRIS: I am convinced that no one can possibly identify the interaction of individuals with instructional programs in the twentieth century in terms of what we know about statistics. Now, if you are talking about types of individuals, like high IQ, low IQ, that's all right; but everybody is talking about the interaction of individuals with instructional programs. That information is completely inaccessible.

Everybody is talking about individual students interacting with treatments. This is a complete nonsense statement. You can talk about typologies of students, high IQ's, low IQ's, middle IQ's, interacting with treatment, and so forth. When you do that, you can get that information to a greater or lesser extent. That still doesn't tell you anything about the individual student. I thought one of the things that we drifted away from was that Bob Glaser was claiming that he has a model in which you get down to instructing the individual and choosing these things in terms of an individual, not in terms of his category.

GAGE: Would you be happier, then, with the term *typologizing instruction*?

C. HARRIS: This is what these interactions are, but they talk about them as interactions of individuals.

LORTIE: I would like to return to our discussion of behavioral goals. I wonder if there isn't another dimension than rationality and irrationality, that is, static versus developmental, in this notion of the statement of behavioral goals.

I can think, for example, of the situation where you say, "Ideally, in this specific classroom in this specific year, I want to teach such-and-such during the year." Then the teacher, during the year in the course of trying to communicate with the students, finds that either something that was supposed to be in the plan didn't get into their heads, or the engineers of the plan never thought of it. At that point he stops there and works on this. That's rational, isn't it?

The teacher's taking corrective action is as rational in the problem of behavior as is imaginable. I am getting a little bit leary of the notion of the prior statement about the objectives, that this is rational and the opposite is not. It seems to me you have to take account of any rational scheme of new perceptions in the course of greater engagement in it.

This is what bothers me a little bit about your notion that you can treat objectives strictly in terms of individual kids, because you can't. In fact, many teacher decisions have to be made, in 95 percent of the teaching situations, in terms of group contexts, in terms of the meaning of this behavior with this child for twenty-nine other students and how it is going to either constrain or add to future options. These steps are taken not in isolation to each child at the time but vis-à-vis the group.

The diagnostic, the relationship between diagnosis and schools as they now exist, and the taking of corrective action, can never, it seems to me, be in individualistic terms.

MCDONALD: After listening to this discussion, I am wondering whether the argument about specifying objectives isn't really disguising a more fundamental disagreement of the group. It seems to me the argument is over what is meant by evaluating to improve instruction. Some people, like Bob Glaser and Art Lumsdaine, and some other people whom I needn't identify, will say what you mean by the improvement in instruction is the change in the child. Specifying objectives and laying out programs clearly follows from that. But I thought I heard Bob Stake and Gene Glass saying that improvement in instruction was something more than that, and I'm not at all clear what that "something more" is, although it has been asserted on occasion here, I think.

STAKE: I claim that evaluation of instruction should reveal what it is that has happened and the satisfaction and dissatisfactions it has brought. Change in the child is one thing that happens. We should measure that change as best we can. But also, we should measure how important that change is. How different people see the value of that change is part of the evaluation.

If the evaluation report is to be useful to other educators, it should show what happened in the classroom. It should describe the classroom, the community, and whatever conditions might help explain the outcomes. It should report the hopes and expectations and doubts of various participants and spectators. Attention to these environmental factors and value judgments does divert attention from changes in the individual children. I think the fundamental disagreement here concerns whether to look closely at instruction's intended changes or to look broadly at instruction in a social context. To me, evaluation is an attempt to indicate whether or not an individual child or a community is getting its "money's worth" from an instructional program.

PART III

Instructional Variables

CHAPTER 4

Instructional Variables and Learning Outcomes

ROBERT M. GAGNÉ

Evaluation is a word commonly used to refer to a great variety of activities connected with educational programs. In its broadest sense, it has to do with valuing, or determining the worth of, educational courses, programs, or even whole systems. It has, however, a considerably more modest meaning when applied to the appraisal of a very important, although sometimes small, segment of a total program or system; namely, of the extent to which specified instances of learning have occurred.

Although one can conceive of "evaluating" learning outcomes in something like a cost-effectiveness sense, this is not usually what one wishes to do. Instead, interest often centers upon the accomplishment of certain human performance objectives as a part of a set of more comprehensive goals. For example, a learning outcome pertaining to a student's mastery of differential equations may be merely a portion of a larger goal of producing a capable mechanical engineer. When considered in relation to this kind of specific learning outcome, it may be that evaluation is better expressed as assessment. The latter word may imply the desirable characteristic of objectivity (as opposed to the subjective nature of "valuing") and at the same time carry an implication of the importance of such an activity to the larger evaluation goal.

So long as one looks upon education, or perhaps only schooling, as a system having a definable social purpose, whose functions and components are subject to planning and design, assessment of learning outcomes may be seen to have an essential importance within the system. One can, of course, study separately the characteristics of certain other parts of the system, such as the method of communicating, the subsystem of guidance, or the functions of the teacher. One can even study separately the processes that take place during system operation, such as student-teacher interactions or teacher-administrator interactions. All of these are useful to know about. But, so far as I can see, nothing can take the place of the student's performance as an absolutely essential criterion of system or subsystem functioning. There may be many reasons to know how teachers are conducting their questioning, how administrators react to an innovation, or whether students enjoy going to class. But none of these can take the place of learning outcomes as an essential part of any seriously purposed "evaluation" of educational systems or subsystems. By definition, the effecting of externally stimulated behavioral change in students is a major purpose of education, and this implies that behavior assessment must be undertaken.

Obviously, one can assess outcomes soon after the occurrence of some educational processing, or at a later time, even considerably later. There is often a need to discover, for example, not simply whether a method of solving differential equations was mastered immediately following a period of time devoted to its learning, but also whether it is remembered several weeks later when the student is faced with learning a more complex method incorporating the formerly learned technique as one step. Or again, one may be interested in whether, at a later time, the method of solving differential equations can be recalled and used in connection with quite a different situation, like that involving the rotary motion of a body or the rate of a chemical reaction. The question of assessing learning outcomes evidently must include those human performances affected by the processes of retention and of transfer of learning.

THE PROBLEM OF MEASUREMENT

Scientific measurement is generally agreed to be fundamentally a matter of counting units that are agreed upon as being generated by the same operations. As the writings of Campbell (1957) indicate, the operations applied to counting the measures referred to as length, mass, and time have been fairly easy to agree upon, and, therefore, may perhaps deserve to be called "fundamental." Most measurement in science, however, is not of this fundamental sort, but instead is derived from it. For example, the chemist considers that he has a satisfactory measure, let us say, of the "strength of a solution" when he performs those operations that extract the solid components and then relates the mass of these components to the total mass of the solution. Or the biologist may construct an indirect measure of the "adiposity" of tissue by ascertaining the proportion of area in cells observed under a microscope taken up by material that is stained a particular color. In such instances, and there are many of them, the scientist is constructing a measure of some entity by demonstrating its relationship to an operation of counting.

It is apparent that what is done in measurement, so far as intellectual operations of a measurer are concerned, is that an inference is made. The chemist infers the variable "strength of solution," the biologist, the variable "adiposity." These variables are not directly observed, as for example, color, shape, and numerosity may be; each is an inference depending upon a chain of reasoning. In the same manner, the psychologist infers the variables of learning, retention, and transfer of learning. None of these variables is observed directly. Each of them is measured indirectly by being related rationally to operations that include counting.

One of the major implications of this line of reasoning is the following: in undertaking measuring, one must be prepared to answer two questions, one of which precedes the other. The first question is, "What is being measured?" There must be, in other words, agreement among those who use measurement that the units defined by a set of operations are the same and, therefore, can be given a common name. One measures length by counting units that can be matched and thus readily agreed upon as being the same. But indirect measurement, as in the case of measures of "solution strength," "adiposity," or "learning," may offer a much more difficult problem of agreement, because a more complex set of operations is involved. Accordingly, the answer to the question "What is being measured?" is often not an easy one to determine. It seems probable to me, for example, that virtually all controversy in the field of learning research over the past several decades could be categorized in the question "What is being measured?"

The second question of measurement is "how much?" When measurement is indirect this too is not always an easy question to answer, even when the operations are agreed upon, because of the problem of size of unit. If the unit, for example, is an apple, there are problems about what will be agreed upon as a "standard apple," how one will handle variations in the size of apples in applying such a unit, and so forth. But even when such measurement problems are encountered, they fade to insignificance beside the monumental confusions in measurement that derive from mixing apples and bananas. This is why the question "What is being measured?"

is the first question, and in that sense the more important one. To worry about the scaling of units for a mixture of apples and bananas is really quite ridiculous. The first problem is one of demonstrating agreement that one indeed has something called "apples" and something called "bananas" to measure.

Indirect measurement, then, requires that there be a defined set of operations as a basis for agreement on the inference as to what is measured. Before one worries about how much, it is necessary to distinguish the measurement operations for one inferred entity from those for another, as well as from what may be called the "noise" in the system as a whole. This thought may be summed up by saying that two primary criteria of measurement are (a) *distinctiveness* and (b) *freedom from distortion*. These two criteria need to be applied if we are to have measurement at all.

Learning, Retention, Transfer

For three rather gross classes of behavioral inferences, it should be possible to apply these primary criteria to the question of what is measured. It would not seem to be too difficult a task to show that the categories called learning, retention, and transfer of learning can be examined by means of these criteria. And if this is so, perhaps finer inferential categories (such as varieties of learning) can be similarly examined.

Learning. The inference called learning appears to depend upon the following set of operations. First, it is determined that an individual cannot do a particular performance A. (The operations used to make this inference are themselves specifiable, as will become apparent.) Second, the individual is provided with a certain sequence of stimulation, and it is determined that he is attending to this stimulation. Again, the operations required to demonstrate attention are simply mentioned here, but are capable of being specified. Third, another set of operations is used to determine that he is motivated to perform. Finally, the observation is made within a specified brief time that the individual either does or does not exhibit performance A. To be complete, one also makes the observation that he exhibits performance A′, another member of the class A (and perhaps also that he exhibits performance A″). As a result of these last observations, it would be generally agreed that the inference is justified that the individual possesses performance capability *a*. In other words, his nervous system, at least during this brief time, has a capability that makes possible performances of the class A.

Has capability *a* been learned? This is the inference sought. In order to make it, however, one must carry out still another operation on the same kind of individual by repeating the total procedure but omitting the second step, the sequence of external stimulation. This control makes it possible to infer learning rather than growth. Of course, this operation is often assumed rather than actually carried out, as is true with some of the other steps. When the measurer is satisfied on this point, he may then make the inference that capability *a* has been learned.

Distortion. Distortion of measurement is avoided in these operations by procedures used to insure that attention is in effect, that there is motivation to perform, and that more than a "chance" performance has been observed. The inference of learning is not justified unless these means are taken to insure that the measurement is free from distortion. If one is concerned with "How much?" obviously the factors of motivation, attention, and variability of response can affect the measurement. But more important is the fact that distortion can reduce the amount to zero, and thus have a direct affect on the question "What is measured?"

Distinctiveness. Distinctiveness of measurement pertains in this instance to the distinction between learning and growth as justifiable inferences. It is noteworthy that the demonstration of distinctiveness in this case ideally requires a "control" operation, which in some circumstances becomes a control group. A large performance change takes place over a relatively small, arbitrarily chosen period of time, which in most cases can be agreed upon as not produced by growth. For this reason the control operation is frequently not actually carried out. Nevertheless, it is of considerable importance to recognize that it is rationally demanded, and cannot be ignored. Its assumption needs to be explicit.

Retention. Retention is inferred from a set of operations somewhat as follows. First, there is a measure of what may be called "immediate learning effects," taken in accordance with the procedures previously described, within a specified time—usually a few minutes following the application of the stimulation situation for learning. (As studies of "short-term memory" make us aware, it is important that the time for this measure be set at a few minutes rather than at a few seconds; further discussion of this point, however, will not be undertaken here.) Here is another instance in which it is necessary to make the measurement of immediate learning outcome in a separate equivalent subject or group, in order that the measure of retention remain uncontaminated. There are scores of studies in the older literature that suffer from this methodological defect in the measurement of retention.

After it has been demonstrated that there has been some immediate effect of learning, the measurement of retention may be undertaken at some specified time—hours, days, or months after the learning session has been completed. Again, interest centers upon the inference that capability a has been retained, as shown by the execution of performance A. For such an inference to be valid, the performance measured after the intervening time must, of course, be the same as that measured "immediately."

The inference about retention of capability a, however, is not quite this simple, and usually certain other precautions of measurement must be observed. This is because what happens to the learner during the intervening time has some marked consequences. As a single example, it is known that the learner may engage in "internal rehearsal"; in fact, it is difficult to prevent him from doing so (Murdock, 1963). In addition, it is known that different kinds of intervening activity, introduced with the purpose of preventing such rehearsal, have different effects on retention as finally measured (Loess and McBurney, 1965). At the very least, it may be said that a measure of retention is uninterpretable without a specification of what has happened to the learner in the period between learning and the measurement of retention.

Again in this instance of measurement, one can see the need to apply the criteria of freedom from distortion, and distinctiveness, in order to be sure about what is measured—before one faces the question "How much?" Distortion is prevented by operations that control the opportunities for "internal rehearsal," and that also control the kind of intervening activity known to produce varying amounts of interference (compare Postman, 1961). Distinctiveness is insured by control-group operations that make possible the inference that that capability which has been learned in the first place has (or has not) been retained.

Transfer of Learning. Measuring transfer involves many of the operations previously mentioned, and others besides. The inference one wishes to make is that some capability a, exhibited in performance A, having been learned and retained, has an effect on the learning of capability b (in some performance B'). The capabilities a and b are different in some respects that are specifiable. It is evident that the inference of transfer depends upon measurement operations that involve the demonstration that learning and retention are present as prior events. Otherwise, of course, one may not know whether what is hypothesized to transfer is present in the first place. Transfer is also markedly subject to contamination by intervening events, as is the case with the measurement of retention. Studies of retroactive inhibition (compare Keppel, 1968) provide the classical setting for the masses of evidence bearing upon this measurement problem.

In this case, too, the question of what is measured is subject to the criteria of freedom from distortion and distinctiveness. For the former, one must design operations to demonstrate that learning has occurred, that retention is possible, and to control and specify intervening events. Distinctiveness of measurement must be insured, as was true with learning and retention, by the use of a control subject or group that demonstrates the absence of effects from sources other than the capability on which interest centers. One must bear in mind that one wants to make the inference that capability *a* has transferred, not simply that capability *b* has been facilitated or interfered with.

CLASSES OF LEARNING OUTCOMES

It appears to be so, then, that the distinguishing of learning outcomes into the gross categories of learning, retention, and transfer requires measurement operations that are designed to prevent distortion and to insure distinctiveness. To be sure of clarity, let me try to define these two terms formally, although their meaning may already have been deduced. Keeping measurement *free from distortion* means insuring that the performance observed in the act of measuring has not been influenced by some class of variable other than a capability of the general sort which is the focus of interest in studies of learning. Examples, some of which have previously been mentioned, are attention, set, motivation, rehearsal, interference. Also included might be other factors affecting the measured performance which cannot be exactly specified, that is, "chance" factors. *Distinctiveness* in measurement has the aim of ruling out the observation of one category of capability as opposed to some other capability. Thus measurement seeks to insure that a learned capability is observed rather than one which is grown, or that a retained capability is one that was learned in the first place, or that a transferred capability is the one that was initially learned and transferred, and not some other.

By applying the criterion of freedom from distortion, one attempts to insure that the inference from performance to capability is valid. By applying the distinctiveness criterion, the effort is made to assure that the inferred capability has been properly identified.

Some Additional Distinctions

In measuring the outcomes of learning, there is very often an interest in making even finer classifications of the capabilities being inferred. For example, those who have studied maze learning in animals have traditionally been interested in designing measures to distinguish "place" learning from "sequence" learning. Hunter's (1913, 1920) studies of delayed reaction and double alternation were designed to distinguish between the learning of discriminations and "representative process." Harlow's (1949) work on monkeys proposed to draw a distinction between "discrimination habits" and "learning sets." Investigators of the learning of verbal sequences are concerned with devising measures that will distinguish the learning of sequence from the learning of item position (Jensen and Rohwer, 1965). Many other examples could be given.

In my work (Gagné, 1970) I have suggested eight different kinds of inferences that seem to me to be generally useful distinctions to make throughout the field of learning as a whole, particularly as they are relevant to school learning. I am prepared to think that more than eight distinctions may be important to make, and that there may be several reasons for making them. Nevertheless, it still seems to me that these eight categories are of particular significance to learning research and theory, as well as to the particular affairs of education.

In repeating these categories here, I do not wish to cover old ground. Rather, I should like to examine specifically the question of distinctiveness between pairs of these categories. As is true with other classes of learning outcomes, each of these inferred capabilities carries its own set of problems with respect to the criterion of distortion (that is, effects of other variables on performance). But it would be too long a job to consider these distortion effects here. The question of distinctiveness, however, seems to be of particular relevance to a consideration of "what is measured" when interest centers upon "what kinds of capabilities can be inferred?"

The distinctions among inferred capabilities that should be described for present purposes are as follows:

1. The classical conditioned response ("signal learning") versus the operant conditioned response ("response learning").
2. The operant conditioned response versus the motor chain; or versus the verbal sequence.
3. The single response or chain versus the multiple discrimination.
4. The multiple discrimination versus the concept.
5. The concept versus the principle.
6. The simple principle versus the abstract (or higher-order) principle

Two Types of Conditioning. The problem of distinguishing the measurement operations for classical and operant conditioning has a long history, extending back to Skinner's (1935) landmark paper, and even before that. Modern writers (for example, Kimble, 1961; Grant, 1964) state the major distinctive operations to be somewhat as follows: In the classical conditioning situation, the conditioned response being observed is maintained by the pairing of conditioned and unconditioned stimuli, where such pairing is independent of the learner's response; in operant conditioning, the maintenance of the learned response depends on presentation of the "unconditioned stimulus" in a manner that is contingent upon the occurrence of that response. What is most notable about this distinction, for present purposes, is that it takes at least two observations to establish distinctive measurement. One must know, first, that the learned response does depend upon the presentation of a conditioned stimulus, and second, that the learned response either is or is not maintained when the contingency of conditioned response followed by unconditional stimulus does not obtain.

Single Connection and Chains. The question of distinctiveness also arises in connection with the learning of a single connection versus the learning of chains. In motor learning, such a demonstration could presumably be carried out by showing that a set of describably different responses forming a sequence (such as unlocking a lock with a key) can each be initiated by a separate stimulus. If each element or link in the chain can thus be separately demonstrated, then each may be contrasted with the total sequence as a single connection. Of course, one may continue the measurement process by seeing whether each "single" connection may, in its turn, be further broken down into two or more additional links. Presumably, there is at least a practical limit as to how far this process may be carried.

Another important example of the distinctiveness criterion occurs in the learning of verbal paired associates (verbal chains). Whereas for many years the paired associate was treated as a single connection, the studies of Underwood and Schulz (1960) have demonstrated the necessity of observing at least two links in a chain. Thus, operations were devised to measure "response learning" separately from "association learning," and no modern investigator would think of ignoring this distinction. Nowadays, a number of procedures are used to insure that measurement is either directed primarily at the "associative phase," for example, by using response words that are known to be previously well-learned; or else at "response learning" itself, by having the learner recall freely a set of originally unfamiliar syllables. Establishing the distinctiveness of single connections and verbal chains is usually either a two-stage measurement process, or one which accomplishes a similar purpose by the use of experimental and control groups.

Single Connections and Multiple Discrimination. Studies of discrimination learning in both animals and human beings usually make the distinction between single connections and multiple discriminations quite clear. Typically, this is done by using the kinds of single connections that are already known to be well-learned, or which can be shown to be. Discrimination in a white rat, for example, can be measured by testing whether he jumps to the right or left, or perhaps presses a lever with a vertical or horizontal push. In either case, one attempts to observe the discrimination only after assuming that the jumping, or the lever-pressing, has been previously learned. When such prior learning of single connections (or chains) cannot be assumed, it must first be demonstrated. An investigator would not try to observe discrimination learning unless the differential responses called for could not be shown separately as being already present in the animal's repertoire.

Lists of verbal associates also fall into the category of multiple discrimination. Each single pair, provided its component links are previously learned, is retained with near-perfection for a short time following a single presentation (Murdock, 1961). When one or more pairs is added, the increased difficulty in learning that occurs is one of the best-known phenomena in the verbal learning field. Difficulty of learning increases with length of list (McGeoch and Irion, 1952). The effects of intralist similarity of interferences among items have also been extensively studied (compare Underwood, 1964). Without attempting to describe further the various findings bearing on this point, let me simply say that investigators of paired-associate learning are careful to distinguish the measurement of single verbal associates from the measurement of sets of associates, which I here put in the category of multiple discrimination. The single verbal chain is learned in one trial, and this usually serves as a standard against which to measure the learning of sets of associates that are greater than one.

The Use of Control Techniques

These brief descriptions of measurement techniques applicable to single connections, chains, and multiple discriminations have been included not with the intention of an exhaustive consideration of their measurement problems, but rather to provide a background for discussion of the measurement of more complex learning outcomes. It seems to me that the learning of concepts and principles, the major domain with which school learning is concerned, is likely to face similar measurement problems and be subject to similar criteria, as are these simpler kinds of learning. If there are techniques for applying the criterion of distinctiveness to measuring these simpler kinds of learning outcomes, similar techniques should at least be tried in the measurement of more complex capabilities.

I refer to concepts and principles as being more complex than connections, chains, and discriminations for the very simple reason that they appear to require the inference, or the postulation, of more elaborate mechanisms to account for them. In other respects, they may not be more complex; for example, the conditions typically required to bring them about by learning may actually be simpler to describe. Whatever the case, it is certainly true that they have been studied less, and one has many fewer pieces of evidence to call upon in identifying appropriate measurement procedures.

What does the scientific literature on simpler learning processes suggest about the measurement of concepts and principles as outcomes of learning? What kind of extrapolations can be made concerning the problem of distinctive measurement, of identifying precisely what is being measured?

The theme of methodology running through the application of measurement to simpler capabilities appears to be this: the criterion of distinctiveness requires that a control be employed before a dependable conclusion can be drawn about what is measured. Sometimes it is possible to make this control measurement on the same person, sequentially with the second measurement, which more specifically encompasses the learning outcome of interest. When this is possible, one may think of distinctive measurement as a two-stage process, the first (control) stage of which must be done before a firm conclusion can be drawn from the second stage. In other instances, control takes the form of using another (equivalent) individual, or another group. In such instances, the two measurement procedures, control and "experimental," can be applied at the same time or within the same experimental context. But in either case, the purpose is the same: it is to measure the capability distinctively; to insure that what one wants to measure is not in fact something else.

Let me state this proposition more specifically. Control procedures of measurement are used to distinguish classical and operant conditioning; if the latter is being measured, one must either first or independently demonstrate that the response being observed does not occur when the contingency of instrumental production of the unconditioned stimulus is made impossible. Only then is one justified in being convinced that what is being measured is an operant response. Similarly, control procedures are used to distinguish single connections and chains; one can legitimately speak of chain learning only when independent measurement has shown that the component links in the chain have been previously learned. Distinctive measurement procedures also apply to single connections and multiple discriminations: one measures discrimination learning only when independent methods have been used to demonstrate that the single connections or chains that make up the multiple set to be learned have already been acquired. (In animal learning studies, the control operation is usually specifically carried out; in human verbal learning, it is usually assumed to require a single trial.)

When one turns to the procedures used in observing concepts and principles as learned outcomes, one is immediately struck by the fact that control measures are often not employed. Instead, the general picture seems to be dominated by quite a different set of procedures, derived from other kinds of considerations. One begins to encounter measurement instruments described as "multiple-choice tests," "completion questions," or "matching questions." These may well be useful ways to apply measures, and nothing can be immediately perceived as wrong with them. But still another characteristic of measurement emerges in the fact that these techniques are not usually employed in such a way that controls are present. The single "item" of a single type appears to be employed as the unit of measurement, rather than a two-stage technique or a control procedure. To be sure, more than one item is usually employed, but the justification for this is reliability (a variety of the freedom from distortion criterion), as opposed to distinctiveness of measurement. Logically, no amount of concern with reliability can provide a solution to the problem of identifying what is measured.

There is, then, an apparent discrepancy that needs to be further examined. The kinds of learning outcomes most frequently measured in laboratory studies are usually subject to the criterion of measurement distinctiveness. This requires some kind of control technique to insure the distinction between one kind of learning outcome and another. In contrast, the kinds of learning outcomes most frequently encountered in educational settings are typically measured with techniques that do not involve control procedures. Is it possible that such procedures are unnecessary with these more complex kinds of learning? Can suitable assumptions be made to make them unnecessary? Or has their applicability been somehow overlooked?

MEASURING CONCEPTS AND PRINCIPLES

It is now time to examine more closely the kinds of distinctiveness considerations that may be applicable to the measurement of concepts and principles, and in addition, their desirability as criteria of measurement. In doing this, I shall discuss the distinction between multiple discrimination and concepts, concepts and principles, and among different classes of principles.

Multiple Discriminations and Concepts

In dealing with concepts, as a first step it is desirable to define the term "concept." By a concept I mean the kind of capability that enables an individual to identify (by class name or otherwise) a specific member of a class of objects, object properties, actions, or events, when that specific member is new to him. This is the kind of entity the psychologist studies, usually in children, when he deals with the learning of colors, shapes, textures, positions, and directions. A somewhat special category of such concepts, with which I shall not deal further here, are the kinds of concepts that have designated combining rules, such as "conjunctive concepts" (yellow and bordered), "disjunctive concepts" (either yellow or bordered), and the like (compare Bruner, Goodnow, and Austin, 1956). In still another and quite different category are concepts that cannot be conveyed by giving experience with specific members of a class, but which must be communicated by *definition* (compare Gagné, 1966). The simpler kinds of concepts, having concrete referents, are what I have in mind to discuss here. Defined concepts, which appear to be formally identical with principles, will be dealt with later.

In order to make an observation to detect whether a concept has been learned, one must in effect ask the question: "Among this variety of objects (object properties, actions, events) that I show you, which are bilpads?" (The final word represents a name for the class.) I say "in effect," because it seems evident that such a question can functionally be asked of an animal who does not understand language, as was true of Harlow's (1949) monkeys, who learned to respond to concepts such as those we call "right," "left," and "odd."

However, it is at once apparent that asking a question like "Which are bilpads?" is in itself an insufficient condition for making a distinctive measurement of the concept. Suppose that "bilpad" means a particular shade of tan, and that objects having a somewhat different shade of tan are not "bilpad." The individual who has not previously learned to discriminate these shades of tan will not make correct identifying responses and, thus, will not have learned the concept according to the measurement applied. A recent analysis by Martin (1967) relates the concept to multiple discriminations in terms of $S–R$ connections. While Martin's hypothesis of mutual inhibition is not essential to the conception of concept here being discussed, his clear exposition of the necessity of discrimination as a prior condition of concept acquisition is highly relevant.

The purpose of distinctive measurement of a concept capability is, after all, to assess the effectiveness of some particular learning situation. Suppose that the learners have been placed in this learning situation, designed to have them acquire some designated concept. When measurement operations are applied, it is found that some have acquired the concept, while others have not. But of those who have not, there are two kinds, and a single-stage sort of measurement will not be able to distinguish them. Specifically, there will be learners who (a) have previously acquired the necessary discriminations, but who do not know the concept, and learners who (b) have not previously acquired the necessary discriminations and who do not know the concept.

Single-stage measurement, of the sort that simply tests whether or not learners correctly identify "bilpad," or some other concept, is not distinctive measurement. Such single-stage operations do not distinguish concepts from multiple discriminations or, more specifically, the absence of concepts from the absence of multiple discriminations. The design of distinctive measurement seems a relatively simple matter, but it must involve a control that determines the presence or absence of concepts. A two-stage operation would probably be simplest to use—one which first measured the presence of multiple discriminations, and then the presence or absence of the concept.

I see no reason why this line of reasoning does not apply directly to the measurement of concepts that are learned in school, whether they are very simple ones such as the printed letters learned in the early grades, or more complex ones like "cell nucleus" learned in some later grade. Again, the criterion of distinctive measurement requires a distinction to be drawn between those performances that fail to identify members of the class "cell nucleus" when the learners *can* make the necessary discriminations, and those performances that fail to identify the concept when the learners *cannot* make these discriminations. Two-stage measurement would appear to provide a way of achieving such distinctiveness.

Concepts and Principles

I should now like to consider the measurement of principles, or ideas, as contained in such simple statements as "leaves grow on trees," "airplanes fly in the sky," or "a nervous impulse is a wave of electrical dipolarization propagated along the membrane of a neuron." It is evident that measurement of such principles also presents very similar problems so far as the criterion of distinctiveness is concerned.

Each principle is composed of concepts. The principle "leaves grow on trees" is, very simply, composed of the four concepts, "leaves," "grow," "on," and "trees." Since concepts are involved, a single-stage measurement operation simply does not provide distinctive measurement, because the failure of a learner to demonstrate that he "knows the principle" may mean that he does not "know the concepts." The principle that "a parallelepiped is a prism whose bases are parallelograms" may obviously not have been learned because the learner does not have one or more of its component concepts, whether "prism," "base," or "parallelogram." Distinctive measurement of what is learned would seem to require two-stage measurement, the first stage devoted to assessing whether the concepts have been acquired, and the second to whether the principle is known.

Still another problem of distinctive measurement occurs with principles. This is the problem of distinguishing the measurement of principles, not from concepts, but from verbal associates. This problem occurs particularly because of the fact that verbal items are typically and widely used to measure the acquisition of principles. Accordingly, the problem is to distinguish knowing the principle from knowing the names of the concepts that make up the principle. Obviously, a test item like the following,

Leaves grow on _____.

or any variants of this item using multiple-choice alternatives, may be measuring the verbal association "leaves-trees" rather than the principle itself.

Ideally, this difficulty would be overcome by using actual members of the classes of concepts involved (that is, real trees, real growing, and real leaves) to make up the stimulus situation in which the measurement is taken. Employing a two-stage process, the concepts themselves would first be identified by the learner, who would then be asked to demonstrate the principle. Under certain other assumptions, distinctive measurement of a principle can be carried out by asking the learner to demonstrate by means of a picture. For example, the instruction may be given to a child (following upon a first stage of concept measurement): "You have learned that leaves grow on trees. Draw a picture to show this."

The criterion of distinctiveness in the measurement of principles has often not been followed in experimental studies of substance learning. In their review of investigations thirty years ago, Welborn and English (1937) mention several widely used methods of measurement, including (a) verbatim recall with verbatim scoring; (b) free recall with scoring for main ideas; and (c) recognition measures employing multiple-choice tests. More recent examples of each of these methods can also be readily located, such as Newman (1939), Ausubel, Robbins, and Blake (1957), and King and Russell (1966).

It appears evident at once that the verbatim method of scoring fails to distinguish between the retention of verbal chains and the retention of principles. The employment of control procedures to measure these two outcomes separately is deliberately undertaken in some studies (for example, Cofer, 1941; King and Russell, 1966), and these procedures surely acknowledge the problem. It is not quite so evident, however, that all investigators who have used this kind of control are entirely clear about what it is they want to measure. Even less useful, from the standpoint of distinctive measurement, is the method of recognition using multiple-choice tests. Such items do not require the recall of a principle, since the major portion of the principle is included either in the stem of the item or in one of the alternatives. If such a partial statement of the principle repeats the learning statement verbatim, we again face the problem of indistinguishability from verbal sequence learning. On the other hand, if the partial representation of the principle contained in the test item is a paraphrase, the recognition of the missing word may be a matter of identifying a concept, rather than a reinstating of the principle.

I am led to the belief, therefore, that measuring the learning outcome of principles must be accomplished in some way or other that requires the learner to demonstrate the *idea* of the principle, and that this must be distinguished by suitable control procedures from both verbatim learning of a verbal sequence and from the learning of the concepts that make up the principle. One method, already suggested, would require identification of the concepts as a first stage, followed by some sort of representation (as in drawing) of the principle as a second. Assuming that a suitable first stage is employed, the second stage might well take other forms, one of which is paraphrasing (as used, for example, by English, Welborn, and Killian, 1934).

Another instance of failure to describe and exemplify distinctive measurement of principles occurs in the work of Bloom and his collaborators (1956), in their treatment of a taxonomy of learning tasks. These authors equate the category of "knowledge" with "recall of ideas," and illustrate their measurement mainly with multiple-choice test items. One simply does not know what these items measure. Here is an example (Bloom, 1956, p. 81):

Magnetic poles are usually named:	3. east and west
1. plus and minus	4. north and south
2. red and blue	5. anode and cathode

An item such as this might be measuring the verbal association "magnetic pole—north, south." Many people would probably say that is what it does measure. If so, then it can hardly be considered to constitute adequate measurement of a principle. One can imagine an item in this general category designed to measure a concept, as in the following instance:

(Picture of a magnet, with lines of force)
Label the poles of the magnet by their usual names.

However, it is apparently not possible in this instance to turn such an item to the purpose of principle measurement because it simply does not imply a principle. One can imagine an item designed to measure such a principle as the following: When two bar magnets are allowed to attract each other, the north pole of one will be adjacent to the south pole of the other. The item would be:

(Picture of two bar magnets)
The two bar magnets in the picture have come together by attraction. Label the poles of each.

These examples illustrate one way in which two-stage measurement might be employed. First, a measure is applied to determine whether the individual possesses the concept of magnetic poles. If he knows this, it is then possible as a second step to attempt to test whether or not he has learned a principle. Obviously, if the second step is undertaken without the first, the results are ambiguous. They do not enable us to distinguish learners who have not learned the concept "magnetic pole" from learners who have learned this concept, but who have not learned the principle.

Distinctions among Principles

In the field of achievement testing, it is not difficult to find examples of measurement that do not meet the criterion of distinctiveness. Often these instances fail to distinguish a simpler, more concrete principle from a more abstract one. More generally, they attempt to measure more than one principle at one and the same time. An example I have used before is the following (Gagné, 1965, p. 259):

(Diagram of a pipe, showing a cross section)
Find the thickness of a pipe whose inner circumference is 9_π, and whose outer circumference is 21_π.
(a) 12_π; (b) 12; (c) 6_π; (d) 6; (e) 3.

This item fails to distinguish measurement applicable to two different principles. First is the principle relating circumference to diameter, that is, $C = \pi d$. Second is the principle, rather readily applicable to the accompanying picture, that the outer diameter of a pipe equals the inner diameter plus twice the thickness of the pipe.

Clearly, if one wishes to know whether these two principles have been learned, they must be measured separately. Again in this instance a two-stage measurement operation, or some other form of control, is called for. If the individual fails this item, we do not know whether (a) he did not know the first principle; (b) he did not know the second principle; (c) he did not know either principle; or (d) he knew both principles, but was unable to put them together in solving a new problem. The criterion of distinctiveness in measurement is not met by items such as this, which try to combine too many measurement operations into one.

REQUIREMENTS OF LEARNING MEASUREMENT

The substance of what I am saying is this: Measurement of learning outcomes in laboratory studies of such varieties of learning as connections, chains, and multiple discriminations has generally been characterized by careful attention to what is being measured. For those varieties of learning in which such analysis and definition of outcome has not been true in the past, one can readily see pronounced trends in this direction at present. Measurement of these simpler sorts of learning events appears to be subject to the criteria of (a) distinctiveness, by which is meant operations that distinguish one class of learning outcome from another; and (b) freedom from distortion, involving a set of operations that distinguish learning from the action of other variables of various sorts.

The criteria of distinctiveness and freedom from distortion, when applied to these relatively simple kinds of learning, appear to require the use of control operations as essential parts of the measurement itself. Often, this means the employment of control individuals or groups. In other instances, control is exercised by using the same individuals, but making the necessary operations in two stages. The first stage is the control measurement, and the second is the measurement that is the center of interest.

When one looks at more complex varieties of learning outcome, it appears that control operations are equally applicable and equally necessary, if one is going to be confident about what is measured. Thus, it is possible to design control operations for measurement distinctiveness that make possible differentiation between concepts and multiple discriminations, between principles and concepts, between principles and verbal sequences, and between principles of differing levels of abstractness. Although not elaborated here, it is not difficult to believe that operations to avoid distortion of measurement are similarly feasible for these varieties of learning.

Such measurement operations for concepts and principles are possible; however, they appear not to have been much used. Instead, there is what I would characterize as a regression to the use of inexact techniques originally designed for quite different purposes. These techniques are those of mental testing, which were designed primarily for the purpose of predicting performance, rather than of measuring learning outcomes. If one is concerned with prediction, it is likely to make little difference whether a distinction can be drawn between the learning of, say, a concept, and the learning of a principle. In brief, the individual who "knows more" is going to exhibit faster learning and a better ultimate performance, regardless of what the particular components of his capability are.

It should be clear that the purposes of achievement measurement in the schools are not always those of prediction. In many important instances, the purpose is to identify what has been learned, and by so doing to relate it to that which was intended to be taught. Thoughtful writers on achievement testing have usually given considerable emphasis to this distinction. Lindquist (1951), for example, states that the first step in designing achievement tests must be that of determining what is to be measured. Nevertheless, having acknowledged this idea, most writers on achievement measurement proceed blithely to describe techniques of test design that pay no further heed to the methods of distinctive and distortion-free measurement.

Dependence upon imprecise techniques of mental testing for the measurement of concepts and principles has led to the ignoring of the requirements for control procedures that have come to be standard features of measurement techniques used with other simpler kinds of learning outcomes. The single item used in traditional achievement testing constitutes an uncontrolled, ambiguous measure that can only in rare instances be shown to be related directly to the learning outcome of interest. Partly as a consequence, perhaps, there is appeal to "scores" from a set of items that must be shown to have elaborate statistical relationships to each other. Statistical methods are used in the attempt to increase precision of measurement, when in fact the problem of achieving distinctiveness and freedom from distortion could best be accomplished by direct control procedures.

What is suggested by this review is that techniques of control need to be developed and used for the measurement of concepts and principles as outcomes of learning. In particular, the notion of two-stage measurement, rather than dependence on the single item (alone or in collections), seems to offer greatest promise of a feasible solution. Of course, if this suggestion were followed, it would lead to new kinds of tests for achievement, as well as new kinds of scoring procedures. Neither of these are now in existence, but they appear to be technically possible.

I need to mention again the question of measurement of "How much?" There are some highly interesting problems involved in this question, but I cannot begin to deal with them here. Their neglect should not be interpreted as indicating, however, that I consider them unimportant. Instead, I have simply followed the advice of other investigators of measurement, and attempted to give priority to the question of what is measured. If this priority matter can be clarified, it should not be difficult to devise clear definitions of what may be meant by degree or amount of learning.

Designing techniques to measure learning outcomes seems to me to be a most important requirement for research on complex forms of learning, and consequently also for the practice of educational measurement. We need some new procedures, based upon the criteria of distinctiveness and freedom from distortion, to accomplish the measurement of concepts and principles. These procedures should take into account the use of controls that characterizes the experimental measurement of such learning outcomes as connections, motor and verbal chains, and multiple discriminations in laboratory studies. In this way, a consistent logic of measurement may ultimately come to pervade the entire field.

REFERENCES

Ausubel, D. P., Robbins, L. C., & Blake, E., Jr. Retroactive inhibition and facilitation in the learning of school materials. *Journal of Educational Psychology,* 1957, *48,* 334–343.

Bloom, B. S. (Ed.) *Taxonomy of educational objectives. Handbook I. Cognitive domain.* New York: David McKay Company, Inc., 1956.

Bruner, J. S., Goodnow, J. J., & Austin, G. A. *A Study of thinking.* New York: John Wiley & Sons, Inc., 1956.

Campbell, N. R. *Foundations of science.* New York: Dover Publications, Inc., 1957.

Cofer, C. N. A comparison of logical and verbatim learning of prose passages of different lengths. *American Journal of Psychology,* 1941, *54,* 1–20.

English, H. B., Welborn, E. L., & Killian, C. D. Studies in substance memorization. *Journal of General Psychology,* 1934, *11,* 233–259.

Gagné, R. M. *The conditions of learning.* (2nd ed.) New York: Holt, Rinehart and Winston, Inc., 1970.

Gagné, R. M. The learning of principles. In H. J. Klausmeier and C. W. Harris (Eds.), *Analyses of concept learning.* New York: Academic Press, Inc., 1966. Pp. 81–95.

Grant, D. A. Classical and operant conditioning. In A. W. Melton (Ed.), *Categories of human learning.* New York: Academic Press, Inc., 1964. Pp. 3–31.

Harlow, H. F. The formation of learning sets. *Psychological Review,* 1949, *56,* 51–65.

Hunter, W. S. The delayed reaction in animals and children. *Behavior Monographs,* 1913, *2,* 1–86.

Hunter, W. S. The temporal maze and kinesthetic sensory processes in the white rat. *Psychology,* 1920, *2,* 1–17.

Jensen, A. R., & Rohwer, W. D., Jr. What is learned in serial learning? *Journal of Verbal Learning and Verbal Behavior,* 1965, *4,* 62–72.

Keppel, G. Retroactive and proactive inhibition. In T. R. Dixon and D. L. Horton (Eds.), *Verbal behavior and general behavior theory.* Englewood Cliffs, N.J.: Prentice-Hall, Inc., 1968.

Kimble, G. A. *Hilgard and Marquis' conditioning and learning.* New York: Appleton-Century-Crofts, 1961.

King, D. J., & Russell, G. W. A comparison of rote and meaningful learning of connected meaningful material. *Journal of Verbal Learning and Verbal Behavior,* 1966, *5,* 478–483.

Lindquist, E. F. Preliminary considerations in objective test construction. In E. F. Lindquist (Ed.), *Educational measurement.* Washington, D.C.: American Council on Education, 1951, 119–158.

Loess, H., & McBurney, J. Short-term memory and retention-interval activity. *Proceedings of the 73rd Annual Convention of the American Psychological Association,* 1965, 85–86.

McGeoch, J. A., & Irion, A. L. *The psychology of human learning.* New York: David McKay Company, Inc., 1952.

Martin, E. Formation of concepts. In B. Kleinmuntz (Ed.), *Concepts and the structure of memory.* New York: John Wiley & Sons, Inc., 1967. Pp. 33–67.

Murdock, B. B., Jr. The retention of individual items. *Journal of Experimental Psychology,* 1961, *62,* 618–625.

Murdock, B. B., Jr. Short-term retention of single paired associates. *Journal of Experimental Psychology,* 1963, *65,* 433–443.

Newman, E. B. Forgetting of meaningful material during sleep and waking. *American Journal of Psychology,* 1939, *52,* 65–71.

Postman, L. The present status of interference theory. In C. N. Cofer (Ed.), *Verbal learning and verbal behavior.* New York: McGraw-Hill, Inc., 1961. Pp. 152–179.

Skinner, B. F. Two types of conditioned reflex and a pseudo type. *Journal of General Psychology,* 1935, *12,* 66–77.

Underwood, B. J. The representativeness of rote verbal learning. In A. W. Melton (Ed.), *Categories of human learning.* New York: Academic Press, Inc., 1964, 48–78.

Underwood, B. J., & Schulz, R. W. *Meaningfulness and verbal learning.* Philadelphia: J. B. Lippincott Company, 1960.

Welborn, E. L., & English, H. B. Logical learning and retention: A general review of experiments with meaningful verbal materials. *Psychological Bulletin,* 1937, *34,* 1–20.

Comments on Professor Gagné's Paper

RICHARD ANDERSON

Since I find myself in substantial agreement with Professor Gagné, my remarks will be more an extension of what he said than a critique.

I have three kinds of comments to make. First, I shall comment on Gagné's classification scheme with respect to the varieties of learning outcomes. Second, I shall try to give concrete illustrations of what I regard as the main theme of his paper; and third, I shall comment on an appropriate kind of research design for instructional research studies. My remarks will generally have more directly practical implications than either Professor Gagné's or Professor Postman's remarks.

I would like you to assume that some students have received a verbal lesson and that some tests that have entirely verbal content are given. Now, it would be said by a specialist in the subject matter of the discipline being taught that the lesson contains statements, some of which are descriptions and definitions. Other statements would be said to express concepts and principles.

In his hierarchical classification Robert Gagné has described such categories as *S–R* connections, simple chains, concepts, and principles. It is tempting to believe that there is a one-to-one correspondence between the statements in the subject matter, that is, in the object discipline, and the categories in Gagné's system.

My first point is that we certainly cannot assume such a one-to-one correspondence, and I am not trying to suggest that Gagné implied that we could. In fact, I think the whole point of his paper was that we cannot take statements from an object discipline and characterize them on the basis of an inspection of the statements alone. Let us be specific. A botanist might, in the course of a lecture, make the following two kinds of assertions: (a) "Palmate leaves are hand shaped," and (b) "Gene pools tend to remain stable over time." He might regard the first statement as a definition or a descriptive statement; he might regard the latter as a broad principle, a cornerstone of his discipline. We cannot assume in terms of Gagné's classification scheme that the definitional statement is learned as an *S–R* connection or a simple chain and that the botanist's principle is learned as a principle in Gagné's sense. Both or neither of the statements in the discipline could be learned as simple *S–R* connections or as principles. I fear that Professor Gagné has been widely misunderstood on this point. Educators from various subject matter areas try to match what they call concepts and what they call principles with the categories so designated in his system. Hereafter when I use the word "principle," I will be referring to a statement in the subject matter being taught.

My second comment deals with what I regard as the main theme of Gagné's paper: namely, that we should be applying the logic of experimental analysis to instructional research, most particularly to evaluation and assessment problems. This is a position that I heartily endorse. What I want to do today is to make concrete some of Gagné's suggestions.

Consider first the distinction between the instructional stimulus and the test stimulus. This is the distinction upon which depends the differentiation between learning and retention, on the one hand, and transfer of training on the other hand. Test items that entail verbatim repetition of an instructional stimulus can easily be distinguished from items that entail paraphrases or transformations of the verbatim statement as it appeared in instruction. In other words, the instructional statements and statements in test items can be stated in different words that will be judged to mean the same thing by a person who is an expert in the appropriate discipline.

It will be said by a person operating within a subject matter that principles and concepts apply to classes of examples or instances. A test item may repeat an example included within instruction, or it may involve a new example not included within instruction.

We have here, simply, the difference between lack of understanding and understanding—a person who "knows" a principle can perform in a manner consistent with the principle, no matter what words are employed to express it. A person who "understands" a concept should be able to correctly classify new instances that he did not encounter during the course of a lesson. Technically, the distinction between an instructional stimulus and a test stimulus is a prerequisite for distinguishing between transfer of training and learning or retention.

Several other distinctions can be made. Within instruction we cannot easily distinguish between the stimulus and the response, but we can make this distinction with respect to test items. For example, one can present the definition of a technical term within an item stem and call for the technical term from the student, or one can give the technical term as the test stimulus and call for the definition from the student.

Test items can be distinguished in terms of whether the student must select an alternative, as in a multiple choice item, or supply the response word or phrase, as in completion items. Evidence is beginning to accumulate in my laboratory and elsewhere that the response mode of test items interacts with instructional variables.

A variety of kinds of item types can be generated by applying simple operations of the sort outlined above to instructional statements. Table 1 illustrates the items that may be obtained (a) by varying the segment of the instructional statement which comprises the test stimulus, (b) by allowing either a constructed or selected response from the student, (c) by including verbatim or transformed instructional statements, and (d) by employing repeated examples or new examples. I do not mean to suggest that this analysis is complete; however, it should be possible to develop a taxonomy of kinds of test items by making distinctions such as I have made.

Table 1

Item Types Generated in an Analysis of Principle Statements in an Object Discipline

PROTOTYPE	SAMPLE ITEM
1A. Given the *verbatim* statement of a principle, the student can *supply* the name of the principle.	1A. Behavior which leads to a satisfying state of affairs is strengthened. Behavior which leads to an annoying state of affairs is weakened. The principle is called _____.
1B. Given a *verbatim* statement of the principle, the student can *select* the name of the principle.	1B. Behavior which leads to a satisfying state of affairs is strengthened. Behavior which leads to an annoying state of affairs is weakened. This principle is called: (a) The Law of Effect (b) The Law of Contiguity
2A. Given a *transformed* statement of the principle, the student can *supply* the name of the principle.	2A. Rewarded responses tend to be repeated. Punished responses tend to be suppressed. This principle is called _____.
2B. Given a *transformed* state-	2B. Rewarded responses tend to be re-

Table 1

Item Types Generated in an Analysis of Principle Statements in an Object Discipline—Continued

PROTOTYPE	SAMPLE ITEM
ment of the principle, the student can *select* the name of the principle.	peated. Punished responses tend to be suppressed. This principle is called: (a) The Law of Effect (b) The Law of Contiguity
3A. Given the name of the principle, the student can *supply* the *verbatim* statement of the principle.	3A. Define the Law of Effect (in Thorndike's words).
3B. Given the name of the principle, the student can *select* the *verbatim* statement of the principle.	3B. Which of the following is the best definition of the Law of Effect? (a) Behavior which leads to a satisfying state of affairs is strengthened. Behavior which leads to an annoying state of affairs is weakened. (b) When a neutral stimulus is repeatedly paired with an unconditioned stimulus, the former stimulus acquires the power to evoke the conditioned response.
4A. Given the name of the principle, the student can *supply* a *transformed* statement of the principle.	4A. Explain the Law of Effect in your own words.
4B. Given the name of the principle, the student can *select* a *transformed* statement of the principle.	4B. Which of the following is the best definition of the Law of Effect? (a) Rewarded responses tend to be repeated while punished responses tend to be suppressed. (b) Any stimulus can become a "signal" for a second stimulus if the first one accompanies or slightly precedes the second one enough times.
5A. Given an example *included within training,* the student can *supply* the statement of the principle.	5A. A pigeon receives a pellet of food for some but not all of the pecks it makes on an illuminated key. When the food is terminated, the pigeon continues to peck the key for a number of hours. Explain what has happened in technical, psychological terms.
5B. Given an example *included within training,* the student can *select* the statement of the principle.	5B. A pigeon receives a pellet of food for some but not all of the pecks it makes on an illuminated key. When the food is terminated, the pigeon continues to peck the key

Table 1

Item Types Generated in an Analysis of Principle Statements in an Object Discipline—Continued

PROTOTYPE	SAMPLE ITEM
	for a number of hours. Which of the following is the best explanation of what has happened? (a) Keypecking behavior has been reinforced intermittently with food: therefore, the behavior is resistant to extinction. (b) The previously neutral stimulus, the illuminated key, has acquired the power to evoke keypecking behavior which, therefore, continues when food is terminated.
6A. Given a *new* example, the student can *supply* the statement of the principle.	6A. Mr. Jones has had frequent trouble starting his car. Sometimes it starts immediately. Sometimes it doesn't. On one particular occasion it fails to start immediately. Mr. Jones continues to try to start his car for nearly a half an hour before calling a taxi. Explain what has happened in technical, psychological terms.
6B. Given a *new* example, the student can *select* a statement of the principle.	6B. Mr. Jones has had frequent trouble starting his car. Sometimes it starts immediately. Sometimes it doesn't. On one particular occasion, it fails to start immediately. Mr. Jones continues to try to start his car for nearly a half an hour before calling a taxi. Which of the following is the best explanation of what has happened. (a) Attempts to start the car have been reinforced intermittently; therefore, this behavior is resistant to extinction. (b) A previously neutral stimulus, the car's starter, has acquired the power to evoke starting behavior; therefore, attempts to start the car continue even when it fails to start immediately.
7A. Given a statement of a principle, the student can *supply* an example *included during training*.	7A. Intermittent reinforcement causes resistance to extinction. Give a concrete example of this principle (which appeared in your reading).
7B. Given a statement of a principle, the student can *select*	7B. Intermittent reinforcement causes resistance to extinction. Which of the follow-

Table 1

Item Types Generated in an Analysis of Principle Statements in an Object Discipline—Continued

PROTOTYPE	SAMPLE ITEM
an example *included during training.*	ing best illustrates this principle? (a) A pigeon occasionally receives food when it pecks an illuminated key. When food is no longer given, the pigeon continues to peck the key for a number of hours. (b) Shortly after a buzzer sounds, a dog is shocked unless it jumps over a barrier. After the shock is discontinued, the dog continues to jump when the buzzer sounds for a number of hours.
8A. Given a statement of a principle, the student can *supply* a *new* example.	8A. Intermittent reinforcement causes resistance to extinction. Give a concrete example of this principle which was *not* included in your reading.
8B. Given a statement of a principle, the student can *select* a *new* example.	8B. Intermittent reinforcement causes resistance to extinction. Which of the following best illustrates this principle? (a) As the number of hours since the baby was last fed increases, the frequency and intensity with which it cries are observed to increase. (b) In order to keep him quiet, Mrs. Jones sometimes gives her son candy when he throws a tantrum. She stops this practice on the advice of a psychologist; however, the tantrums are observed to continue.
9A. Given a *new* example of the antecedent of a principle, the student can *supply* the consequent.	9A. A person selling life insurance will make a sale to only a small proportion of the prospects he contacts. Describe the probable behavior of a seasoned life insurance salesman who fails to sell a policy for a number of days.
9B. Given a *new* example of the consequent of a principle, the student can *supply* the antecedent.	9B. A seasoned life insurance salesman fails to sell a policy for a number of days. Nonetheless, he continues to make contacts in the attempt to sell. Suggest in concrete terms a possible explanation of why he continues to try to sell instead of, for instance, taking another job.

Table 2 lists kinds of information about testing procedures that people performing instructional research could provide. In the second column is my guess as to how frequently this information is indeed provided. I shall comment briefly on the fourth entry regarding "Test Development Procedure." The psychometrician reigns supreme here. When there is any talk of how achievement tests are developed, there is usually talk of selecting items in terms of difficulty levels, item-total correlations, and discriminating power. I think the thrust of Gagné's analysis is that the first order of business is a qualitative and a logical analysis, that the discriminating power of items should be given zero weight until the qualitative and logical questions have been satisfactorily answered. Then, with what freedom remains, there presumably is no objection to optimizing discriminating power.

With respect to the fifth entry, "Assumed Level of Psychological Process," the implication of this analysis is that one can make no statement about psychological process without a consideration of experimental operations, control operations, and measurement operations. Distinctions between processes depend upon experimental design. Such distinctions cannot be made from inspection of the test items alone.

Finally, I shall claim that most instructional research should involve a transfer of training design. When we talk as Gagné does about concepts and principles, we imply transfer of training as an underlying process. When we talk about analysis and synthesis, such as Bloom and his associates have done, once again transfer of training is implicated.

Educators generally hope that the student will be able to deal with new configurations of material different from those he encountered during in-

Table 2

What Information Is Provided Regarding Testing Procedure in Published Reports of Instructional Research?

TYPE OF INFORMATION	FREQUENCY
1. Response mode	Always
2. Number of items	Usually
3. Internal consistency reliability	Often
4. Test development procedure	Often
item difficulty	
part-whole correlation	
5. Assumed level of psychological process	Occasionally
6. Topical content analysis with number of items per topic	Rarely
7. Systematic analysis of test items in relation to instructional content	Never

struction. Transfer of training is usually a goal of instruction. Two-stage measurement of the sort that Professor Gagné is suggesting seems necessary to distinguish between learning and transfer. To be determined at the first stage is whether the student can deal successfully with verbatim statements and examples from the lesson. Then, at the second stage, it is determined whether he can handle transformed statements of principles and new examples of the principles hopefully taught within the lesson. With respect to two-stage measurement, there is at least one complicating consideration: the possible reactive effects of testing. There can be a facilitative effect from merely working through a sequence of items. Split-sample designs, in which some students get some items and other students get other items, could be used to control for facilitation due to repeated exposure to similar test items.

In conclusion, the one point that I wish to stress is the importance of systematic analysis of test stimuli in relation to instructional stimuli. The distinction between learning or retention and transfer of training cannot be made without such analysis.

Comments on Professor Gagné's Paper

LEO POSTMAN

Professor Gagné has presented to us a very useful conceptual framework for the assessment of learning outcomes. I find myself in full agreemeet with his view that the valid measurement of learning outcomes is an essential and, indeed, a critical part of the evaluation of educational systems. I want to underscore especially his call for the use of measures of retention and of transfer in the assessment of learning outcomes. Since the objective of instruction is preparation for future activities, long-term retention and the potentialities for transfer to the mastery of new tasks must be the primary criteria of the success of our methods of teaching.

A major value of Professor Gagné's contribution lies in the combination of a general analysis of principles of measurement with the development of an orderly system for the classification of learning outcomes. There is likely to be wide agreement on his formulation of the criteria that must be met by valid measures of learning outcomes, namely, distinctiveness and freedom from distortion. It is, indeed, essential to differentiate as precisely as possible the measuring operations for various classes of learning outcomes and to minimize the influence of uncontrolled and irrelevant variables on performance.

We would expect less consensus when we consider the translation of these general principles into specific operations. The choice of categories of outcomes and of defining operations is based both on theoretical pre-suppositions and on generalizations from available empirical findings. There will be legitimate differences of opinion regarding the most useful cate-gorization of learning outcomes and the empirical generalizations supported by the experimental evidence. The discussion of such differences in opinion should in the long run contribute to the improvement of our methods of assessment. With this objective in mind, I should now like to comment on some of Professor Gagné's proposals for the application of the basic cri-teria of measurement to the systematic assessment of learning outcomes. My purpose will be not so much to disagree with the substance of his rec-ommendations as to emphasize the close interrelations between theory, inferences from available empirical data, and the establishment of criteria for new measurements. The burden of my argument will be that the cate-gorization of outcomes and the measuring operations coordinated with them should be regarded as flexible heuristic devices, and that it will be well to guard against the risk of standardization. I believe that is also Professor Gagné's intention, but it may be useful to focus explicitly on this point.

Let us consider first the measurement of the three broad classes of out-comes distinguished traditionally in our experimental investigations: learn-ing, retention, and transfer. To measure each of these outcomes distinctively requires the performance of a control operation to support the conclusion that the observed outcome reflects the process under study rather than some other process. Once this requirement is accepted, the choice of the appropriate control operations is not necessarily self-evident and often must be based on theoretical decisions. Take the distinctive measurement of transfer as an example. As Professor Gagné formulates the problem, "The inference one wishes to make is that some capability a . . . has an effect on the learning of capability b. The capabilities a and b are different in some respects that are specifiable." To insure distinctiveness, a control group is used to demonstrate that without prior acquisition of a there is no effect on the learning b. And the control operations must be such as to permit the inference that "capability a has transferred, not simply that capability b has been facilitated or interfered with."

These defining operations are clearly appropriate to the measurement of specific transfer, that is, transfer based on the similarity relations be-tween elements in the successive tasks. The capabilities a and b are different in specifiable ways. The transfer of *a* influences the learning of *b* because there is some systematic relation between these different capabilities. Facilitation of *b* or interference with *b* is not included within the domain of transfer. The classical paradigms of specific transfer, such as the learning of old responses to new stimuli, can be readily subjected to tests of distinctiveness implied by these boundary conditions. However, it would be difficult to apply these particular criteria of distinctive measurement to another type of transfer which contributes heavily to the progressive improvement of the learner in the performance of successive tasks, namely general transfer or learning to learn.

In studies of learning to learn, the experimental procedures are explicitly designed to minimize the possibility that the observed improvements reflect the transfer of specific components from earlier tasks; thus, every effort is made to eliminate overlap of elements or similarities between the units in the successive tasks. As the individual goes from task *A* to task *B,* the corresponding capabilities *a* and *b* are assumed to be instances of the same class with reference to general transfer or learning to learn. The question at issue is whether the individual changes his mode of attack on *B* as a result of his experience with *A*; in that sense transfer is the facilitation of *b* rather than the carry-over of a specific *a*. It is our hope, of course, to be able through experimental analysis to break down general transfer into component habits and skills. However, in embarking on studies of learning to learn we were unable to specify these component habits and skills in advance. Rather, the component sources of transfer must be induced gradually from the conditions and characteristics of improvement and the validity of the inductions when tested experimentally. Thus, as our knowledge of general transfer increases, the experimental paradigms used in its analysis progressively approach those of specific transfer.

The basic point here is that the control operations designed to demonstrate distinctiveness will be different for specific transfer and for general transfer. In fact, it is now standard procedure in experiments on specific transfer to include control operations to parcel out the effects of general transfer. Thus, I am in no way questioning the defining operations for transfer proposed by Professor Gagné but am merely trying to delimit the domain of outcomes to which they apply. It is important that our approach to the problem of transfer be in no way constrained by any existing set of criteria of distinctiveness. The same applies, of course, to other learning outcomes. It is a truism worth emphasizing that theoretical considerations must take precedence over the constraints imposed by conventional operational definitions.

While the criterion of distinctiveness must be recognized as essential for orderly measurement, we must also guard against the possibility that a compartmentalization of outcomes unduly restricts our inferences about the effects of training. It is possible to point to situations in which outcome *B* provides the best, and perhaps the only means for establishing the existence of outcome *A* because the usual criteria for *A* lack sensitivity. Consider the situation in which an individual is given several practice trials on a task, say on a list of paired associates. An examination of his performance on these practice trials shows that there are a number of items that he never gave correctly, and he is also unable to recall any of these items correctly on a test of retention immediately after the end of practice. By the usual distinctive criteria, he has failed to learn these items. There is clear experimental evidence, however, that under these circumstances a test of transfer will show that some degree of learning for these items did occur on the practice trials. For example, if the stimuli in these items are paired with new responses, there will be significant negative transfer relative to an appropriate control base line. The degree of learning on the practice trials was insufficient for the performance of the prescribed task, but it was great enough to result in a significant amount of transfer. It may be mentioned in passing that the use of a transfer test for determining whether or not learning has occurred has become an accepted procedure in experimental evaluations of the hypothesis that association is an all-or-none process.

More generally, a transfer test must typically be used to decide between alternative interpretations of what an individual has learned in a given training situation. The analysis of stimulus selection is a case in point. Suppose the learning task consists of paired associates in which the stimulus terms are nonsense syllables presented against colored backgrounds, these colors being clearly different for each syllable. Once the subject has mastered the list, the question arises of what stimuli he has learned to respond to—the syllables, the colors, or both. That is, did he select one of the components of the stimulus terms and associate his responses to that component? The answer to the question of what he has learned depends on whether and to what extent there has been such stimulus selection. And the answer can be obtained only by a test of transfer, that is, by determining the subject's ability to give the correct responses to each of the components separately and in combination. Thus, the logic of the experimental question makes it necessary to draw inferences about learning by means of the distinctive operations of transfer. It is always necessary to insist that the operations of measurement be distinctive, but the acceptance of the criterion of distinctiveness does not entail an invariant identification of a given type of outcome with a particular set of measuring operations.

When the criterion of distinctiveness is applied to measures of outcomes of varying complexity, as is done in the hierarchical scheme proposed by Professor Gagné, it is important not to assume on a priori grounds that the more complex outcomes represent a compounding of the less complex ones. Suppose that a response chain has been established and that it is possible to specify and to measure independently and distinctively each of the links in the chain. We must be cautious about making the inference that the integrated chain represents a summation of these independent elements, and the same holds for any capability that can be analyzed into distinctive and independently measurable components. The two-stage conception of paired-associate learning to which Professor Gagné refers is a case in point. The distinction between response learning and associative learning has proved very useful in the analysis of the conditions and characteristics of paired-associate learning. Each component can be measured independently, for example, by free recall of the responses on the one hand and a test of stimulus-response matching on the other. But it is also a fact that at a given stage of practice the subject's performance in the paired-associate task does not represent a simple summation of the two components measured independently. When a high-order capability is critically dependent on the interaction of conceptually distinct components, two-stage measurement yields only limited information about the status of such a complex capability. The need then arises for the development of distinctive measures directed at the assessment of the interaction of the components.

The decisive influence of theory on the formulation of the criteria of valid measurement is exhibited most clearly in relation to the requirement of freedom from distortion. To avoid distortion of measurement we must choose a set of operations that distinguishes the outcome under study from the action of other variables. To apply this principle we must then distinguish between relevant and irrelevant variables, and that is clearly a theoretical decision. Such decisions will obviously be subject to disagreement on theoretical grounds. I will limit myself to one illustrative example where I found myself in disagreement with Professor Gagné's specification of potential sources of distortion. In describing the measuring operations for the assessment of retention, he states that distortion is prevented by operations that control, among other things, the kind of intervening activity known to produce varying amounts of interference, that is, retroactive inhibition. But according to at least one theoretical view, forgetting is always the result of interference, whether this interference is produced by formal laboratory tasks or by the activities of the learner outside the laboratory. On this theoretical assumption it becomes impossible in principle to eliminate, or to hold strictly constant, interference from intervening activities in the measurement of long-term retention. One can try to influence the probability of interference by choosing materials assumed to have certain similarity relations to the learner's outside activities. Clearly, an interference theorist, a decay theorist, and a consolidation theorist will have quite different conceptions of what are distortion-free conditions for the measurement of retention. Given the lack of theoretical agreement among experimental investigators, the same would hold true for most if not all outcomes of learning.

As I indicated at the outset, I find myself in substantial agreement with Professor Gagné's basic approach to the measurement of learning outcomes. In dissenting from some of his proposals, it has been my intention to bring to the fore the inevitable theoretical basis of decisions about measurement. A good theory will generate appropriate methods of measurement, but the continued acceptance of currently successful measuring operations will not necessarily lead to better theories.

Comments on Professor Gagné's Paper

JOHN BORMUTH

It seems pretentious for us to claim that we can evaluate either the effectiveness of instruction or the achievement of students unless we can specify what our test items actually measure. Gagné has provided us with a clear statement of why this cannot be done using current testing methods. At the same time he has provided us with an analytic device by which we can not only reduce the ambiguity in the interpretation of tests but also add greater power to our testing procedures. In my remarks I will examine one or two points in his logic and then point out some ways Gagné's analysis may be further developed.

It is necessary to begin by making explicit some of the features of Gagné's analysis. He began by pointing out that many of the capabilities we teach can be analyzed as being hierarchical. Figure 1 may be interpreted as the diagram of some simple behavior hierarchy such as answering a long division problem in arithmetic. The diagram is interpreted in this manner. Each letter represents some behaviorial capacity. Behaviors of the types labeled A and B provide the input upon which behaviors of type D operate, behaviors of type D provide the input for behaviors of type F, and so on. Explicitly, an instance of a correct behavior of any type de-

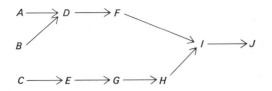

FIGURE 1 *Diagram of a behavior hierarchy.*

pends upon the correct performance of the behaviors connected to it on the left.

These behaviors are operationalized using achievement tests. Figure 2 shows a behavior chain which has been operationalized by including test tasks, T_X. The test task may be analyzed as distinct from the capacity it presumably tests, because it is possible to devise more than one item for observing a given capacity. The upper case letters represent the capability and the lower case letters represent the observable response. It is standard practice to label a capability by giving it the name of the ultimate behavior in its hierarchy. Thus, the chain extending from C to G is named G just as answering long division problems are called division even though their solutions also require the capabilities to add, subtract, and multiply.

Next, Gagné points out that responses to test tasks are ambiguous. A correct response can be interpreted as showing that the student either (1) has acquired the capability represented by the item or (2) has obtained the answer by exercising some other capability such as by copying, by being told the answer, or by using any capability other than the one we hope underlies the response. An incorrect response may mean that the student either (3) has failed to learn just the ultimate behavior in the hierarchy, the behavior that gives the hierarchy its name or (4) has failed to learn one of the capabilities to the left of the ultimate capability.

Only alternatives 1 and 3 provide information that is useful for making educational decisions, making it essential to exclude interpretations 2 and 4. For example, it is impossible to interpret a test performance as an evalua-

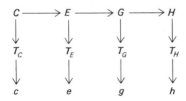

FIGURE 2 *Operationalization of a behavior hierarchy.*

tion of a student's performance or of the instruction if it cannot be determined whether the student obtained the answer by using the capability presumed to have been tested by the item. Similarly, an incorrect response cannot be attributed to a failure in the program to teach a particular capability, say G, unless we can exclude the possibility that it was really a failure of the program to teach one of the behaviors to its left, in this case C and E.

Finally, Gagné proposed that multiple stage measurement operations can be used to eliminate the ambiguous interpretations that can be made of a response to an item. Actually multiple-stage measurement operations can exclude only some of the interpretations of a response, but it is logically impossible to eliminate others. Consider a simple two stage operation in which we test students on some capability that we define as the ultimate capability in a hierarchy and also test them on its penultimate capability. The patterns of responses to the item testing the ultimate capability can then be interpreted. Table 1 shows some of these interpretations. Additional interpretations are possible but their discussion is not necessary to demonstrate the point being made here.

Notice that the two-step operation cannot conclusively refute all of the possible interpretations of a response to the item testing the ultimate capability. We can conclusively refute the proposition that the student has acquired a capability (provided we consider just those interpretations shown in the table). But when he answers correctly the item testing the ultimate capability, we are still unable to assert with assurance that he has indeed learned the ultimate capability. And no amount of additional testing will prove this statement, for there can always remain some possibility that the student obtained his answer using some capability other than the ones our multistage testing operations have excluded. This should be recognized as an instance of the familiar fact that a false theory can be refuted but a true theory can never be conclusively proven true. However, testing the capabilities to the left does put our theory to an experimental test and with each experimental test the statement survives we increase our confidence in its truth.

Similarly, we cannot conclusively prove that a student has failed to learn just an ultimate capability because proving this involves proving that the student has indeed learned its penultimate capability, another instance of proving a correct theory to be true. But we can prove that he has failed to learn some capability to the left of the penultimate and thereby exclude the possibility that he has learned the penult.

This should make it clear that multistage measurement operations increase the interpretability of responses to items, but it is logically im-

Table 1

Interpretations Placed on the Patterns of Responses Observed on Items Testing
an Ultimate and its Penultimate Capability

SCORES OF RESPONSES		INTERPRETATIONS
ULTIMATE	PENULTIMATE	
Pass	Pass	It is possible that the student acquired the ultimate capability, because he was able to exhibit a correct performance both on the item testing the ultimate capability and on the item testing the penultimate capability whose acquisition is prerequisite to the acquisition of the ultimate capability. But this interpretation is not certain because there remains the logical possibility that either item could have been answered using some capability other than the ones being tested.
Pass	Fail	(a) The ultimate capability was not learned because the student was unable to demonstrate correct performance on the item testing the penultimate capability which is a necessary prerequisite to the acquisition of the ultimate. (b) The correct response to the item testing the ultimate capability was obtained using some capability other than the ultimate.
Fail	Pass	(a) The ultimate capability was not learned. (b) It is possible but not certain that failure to exhibit the ultimate capability was due to a failure to learn just the ultimate capability rather than to a failure to learn some capability to its left.
Fail	Fail	(a) The ultimate capability was not learned. (b) Failure to exhibit the ultimate capability was due to a failure to learn some capability to its left.

possible to remove all ambiguity from all response patterns except the interpretation that a student has failed to learn a capability. That is, we can interpret only the incorrect responses unambiguously. This result is rather interesting in view of the fact that test performance is almost universally interpreted in terms of items answered correctly, the very responses which are least interpretable. Before leaving this topic, it should be mentioned that for reasons not considered here, similar ambiguities occur in the interpretation of the incorrect response.

The Gagné analysis can also be used to improve other aspects of the design of tests. To be useful in making educational decisions a test should provide us with a maximum amount of information necessary to design instruction for a group and for individuals in the group. That is, it should provide us with a detailed inventory of the capabilities a student has failed to acquire. Scores that merely rank students are of marginal usefulness and inventories of the items a student answered correctly are logically ambiguous and of only marginal usefulness, for instruction is designed to teach those capabilities which a student has not learned, not those that he has learned.

Consider two characteristics commonly found in current test designs. First, when test items are ordered at all, they are arranged in a sequence so that students begin with easy items presumably testing simple capabilities (those having fewer capabilities to the left in their hierarchies). The student then proceeds to items testing more difficult and presumably more complex capabilities. Second, instead of presenting the student with items testing all the capabilities taught, a small sample of items is selected in a manner which may or may not be representative of the capabilities taught.

When the Gagné analysis is used to evaluate the design of tests currently in use, it is difficult to justify these traditional methods. In subject matter areas where the capabilities taught are hierarchical, it would seem more rational to test the complex capabilities first and then have the student proceed to the left, stopping when enough correct responses have occurred in succession to permit fairly sound extrapolations to the capabilities remaining to the left. This strategy would probably result in the student dealing with fewer items, since there are usually far more simple than complex capabilities in any hierarchy. And, if the instruction is reasonably effective, most of the simple capabilities would have been learned.

Since this strategy would probably produce the greatest amount of parsimony, it may permit testing the student for all the capabilities taught even though he is not given all of the items. It is true that we cannot extrapolate to the simple items with perfect logic. But we can perform this extrapolation to untested items with considerably greater logical support than we can using present test designs. Furthermore, the responses we do observe, the errors, are less ambiguous and more directly useful in designing instruction.

There will undoubtedly be objections that constructing tests of this sort is extremely difficult. It is true that the application of Gagné's analysis is not a simple matter. New formats will be required; much more attention must be given to the structure of content; and the design of the test will be far more complex. However, we should focus our attention on the facts that the most commonly used achievement tests are almost useless for determining the effectiveness of instruction or for deciding what instruction a student should have. In this context it seems difficult to see how we can escape attempting to develop and exploit the implications of Gagné's analysis.

Open Discussion of Gagné's Paper and of Anderson's, Postman's, and Bormuth's Comments

MCDONALD: As I listened to Bob Gagné, I heard quite a different conception of what constitutes measurement and evaluation than we had heard earlier. What Bob said, in his urbane and courteous way, was that most measurement procedures are, as we now know them, irrelevant to evaluation of instruction. As it has been developed, we like to conceive of testing as useless for inferring whether or not learning has occurred.

I think the other point is the extent to which one's conception of learning (and Leo Postman elaborated Bob's idea) determines the method of measurement. I hear all the speakers stating very clearly that what you think about learning is a prior consideration, and that methods of measurement follow from that. If one looks at the categories of validity used in psychometrics, they seem to be irrelevant to this conception.

GUILFORD: Firstly, I would like to welcome Gagné to the camp of what I call informational-operational psychology. He is talking my language, in this sense: he is talking about the learning of classes, the learning of relations, the learning of systems. This fits my theory of learning, exactly. In my theory, the things learned are the products of information. When Gagné speaks of distinctiveness as being a property of learned material, he is giving almost identically my definition of information, which is that which the organism discriminates. The better learned a thing is, the greater the distinctiveness achieved.

I was struck by the fact that, in his discussion of the thinking that goes into the development of measures of achievement of particular information systems, he is indulging in precisely the kind of thinking that we engaged in when developing tests for the general abilities in these particular areas.

And, about his comment on transfer, I would say that, in addition to the transfer that is proposed by stimulus-response psychology, there is also a kind of transfer based upon the learning of products. The more relations a person learns, the better he is able to learn new relations, for he has a greater fund of relations in his memory; also because he has, in the process, learned some strategies for learning relations that will apply in learning new relations. The same thing can be said for principles or for other products of information.

I should say that the theory does include associational interpretations. What I call implications are what used to be called associations. Transfer of learning occurs, then, from the learning of particulars, which also has the general effect of equipping a person for learning more of the same kind of information.

One short comment on Anderson's handouts and his discussion: I am very happy to see this exhibit of divergent production on the part of one who develops items for measurement of the effects of learning. He does get over into what I would call productive abilities in many of the items. They are not all cognition items, as is so often true of other examinations.

GAGNÉ: Let me make a statement here that I think will arouse people, if you want them to be aroused.

You see, I have the notion that the way achievement examinations are made is that a group of experts get together to say, "Now what we want to do is write an item covering this particular concept: that responses tend to be repeated."

And they say, "How will we measure that?"

"Well, we will sit down and we will make items that somehow are at a particular level of difficulty."

I am saying difficulty is an irrelevant idea. You shouldn't even consider difficulty, at that point, anyway. I might admit that you can consider it later, but at that point it is nonsense. It isn't the question. The question is, what do you want to measure? And difficulty has nothing to do with this question.

GLASER: I agree with what you said, but there is a difference between scientific experimental psychology and the engineering of instruction. The operation you use for experimental control is not directly applicable nor exact for the engineering of instruction. So, the methodology used for instructional research or learning research seems to apply to measurement; but it is not a direct translation all the time.

GAGNÉ: I certainly agree, Bob, that one has a different goal from the other, one being, as you say, an applied engineering operation. Yes, you may be engaged in applied operations, but one has to use whatever knowledge he has to make the measurement distinctive, even if it is only of the sort that Leo mentioned, that is, being able to distinguish only that this may be distinctive (or specific) transfer, and the other may be general transfer of the sort we are not able to analyze very well at the moment.

GAGE: I would like to have Bob Gagné speak on the question of whether the way in which he regards the difficulty of a question as irrelevant also assumes that there is no correlation between the level of a test item—this continuum in Dick Anderson's prototype from 1 to 10—and the difficulty of the item. If you made up 100 items, 10 at each of these levels of difficulty, and had normal people doing them, there would probably be a correlation of about .8 between the difficulty of the items and their rank on his continuum from 1 to 10. In that case, would your point about the irrelevance of difficulty still be made? I want to say that I think it would be pretty hard to write items at his point 10 which are typically as easy as the item that is at level 1.

If so, is your comment about the irrelevance of difficulty exactly what you mean to say?

GAGNÉ: Well, you see, essentially what Dick has stated here are different objectives, so that I guess I would think that each one of these could be distinctively measured. The question of difficulty comes in because items assigned to be at a particular level of difficulty simply wander away from the point. The difficulty in attempting to introduce a determined level of difficulty is that it really produces an item that is not relevant or is not measuring what was initially intended.

GLASER: Nate, I could concur with Bob this way: often difficulty is manufactured in an item by manipulating a stem so you introduce high "g" components. It is initially irrelevant.

BLOOM: Is there a distinction between the complexity of the idea and its difficulty? Are you quite prepared to have your test makers make a highly complex problem because they think this is the kind of learning they seek, which may be very simple or very difficult in terms of actual percent of students passing?

GAGNÉ: I think the two are different kinds of decisions. I talked about a principle, you see, and I gave examples of several principles. Now, obviously, some of these are much more complex than others, and the question as to whether one wants to measure the complex principle as opposed to the simpler one is simply a matter of, "Well, have you tried to teach the simpler one or have you tried to teach the more complex one?"

BLOOM: You would have no objection to the test maker trying to work on the complexity of the idea he wishes to get at, whether it is difficult or simple in the end?

GAGNÉ: No, provided this could be related to the objectives of instruction. No, I wouldn't.

GUILFORD: With regard to the question of simplicity and complexity, I would like to suggest that the simple constructs you are talking about might be just relations, implications, or simple classes, whereas the complex ones are either systems, such as a hierarchy of classes, or a complex set of relations involved in a problem.

GAGNÉ: Yes, I tend to make the distinction on the basis of verbal statements that are used to represent a principle.

GUILFORD: My point is that they are qualitative differences, not just quantitative, for different kinds of products are involved.

GAGNÉ: I would have to talk to you more about that. I think that is an interesting point.

PART IV

Contextual Variables

CHAPTER 5

The Cracked Cake of Educational Custom and Emerging Issues in Evaluation

DAN C. LORTIE

The changes taking place in American public schools today have a familiar ring. Contact replaces isolation as new social groups (business, federal agencies) engage themselves in school affairs. Heterogeneity displaces homogeneity when school staffs expand to include people from different occupations (social work, psychology, library work) and teachers are more diverse in social and educational backgrounds.[1] A hierarchical, paternalistic authority system is challenged by subordinates who clamor for a say in decision-making. Interaction within the subsystem quickens as new kinds of buildings and work patterns (team teaching for example) eliminate the walls separating fellow teachers and fellow students. Age-old pedagogical conventions are discarded as students are turned loose to teach themselves with the help of complicated, expensive machines. All these juxtapositions have been witnessed before by anthropologists and sociologists studying cultural and social change; the analogy to processes of modernizing societies is striking. In Walter Bagehot's phrase (1948) "the cake of custom is cracking."

[1] A national survey of teachers conducted by the NEA disclosed that teachers come close to a representative sample of Americans in general in terms of the social class status of their parents. Many observers believe that this represents a broadening of the teacher base. Undergraduate schooling today is considerably more diverse than it was several decades ago; today there are relatively few beginning teachers who have been trained in "single purpose" institutions. See National Education Association, Research Division, "The American Public School Teachers, 1960–1961," Research Monograph 1963-M2.

149

Cultural and social change involves shifts in how people assign value to various parts of their world, ambiguities arise as old certainties melt. This paper explores this process as educational evaluation confronts a system in transition; it focuses on issues that arise as a consequence of change.[2] Such analysis requires more than mere assertion that changes are taking place; the trick is to trace their specific effects. There is the temptation, often yielded to by sensational journalists, to see a revolution in every protest rally. Conservatism seems indicated. I shall, therefore, limit my observations to trends that are already visible and, in sketching out probable effects, eschew long lines of inference. It is, in fact, very doubtful whether social science theory permits us to gauge anything more than such first-order effects. Yet it is interesting that the implications of current educational change are such that even a prudent approach produces a set of rather complicated possibilities.

ORGANIZATIONAL TRENDS AND EVALUATION

Using the local school district as our point of reference, we can classify organizational trends occurring today as "external" and "internal." We begin with events taking place in the external system. There seems little doubt that the augmented roles of the federal government, business corporations, and universities will have important effects on the public schools.

The activities of the federal government erode educational tradition. We can see this as the government legitimates and diffuses that set of ideas symbolized by the phrase "research and development." This conception of educational practice stresses a core idea of rationality in governance; it applies scientific ways of thinking to the appraisal of alternatives and to the making of decisions. This viewpoint is not new to university professors. Yet as a statement of official government policy, backed by public tax monies, it is novel for the public schools. The research and development viewpoint has migrated from universities and industry to school boards justifying their claims for federal grants. It becomes part of the working reality of school officials because it is built into the rhetoric of applying for funds and undergrids the logic of allocation used by federal agencies. We need not argue that school officials understand it fully to argue that it influences their actions. Thoughtways can affect organizational behavior

---

[2] "Evaluation" and "assessment" are given broad definition in this paper, for evaluative acts are intertwined with most educational decisions. The writer assumes, however, that technical evaluation involves some measurement of effects of programs, and so forth, on students. I have omitted references to the evaluation of personnel since I see it as a somewhat different kind of administrative function.

even where understanding is incomplete (Callahan, 1962). It is becoming routine for federal agencies supporting new programs to require recipients to build in evaluation procedures. Such requirements force compliance to the new ideology and undermine belief in tradition as the warrant for educational practice.

Federal activities in education are conducted by a variety of agencies featuring a variety of primary objectives.[3] It seems that once an agency takes on the foundation function, its officials begin to act like foundation men; they prefer to back undertakings that are original and, if possible, dramatic. Thus, new funds, coupled with diverse sponsors who bend toward the novel, produce an increased number of institutional options and thereby add to the alternatives confronting decision-makers in local school districts. Such an increase in options reinforces notions of rationality conveyed by the research and development ideology. The necessity to make choices forces people to attend to the grounds for choice. The larger the number of alternatives, furthermore, the more those who would prefer to "stand pat" must defend their inactivity as a choice in and of itself. This is not to say that the availability of options carries assurance that all or even most will be adopted by local school officials. But when we recall the potency of incentives possessed by the federal government (that is, large amounts of new monies, a capacity to give national publicity to selected school systems), it seems reasonable to expect at least some of the new approaches to enter school decision-making. It is theoretically possible, moreover, that some highly innovative school systems will make radically divergent initial choices (for example, Pittsburgh's commitment to educational parks) and, constrained in the selection of subsequent solutions, will ultimately branch into highly divergent overall solutions. It is probably too early for us to conduct empirical studies of radical branching, but it is a possibility well worth keeping in mind.

Business corporations dealing with educational matters will add to the number and range of instructional practices and solutions; individual firms, in fact, will do so or go out of business. The new firms combining publishing and electronic resources, moreover, frequently have vast financial resources available for development, production, and sales. Competition between firms is likely to be fierce, particularly as each battles to get and hold as large a share of the market as possible. Recall as well that when businessmen talk about "merchandising," they are describing effective techniques for disseminating practices. If we can assume that no single firm or coalition of firms monopolizes sales, the outcome will be further differen-

[3] Compare, for example, the preoccupations of the National Science Foundation with those of the Office of Economic Opportunity.

tiation among school systems as patterns of purchasing and implementation vary.

It is many years since Veblen showed that universities act like business corporations in struggling for prestige, wealth, and influence (Veblen, 1957). They, like business organizations, are under pressure to come up with differentiated "products" for the educational market. Universities have their own resources in countering competition from government and business; they export highly trained persons as well as ideas. Graduates of a particular university can be uniquely competent in implementing and refining an approach developed at their institution; professors acting as consultants widen the institution's sphere of influence. Competition between universities is, of course, softened by cooperation among specialists from different institutions (for example, the professor-developed curricula), but the net effect is similar for local school officials. They confront not only diverse university programs but demands for more and more student time issued by competing hands of university scholars. Professors engaged in public-school affairs produce alternatives that must be considered by those governing school districts.

Changes in the external system, then, point to greater pressures on local decision-makers to deal with ever more possible lines of action. School officials will probably look for ways to reduce those pressures; inquiry would probably reveal that structures are being constructed now to filter and contain innovative forces.[4] Yet the external system, primarily because it is external and largely outside the power system of local officials, can stay with its self-appointed function of generating new ways to keep school. School officials, whether they wish change or prefer continuity, will have little choice but to examine an expanding number of instructional approaches in the years ahead.

The examination of new alternatives will require considerable increases in the amount of evaluative activity carried on by school personnel. The justification of a particular choice requires comparisons between alternatives and the explication of general grounds for choice; effects on students and the rating of effects as more or less desirable will be difficult to avoid. Thoughtful school-board members, administrators, and teachers will be skeptical of claims made by sponsors of any given approach. Less thoughtful colleagues may find that the public expects them to appear as if they are giving careful consideration to new possibilities. One does not need to be a specialist in evaluation to realize that tradition is no guide in choosing between competing novelties..

[4] One might, for example, review the activities of the Education Commission of the States from this perspective.

The evaluative load will increase most dramatically where school systems undertake large-scale changes. The simultaneous introduction of innovations creates a special and demanding evaluative problem, for one must take account of local circumstances and interaction effects among innovations. For example, a school system might decide to combine educational parks with computer-assisted instruction. What affective outcomes flow from impersonalities associated with man-machine systems and sharp increases in the number of fellow students? Situations of this sort do not permit local officials to apply evaluations developed elsewhere; they must do their own digging.

Two major trends are taking place in the internal system of public schools, and both are likely to have serious implications for the conduct of evaluation. The first, functional differentiation, develops quietly and may go unnoticed. The second, "teacher militancy," hits the headlines almost daily. Both trends, however, seem to share a common effect. They weaken familistic and paternalistic conceptions of authority relationships among people working in schools.

The history of American school organization is largely the story of increasing specialization in the knowledge to be transmitted and in the tasks of those engaged in transmitting that knowledge. Contrast, for example, the one-room school house of the nineteenth century with its modern counterpart, the rural regional school. Grades, subjects, and teaching tasks have all been subdivided. Today, specialists counsel students, supervise their health, store and distribute books, purchase and distribute audio-visual equipment, and visit families with problems. These specialists, moreover, have separate occupational associations concerned with "professionalizing" each subfield. One influential spokesman has called for the creation of a national system of specialty boards for various categories of teachers (Liberman, 1960).

Yet the division-of-labor we see today may prove to be but a pale prologue to much greater differentiation in the future. Functional differentiation among school professionals, so far, has tended to be differentiation among equals. But now we see new forms of stratification being introduced as specialists of lower or higher status are hired. Some school systems, for example, are employing teacher aides whose credentials make it very unlikely that they will ever move into teacher ranks (Leggatt, 1966). Team-teaching arrangements in some places, on the other hand, involve higher status for team leaders and senior teachers (Shaplin and Olds, 1964). New technologies bring specialists, sometimes of higher rank, in their wake; we now have television teachers, programmers of instruction, and computer experts. Similar things are happening in central offices where superintendents look for men to specialize in relationships with the federal government, experts in collective bargaining, and men who can design program budgets. *The pace of role differentiation is quickening.*

Problems of communication and conflicts in orientation occur more readily when systems become internally differentiated.[5] Occupational differentiation produces specialisms not only of skill but of perspective, of moral outlook.[6] Additional layers of authority in organizations complicate communication within by producing more blockages in the flow of information and affect (Gardner and Moore, 1955). Thus, we can look ahead to schools and school systems where people of diverse outlook and rank find it harder to agree on instructional matters. We expect that mechanisms will be developed to cope with this problem. Building such mechanisms, however, requires considerable time, and it is debatable whether they ever attain the easy consensus associated with earlier social homogeneity.

Perhaps "teacher militancy" is a special case of role differentiation; in any event, it is clear that teacher demands are producing controversy over instructional matters as well as salaries and working conditions. The New York City strike is a recent example. There the union bargained hard and long over whether the More Effective Schools Program would receive additional financing. Nor is New York unique, for state after state is making legal provision for the participation of teacher groups in setting school policy.[7] Other categories of school workers are also agitating for more influence in instructional matters.[8] It is ironic that the external system should begin to produce increased options at that point when overt conflict on instructional policies emerges within the internal system.

Evaluation will undergo alterations where instructional policy-making is colored by conflict. Spirited advocacy by opponents will make policy deliberations more like courtroom trials and legislative battles. Protagonists, eager to cloak their positions in the garb of educational superiority, will buttress their beliefs with evaluations.[9] Overt conflict may lead to debates

[5] Several sociologists of note have made this point. Emile Durkheim was among the most prominent, as in his *The Division of Labor*. New York: The Free Press, 1947.

[6] One of the earliest statements of this is found in Hughes, E. C., Personality and the Division of Labor. In E. C. Hughes (Ed.), *Men and Their Work*. New York: The Free Press, 1958.

[7] The author recently heard a report on this topic by James Guthrie presented at the Annual Social Science Institute of the University of California, Berkeley.

[8] There are indications that principals may become a special interest group. In Michigan, for example, they find themselves caught in cross-pressures of bargaining and are considering the possibility of forming their own professional association.

[9] The New York City teachers' union was undoubtedly hampered by the somewhat negative report on the M.E.S. program submitted by the Center on Urban Education. One presumes that next time, they will present evaluative studies of their own!

in which discrepant evaluations of the same program are presented. Since judgments made by contending parties can affect the interests and prestige of combatants, the process of evaluation could itself become embedded in controversy. Should this occur, the public and its representatives, confused by competing claims, will call for clarification, for disinterested and objective assessments upon which they can rely. Controversy makes it essential that some evaluators be regarded as men of probity and objectivity. The educational system must find a way to solve the problem of integrity-trust in the performance of the evaluative function.

PROCESSES OF INNOVATION AND EVALUATION

Two facets of the current emphasis on change deserve attention in our consideration of emerging issues in evaluation. The first is the fact of the ferment itself—of the interest in finding and carrying out new ways of instructing children. The second has to do with the scope of changes now underway, with the emergence of large-scale, structural changes. Both aspects of the innovative thrust have important consequences for the conduct of evaluation.

In the decades immediately preceding 1950, public education was characterized by a relatively slow rate of change. Despite the ideological concerns of the twenties and thirties, the principal chronicler of that period does not point to consequences that followed in the actual conduct of school affairs (Cremin, 1961). Callahan argues, in fact, that school practice was heavily influenced by a simplistic conception of business efficiency (Callahan, 1962). Although one can find changes in curricula, textbooks, teacher training, and the like during this period, it is difficult to identify significant structural changes.[10] The energies of American school men and women were absorbed in constructing a vast system of public education along previously conceived lines; the years between World War I and 1950 were years of extending rather than reorganizing a social form.

Although it is difficult to be certain (we lack empirical studies on the conduct of evaluation during this period), evaluation appears to have been part of a system of decision-making adapted to slow rather than rapid change. The 1930s and 1940s saw the emergence of "democratic administration," of a preoccupation with winning the support of diverse groups for school activities. The superintendent, by this doctrine, should "involve" a wide variety of publics in school affairs and "harmonize" them into a

[10] A possible exception is the introduction of the junior high school.

trouble-free consensus.[11] The curriculum committee is symbolic of this ideology. The composition of that body might include citizens at large, teachers, parents, professors, representatives of special interest groups, and so forth. Curriculum was not an area for the application of esoteric knowledge and research skills. One might, of course, consult an expert in evaluation or curriculum, but the basic mechanism in resolving issues was the vote rather than recourse to "professional opinion."

Whatever the strengths and weaknesses of the participatory model may have been, it cannot be effectively argued that it fostered rapid change. Its very composition and organization conforms to those bodies that Blau describes as least likely to act with dispatch (Blau, 1956). The emphasis on consensus did nothing to advance techniques of evaluation. One gains the impression, in fact, that considerably more effort was expended in verbalizing objectives than in operationalizing them. Robert Wood was led to comment, rather in exasperation, that "public education is a continuing constitutional convention."[12]

Change begets more change. For as social systems shift to new and different ways, solutions to problems produce new problems demanding new solutions. Inasmuch as education is engaged in serious change, pressures for more expeditious evaluation will mount. School officials, pressed for more rapid action, will skirt cumbersome participatory methods and favor rapidly obtainable expert advice. Other factors make it likely that evaluation will become defined as an area for expert treatment. The diffusion of the research and development orientation, coupled with increasing public awareness of statistics and behavioral science as fields in their own right, will help to define evaluation as "specialized" work. I consider it extremely probable that the expert, highly trained evaluator will come into his own.

Some instructional changes taking place today alter student experience in much greater ways than in the past. Most evaluative work has concentrated on differences between one more-or-less similar component and another; one measured, for example, the efficacy of a given French curriculum over another. Large-scale changes, however, disturb aspects of student experience and socialization that, previously constant, could be reasonably ignored. Since we did not propose to alter them, they did not matter. But large-scale change makes previously latent functions relevant to evaluative

[11] Practically any textbook in educational administration published during the period will serve as an example. See for example, H. Hunt and P. Pierce. *The Practice of School Administration.* Boston: Houghton Mifflin Company, 1958.

[12] I heard Robert Wood make this statement in a public address in Cambridge, Mass., about 1959.

actions, for to change them without considering the effects on students may be to alter socialization in unintended ways. We can illustrate this process with concrete examples.

The serious introduction of team teaching is manifestly a major change in collegial and student-teacher relationships. Yet our grasp of the meaning of the change for student socialization is limited by our ignorance of the latent functions served by the self-contained classroom pattern. Is Parsons (1959) right, for example, in implying that it requires a relationship to one nurturant teacher to move the student from the ascriptive world of the family to the achievement world of the higher grades and work?

Could evaluators make initially positive reports on teaming in the early grades and miss effects that become observable, let us say, only during adolescence? What are the latent effects in grading children by age and having them move, almost regardless of ability, at the same rate as their age cohorts? Will self-paced study and nongraded arrangements, in increasing the performance gap between those of the same age, augment or diminish net self-esteem among school children? It would not be hard to produce a long list of such questions—questions that point to our lack of knowledge about the functions of existing arrangements. How effectively can we assess serious change in light of our weak grasp on present learning structures?

Social forms used in instruction can "contain" some values and exclude others apart from the explicit content communicated within the form. A given learning structure, I submit, may "instruct" persons in values considered important by the society; yet not be explicitly planned nor consciously evaluated. Note, for example, how different professions use different forms in their professional schools without explicit theoretical justification.[13] Graduate departments in arts and science "automatically" rely on seminars and laboratories; military academies cling to recitation long after other institutions have forsaken it; schools of architecture organize instruction around student projects, and medical schools elevate the importance of the clinic and operating room. Are such choices merely "technical" or "accidental"? Could it not be that the selected forms inculcate, by the very rules that exist within them, implicit conceptions of occupationally appropriate beliefs on such questions as the relationship between knowledge and action or their relative importance? What underlying assumptions about structure and values lead graduate students, asked to design single-purpose schools, repeatedly to link loyalty induction to strict hierarchical organization, or creativity as a goal to structural looseness and

---

[13] These observations are based on a pilot study conducted by the author of some twenty fields in which vocational training occurs in universities.

equality?[14] Breer and Locke have shown that temporary, experimental involvement in divergent task configurations tends to change attitudes in divergent directions (Breer and Locke, 1965). It is not likely that protracted engagement in particular learning structures has considerably greater effect on student attitudes and values?

The state of knowledge on interpersonal structures and socialization outcomes forces us to raise questions rather than cite propositions. Yet the probability that structures influence students in as yet unknown ways is, to my view, great enough to have significance for evaluators. To the extent that alternative social forms actualize different values, evaluating "pedagogical means" turns out to be, in fact, the evaluation of "educational ends." Evaluators claiming to assess the effects of large-scale changes should examine functions in depth and decipher effects on latent as well as manifest levels. To ignore such value implications, perhaps by using such a single dimension as cognitive learning, could result in missing unintended and perhaps undesired effects. Large-scale changes make it inappropriate for evaluators to adopt a narrowly technical conception of their role, for such changes add moral complexities to the work of the evaluator.

BROADER GOALS AND EVALUATIVE EXPERTISE

Schooling is more and more a matter of broad societal concern; today, the specification of educational objectives includes references to wider social, political, and economic problems. The schoolhouse is no longer an isolated establishment holding interest only for its students, teachers, and parents; the issues that arise there arouse excitement in many sectors of our society.

Examples of the newly perceived closeness between school and society at large are easy to find. The writer recalls that his undergraduate professors of economics depicted education as a luxury, as an activity using up scarce goods to economically questionable ends. Today economists pay close attention to the role of education in developing societies and urge heavy investment in it; Schultz and others argue that education contributes directly to human capital formation (Schultz, 1963). Time-worn phrases about "equality of opportunity" take on pungency when the federal government commissions James Coleman to measure departures from that ideal in the conduct of public education (Coleman, 1966). The report that resulted

---

[14] I have asked students, subdivided into groups of four or five members, to design the curriculum and structure of a school system dedicated to one major purpose, for example, induction of piety, cognitive mastery, creativity in the arts, and so forth. This has been done four times, and on each occasion students moved toward similar structures for the same overall purposes.

affects our view of educational goals and processes; we are now more likely to concentrate on the output of self-confidence and the relative contribution of institutions (for example, the family) outside the formal educational apparatus. Education is involved deeply in other questions of our time, from structural unemployment to crime prevention, from producing more scientists to early identification of emotionally disturbed children.

It is not difficult for educators in convention to write statements outlining education's manifold responsibilities. It is quite another matter, however, to calibrate specific instructional choices with particular social or economic or political goals. Past practice has been based on the general idea that mastery of conventional knowledge and/or training in a particular trade would result in students prepared for adult life. What happens when the boundaries of conventional knowledge explode? Or what decisions must be made when traditional occupational lines melt under the impact of automation? Such events make the design of study programs extremely problematic and complicate the evaluative criteria to be used. The educator must become expert in gauging events outside of school affairs, in predicting what knowledge will prove basic, what core skills will have generality in the labor market, and what educative experiences will prove to be of persisting value.

The verbal broadening of educational objectives will make no discernible impact until specific instructional practices are aligned with specific social goals. Should demands for such refined interconnections develop, acts of evaluation will take on new dimensions of substantive expertise. Evaluators familiar only with procedures organized around in-school events will find themselves puzzled in translating tests or whatever into meaningful indices of relevance to those demands. The question is, what substantive knowledge will prove vital in such assessments? Should that knowledge prove to be various and broad, educational evaluation, as a field of expert study and practice, may itself break down into a series of subspecialties organized around substantive fields and particular societal problems.

SOME NOTES AND QUESTIONS

It is clear that the writer believes evaluative functions will become more critical in the years ahead; rational decision-making will hinge largely on whether they can be performed in an effective way. I wish to conclude this paper somewhat unsystematically by making additional comments on emerging issues and by raising a few questions that deserve the close attention of educators. The aim is not to design a general evaluative scheme but to stimulate thought and discussion in the hope that those responsible for governing schools will begin work on needed solutions.

1. We noted that there will be more options available to school personnel. There are forces at work that will enhance the role of evaluators and move evaluation toward greater expertise and specialization. Yet we must not overlook the great likelihood that all persons working in schools will be affected by the presence of more options. Administrators, teachers, and specialists will perceive more personal possibilities in their respective roles; the public at large, long exposed to claims of professionalism, will expect educators to be ready with informed judgments on alternatives. Scarcities in highly trained personnel make it unlikely that there will be enough specialized evaluators around to relieve other educators of all such pressures. Effective evaluation, furthermore, will proceed only as those who are not specialized come to understand enough about assessment problems and techniques to initiate useful questions and make sensible use of findings.

We may see a collision between the proliferation of options and the subculture of those working in public schools. There is, to my knowledge, no tradition of tough-minded empirical evaluation among American teachers and administrators. Their subculture seems to stress the merits of intuitive judgment based upon experience.[15] Yet experience is of little use in predicting the potential costs and benefits of novel alternatives. How will school people react to problems they cannot resolve through experience? One possibility is firm and unyielding attachment to the status quo. Another, likely to occur where pressures for change are powerful, is the arbitrary adoption of what appear to be politic programs of action. The writer is willing to wager that such faddism will increase in the years ahead.

Those who have a special concern with evaluation, then, face allocative dilemmas in making the best use of scarce teaching resources in their field. Granted that some upgrading of teacher and administrator knowledge of evaluative basics is needed, what weight should be assigned to that need in comparison to the production of able specialists? Given the massiveness of the educational establishment and the extreme improbability of reaching two million teachers and administrators, which groups have the greatest potential for furthering effective evaluation? Presuming that resources will never be sufficient to find and train "enough" specialized evaluators, how can specialists be deployed to attain maximum effectiveness? In view of the long lead-time required to create new resources of high skill, early attention to such questions seems indicated.

2. The quantity of evaluative work is likely to make it a routine rather

[15] This impression is based on interviews conducted as part of the writer's research on teaching as an occupation.

than occasional activity of local school districts. It is also highly probable that evaluators will become key members of the administrative group that concerns itself with policy recommendations. Evaluators will need considerable influence if they are to perform well, for they will need control over how innovations are instituted and conducted in order to generate reliable data. Thus, evaluators will take part in setting up record-keeping systems, experimental controls, and so forth, in order to ensure relevant and dependable feedback on programs and their effects.

Constructing evaluative systems is no novelty to American businessmen and government officials. In business, we find elaborate and precise accounting systems, production records, sales statistics, merchandising data, and so forth, integrated into overall statements that are highly useful in executive decision-making. The "art" of business management is more and more the "art" of interpreting quantitative data and making inferences about their meaning for corporate action.[16] Federal agencies frequently possess complex machinery for evaluation and control of operations (Kaufman, 1960). The diffusion of rational modes of decision-making in public schools will also require the development of feedback systems useful to decision-making.

Moving to the rational model is not without complication, however, and this is especially true in education. Business and government systems occur where there is little dispute over the propriety of hierarchical authority and organization—both tend to emphasize centralized decision-making. The introduction of effective evaluative controls in education could, in fact, centralize decision-making without that being anyone's intention: Rourke believes that this is currently taking place in universities as a consequence of the administrative use of computers (Rourke, 1967). Ironically, demands for careful evaluation are arising in education at the point where monolithic and bureaucratic forms of administration are coming under attack from teacher associations, professors, and others.

It would ill-suit evaluators with their passion for objective assessment to prejudge an issue as complex as the relative merits of centralized and decentralized decision-making in schools. They had best step gently in designing and implementing systems of data gathering and program control. This problem raises particularly vexing and subtle questions about designing evaluative systems for studying school programs; it looks as if special ingenuity in design will have to be accompanied by special understanding of the dynamics of organization and decision-making.

---

[16] The Harvard Business School, long associated with case instruction, recently augmented the amount of quantitative material to be taught their master's students. There was also a special program instituted to train faculty members in the newer quantitative techniques.

3. Unchecked controversy over the conduct of educational evaluation could result in the loss of public confidence. Ways should be found to limit conflicts over the evaluative process itself. The issue of integrity-trust may require considerable attention in the years ahead.

The problem arises from the principle that persons and organizations cannot be trusted to act as judges in their own case (Parsons, 1958). This rule controls financial accountability in our society. No matter how intricate the system of internal audits or how secure the reputation of officials, corporate bodies employ outside accountants to review and report on their financial status. By analogy, we cannot expect protagonists in policy disputes or members of the general public to accept a school system's self-appraisals without question.

Are existing organizational resources adequate to solve the integrity issue, or are new social forms needed? It may be, for example, that critical evaluations will occur infrequently and will be sufficiently independent of university interests so that professors can serve where outside, expert judgments are needed. On the other hand, the volume of work and the consequent necessity for regular "audits" may strain readily available resources in universities and research centers.

What of models from other fields? Medicine, for example, has impressive controls based largely upon the work of pathologists in reviewing surgical tissue and diagnoses through post mortem examinations. But medicine is organized on the basis of sharp autonomy from public inspection linked to a high degree of internal, collegial control, a debatable model for schools that are part of local government. The role of the certified public accountant is more suggestive. A fee-for-service professional, he reports in standard ways understandable to those who choose to learn the elements of accounting rhetoric. Assuming that enough work would be available to give them autonomy from any single client, fee-for-service evaluators could be employed by school boards or, in some cases, dissident groups, to render a public and disinterested accounting. Such an arrangement might forestall pointless controversies where arguments center on the facts of the case rather than issues of policy.

4. Issues of moral complexity stemming from ends-means ambiguities are difficult to resolve by examining models outside education. It seems that other fields can use simple dichotomies (profit–loss; sick–healthy), which would be gross oversimplifications in education.

Could evaluative reporting, however, pay closer attention to this question of moral complexity by reporting empirical results in several ways? What I am wondering is whether alternative value schemes could be represented by statistical weighting schemes. Thus a single report might review the data gathered from several perspectives and in terms of several generally recognizable educational positions. The reader would be free to introduce his own dichotomies if he chose; the evaluator would, on the other hand, avoid sacrificing complexity for "a clear answer."

I can see several problems in this approach. Considerable work would be needed to find and express moral positions that are meaningful to the key publics involved in public education. Open identification would undoubtedly stir up debate that is currently minimized by fuzzy statements of both goals and outcomes. But might the long-term gains in the quality of public discourse justify short-term conflicts? There is risk in the present course of overlooking value conflicts; evaluation may eventually suffer "whip-lash" from publics who realize later that they do really want *that* particular set of values.

An adequate system of evaluation, whatever its formats for reporting, will have to cope with shifts in the latent functions of instructional forms. But does current knowledge and research permit us to undertake such analysis with confidence? How much does social psychology tell us about relationships between socialization and educational structures? If it tells us too little, what basic research is needed, and what responsibility do evaluators have to further such research?

5. Broadened educational goals raise the question of evaluator expertise. To what extent should evaluators working outside the traditional domains of education (the economy, crime prevention, race relations) possess substantive knowledge, which is especially relevant to the problem area?

This is delicate territory for those who, like myself, lack expertise in evaluative methodology. How generally applicable are models used in the field? Has the historic link to educational psychology institutionalized data-gathering techniques and analytic habits that are better suited to in-school than out-school considerations? Can evaluators absorb specialized knowledge about new sectors and problems rapidly enough to practice on a variety of fronts?

Those who have intimate knowledge of the field are better equipped than I to answer these questions. The possibility of specialization within evaluation is, however, an issue that should receive very careful thought. Should such specialization prove desirable, it would have important implications for the training of evaluative specialists and would point toward greater exposure to a wide variety of university-based disciplines.

Speculative analyses are high-risk undertakings; there is no assurance that the method, no matter how prudent, discerns the truly vital issues. But I can conclude with one certainty. To crack the cake of educational custom is to release forces that, by comparison, make the occupants of Pandora's box appear to be docile, innocent, and amusing creatures.

REFERENCES

Bagehot, W. *Physics and politics.* New York: Alfred A. Knopf, Inc., 1948.

Blau, P. *Bureaucracy in modern society.* New York: Random House, Inc., 1956.

Breer, P., & Locke, E. *Task experience as a source of attitudes.* Homewood, Ill.: Dorsey Press, 1965.

Callahan, R. E. *Education and the cult of efficiency.* Chicago: University of Chicago Press, 1962.

Coleman, J., and others. *Equality of educational opportunity.* Washington, D.C.: U.S. Government Printing Office, 1966.

Cremin, L. *The transformation of the school.* New York: Alfred A. Knopf, Inc., 1961.

Gardner, B., & Moore, D. *Human relations in industry.* Homewood, Ill.: Richard D. Irwin, Inc., 1955.

Kaufman, H. *The forest ranger: A study in administrative behavior.* Baltimore: Johns Hopkins Press, 1960.

Leggatt, T. W. The use of non-professionals in public education. Unpublished doctoral dissertation, University of Chicago, 1966.

Liberman, M. *The future of public education.* Chicago: University of Chicago Press, 1960.

Parsons, T. Some ingredients of a general theory of formal organization. In Andrew Halpin (Ed.), *Administrative theory in education.* Chicago: Midwest. Administration Center, University of Chicago, 1958.

Parsons, T. The classroom as a social system. *Harvard Educational Review,* Fall 1959.

Rourke, F. E. Computers and university administration. *Administrative Science Quarterly,* March 1967.

Schultz, T. W. *The economic value of education.* New York: Columbia University Press, 1963.

Shaplin, J., & Olds, H. (Eds.) *Team teaching.* New York: Harper & Row, Publishers, 1964.

Veblen, T. *The higher learning in America.* New York: Sagamore Press, 1957.

Comments on Professor Lortie's Paper

C. WAYNE GORDON

Dr. Lortie's shadow has preceded him; his influence is already apparent in its effect on evaluation. From what I have heard around the country he has had his finger in the cake and has been helping practice the practice of evaluation in his own right.

He disturbs me, however; and this is not a prologue to saying I agree with everything he said, with the monstrous complexity with which he confronts us.

At this point, the evaluator must feel like the centipede who looked out in the morning to see which foot to put down and had to make a decision. He was so cantonized he didn't get up all day.

Fortunately, Lortie has given us a foot or two to put down. I would like to put one or two of them down at the risk of recapping the main set piece for discussion—that is, change. He rather belatedly introduced the dynamic force for economic change in the new discussions and the new discoveries, but the change itself has taken on a value. It is like the new tide—better than the old.

He gives us a set of competing sources for the alternatives we seek. These are largely external to the system—government sources, commercial activism, and even the universities with their wares.

These competing sources are not just standbys; they are sources of control as well. These are not alternatives that the educator-administrator is free to accept without some coercion. He is obliged to get a grant to develop his particular program. To that extent we do have a new situation, I think; and one which has powerful control implications, powerful for elevating the role of evaluation.

So, we have this harassed educator-administrator who must make decisions; and because there is contention in the system he must make not only correct decisions, but ones that have legitimacy. These won't necessarily be the same. In other words, the most acceptable answer and the basis for having supplied it will not always depend on the validity of the answer or the evidence used to support it.

The professional evaluator is going to be the handmaiden who plays the appropriate pattycake with the educator-administrator's problems. He is like an umpire in the final game of the World Series. He not only has to make the right decision, but he has to have good eyesight.

So, we come to integrity; we must have integrity in this process. But because the administrator has to make choices, we are in the short run faced with heavy demands on evaluation services. Their decisions have to be defended in the face of competing alternatives.

We have set the stage for objectivity and rationality in science and truth. For the first time we have a structural determinism, which forces people to be both honest and correct because of the disadvantages of bad choices and bad decisions. We have powerful resources that place demands on us at the highest level of integrity—science and truth.

I notice that Lortie doesn't believe that he wants that much truth or that much knowledge. He says, "The thoughtful school board members, administrators and teachers will be skeptical of plans made by sponsors of any new approach"; and, "The less thoughtful colleagues may find that the public expects them to appear as if they are giving careful consideration to new policy builders." Here I find the latter point of view the more typical possibility.

I just don't think this variety of decision-making will afford the luxury of evaluative systems of the kind he describes. The demand in this market isn't entirely for the kinds of product he suggests.

Now, even so, it seems to me that he has opted for a classic solution. It's for rationality; it's bureaucratic; he has decisions to be made based on expertise, honesty, and integrity. And we have a profession prepared to provide this expertise. But then he introduced a new problem. He said, "He not only needs answers, but he needs answers to questions that are infinitely more complex than the ones that he has decided." Lortie hinted at the problem of functional analysis of many outcomes, including unintended effects of instruction. If he had pursued this line of reasoning, he would have been led into an entirely new analysis of the justification for complexity of evaluation. I then could have accepted his concern for expanding the range of variables and values.

That is where my centipede arises. The user, the educator-administrator, doesn't want that much knowledge. Yet we must, as Professor Gage says, talk about basic research methods rather than value judgments. The administrator needs quicker, shorter, and more simple-minded answers.

I have another concern. It is for the evaluator because Lortie has made his problem complicated. The evaluator has a stock in trade. In most cases he has a gimmick, a system, a line of goods that he is prepared to provide in this market. We have some symmetry in the insincerity of the request for evaluation and the incapacity of the evaluator to fulfill the demand.

I think the evaluator is a bit like the policeman who found a dead horse on Potawotomi Street. He couldn't spell "Potawotomi" and had to make a report; so he dragged the horse to First Street and wrote the report.

If the demand for the rationality, if the integrity of the answer is not sought to that extent, the educator-administrator can probably do well at a different kind of hot dog stand. He will seek someone more willing to serve in this market, who will not impose on him the complexity which Lortie suggests, nor will he impose on him the embarrassment of going to the public with his problem.

Lortie has added another complexity that is even more difficult, and that is elaborate studies designed to fit the uniquely different facts of the case. This again is messy, difficult, demanding, time consuming, and costly. As you try to prescribe for him the package that will be important for his immediate need, the evaluator is not listening. He is waiting for another kind of advice—how to get the contract renewed.

Now, may I give one more thought? Lortie suggests a rather facile way to get out of the dilemma of how the evaluator can avoid being caught providing unpopular conclusions because of the values present in the package. Lortie has suggested a weighted system of assessing the results in terms of different value perspectives. He neutralizes the necessity for having values themselves. The evaluator is going to be an operator of relative perspectives from which he derives objectives to assess.

Maybe this is the only way to avoid the dilemma. But would you be willing to consider the kind of optimism which says, let's include enough of the dependent variables in the value area—a smorgasbord of values; that is, let's get some criteria in there that we haven't been asking about; and then let's observe which independent variables are probable for the best predictions. Could we expect eventually to get a sufficiently generalized system of variables on both sides of the system, independent and dependent, that would achieve an objectivity in which even the evaluator or the researcher would propose values and possible effects that transcend the parochial foci of controversy? At least then we could rest a bit on the possibility that we are not so subject to the winds of the conflict and the controversy that he proposed that we have nothing to offer but to follow the fads that are going to be proposed.

Comments on Professor Lortie's Paper

N. L. GAGE

Professor Lortie has presented an incisive analysis of the forces operating to make evaluation a central concern of contemporary educational enterprise. Applying the conceptual tools of the sociologist, he has furnished what might be called an apologia pro centro UCLA. That is, one leaves his paper with the feeling that whatever else may occur in American education in the years ahead, a major part of it will consist of evaluation.

AN OVERVIEW OF LORTIE'S PAPER

External trends resulting from federal activities, business corporations, and universities are increasing the pressure to evaluate because of the many new alternatives that they are placing before school personnel. And the trends internal to the school system, such as the specialization and stratification of educational workers and the increase in teacher militancy, will also enhance the need to evaluate because the rivalries among different categories of educational workers will lead them to attempt to strengthen their positions by means of evaluative data.

Further, the increased rate of change in American education, resulting in part from the development of substitutes for the old participatory model of school administration, has brought about greater reliance upon evaluative efforts by specialists in such work. Similarly, the enlarged scope of change in education, which affects previously untouched aspects of student life, calls for increased emphasis on evaluation. Team teaching, nongraded classrooms, and the particular social forms of a given kind of professional training all tend correspondingly to broaden the scope of the variables with which evaluation workers must be concerned.

Dr. Lortie's third section deals with the effects on evaluation work of the increasing recognition of education as a system of forces affecting every aspect of society—economic, social, political, and cultural. Education, in turn, is influenced by a similarly broad array of forces, ranging from explosions in population and knowledge to the computer revolution and the labor market. The kinds of concerns important to evaluators are similarly enlarged; it will no longer suffice to concentrate merely on what goes on in schools and classrooms if evaluation is to have a correspondingly broadened scope.

Next, Dr. Lortie asks where the increased amount of evaluative talent is to originate, how greater knowledge and understanding of evaluative procedures can be disseminated, and how more specialists can be produced and deployed. Second, evaluation workers may need to concern themselves with decision-making processes in education and their relationship to the feedback of evaluative data on proposed changes. Third, he sees the problem of maintaining public confidence in the integrity and validity of educational evaluations made by outside experts. Models of such efforts in medicine, accounting, and other fields suggest the emergence of a fee-for-service profession of autonomous evaluators. Further, Dr. Lortie pointed to the issues of moral complexity involved in evaluation against any set of objectives to be attained by a set of means. For many of these means-end combinations we do not know enough about their latent functions to have confidence in our value judgments.

Finally, Lortie raises the question of whether many of the kinds of expertise needed in adequate evaluation must be drawn from other domains, such as economics, crime prevention, or race relations. If so, the implications for specialization and training of evaluation workers must be given thought.

A DISCUSSION

I can find no reason to take serious exception to most of what Dr. Lortie has offered. But there are some aspects of his analysis that seem to rest on assumptions that ought to be made explicit and perhaps be subjected to some questioning.

1. It seems he implies that every school district, or, indeed, every school, will need to evaluate independently all innovations or educational alternatives that may be developed and offered in the years ahead. It is almost as if he saw the need for each school board to operate its own consumer's union for the evaluation of new developments, procedures, and products offered to the schools.

It is unclear to me whether he predicts or supports any such conception of the role of evaluation, which, in either case, ought to be severely questioned. Surely, the differences between our school districts are not so great in any of the relevant dimensions that they require each district to make its own independent evaluation of proposed innovations in the schools. It must be possible for any given school district to learn something from the experience of others, that is, from the reports of large-scale evaluative efforts conducted in representative samples of school districts and classrooms. Just as every prospective car buyer need not be an expert in compression ratios and crankshaft bearings, so every school board need not arrange for its own evaluation of team teaching or the nongraded classroom.

Perhaps a distinction ought to be made between the evaluation of an innovation in its general form and the evaluation of how it is working in a particular and local situation. Such a distinction would be analogous to that between the kind of evaluation made by Consumer's Union, concerning how good the 1968 Fairlane is in general, and the evaluation made by the owner and operator of a particular Fairlane concerning how well his own car is working. For the former kind of evaluation, large-scale programs of evaluation by experts ought to do the job for 10,000 school districts at a time; for the latter kind of evaluation, each school district, school, administrator, or teacher will need to know how to tell whether a given practice, old or new, is working well and when something is seriously wrong. It is the difference between the kind of evaluation made by the automotive engineer and that made by you and me, who know enough to get worried when the exhaust from our car gets too black.

2. Another question can be raised concerning Dr. Lortie's implicit conception of evaluation. If I understood the connotations of his discussion, he sees evaluation as consisting of a kind of posttesting applied at the end of the operation of a given kind of educational innovation or program. But many students of evaluation have questioned this sort of conception. They say that evaluation merely at the end of a curriculum development program is often ineffectual. Evaluative effort ought to be poured into educational innovations while they are being developed, as part of the developmental process itself. The evaluation worker ought to work with the educational innovator, the developer of a new kind of evaluational procedure or material. In this sense, evaluation takes place much more frequently on the basis of a much wider variety of evidence. The analogy that occurs to me here is the difference between the kind of evaluation of a student's learning that takes place after each frame in a body of programmed instruction and the kind of evaluation that takes the form of a final examination at the end of a course. If I understand him, Dr. Lortie deals only with the latter kind of evaluation. It would have been desirable if his analytic effort had also been turned to the former.

3. Next, I should like to raise the question of what happens to evaluation when it finds, time after time, that a given kind of educational innovation or alternative does not seem to make any difference. J. M. Stephens, in his recent little book, *The Process of Schooling,* has pointed out that most evaluations of educational innovations have yielded negative results. Stephens documented his position with references to summaries of studies of a host of specific educational variables, procedures, practices, and orientations. That is, he summarized the summaries of studies of school attendance, instructional television, independent study and correspondence courses, size of class, individual consultation and tutoring, counseling, concentration on specific students, the students' involvement, the amount of time spent in study, distraction by jobs and extracurricular activities, size of school, the qualities of teachers that can be rated by principals and supervisors, nongraded schools, team teaching, ability grouping, progressivism versus traditionalism, discussion versus lecture, group-centered versus teacher-centered approaches, the use of frequent quizzes, and programmed instruction. According to Stephens, studies of all these have failed to show that they make a consistent and significant difference.

Stephens briefly considered the possibility that the negative results are due to methodological errors such as concentration on one narrow segment of achievement, using insensitive tests, employing poor controls, exerting overcontrol that holds too much constant and so restricts the differences, or using a too stringent criterion of statistical significance. Stephens concluded that negative results are only to be expected, because "in the typical comparison of two administrative devices (such as teaching methods) we have two groups that are comparable in the forces responsible for (say) 95 percent of the growth to be had and which differ only in the force that, at best, can affect only a small fraction of the growth" (Stephens, 1967, p. 84).

This is not the place for any extended discussion of the exact merits of the details of Stephen's argument. But I cannot disagree with his statement that, by and large, evaluations of innovative efforts in education have yielded a "flood of negative results." Instances come to mind almost every day. Recently, for example, the "More Effective Schools" program in the New York City schools was found by the Center for Urban Education to make no significant difference in the achievement of the pupils in the participating schools. Evaluations of Project Head Start have been more noteworthy for their failure to reveal significant differences than for anything else.

If so, what are the implications for evaluation workers? Are they willing to be cast in the role of the spoilsport, who continually finds nothing in favor of, as well as nothing much against, the shiniest products of the ingenious innovator's art? Will evaluation come to be regarded, even more than it is now, as a threat to the fondest hopes of the educational thinker, research worker, and developer? Will mechanisms be developed to rationalize, even more than is now the case, the unwillingness of the educational worker to subject his pet scheme to the kinds of tests that, nowadays at least, 95 times out of 100, reveal no statistically significant difference, one way or another? If as Dr. Lortie said, there is "no tradition of tough-minded empirical evaluation among American teachers and administrators" (p. 18), perhaps the reason is that they so often in the past gone without reinforcement when they have exhibited evaluative behavior.

But another question also seems to arise almost inevitably. One wonders whether the failure to find significant results when educational innovations are evaluated stems not from some weakness of the innovations, as Stephens thinks, but rather from some weakness in the kinds of evaluations that are made. Perhaps the gross kind of measure of the effect of a given innovation is, indeed, too insensitive to reveal the effects of that treatment. Perhaps we need to become much more modest in the kinds of effects we seek. Perhaps we need to bring them much closer in time, space, and conceptualization to the operation of the kinds of educational variables that are manipulated in our experiments.

My analogy here is to the difference between seeking the effect of dropping a rock on the surface of a lake within twenty feet, or seeking its effect a mile away. In principle the rock does affect the water a mile away, but the effect has become much too attenuated at that distance to be discernible. Similarly, the effects of team teaching or the nongraded classroom or programmed instruction ought not to be sought at the end of the school year in terms of the mean score differences between an experimental and a control group; rather, they ought to be sought in the day-to-day behaviors of teachers and pupils—an approach much closer in time, space, and conceptual relevance to the kind of innovation being studied. Someday, understanding of these more modest kinds of effects will culminate in an understanding of the chain of effects with long-range and large-scale significance of the kind that is nowadays more often evaluated. But in the meantime it might make better sense, and lead to less frustration caused by negative results, if evaluators focused more sharply on variables that have some chance of being affected by the kinds of innovations they study.

Dr. Lortie paid no attention, as I understood him, to the role of evaluation in improving scientific understanding of educational processes as separate from the role of evaluation affecting practical decision-making in the schools. Yet the concerns of the former kind of evaluation may in the long run be more important than the latter. Such evaluation for the purposes of scientific research can lead to greater understanding of pupils and better theory about what occurs in classrooms, schools, and school districts. It is surely unnecessary to defend, before this audience, the values for educational practice of improved theoretical formulations.

Open Discussion of Lortie's Paper and Gage's and Gordon's Comments

LORTIE: Professor Gage has an unhappy knack for landing on just those points where, in my preparation, I thought, "Well, if I had more time I would go into that."

In my informal observations based on contacts with school administrators, I have been impressed by the discontinuity and irrationality in the flow of information. There doesn't seem to be currently existing any coherent or well-organized system for distributing reliable information. The inter-personal relationships among superintendents and their friendship patterns, probably have more to do with the reputation of a given innovation than does the solid work of evaluators. I would like to see evaluators in local school districts because, by virtue of their role and position, they would have to be spokesmen for rationality. Other than the business manager, there is no local figure arguing for the careful and steady use of data in decision-making in the local school.

Whether or not it is practical to have an evaluator in each school, I am not sure. There are far too many school districts for there to be a talented evaluator in each. But frankly, in real politic terms, I would like to see more scientifically trained evaluators right there where decisions are made.

Now, let's proceed to this thorny second question you raise about the role of the evaluator in developmental evaluation versus ultimate or summa-tional evaluation. I have written on this subject in connection with team teaching in the old Shaplin-Olds volume. I argued there that there should be two kinds of social researchers, and I can extend this argument by analogy.

If you are undertaking a difficult structuralization, I think you do need an evaluator to participate as it unfolds; but I would not expect the public to accept that evaluator at the end of the process as a true reporter on its effectiveness or ineffectiveness. We can't have that cake and eat it, too.

On the third point, I think we are all being humbled on the question of how much effect school has anyway. When you take a fraction of the school, how much effect do you have? This is the way things are now. If we move toward true rationality, in the sense of a willingness to scrap existing institutional forms and become genuinely experimental, I still man-age to maintain a ray of hope.

Surely, nothing I've said indicates that I am not concerned about the development of better theory. I am quite sympathetic to the need for ivory tower evaluative work, in a sense, from the practitioner's point of view. But I would also make a plea for more effective diffusion, not only of the findings of evaluators, but of the thought ways. My contact with school people is discouraging, from this point of view. The standards of thought and assessment that a group like this takes for granted are rare where the decisions are made. It disturbs me that this very useful ultimately disciplined force of intellect is not being used at the spot where kids are getting schooled.

In response to Gordon's remarks, I have a funny view of rationality. I would not bank on people's innately wanting rationality. I would, however, see some optimism because of the conflict and sheer fatigue that is more and more becoming the role of the superintendent. Frankly, I think it is going to become more convenient to be honest. That's very optimistic, I know. But the way the forces are heading, I see a situation where it may actually prove politic to be rational.

I do not know how the evaluator will solve the technical problems you raise—the difficulties of his own conceptual knowledge and his own technical expertise.

The initial evaluations of large-scale structures are going to be really hard ones. It is going to be rugged the first time that one tracks out, say, the relationships between ranking systems or grading systems and net self-esteem loss or gain. All I can hope is that there will be an accretion in skill and sophistication available to the evaluator.

I would like to see the evaluator in the role of the elevator of public discourse. This may be a naïve eighteenth-century conception of rational democracy, but if we did feed specific information to those who seriously think about school affairs, the quality of discourse and decision-making would rise. That hope leads me to suggest that he act as an explicator of values and identifier of consequences, rather than as philosopher king.

FESHBACH: Will evaluation itself become a conceptual variable by nature of how the evaluation system is directed and how it affects the association?

LORTIE: Fantastic! Right. A fully developed system of routine evaluation has fantastic consequences for life careers, for the subculture; many of them will be difficult to anticipate until we actually see how it is conducted. Dalton's study of "Men Who Manage" shows that businessmen do not sit by passively while everybody is assessing their activities. They are very hard-nosed, true politicians. They use coalition behavior, and they sometimes use tactics of intimidation.

This is an active, dynamic kind of situation, and the evaluator is going to have to live with that reality. He is not, in practice, going to be able to be completely remote from it.

So I am not predicting a dry, automatic system but one in which the evaluator will make decisions whose consequences he will soon learn about in political and direct terms. He is going to have to be a hard-nosed guy.

TROW: One important device the educational administrator has available to him in dealing with the heterogeneous public is the diffuseness and ambiguity of the goals. I can think of few things that would be more dysfunctional for his everyday activities than making explicit the priority of his goals.

LORTIE: This is a very real problem. More and more the forces interested in making money out of schools are bypassing the school man. They are appealing directly to the consumer, the taxpayer. Magazine ads are influencing people in many communities. I think we are going to see more and more drumming at the influential citizen for him to decide, by gosh!

The superintendent is already beleaguered and often has limited power. If he has to choose between further erosion of his role through external pressures, if at the same time his training and preparation veers, as it is beginning to in some major universities, toward more skill in analysis of policy issues, more forensic ability in making images he likes smell good, if, in a sense, the superintendent becomes more lawyer-like, we may see him opting for the forum, for the conflict, where at least he has some sense that he might win.

ANDERSON: I want to say, as a narrow technologist, I very much appreciated this broader perspective on evaluation problems, and I think for those of us with a narrower or more delimited role, there are issues here that must be faced. We who collect facts have to confront issues of values, we have to make our facts relevant to policy decisions, and we have to use them in the light of ethical considerations.

LUMSDAINE: I would like to agree to a prior point and then return to the point that Dick made; it is quite important that the concept of a formative evaluator, in Scriven's terms, be kept quite separate from the evaluator who is assessing the overall output of the system. This separateness, however, I think is only one aspect of the separation of roles that may be needed to avoid some of the difficulties of challenge of integrity.

Specifically, there is much wisdom in the lexicographer's distinction between the two meanings of evaluation: that is, determining the worth of something versus reducing it to numbers. We should consider quite seriously whether the evaluator's role of reducing something to numbers—measuring the effects of an educational program—ought to be kept quite separate from the function of choosing among alternatives, given the facts about the effects of the program. I fear that if these functions are not kept separate, the inevitable uncertainties and shifting winds that will surround the question of which values ought to be achieved will tend to discredit the factual basis of evaluation, that is, the data.

This factual basis—and I don't think this is a narrow technicality—must be kept unchallenged, at least unchallenged for improper reasons. The administrator must see that *only by keeping facts separate from interpretations can he defend the integrity of the facts.* This does not by any means deny the importance of the need for the evaluator to deal with values. He can collect relevant data about the outcome of an educational program, not just about narrow academic outcomes but also about those properly relevant to values.

Maybe I could clarify this by adding one more to our long string of automotive analogies. In the Consumers' Union business there is a distinct tendency (although they do infrequently muddy it a bit by stating that this is the "best buy,") to write "This one goes the fastest," "This one has the best economy," "This one corners the best," and "This one has the softest cushions." These specific points of information provide each customer a basis for making his own overall valuation in terms of the relative importance he attaches to each characteristic—economy, speed, and so forth.

The facts, or data, are provided objectively by an impartial investigating body; one presumably does not debate the facts as such, though there may be plenty of disagreement as to which features should be given most weight in arriving at an overall evaluation. We do not want to confuse the question of which outcomes are preferred with that of which outcomes occurred.

BLOOM: Dan, I am somewhat concerned about the latent effects. To use our automobile analogy again, there is a whole set of consequences of the automobile; the latent effects of technology, expressways, and everything else. But it seems to me that the evaluator in that situation is not asked to look at all of the long-term consequences over the next ten, twenty, or thirty years of the adoption of automobiles or fast automobiles versus slow automobiles, and so on.

Why do you insist that the evaluator has to look at the latent effects?

LORTIE: I would make a distinction here between the public sector and the private sector. Where we are acting in the public sector, where we are influencing or exercising authority by virtue of governmental policies, it seems to me that there is a clear-cut element of responsibility which, fortunately or unfortunately, has not been true in the case of private industry, where the rules of *caveat emptor* apply.

I don't believe *caveat emptor* can apply in education. The buyer is constrained in the law; the buyer is a minor and is presumably irrational because he needs education. Where the buyer is thus vulnerable, I think we have a special responsibility as much as we can, to make our decisions in the light of the total range of consequences to and for him.

On another level, I am more concerned about the growing relevance of education in shaping the future of society, not because I think the school should serve in a particular direction, but because I am nervous that we could act without choice. My basic value is that we should exercise conscious, repeated choice, that is, know what we are doing. I would like to see an increase in awareness of the range of effects that we are bringing about and an improvement in the channels for reflecting upon those.

BLOOM: Do we then have to be closer to the pharmaceutical industry, or the controls over the pharmaceutical industry, in which you get this mean, and then these negative answers?

LORTIE: That is a nice model. I hadn't thought about that.

GLASER: Mine is a small point.

I want to respond to Nate Gage's reaction to Stephens' comments about the lack of significant results, and to his suggestion for moving in and getting an accumulation of small-range effects that he hopes eventually will result in a very large-scale change effects.

If you make the assumption that there are many things that you don't like about the present organization of instruction in the schools, and then move in to look at these small-range effects, you are up against a very long and almost impossible task. It seems that what you have to do first is to implement a massive change, some experimental massive change, like a totally reconstituted kind of school organization, and then once you have that operating, correct it by measuring the small-range effects, which are easy to do while something is operating.

GAGE: I think that's a good point.

MESSICK: I want to comment on Nate's remarks as well.

One possibility, as we attempt to cope with Stephens' general conclusion about the overall ineffectiveness of educational variables, may be that we have been looking in the wrong place in the wrong way. Although the effects may be there, something may be happening to attenuate them or wash them out, so we will have to change our perspective to make them visible.

As you went through that summary of negative findings, it reminded me of the same kind of bleak inventory of variables showing no results in psychotherapy research, and both of those things reminded me of a story. I think it has an important point with respect to the black picture that Stephens has painted.

It is the story of a rabbinical student coming up for his examination in Wisdom. The senior rabbi asked him only one Wisdom question, which was, "Ezekiel, two men fall down a chimney. One comes out clean; one comes out dirty. Which one gets washed?"

Ezekiel thought a moment and replied, "It is obvious, Rabbi. The one who is dirty gets washed."

The senior rabbi shook his head and intoned, "Ezekiel, you are very quick, perhaps much too quick. But just stop and think. Two men fall down a chimney. One comes out clean; one comes out dirty. The man who is dirty looks at the man who is clean. He thinks, 'He is clean; I must be clean.' He does not get washed. The clean man who is clean looks at the man who is dirty and thinks, 'He is dirty; I must be dirty.' He gets washed. Go home and meditate. Come to me again in one month, and I will give you another examination."

One month later Ezekiel came back. The senior rabbi said, "Are you ready for your examination? Two men fall down a chimney. One comes out clean; one comes out dirty. Which one gets washed?"

Ezekiel smiled and said, "Thank you, Rabbi. I really appreciate this. The man who is dirty looks at the man who is clean and thinks, 'He is clean; I must be clean.' He does not get washed. The man who is clean looks at the man who is dirty and thinks, 'He is dirty; I must be dirty.' He gets washed."

The rabbi moaned and said, "Oh, Ezekiel, smart you are, but wise you are not. Stop and think. Two men fall down a chimney. One comes out clean; one comes out dirty. How can that be?"

A host of educational variables and none has any significant effect. How can that be?

GAGE: Stephens has a theory called a theory of spontaneous schooling, of how it can be that all of these things don't have any effect. (He is talking primarily about the effect on achievement in schools measured by multiple-choice tests.) His theory is roughly this. The major determiners that account for 95 percent of the variance are: (a) maturation, which I suppose would be hereditary variables; plus (b) the natural, spontaneous, automatic tendencies of teachers since the ancient Egyptians to talk about their subject, to praise a student who makes a correct response, to criticize him and correct him when he makes a wrong response; and (c) the natural, spontaneous, and automatic tendencies of pupils to continue doing what they are praised for and to change what they are criticized for.

The fourth major variable is (d) the nature of the school as an institution in societies throughout history, an institution that contrains behavior in certain ways, that is the scene or the site in which school subject matter is dealt with. By the time you get all these major forces operating, schooling is 95 percent determined. The variables I quoted from his long list are, in a way, the icing on the cake, or the visible part of the iceberg. That's what educators are studying, and they are not very important variables.

Even programmed instruction—he sounds a little bit less sure of his dismal conclusions on that subject as compared with all the others—or the kind of things Bob Glaser has in mind, the nice big boulder, which would be individually prescribed instruction as now being practiced at the Oak Leaf School, won't have any major effect, according to Stephens, if I understand him.

He may have dealt with individually prescribed instruction or other things that in their day looked as massive as individually prescribed instruction does. But Stephens says there are no landslide results in our literature of educational research or evaluation of innovation. We never get any enormous tidal wave. We haven't been able to design any landslides or boulders big enough to produce tidal waves, even when all the theory goes into developing something as revolutionary, plausible, and promising as individually prescribed instruction. My scant knowledge of the evidence indicates that at the Oak Leaf School they are not getting any landslide results.

I hope Stephens is wrong. I think we are all basing our careers on the hope that Stephens is wrong, but maybe we are fiddling around with the icing on the cake.

MESSICK: Or fiddling around with the wrong questions.

STAKE: Our comments go from topic to topic, and I apologize for not following up on that one.

I am concerned about the role of the evaluator. The choice is between the role of decision-maker and the role of information-purveyor. I feel that it is appropriate for the evaluator to assume the role of the information-purveyor. But, of course, he has to make decisions, as any purveyor does. It seems to me that the subjectivity of the evaluator's decisions is about what a number of us are concerned.

The fact that a social scientist works with opinions and values does not force his methods to be subjective. The social psychologist has shown otherwise. The subjectivity of judgments about the school curriculum is not what makes the methodology of evaluation subjective.

The subjectivity of evaluation is very similar to the subjectivity of basic research. There is a great subjectivity in picking out what problem is worth working on. More specifically, the subjectivity of evaluation lies in picking out the variables that will be examined. An evaluator has no license to ignore the objectives (variables) of the educator but he is going to go beyond them. There is a great deal of subjectivity as to what he will see. He is subjective in picking the sources of statements of objectives and sources of other information. He has subjective decisions to make in the instrumentation. There are value-choices operating when we go about translating goals into operational behavioral manifestations. I don't see any of us avoiding that subjectivity and those values as a part of research. It would be unreasonable for us to abhor that subjectivity in evaluation.

MCDONALD: In some of this discussion of values, we confuse values with choices. One of the responsibilities of the social sciences is to point to the consequences that the general public or administrator is totally unaware of—the subtler aspects of changes in personality, or social consequences to teachers. As social scientists, we can't avoid pointing out that these are events of which we should be aware. At that point I don't think we are intruding on choices.

One other responsibility we have is to demonstrate whether certain kinds of consequences associated with value choices can be measured. Certainly, we would say you can have this kind of information to use in making your choice.

The third thing we ought to be aware of is that what we call facts indicate certain already accepted value choices. This is subjectivity. If we want to measure the softness of cushions, that presupposes that at least somebody thinks softness of cushions is an important variable.

Finally, we might be able to show that measurement interventions, as was mentioned earlier, also produce consequences. I don't see how knowing that there are these consequences deprives the public, which in the last analysis is us, of any choice.

WITTROCK: It should make the choices more meaningful.

PART V

Criterion Variables

CHAPTER 6

The Criterion Problem in the Evaluation of Instruction: Assessing Possible, Not Just Intended, Outcomes[1]

SAMUEL MESSICK

This paper will discuss cognitive styles and affective reactions as two major classes of criterion variables that should be taken into account in the evaluation of instruction. These two types of variables are emphasized because of their bearing upon questions that should be asked in evaluation studies—questions that stem from particular views about the diversity of human performance and about the role of values in educational research.

INDIVIDUAL DIFFERENCES IN RESPONSE TO EDUCATIONAL TREATMENTS

Traditional questions in education and psychology have frequently spawned answers that are either wrong since they summarize findings "on the average" in situations where a hypothetical "average person" does not exist, or else are seriously lacking in generality because they fail to consider the multiplicity of human differences and their interactions with environmental circumstances.

Consider the kind of "horse race" question typical of much educational research of the past: Is textbook A better than textbook B? Is teacher A better than teacher B? Or, more generally, is treatment A better than treatment B? Such questions are usually resolved empirically by comparing aver-

[1] The preparation of this paper was supported in part by the National Institute of Mental Health under Research Grant MH-4186.

183

age gains in specific achievement for students receiving treatment *A* with average gains for students receiving treatment *B*. But suppose treatment *A* is better for certain kinds of students and treatment *B* better for other kinds of students. Depending upon the mix of students in the two groups, the two treatments might exhibit negligible differences on the average while producing wildly different effects upon individuals. An entirely different evaluation of the treatments might have resulted if some other questions had been asked, such as "Do these treatments interact with personality and cognitive characteristics of the students or with factors in their educational history or family background to produce differential effects upon achievement? Do certain student characteristics correlate with gains in achievement differently in one treatment than in the other?"

From the vantage point of differential psychology, it would appear that educational researchers frequently fail to take proper account of consistent individual differences. They tend to assess treatment effects on the average, presuming that variations in performance around the average are unstable fluctuations rather than expressions of stable personal characteristics. Developmental psychologists, on the other hand, survey essentially the same arena with their own limited purview. They not only frequently make the same assumption about individual variation but also the obverse concerning environmental variation. They seek to uncover for the generic human being general laws of learning and cognition—at best a small number of different laws for assorted idealized types of individuals—and to delineate mental development *on the average,* where the average is taken over all the differential educational experiences and environmental impacts that might interact with current psychological status to moderate change.

To evaluate educational treatments in terms of their effects upon individual students requires not only the assessment of variables directly related to specific treatment goals, such as achievement level, but also the assessment of personal and environmental variables that may moderate the learning. Similarly, to formulate the psychology of the development of cognitive or personality characteristics over a fixed period may require information not only about individual differences in the trait in relation to other traits at different times, but also about the educational treatments and environmental variations accompanying the change. Information about the trait's previous development and the personal, social, and environmental factors associated with prior growth may also be necessary.

If concerns about personal, social, and environmental characteristics were systematically combined with concerns about the effects of educational treatments, a conceptual framework for educational and psychological research would result, stimulating questions about interactions among these components, such as "What dimensions of educational experience are associated with growth on dimensions of cognitive functioning or with changes in attitude or affective involvement, and what social and environmental factors moderate these effects?" The need for such a multivariate interactional approach derives from the view that in education and psychology we are dealing with a complicated *system* composed of differentiated subsystems; even in research on presumably circumscribed issues it is important to recognize the interrelatedness of personal, social, environmental, and educational factors. In such a system it is possible that compensating trade-offs among variables will occur under different conditions to produce similar effects, and that particular outcomes will frequently be multiply determined. This is not to say that overall main effects due to specific educational treatments will not occur or that no personal characteristics will prove to be general over situations, but rather that interactions between treatment variables and personal or environmental factors are probable and should be systematically appraised in evaluating treatment effects.

The major thrust of this approach is that evaluations of the significance of changes in performance or attitude over a given time period as a presumed function of a specific instructional program should consider other changes in human characteristics and environmental influences active at the same time. Educational growth should not be viewed as independent of human growth, and the effects of instructional experiences should not be viewed as independent of other life experiences.

These multiple influences upon behavior should not only be considered at the level of systems analysis, but also at much simpler levels, such as in developing and evaluating a measure of academic achievement, where we sometimes forget that even specific responses are frequently complexly determined and buffeted by many environmental influences. Consider a researcher who attempts to assess quantitative reasoning in a lower class, culturally disadvantaged child by inquiring, "If you had seven apples and I asked you for two, how many would you have left?" The answer comes quickly and triumphantly—"Seven!" Hopefully, of course, we would never use such loose phrasing in our questions, but the example illustrates the point. We often fail to appreciate the extent to which the respondent's affect will be engaged by the content of a question and the extent to which personal, social, and economic factors will focus his attention upon problems quite different from the ones we thought we had posed.

When the efficacy of instruction is evaluated in such a multivariate framework, cognitive styles and affective reactions assume particular interest: (a) as personal characteristics that may interact with treatment variables to moderate learning, retention, and transfer; (b) as dispositions to be monitored to detect any possibly undesirable side effects of instruction; and (c) as qualities to be fostered either directly as specific objectives of the instructional program or indirectly as by-products of other efforts. This latter possibility of fostering stylistic and affective qualities appears to be consonant with general educational aims and the desirability of developing positive attitudes toward school, learning, subject matter, or self. But with respect to cognitive styles there is much less consensus, for we are not sure whether to emphasize particular styles or flexibility in the use of multiple styles, nor are we sure what the options are for changing styles. This problem will be discussed in more detail after we have considered the nature of cognitive styles and some reasons why individual differences in characteristic modes of cognition are relevant to educational practice.

THE ROLE OF VALUES IN THE SCIENCE OF EDUCATION

To suggest that cognitive styles and affects might serve as additional criteria in the evaluation of instruction is a value judgment; but value judgments abound in the evaluation process, and appear to be made with hesitancy only at the end of the enterprise when a decision about the worth of the program is required. Value judgments are usually made explicitly when the specific goals of the instructional program are outlined and when particular standards of excellence are accepted for judging success; but they are also made, usually implicitly, when criterion instruments are selected to assess the intended outcomes, when additional criterion measures are chosen to appraise side effects, when particular teaching methods, media, or materials are scrutinized during the course of instruction, and when certain types of transactions between the student and other persons are observed (Stake, 1967)—in short, whenever a subset of the possible alternatives is marked for special attention.

The selection of a subset from the range of possibilities implies priorities—that some things are more important to assess than others. But it is not enough to label such decisions "value judgments" and then proceed with the assessment. If it were, evaluation would be a straightforward affair indeed: we could specify the goals of the instructional program as we intend them and select criterion measures to assess those outcomes that seem directly relevant to the stated objectives. This is what Scriven has called "estimation of goal achievement" in contradistinction to evaluation proper. All appraisal in this case is relative to the stated goals, and the concern is with how well the program achieves its intended objectives. In addition, however, we should inquire to what extent the objectives are worth achieving and, in general, should endeavor to include in the evaluation process provisions for evaluating the value judgments, especially the goals (Scriven, 1967).

An important step in this direction is to be concerned with *possible* as well as *intended* outcomes. Evaluation comprises two major functions—to ascertain the nature and size of the effects of the treatment and to decide whether the observed effects attain acceptable standards of excellence. These two components have been termed "description" and "judgment" by Stake (1967). The point here is that the descriptive phase of evaluation should be as complete as our art and resources allow. In this instance the evaluation specialist should be, in Bruner's words (1966), a "diviner and delineator of the possible"—he should "provide the full range of alternatives to challenge society to choice." This attempt to describe the full range of possible effects of instruction is an important prerequisite for the judgmental phase of evaluation, since it might unearth alternatives that ought to be weighed in reaching the final appraisal. As Henry Dyer (1967, pp. 12–24) has emphasized, "Evaluating the *side* effects of an educational program may be even more important than evaluating its intended effects." Dyer (1967) also pointed out that such broad assessment of the possible effects of an educational program should contribute to an evaluation of its goals. Inverting the customary prescription that one must determine the objectives of instruction before developing measures of instructional outcomes, Dyer suggested that it may not be possible to decide what the objectives ought to be until the outcomes are measured.

In practice, of course, evaluation studies rarely approach completeness. We include in any feasible assessment program only a selection of criterion variables—those that reflect our current view of priorities or our attempt to represent several diverse viewpoints. Again it is not enough just to admit that practical considerations demand selectivity. To develop a science of evaluation, we should endeavor to justify these value judgments on rational grounds in terms of the specific objectives of the instructional program in question and of goals of education that transcend the particular course (Scriven, 1967). It is important not only to explicate the separate value judgments implicit in the choice of each criterion variable, but also to consider interrelations among them. Values rarely exist in isolation. They are typically part of ideologies that provide characteristic ways of thinking about man and society. In considering the assortment of variables to be assessed in a particular evaluation study and the goals that the instruction might serve, we should inquire to what extent do the possible outcomes reflect divergent value systems that "need to be reconciled or compromised and to what extent do they represent simply different frames of reference for compatible goals" (Proposal for a Research and Development Center, 1965).

Incidentally, the particular teaching methods chosen for an instructional program should also be evaluated for their compatibility with multiple goals and values. Even though two goals are reasonably compatible, the method of instruction may foster one aim and hinder the other. Wallach, for example, is concerned that modern methods of teaching, especially those using programmed materials and teaching machines, so emphasize accuracy of responding that the student is likely to acquire a generalized intolerance of error and consequent decline in his originality of thinking. Some other method or combination of methods might be used to develop facility in the analysis of logical implications without diminishing fluency in the generation of conceptual possibilities (Wallach, 1967, pp. 36–57).

Since educational values derive from broader systems of social values, it is appropriate to evaluate goals and criteria for instruction not only in terms of specific educational implications but also in terms of more general social implications. The suggestion that cognitive styles and affective reactions be used as criterion variables in the evaluation of instruction, for example, should be upheld in precisely such terms, but a consideration of the educational and social implications of these dimensions must await a more detailed discussion of the nature of the variables themselves.

COGNITION, AFFECT, AND PERSONALITY

In recent years we have seen the isolation of several dimensions of individual differences in the performance of cognitive tasks that appear to reflect consistencies in the manner or form of cognition, as distinct from the content of cognition or the level of skill displayed in the cognitive performance (Thurstone, 1944; Witkin and others, 1954; Witkin and others, 1962; Gardner and others, 1959; Gardner and others, 1960). These dimensions have been conceptualized as *cognitive styles,* which represent a person's typical modes of perceiving, remembering, thinking, and problem solving. Some examples of these dimensions are:

1. *Field independence versus field dependence*—"an analytical, in contrast to a global, way of perceiving (which) entails a tendency to experience items as discrete from their backgrounds and reflects ability to overcome the influence of an embedding context" (Witkin and others, 1962).

2. *Scanning*—a dimension of individual differences in the extensiveness

and intensity of attention deployment, leading to individual variations in vividness of experience and the span of awareness (Holzman, 1966; Schlesinger, 1954; Gardner and Long, 1962).

3. *Breadth of categorizing*—consistent preferences for broad inclusiveness, as opposed to narrow exclusiveness, in establishing the acceptable range for specified categories (Pettigrew, 1958; Bruner and Tajfel, 1961; Kogan and Wallach, 1964).

4. *Conceptualizing styles*—individual differences in the tendency to categorize perceived similarities and differences among stimuli in terms of many differentiated concepts, which is a dimension called *conceptual differentiation* (Gardner and Schoen, 1962; Messick and Kogan, 1963), as well as consistencies in the utilization of particular conceptualizing approaches as bases for forming concepts—such as the routine use in concept formation of thematic or functional relations among stimuli as opposed to the analysis of descriptive attributes or the inference of class membership (Kagan, Moss, and Sigel, 1960; Kagan and others, 1963).

5. *Cognitive complexity versus simplicity*—individual differences in the tendency to construe the world, and particularly the world of social behavior, in a multidimensional and discriminating way (Kelly, 1955; Bieri, 1961; Bieri and others, 1966; Scott, 1963; Harvey, Hunt, and Schroder, 1961).

6. *Reflectiveness versus impulsivity*—individual consistencies in the speed with which hypotheses are selected and information processed, with impulsive subjects tending to offer the first answer that occurs to them, even though it is frequently incorrect, and reflective subjects tending to ponder various possibilities before deciding (Kagan and others, 1964; Kagan, 1965).

7. *Leveling versus sharpening*—reliable individual variations in assimilation in memory. Subjects at the leveling extreme tend to blur similar memories and to merge perceived objects or events with similar but not identical events recalled from previous experience. Sharpeners, at the other extreme, are less prone to confuse similar objects and, by contrast, may even judge the present to be less similar to the past than is actually the case (Holzman, 1954; Holzman and Klein, 1954; Gardner and others, 1959).

8. *Constricted versus flexible control*—individual differences in susceptibility to distraction and cognitive interference (Klein, 1954; Gardner and others, 1959).

9. *Tolerance for incongruous or unrealistic experiences*—a dimension of differential willingness to accept perceptions at variance with conventional experience (Klein and others, 1962).

Stylistic consistencies have also been observed in the differential tendencies of individuals to err by omission or by commission on memory tasks (McKenna, 1967). In addition, several dimensions deriving from the work of Thurstone, Cattell, and Guilford, which are usually considered to fall within the purview of intellectual abilities, also reflect such potential exemplars of style or mode of cognition as speed, flexibility, divergence, convergence, and fluency.

Cognitive styles, for the most part, are information-processing habits. They are characteristic modes of operation which, although not necessarily completely independent of content, tend to function across a variety of content areas. Before considering some possible implications of cognitive styles for educational practice, let us discuss one in more detail to illustrate its generality and breadth of operation. For this purpose the dimension of analytic versus global attitude offers the best example, since it has been extensively studied in various forms by H. A. Witkin and others.

Witkin's early work emphasized individual differences in the characteristic ways in which people perceive both the world and themselves. One of the test situations used was a tilted room in which the subject, seated in a tilted chair, must adjust his body to the true upright. Reliable individual differences were found in this ability; that is, some individuals were reliably more susceptible than others to the influence of the surrounding tilted room. In another test, the subject was seated in a completely dark room and confronted with a luminous rod surrounded by a luminous picture frame; his task was to set the rod to the true vertical position while the frame was set aslant. Again, reliable individual differences were found in this ability, and a substantial correlation was noted between the two tests; the subjects who had difficulty withstanding the influence of the surrounding room while adjusting their body to the upright also had difficulty withstanding the influence of the surrounding frame while adjusting the rod to the upright. These individual differences were initially conceptualized in terms of a differential reliance upon visual cues obtained from the external field as opposed to kinesthetic cues obtained from the subject's own body.

This interpretation of field versus body orientation was extended to a more general dimension of perceptual analysis, however, when it was found that subjects who had difficulty overcoming the influence of the tilted room and the tilted frame also had difficulty overcoming the influence of superimposed complex designs when asked to find hidden simple forms in an embedded-figures test. This extended conception of the dimension was now termed "field dependence vs. field independence": The perception of relatively field-dependent subjects is dominated by the overall organization of the field, whereas relatively field-independent subjects readily perceive elements as discrete from their backgrounds. Sex differences have been repeatedly obtained on the measures of this dimension, with females being relatively more field dependent and males relatively more field independent (Witkin and others, 1954).

Since many correlates for these perceptual scores have been subsequently uncovered in several areas of intellectual and personality functioning, field independence versus field dependence is now viewed as the perceptual component of the broader dimension of *articulated versus global cognitive style.* For example, when the possible relation of field independence to intelligence was investigated, substantial correlations were obtained with some subtests of the Wechsler intelligence scales but not with others. The subtests of the Wechsler scales cluster into three major factors—a verbal dimension composed of the Vocabulary, Information, and Comprehension subtests; an attention-concentration dimension composed of the Digit Span, Arithmetic, and Coding subtests; and an analytic dimension, composed of the Block Design, Object Assembly, and Picture Completion subtests. The measures of field independence were found to correlate substantially with the dimension of analytic intelligence but not with the other two. Thus field-independent subjects exhibited a marked advantage on analytical intelligence tasks, but they could not be characterized as being superior in verbal intelligence or, in a meaningful way, as being superior in general intelligence (Goodenough and Karp, 1961; Witkin and others, 1962).

Children with a relatively articulated mode of cognitive functioning have also been found to have relatively articulated body concepts, as inferred from figure drawings; that is, when asked to draw human figures, these children display more realistic body proportions, more details, and more sex and role characteristics than children with a relatively global mode of functioning. Global subjects also tend to lack a developed sense of separate identity, as reflected in their relative reliance upon others for guidance and support, the relative instability of their self-view, their suggestibility and their susceptibility to social influence in forming and maintaining attitudes and judgments (Witkin and others, 1962; Linton and Graham, 1959).

Developmental studies have indicated that mode of cognitive functioning becomes progressively more articulated, and perception more field independent, with age up to late adolescence. At the same time, however, a child's relative level of articulation vis-à-vis his peers is quite stable. From age 10 to 14, the test-retest reliability of the perceptual index score of field independence was .64 for a group of thirty boys and .88 for a group of thirty girls, and from age 14 to 17 it was .87 for the boys and .94 for the girls (Witkin and others, 1962; Witkin and others, 1967).

In an effort to uncover the possible origins of this cognitive style, Witkin and his colleagues studied patterns of maternal child-rearing practices and mother-child relations. On the basis of interview data, the mothers were classified into two groups: those who fostered the child's differentiation from themselves and who helped him develop a sense of separate identity, and those who did not. In general, this classification of the mothers was found to be significantly related to the performance scores of the children, with the children of the mothers judged to have fostered differentiation being more field independent and cognitively articulated (Dyk and Witkin, 1965).

Differences have been noted in the type of defense mechanisms likely to be adopted by subjects at the two extremes of articulated and global cognitive styles when confronted by conflict and stress. Articulated subjects are more likely to utilize specialized defenses, such as intellectualization and isolation, while global subjects are more likely to utilize primitive defenses, such as denial and repression. No general relation has been found, however, between the degree of articulation of the cognitive style and the degree of personal adjustment or psychopathology. Rather, as with the defenses, when psychological disturbances occur, there are differences in the kinds of pathology that are likely to develop at the two extremes of the styles. Psychopathology in articulated persons is more likely to involve problems of overcontrol, overideation, and isolation; in severe pathological states, delusions are more likely to develop. Pathology in global persons, on the other hand, is more likely to involve problems of dependence, with symptoms such as alcoholism, obesity, ulcers, and asthma; in severe states hallucinations are much more likely to develop (Witkin, 1965). Such findings highlight the fact that styles of intellectual and perceptual functioning are part of the total personality and are intimately interwoven with affective, temperamental, and motivational structures. In some cases, for example, "The general style of thinking may be considered a matrix . . . that determines the *shape* or *form* of symptom, defense mechanism, and adaptive trait" (Shapiro, 1965). In other cases the form-determining matrix may not be a mode of cognition but perhaps a type of temperament or character structure or neurosis—the cognitive style would then be more derivative and would reflect but one component of a broader personality structure that permeates several areas of psychological functioning.

Although in most of this discussion one probably gets the impression that articulated, field-independent subjects have the advantage over their field-dependent peers, situations do exist where a more dependent reliance upon the external field, and particularly a reliance upon social stimuli for guidance and support, is profitable in the accrual of incidental information. Field-dependent subjects have been found to be significantly better than field-independent subjects, for example, in their memory for faces and social words, even though, on the other hand, their incidental memory for nonsocial stimuli is not generally superior (Messick and Damarin, 1964; Fitzgibbon and others, 1965). The fact that certain types of problem situations and certain types of subject matter favor field-dependent subjects over field-independent subjects and vice versa (just as other types of problems might favor broad categorizers over narrow categorizers or levelers over sharpeners, and vice versa) is extremely important, since it highlights the relativity of value of the opposing extremes of each cognitive style. Unlike conventional ability dimensions, one end of these stylistic dimensions is not uniformly more adaptive than the other.

The perceptual and intellectual consistencies just discussed have been interpreted in stylistic terms, which implies, for example, that an individual spontaneously and habitually applies his particular degree of analytic or articulated field approach to a wide variety of situations. Even though a relatively global individual may appear typically global in most situations, it is conceivable that when confronted with a situation that patently demands analysis he might be able to analyze with acceptable skill. Yet in the measurement of this cognitive style, it is usually presumed that subjects who characteristically display an analytic approach will in fact perform better on tasks requiring analysis (such as finding a simple figure in a complicated one) than will subjects who characteristically display a more global approach. Accordingly, most measures of analytic attitude are cast in an ability or maximum-performance framework; if a subject does well at the task, he is assumed to have performed more globally (or to be inadequately applying an unfamiliar, atypical analytic approach). In order to buttress the stylistic interpretation, it would be of interest to relate such maximum performance scores to measures of the spontaneous tendency to articulate the field in a task that ostensibly does not demand analysis.

In one attempt to develop such a task, subjects were required to learn to identify by name (a nonsense syllable) ten complex visual designs, each consisting of a large dominant figure, composed of elements, against a patterned background. In learning to identify these designs, the subject does not have to articulate the component parts, although the instructions do encourage analysis. The subjects are then told that each design was a member of a family of similar designs and that the names they had learned were family names. They are now presented with variations of the original designs (such as the element alone, the form alone, and the form composed of different elements) and asked to identify them in terms of the appropriate family name. In this strategy of test design, it was assumed that subjects who spontaneously articulated the designs during the learning process would be able to identify more variations than subjects who learned to identify the designs in a more global fashion. The total number of variations correctly identified, however, did not correlate significantly with the embedded-figures test. But this was because individuals differed consistently not only in the degree to which they articulated the original designs but in the type of figural component articulated, and the articulation of only one of these components was associated with embedded-figures performance. A factor analysis of variation scores uncovered two major dimensions representing two distinct modes of stimulus analysis, one emphasizing the articulation of discrete elements and the other of figural forms. A third mode reflecting the utilization of background information was substantially correlated with the other two. A significant relation was obtained between embedded-figures performance and the element articulation factor but not the form articulation factor. Although on the one hand element and form articulation are distinct dimensions of stimulus analysis and exhibit different personality correlates, on the other hand they are significantly correlated with each other and combine, along with the background information factor, to form a second-order dimension (Messick and Fritzky, 1963, pp. 346–370).

These findings underscore the fact that the generality of the articulated versus global cognitive style appears at a higher-order level in the factor-analytic sense. Another illustration of this point occurs in a study that attempted to extend Thurstone's perceptual closure factors into the verbal and semantic domains. Thurstone's factor of flexibility of perceptual closure, which is measured by tests like embedded figures, deals with the ability to break one closure in order to perceive a different one and thereby depends upon the capacity to analyze a highly-organized perceptual field. Thurstone's factor of speed of perceptual closure deals with the ability to assemble discrete parts into an integrated, meaningful whole and thereby reflects the capacity to structure a relatively unorganized perceptual field (Thurstone, 1944). The concept of an articulated mode of perception implies facility in both analysis and structuring (Dyk and Witkin, 1965), thereby requiring that the two closure factors be correlated, which usually tends to be the case. When several experimental closure tests were constructed using single words and meaningful discourse as the stimulus fields, factors were also uncovered for both speed and flexibility of verbal closure and for both speed and flexibility of semantic closure, in addition to the two perceptual closure factors. The concept of a general articulated versus global cognitive style requires that all of these closure factors be mutually intercorrelated, which also tends to be the case, although the level of correlation is certainly not uniform. Indeed, some limitation on the generality of the style appeared in a second-order factor analysis, which revealed two relatively independent articulation dimensions, one involving the analysis and structuring of figural materials and the other the analysis and structuring of symbolic materials. In addition, a separate second-order factor of general analytical reasoning was also obtained (Messick and French, 1967).

Studies of other cognitive styles, particularly scanning and breadth of categorizing, have revealed a similar range of involvement in areas of personality and psychopathology. Silverman, for example, found that paranoid schizophrenics exhibited significantly more extensive scanning behavior and utilized significantly narrower categories than nonparanoid schizophrenics (Silverman, 1964). Gardner and Long (1962) reported that extreme scanning was marginally related to ratings of isolation, projection, and generalized delay on the Rorschach. This latter finding that scanning behavior tends to be associated with two different defense mechanisms suggests the possibility that extensive scanning may serve different purposes under different circumstances or, perhaps, that there may be two distinct types of scanning. The association with isolation, which is a preferred defense mechanism of obsessives, suggests that the scanning may occur in the service of information seeking, as reflected in the obsessive's concern with exactness to offset doubt and uncertainty. The association with projection, which is a preferred defense mechanism of paranoids, suggests that the scanning may occur in the service of signal detection, particularly danger-signal detection, as reflected in the paranoid's concern with accuracy to offset suspicion and distrust. Some current research at Educational Testing Service attempts to differentiate empirically between these two possible types of scanning. This is done by use of perceptual search tasks in which the subject is required to locate stimuli (signals) embedded in meaningfully organized visual fields, for example, to locate faces camouflaged in pictorial scenes or four-letter words embedded in sentences. Upon completion of the search task, the stimulus materials are removed, and the subject is then asked specific questions about the content of the scenes or the meaning of the set of sentences. Subjects who incidentally acquire information about the field in the process of scanning can thus be differentiated from those whose concern is apparently limited to detecting the signals.

With this brief characterization of cognitive styles in mind, let us now consider some of their possible implications for educational practice and evaluation. To begin with, cognitive styles, by embracing both perceptual and intellectual domains and by their frequent implication in personality and social functioning, promise to provide a more complete and effective characterization of the student than could be obtained from intellectual tests alone. These stylistic dimensions offer for our appraisal new types of process variables that extend the assessment of mental performance beyond the crystallized notion of achievement levels to a concern with patterns of cognitive functioning. These stylistic characteristics should have relevance, although direct research evidence is admittedly very scanty, not only for the course of individual learning in various subject matter areas, but also for the nature of teacher-pupil interactions and of social behavior in the classroom, the family, and the peer group.

Thus, cognitive styles, by virtue of their widespread operation, appear to be particularly important dimensions to assess in the evaluation of instruction. Yet the very pervasiveness that underscores their importance at the same time interferes with the measurement of other important personal characteristics, such as dimensions of specific aptitude. This is because cognitive styles operate in testing situations as well and frequently interact with test formats and test conditions to influence the examinee's score. Consider, for example, the possibility that the five-alternative multiple-choice form of quantitative aptitude tests may favor subjects who prefer broad categories on category-width measures. Initial, rough approximations to the quantitative items might appropriately be judged by these subjects to be "close enough" to a given alternative, whereas "narrow range" subjects may require more time-consuming exact solutions before answering. Significant correlations between category preferences and quantitative aptitude tests have indeed been found, but the level of the correlation turns out to vary widely as a function of the spacing of alternatives on multiple-choice forms of the quantitative items. Scores for breadth of categorizing were found to be substantially correlated with quantitative aptitude scores derived from a multiple-choice form having widely-spaced alternatives, marginally correlated with scores on a free-response quantitative test, and negligibly correlated with scores derived from a narrowly-spaced form. This suggests that wide spacing of alternatives enhances, and narrow spacing disrupts, the "approximation" strategy that broad categorizers tend to employ on multiple-choice quantitative tests (Messick and Kogan, 1965). Such findings suggest that we should consider the "fairness" of our aptitude and achievement tests not only for different cultures and different sexes, but for individuals having different stylistic propensities. Thus, it is quite possible that cognitive styles are already being reflected in standard evaluation devices; however, their operation under these circumstances is not being assessed for evaluation purposes but serves to contaminate the interpretation of other measures.

Information about cognitive styles offers several possibilities for instructional practice, but choices among them depend upon the results of much needed empirical research. For example, as soon as we are able to assess the cognitive styles of students, we have the possibility of placing them in classrooms in specified ways, perhaps in homogeneous groupings or in particular mixes or combinations. At this point it is by no means clear that particular placements will foster learning for individuals, just as it is by no means clear that homogeneous ability grouping is uniformly beneficial. Similarly, if we can assess the cognitive styles of students, we can also assess the cognitive styles of teachers and consider the possibility of assigning teachers to students to obtain particular combinations of styles that would optimally foster learning. We could also consider selecting particular teaching methods that would be especially appropriate for certain cognitive styles and certain subject matters. As yet, of course, there is very little research to guide us on these points. But even in considering the possibility of matching the student to the teacher or the teaching method, and remembering that with our present assignment procedures some students are in effect so matched while others are not, we should ponder what the criterion of success in this enterprise should be. Should it be the maximal learning of content skills and information?

Consider a possibility that, in the sciences at least, students with an articulated field approach, and perhaps reflective students as well, might learn better with an inductive or "discovery" method of teaching, since it would probably capitalize upon their propensities for analysis and careful consideration of alternatives. More global and more impulsive students, on the other hand, might learn content information better with a directed method of teaching in which rules and principles are specified rather than induced. Consider the likelihood, however, that in our efforts to optimize the learning of subject matter we may so solidify the global child's cognitive style that he may never learn to discover anything in his entire school career. This possibility suggests that teaching to produce maximal learning of subject matter is not enough. We should also be concerned with the student's manner of thinking. One possibility here is that we should attempt to foster alternative modes of cognition and multiple stylistic approaches to problem solving.

Such a goal will not be easily attained, however, since there are many cognitive and personality dimensions that could interact with properties of teaching methods to produce negligible or adverse results. It makes a difference, for example, when and to whom and to what subject matter an inferential discovery method of teaching is applied. Kagan warns us, as an instance, that "impulsive children are apt to settle on the wrong conclusion in the inferential method and become vulnerable to developing feelings of inadequacy. . . ." Since these impulsively derived hypotheses are apt to be incorrect, the impulsive child encounters a series of humiliating failures and eventually withdraws involvement from school tasks (Kagan, 1967; Kagan and others, 1966).

The success of attempts to develop multiple modes of cognition in the individual will depend to a large extent upon the degree to which cognitive styles are malleable. Cognitive styles, as usually conceived, are habits that are spontaneously applied without conscious choice in a wide variety of situations. The possibility being considered here is that through manipulation of educational experience we might convert cognitive styles into cognitive strategies, by which I mean to imply a conscious choice among alternative modes of perceiving, remembering, thinking, and problem solving as a function of the conditions of particular situations. If the cognitive styles are relatively mutable, such efforts at change and multiple development might be feasible at all levels of the educational sequence. If the cognitive styles, or at least some of them, are relatively immutable, it may be necessary to focus attention on the early years and attempt to foster multiple modes of cognition before particular styles crystallize and become predominant. This latter possibility of predominant cognitive styles may be inevitable, regardless of our educational efforts, but we might at least be able to increase somewhat the power of alternative cognitive modes in the hierarchy, thereby reducing to some extent the preemptiveness of habitual thought. As always, however, we must also consider and evaluate the potential dangers in such an enterprise: our efforts to foster multiple modes of cognition in a child may prevent him from soaring in the unfettered application of his preferred style in a particular field.

I have not discussed affective variables at length because most educators, at least when pressed, affirm the importance of enhancing curiosity and of implanting in the student massive and enduring positive affects toward learning and subject matter. Most of us would agree, therefore, that even when an instructional program does not attempt to enhance positive attitudes directly, these variables should still be monitored if possible in the evaluation of the program to guard against unintended decreases in interest or involvement. In the measurement of these affective reactions, however, it seems to me unfortunate that evaluation studies rely so heavily upon the engineering model, which relates inputs and outputs, for there is a marked tendency to assess student achievement and attitudes only at the beginning and the end of the course. As Scriven has emphasized, the medical model is the appropriate paradigm for educational research (Scriven, 1966, pp. 33–49), and one derivative from that model should be an explicit attempt in evaluating a program to take account of the student's attitudes and feelings about the course of the treatment and not just the end result.

I wish to close by underscoring the importance of affect for learning and hence the importance of assessing affect in the evaluation of instruction. This point has been elegantly summarized by John Barth (1964, p. 17) in his novel, *The Sot-Weed Factor*:

> . . . of the three usual motives for learning things—necessity, ambition, and curiosity—simple curiosity was the worthiest of development, it being the "purest" (in that the value of what it drives us to learn is terminal rather than instrumental), the most conducive to exhaustive and continuing rather than cursory or limited study, and the likeliest to render pleasant the labor of learning. . . . This sport of teaching and learning should never become associated with certain hours or particular places, lest student and teacher alike . . . fall into the vulgar habit of turning off their alertness, as it were, except at those times and in those places, and thus make by implication a pernicious distinction between learning and other sorts of natural human behavior.

REFERENCES

Barth, J. *The sot-weed factor.* New York: Grosset and Dunlap, Inc., 1964.

Bieri, J. Complexity-simplicity as a personality variable and preferential behavior. In D. W. Fiske & S. R. Maddi (Eds.), *Functions of varied experience.* Homewood, Ill.: Dorsey Press, 1961.

Bieri, J., Atkins, A. L., Scott, B., Leaman, R. L., Miller, H., & Tripodi, T. *Clinical and social judgment: The discrimination of behavioral information.* New York: John Wiley & Sons, Inc., 1966.

Bruner, J. S. *Toward a theory of instruction.* Cambridge, Mass.: Harvard University Press, 1966.

Bruner, J. S., & Tajfel, H. Cognitive risk and environmental change. *Journal of Abnormal Psychology,* 1961, *62,* 231–241.

Dyer, H. S. The discovery and development of educational goals. *Proceedings of the 1966 Invitational Conference on Testing Problems.* Princeton, N.J.: Educational Testing Service, 1967, 12–24.

Dyk, R. B., & Witkin, H. A. Family experiences related to the development of differentiation in children. *Child Development,* 1965, *36,* 21–55.

Fitzgibbons, D., Goldberger, L., & Eagle, M. Field dependence and memory for incidental material. *Perceptual and Motor Skills,* 1965, *21,* 743–749.

Gardner, R. W., & Long, R. I. Control, defense, and centration effect: A study of scanning behavior. *British Journal of Psychology,* 1962, *53,* 129–140.

Gardner, R. W., & Schoen, R. A. Differentiation and abstraction in concept formation. *Psychological Monographs,* 1962, *76,* No. 41.

Gardner, R. W., Jackson, D. N., & Messick, S. Personality organization in cognitive controls and intellectual abilities. *Psychological Issues,* 1960, *2,* No. 8.

Gardner, R. W., Holzman, P. S., Klein, G. S., Linton, H. B., & Spence, D. Cognitive control: A study of individual consistencies in cognitive behavior. *Psychological Issues*, 1959, *1*, No. 4.

Goodenough, D. R., & Karp, S. A. Field dependence and intellectual functioning. *Journal of Abnormal and Social Psychology*, 1961, *63*, 241–246.

Harvey, O. J., Hunt, D. E., & Schroder, H. M. *Conceptual systems and personality organization*. New York: John Wiley & Sons, Inc., 1961.

Holzman, P. S. The relation of assimilation tendencies in visual, auditory, and kinesthetic time-error to cognitive attitudes of leveling and sharpening. *Journal of Personality*, 1954, *22*, 375–394.

Holzman, P. S. Scanning: A principle of reality contact. *Perceptual and Motor Skills*, 1966, *23*, 835–844.

Holzman, P. S., & Klein, G. S. Cognitive system principles of leveling and sharpening: Individual differences in assimilation effects in visual time-error. *Journal of Psychology*, 1954, *37*, 105–122.

Kagan, J. Reflection-impulsivity and reading ability in primary grade children. *Child Development*, 1965, *36*, 609–628.

Kagan, J. Personality and the learning process. In J. Kagan (Ed.), *Creativity and Learning*. Boston: Houghton Mifflin Company, 1967. Pp. 153–163.

Kagan, J., Moss, H. A., & Sigel, I. E. Conceptual style and the use of affect labels. *Merrill-Palmer Quarterly*, 1960, *6*, 261–278.

Kagan, J., Moss, H. A., & Sigel, I. E. Psychological significance of styles of conceptualization. In J. C. Wright & J. Kagan (Eds.), Basic cognitive processes in children. *Monograph of Society for Research in Child Development*, 1963, *28*, No. 2, 73–112.

Kagan, J., Pearson, L., & Welch, L. Conceptual impulsivity and inductive reasoning. *Child Development*, 1966, *37*, 583–594.

Kagan, J., Rosman, B. L., Day, D., Albert, J., & Phillips, W. Information processing and the child: Significance of analytic and reflective attitudes. *Psychological Monographs*, 1964, *78* (Whole No. 58).

Kelley, G. A. The psychology of personal constructs. Vol. 1. New York: W. W. Norton & Company, Inc., 1955.

Klein, G. S. Need and regulation. In M. R. Jones (Ed.), *Nebraska symposium on motivation*. Lincoln, Neb.: University of Nebraska Press, 1954. Pp. 225–274.

Klein, G. S., Gardner, R. W., & Schlesinger, H. J. Tolerance for unrealistic experiences: A study of the generality of a cognitive control. *British Journal of Psychology*, 1962, *53*, 41–55.

Kogan, N., & Wallach, M. A. *Risk taking*. New York: Holt, Rinehart and Winston, Inc., 1964.

Linton, H. B., & Graham, E. Personality correlates of persuasibility. In I. L. Janies (Ed.), *Personality and persuasibility*. New Haven, Conn.: Yale University Press, 1959.

McKenna, V. *Stylistic factors in learning and retention.* Princeton, N.J.: Edutional Testing Service, Research Bulletin, 1967.

Messick, S. Cognitive interference and flexible control. Princeton, N.J.: Educational Testing Service, Research Bulletin (In preparation).

Messick, S., & Damarin, F. Cognitive styles and memory for faces. *Journal of Abnormal and Social Psychology,* 1964, *69,* 313–318.

Messick, S., & French, J. W. Dimensions of closure in cognition and personality. Paper delivered at the American Psychological Association, Washington, D.C., 1967.

Messick, S., & Fritzky, F. J. Dimensions of analytic attitude in cognition and personality. *Journal of Personality,* 1963, *31,* 346–370.

Messick, S., & Kogan, N. Category width and quantitative aptitude. *Perceptual and Motor Skills,* 1965, *20,* 493–497.

Messick, S., & Kogan, N. Differentiation and compartmentalization in object-sorting measures of categorizing style. *Perceptual and Motor Skills,* 1963, *16,* 47–51.

Pettigrew, T. F. The measurement and correlates of category width as a cognitive variable. *Journal of Personality,* 1958, *26,* 532–544.

Proposal for a research and development center for measurement in education. Princeton, N.J.: Educational Testing Service, 1965.

Schlesinger, H. J. Cognitive attitudes in relation to susceptibility to interference. *Journal of Personality,* 1954, *22,* 354–374.

Scott, W. A. Conceptualizing and measuring structural properties of cognition. In O. J. Harvey (Ed.), *Motivation and social interaction.* New York: The Ronald Press Company, 1963.

Scriven, M. Student values as educational objectives. *Proceedings of the 1965 Invitational Conference on Testing Problems.* Princeton, N.J.: Educational Testing Service, 1966, 33–49.

Scriven, M. The methodology of evaluation. In R. W. Tyler, R. M. Gagné, & M. Scriven (Eds.), *Perspectives of curriculum evaluation.* Skokie, Ill.: Rand McNally and Company, 1967. Pp. 39–83.

Shapiro, D. *Neurotic styles.* New York: Basic Books, Inc., 1965.

Silverman, J. Scanning-control mechanism and "cognitive filtering" in paranoid and nonparanoid schizophrenia. *Journal of Consulting Psychology,* 1964, *28,* 385–393.

Stake, R. E. The countenance of educational evaluation. *Teachers College Record,* 1967, *68,* 523–540.

Thurstone, L. L. A factorial study of perception. *Psychometric Monograph No. 4.* Chicago: University of Chicago Press, 1944.

Wallach, M. A. Creativity and the expression of possibilities. In J. Kagan (Ed.), *Creativity and learning.* Boston: Houghton Mifflin Company, 1967. Pp. 36–57.

Witkin, H. A. Psychological differentiation and forms of pathology. *Journal of Abnormal Psychology,* 1965, *70,* 317–336.

Witkin, H. A., Goodenough, D. R., & Karp, S. A. Stability of cognitive style from childhood to young adulthood. *Journal of Personality and Social Psychology*, 1967, *7*, 291–300.

Witkin, H. A., Dyk, R. B., Faterson, H. F., Goodenough, D. R., & Karp, S. A. *Psychological differentiation*. New York: John Wiley & Sons, Inc., 1962.

Witkin, H. A., Lewis, H. B., Hertzman, M., Machover, K., Meissner, P. B., & Wapner, S. *Personality through perception*. New York: Harper & Row, Publishers, 1954.

Comments on Professor Messick's Paper

PAUL BLOMMERS

In spite of my sheltered life as a statistician rather than as a specialist in measurement, I do not profess to the doctrine of the "average pupil." Further, I am fully cognizant of the importance of the interaction issue, although after more than twenty-five years of statistical consulting with staff and students and serving on countless doctoral examining committees, I cannot recall a single instance of a completely reversible or negative type of interaction.

I find little to quarrel about in Dr. Messick's comments concerning the role of value judgments in both the design and evaluation of instructional programs. I could accept the view attributed to Dyer that "it may not be possible to decide what the objectives ought to be until one has first measured the outcomes." The possible validity of this view, it seems to me, stems largely from man's failure to appreciate or anticipate all the implications of what I shall loosely call his educational decisions, so that the very results of his evaluative efforts may first call his attention to his errors. These judgments must reflect the goals of education in American society; this is no platitude regardless of which dictionary meaning is to be ascribed to platitude.

But while supporting Dr. Messick, these statements primarily are prefatory to his thesis, which, as defended in his paper, is that cognitive style and affective reaction variables ought to be taken into account in the evaluation of instruction. His thesis applies largely to the role of cognitive style in the evaluation of instruction. While affective variables are included in it, their value is treated as more or less axiomatic. Perhaps this is a sufficient and proper treatment, but somehow affective variables do not seem quite to belong with cognitive style. I doubt, for example, that the interaction argument is applicable to them. It is difficult to conceive that enhancing curiosity to a greater or lesser degree could operate in any way save to enhance learning to a greater or lesser degree, which would be true of all types of individuals. It would not apply to all types of individuals to an equal extent, but I doubt the existence of a type of individual who ought to be isolated and shielded from activities which enhance curiosity—whatever such activities may be. On the other hand, I recognize the pertinence of the value judgment argument. Were I a fascist educationist I would certainly restrict the development of curiosity to a limited set of situations; and if I thought that curiosity once developed might be a general sort of phenomenon, I would not be likely to support its development at all— indeed I might rather seek ways of stifling it.

While I have no strong objections to the way Dr. Messick treated affective variables, it does seem to me that his argument is better limited to cognitive styles. This brings me to my final observations regarding his thesis as it applies to cognitive styles. I shall express these observations in the form of questions that are not intended to be rhetorical. I do not know their answers, but answers may exist or may be found.

First, taking a given cognitive style, say articulated versus global, which is it better for an individual to be? If, as Dr. Messick's careful review of the literature appears to suggest, it is better to be articulated for some types of tasks than for others, then I ask for what types of classroom learning tasks specifically is it better to be articulated and for what type is it better to be global? In asking for this specificity I stress the words "classroom learning tasks."

Second, is it possible for a person to shift his cognitive style to optimize his method of attack upon the particular classroom learning tasks confronting him at any given moment?

Third, can I possibly shape his cognitive styles, and if so, by what means? Given this knowledge, is it desirable to do so? Remember that in the case of field independence versus dependence I might make a recluse of him in one way, or an alcoholic in another. I say might because no knowledge about cause and effect exists for these variables.

Fourth, to evaluate efforts to shape cognitive styles, or at least to take them into account in teaching, how do I measure them? Will it cost much to do so, and am I apt to introduce any negative side effects, such as the invasion of privacy?

Fifth, how do I estimate gain in the learning efficiency of my pupils by giving attention to cognitive styles?

Sixth, are cognitive styles relatively independent? If, for example, I somehow make a pupil more field independent am I apt, at the same time, to make him a narrow categorizor, or an intensive scanner? Do these styles complement one another?

Answers to such questions are essential before decisions can be made regarding the role of cognitive styles in the instructional program and in the evaluation of the instructional program. To advocate attention to cognitive styles, while not finding answers to such questions, is not necessarily wrong, but perhaps a bit premature.

I definitely do not wish to discourage further pursuit of Dr. Messick's proposals. As a graduate student in mathematics I remember reading Bishop George Berkeley's indictment of the notion of the square root of a negative number, a notion originally conceived as a purely philosophic extension of the number system, but one which has since come to enjoy great practical value. In this respect, I do not want to be Berkeleian. As of now, I am not yet ready to become an active disciple of taking cognitive styles into account in either the instructional program or its evaluation.

Comments on Professor Messick's Paper

LEONARD CAHEN

In his paper Samuel Messick covers many important aspects of evaluation, and especially emphasizes cognitive styles and affective reactions as they pertain to instructional research. In addition to the commonly assessed areas of pupil achievement, cognitive styles and affective reactions are suggested as further areas of possible assessment in evaluation studies. Among the major themes of Dr. Messick's paper are the need for assessing multiple dimensions of instructional outcomes, the importance of value judgments in instructional systems and their evaluation, and the role that individual differences in cognitive styles and information processing may play in future instructional research.

The idea of assessing the possible and not just the intended outcomes raises some important issues for the evaluator. At a first glance the term "intended" (the counter term "unintended") poses a difficulty. It takes a great deal of wisdom on the part of the evaluator to anticipate the unintended outcomes of instruction and to make the necessary plans for their assessment. In one sense the unintended outcomes may be conceived as unsought "side effects." In a hypothetical example a high school district adopted a new tenth-grade science curriculum. The objectives of the curriculum, among others, were to foster scientific thinking and to develop laboratory skills and an understanding of the scope of science. At the end of the year, the pupils performed satisfactorily on tests designed to measure these objectives. A negative "side effect," however, was seen in the fact that only a small proportion of these tenth-grade pupils elected an eleventh-grade science course the following year. The proportion of these students electing the eleventh-grade science course was significantly smaller than the proportion of eleventh-grade students taking science courses over the preceding years.

The curriculum builders and school administrators felt that there was a cause-and-effect relationship in the situation and decided that it was important to learn more about why the students generally failed to elect an eleventh-grade science course. This negative "side effect" or unintended outcome was assessed by student interview.

A second form of the unintended outcome occurs when the curriculum developer explicitly attempts to develop a certain set of behaviors but not other behaviors. For this example let us assume that he is attempting to develop behaviors A, B, and C but not D. In this case the intended outcomes are A, B, and C where D becomes explicitly stated as an unintended outcome. An example might be found in one of the modern mathematics curricula developed in the early 1960s. Behaviors A, B, and C might be represented by three sophisticated mathematics behaviors such as understanding of different number systems, the development of heuristics in problem solving, and an understanding of mathematical algorithms. Behavior D (the unintended outcome) might be represented by a traditional mathematical skill such as accuracy in routine computations or competence in translating Roman numerals. In the mathematics curriculum, the developer of the instructional program has in part exposed his value system.

The example of the mathematics curriculum represents a common problem that faced evaluators in the 1960s. The problem is manifested in the area of instrumentation where the instructional system or curriculum developer felt that standardized testing instruments failed to measure the dimensions he was interested in—A, B, and C (his intended outcomes)—but measured dimension D (his unintended outcome) with relative precision and validity. The mathematics curriculum suggested has led to considerable debate about the role of comparing outcomes across competing curricula or instructional systems when the competing systems have different intended outcomes.

Michael Scriven (1967) has introduced the terms formative and summative evaluation. Formative evaluation is the gathering of information in the early phases of developing a system of instruction. It is used for

immediate feedback in modification of the materials. Summative evaluation provides information to the potential consumers of the instructional
product. However, as Scriven has pointed out, the distinction between the
two terms is not always clear. If curriculum is to be an ongoing activity,
a summative evaluation will serve as a first stage of a formative evaluation
for the second wave of innovation. In the example of the mathematics curriculum developed above, the evaluator would be asked to provide information on dimension D as well as dimensions A, B, and C if the evaluation
were summative.

The two examples of unintended outcomes are developed to show that
an outcome may be an unsought side effect, unplanned by the innovator,
or may reflect an a priori value judgment by the innovator to exclude certain dimensions from the instructional system.

Dr. Messick has urged evaluators to include psychological as well as
achievement dimensions in the evaluative act. He has proposed that, in
addition to assessing the face-value components of achievement, instructional systems must also focus on processes and psychological variables as
outcomes.

The issue of value judgments in evaluation cannot be overemphasized.
Dr. Messick has pointed out that value judgments are made at many phases
in the development and assessment of instructional systems. Judgments
determine what the anticipated behavioral outcomes are, how they are to
be reached, the components and constructs to be measured, and the selection of instruments or techniques to measure or assess the components and
constructs and, at a later stage, are used to reach decisions from the outcome data matrix. Too frequently value judgments, at least explicitly, are
faced only at the decision-making stages, if at all.

Scriven (1967) has taken the position that the evaluator must play a
key role in the incorporation of value judgments in the evaluative process.
This is not an easy task for the curriculum evaluator, and because he may
not represent the specific discipline underlying the curriculum innovation
he has felt that the judgmental processes must be left to the curriculum
innovator who does represent the field. Robert Stake (1967) has hypothesized that the evaluator might have less access to data if he became identified with the judging of an instructional program. Stake also poses the
problem involved in judging the merit of a program from multivariate data
where some of the outcomes are positive and supportive while other outcomes from the same program may reflect negative findings.

If we are to follow Scriven's suggestion that evaluators play active roles
in the establishment and utilization of value judgments, we will probably
have to give thought to the future sources of evaluators and careful thought

as to their training. In addition, the need for identifying methods to analyze values reflected in a program or instructional system (and across competing instructional systems) will hopefully be given more emphasis in evaluation enterprises of the future.

A proposal is made here that might complement methodologies in evaluating and assessing values in instructional research. The proposal states that outcomes at any stage of instruction can be assessed in terms of how well the instruction has prepared the students for future learning. An assumption is made here that learning is a continuous process and that school curricula will eventually reflect a continuity of experiences rather than inarticulated segments of curricula, that is, elementary school math, junior high school math, and so forth. The success of an instructional program at any level could then be evaluated, in part, in terms of pupils' increased aptitudes for future learning.

I would now like to turn to the problem of utilizing individual difference data as elements in the process of placing groups of students in the most appropriate learning treatment. By most appropriate I mean the assignment of pupils to a learning situation or treatment where the pupil has the highest probability of maximum output or achievement. Dr. Messick has carried his suggestions past the initial stages of evaluation to the stage of implementation.

The model using the interaction of treatment or instruction and selected individual differences of learners has received a great deal of attention recently (Cronbach and Gleser, 1965; and Cronbach, 1966). While there is not always agreement about the results of such an interaction model, the conceptualization does form interesting and explicit hypotheses and requires a major change in the application of quantitative strategies to education. It was not too many years ago that behavioral scientists hoped for nonsignificant statistical interactions in their analysis of factorial designs. Nonsignificant statistical findings at the interaction level allowed them (so they believed) to move on to the clear testing of major effects. Similarly, statistical textbooks frequently emphasized techniques for pooling the lower-order interaction mean squares with the error mean square so that more stable-error terms would be available for testing main effects. This technique of pooling reduced type two errors at the expense of potentially destroying the "nuisance" relationships displayed in interactions.

Dr. Messick has stated that interaction models may be useful in the examination of relationships between teacher and pupil characteristics on cognitive dimensions and in determining how these factors might interact to effect pupil learning. One may also wonder about the possible relationships between different organizations of the teaching act with pupil and teacher characteristics and how these would jointly effect pupil learning. Lastly, one may consider the relationship of individual differences on cognitive dimensions (teacher and pupil) and the structuring of the content of instruction. Might there be ways of organizing and presenting the content of instruction so that it interacts with individual differences of pupils and teachers and teaching methods?

The use of individual difference interaction models will require concentrated efforts by evaluators to develop measures with minimal errors of measurement at the critical positions on the individual-difference scales where decisions are made to assign pupils to learning experiences.

The technique of developing evaluation instruments for reliably measuring individual differences has recently given ground to the development of techniques to assess and evaluate group performance. Evaluation studies will need to determine both the important research questions and what mixture or combination of individual versus group assessments reflect the most appropriate techniques for answering the crucial questions underlying assessment and evaluation of a specific instructional system. The item or matrix sampling model developed by Frederic Lord (Lord and Novick, 1968) is a valuable technique for estimating group performance on many dimensions. Additional sampling combinations of items and subjects (successive matrix samplings) would provide a better estimation of the total covariance structure of the set of behaviors under investigation. However, as Dr. Messick points out, there are limitations and potential dangers in inferring performance of individuals from "averaged" or group assessments. This danger is probably more severe in assessing personality dimensions than in assessing achievement output.

It becomes apparent to the evaluator that there is an almost infinite number of possible dimensions to assess and evaluate. The innovator-evaluator must decide which dimensions have the greatest potential for providing information for himself while also providing multidimensional outcome measures for the potential consumer. Value judgments again must play an important role. Explicit statements from the innovator-evaluator concerning priorities assigned to measures, and facts relating to which evaluative dimensions are not included in the study are crucial.

I would now like to consider a few problems that lie ahead in the utilization of individual difference measures in the cognitive style (nonachievement) areas in curriculum research. The study of individual differences in cognitive styles is in its infancy. Dr. Messick encourages use of longitudinal methods to study the long term interactions between achievement and such psychological processes as cognitive styles. It would be possible and highly desirable to readminister achievement and cognitive batteries over a long period of time and to study the covariance patterns over time within and between the achievement and cognitive domains. The processes underlying achievement and cognitive functions may both be changing, thus making the analyses themselves and the understanding of the analyses very difficult. Witkin and his colleagues (Witkin, Goodenough, and Karp, 1967) have recently reported longitudinal and cross-sectional data on measures of cognitive style. More research of this nature will be needed if we are to utilize and understand cognitive styles and their potential for curriculum research.

Dr. Messick has called to our attention three other aspects related to the role of cognitive styles and curriculum research. He has told us that school experiences should foster an increase in the repertoire of styles for individuals rather than increase the competencies of an individual on a limited set of styles at the expense of other styles. The latter possibility is an inherent danger in the individual-difference interaction model. It might be possible to structure an educational experience so that groups of students develop or increase their cognitive abilities along one dimension while failing to incorporate other styles into their repertoire. The educator must be very careful in structuring these experiences. If we take the dimension of tempo outlined by Jerome Kagan (1966), analytic versus impulsive styles, it is easy to let the semantics of analytic over impulsive determine what appears to be the obvious treatment—and desirable outcome. We must learn to know under what conditions it is favorable for a specific student to act analytically, under what conditions it is best for him to act impulsively, and then to determine a course of instruction that will foster both. It would also be important to teach the student to decide when one style or the other is more appropriate or beneficial.

Dr. Messick has hypothesized that there may be some very important stages in the development of conceptual or cognitive styles, possibly in the very early years, prior to the organism being exposed to formal education. A great deal of research will undoubtedly be devoted to this area in the future.

My final point concerns the difficulty of administering nonachievement batteries in the evaluation of instructional programs. By nonachievement I refer to measures of personality, cognitive style, attitude, and so forth. The problem of invasion of privacy must be considered. In addition, how do students respond to tests not perceived as achievement measures? Students and school administrators will not see the relevance of nonachievement type tests to the evaluation of instructional outcomes.

We will need to convince ourselves first of the utility of individual differences such as cognitive style for instructional research, and then help the innovator to see the value of including these and other process variables in the instructional "package."

REFERENCES

Cronbach, L. J. How can instruction be adapted to individual differences? In R. M. Gagné (Ed.), *Learning and individual differences.* Columbus: Charles E. Merrill Books, Inc., 1966. Pp. 23–39.

Cronbach, L. J., & Gleser, G. C. *Psychological tests and personnel decisions* (2d ed.). Urbana, Ill.: University of Illinois Press, 1965.

Kagan, J. Developmental studies in reflection and analysis. In A. H. Kidd & J. L. Rivoire (Eds.), *Perceptual development in children.* New York: International Universities Press, Inc., 1966. Pp. 487–522.

Lord, F. M., & Novick, M. *Statistical theories of mental test scores.* Reading, Mass.: Addison-Wesley Publishing Company, Inc., 1968.

Scriven, M. The methodology of evaluation. *American educational research association monograph series on curriculum evaluation,* No. 1. Skokie, Ill.: Rand McNally and Company, 1967.

Stake, R. E. The countenance of educational evaluation. *Teachers College Record,* 1967, *68,* 523–540.

Witkin, H. A., Goodenough, D. R., & Karp, S. T. Stability of cognitive style from childhood to young adulthood. *Journal of Personality and Social Psychology,* 1967, *7,* 291–300.

Open Discussion of Dr. Messick's Paper and Blommers' and Cahen's Comments

GLASS: I would like to offer a statement and have you examine it. The statement is: "There is no evidence for an interaction of curriculum treatments and personological variables." I don't know of another statement that has been confirmed so many times by so many people.

A graduate student and I went through many issues of several journals and selected reports of a few hundred experimental studies that used a factorial design consisting of learning treatments crossed with personological variables (Bracht and Glass, in press). We looked specifically for disordinal interactions and found four whose nature may reveal something about what such interactions might be.

The nature of these four or five interactions was that the personological variables and the treatment variables were very narrowly and specifically defined. They were situationally defined. In one study (Kress and Gropper, 1966) programmed instructional training was presented on a television screen to everyone studying in the room. The presentation was in one of two tempos, fast or slow. It had been determined before this instructional period whether a person characteristically worked fast or slowly on programmed instruction, and it was found that matching the tempo on the screen to characteristic work tempo yielded optimal achievement.

Another study showed that initial dispositions, either toward or against an attitude, interacted with attitude change depending on whether the arguments were two-sided or one-sided. You see, these are almost situationally defined treatment variables and personological variables.

This leads me to believe that, if these interactions exist, they exist with respect to very narrow and specific variables, not to the general, factorially complete IQ's and abilities that we typically measure.

In advancing clearer, more detailed definitions of the personological variables, one must break down a lot of human characteristics and traits into very small, narrow variables. I think that is the way to find the interactions necessary to individualize instruction. But there is another side of it, and that side is the treatment variables. As long as they remain complex and broadly defined, it will be difficult to find disordinal interactions of treatment and personological variables.

If at Time 1, one element of the curriculum precedes a flexible person's learning, at Time 2 another element of the curriculum may work against facilitations of his learning. The net effect is to average out the facilitation and the inhibition over the course of instruction, showing no interaction. So, I just don't think we will find disordinal interactions of personological variables with important or realistic treatments.

MESSICK: First of all, if the treatment is really complex so that multiple approaches are included within it, that may certainly be the case. However, there are also treatments adopting more uniform and monolithic approaches throughout, and these are not just limited to brief or circumscribed units of instruction. I'm thinking here of those aspects of educational treatment associated with teaching mode or style.

Consider the use of a directed mode of approach, where emphasis is primarily on the development of comprehension in certain areas (or what Guilford refers to as cognition). The typical procedure here is to present in a straightforward and direct fashion the relevant information and rules that we wish the student to learn. We want to see whether the child can cognize a rule and apply it to appropriate circumstances.

Consider an example that Getzels has used in making a somewhat different point—the problem of finding the area of a rectangle. In the direct approach, the emphasis is upon having the child cognize the principle, so you tell him the rule: "Take the length of the rectangle and multiply it by its height. Now, here are a bunch of rectangles. The height is three inches; the length is four inches; what is the area?"

Next, you are usually concerned with whether the student can retrieve this information, so in a couple of weeks you may ask him the same question again and see whether he can still solve the problem. You might use this general procedure for teaching children all kinds of rules consistently throughout a whole curriculum or sequence. If that kind of consistency occurs, it may have the effect of fostering a particular mode of thinking, one that relies heavily upon the retrieval of previously learned forms, while certain other modes of thinking, such as those involved in creativity and problem solving, may not be simultaneously nurtured—indeed, they may be systematically prevented from flowering. Some children, possibly because of differential experience with varied teaching methods or because of differences in the ability, personality, and cognitive propensities they bring into the situation, might be more constrained than others by this predominant emphasis upon knowledge and memory. They might be better served by a more inductive or inferential approach.

In such an approach, we might proceed by saying, "We are now interested in the area of rectangles, in how much territory is enclosed within the boundaries. Here are a bunch of rectangles, with a number printed on each representing its area in square inches. Let us now see if we can formulate a rule that will enable us to calculate these areas." The students will then measure different properties of the rectangles, trying to induce a rule for finding the area. If successful, they will not only learn the rule but also some general principles about finding such a rule.

If such an inductive approach is used consistently, certain other modes of thinking ought to be fostered, namely those called "convergent" by Guilford, but perhaps at the expense of still other modes of thought, such as divergent thinking and critical thinking. These latter modes, of course, might in turn be stimulated by still other teaching approaches. For example, for divergent thinking we might ask, "How many different questions can we formulate about rectangles?" Under this mode of teaching, if it is consistently applied, children will not only learn how to find the area of rectangles, but also how to stumble upon such notions as, "Is there possibly some proportion of rectangles' height to width that people find more pleasing than other proportions?" The main point of all this is that certain modes or styles of teaching, if consistently applied over an extended time period in the manner I have described, may have a direct influence in fostering certain modes or styles of thinking; and this influence may be differential as a function of the ability and personality characteristics of the students. This differential impact might very well not be revealed, however, in the form of an interaction between teaching mode as treatment and ability or personality characteristics of the students, if the criterion scores employed are gains in subject-matter knowledge. Such interactions may not become apparent until we assess changes in characteristic modes of thinking, more generally, including not only those dimensions that might be directly fostered by the treatment but also those that might be systematically hindered.

An associated point is that in order to capitalize upon the differential impact of instructional treatments, or the apparent lack of it, we may have to broaden our base of measurement even further—beyond the assessment of subject-matter achievement and dimensions of thinking and intellect— to include an array of motivational, behavioral, and situational variables that may help us understand the dynamics of response to educational treatments. This is primarily because of the possible operation of compensating variables that effect trade-off, which produce similar achievement levels for different reasons, thereby obscuring interaction effects. For example, from what we know about the inductive or inferential method of teaching, the analytical and reflective child should find it quite congenial, whereas the more global and impulsive child should have more difficulty learning in this mode. Yet achievement measures may not reveal these differences, because the global child may expend more energy, concentrate more intensely, do more homework, spend more time, seek more help, and so forth. I don't think I have answered your question fully, though.

GLASS: That's true.

MESSICK: Let me try a somewhat different tack. You have emphasized the importance of disordinal interactions for demonstrating differential treatment effects that have educational implications. I don't think we should limit our attention, however, to those interactions where the lines cross in considering the possibility of differential programs. Take as an example a new curriculum, say in social studies, in which everybody does a little better than in the traditional curriculum and some people, say analytic and reflective types, really soar. There is no crossover interaction in relating performance in the two curricula to characteristics of the person, and until we do more work to develop other materials and methods, the new curriculum should be applied to everyone. But one implication of this result is that we should seriously consider doing more work: if we developed ten or a hundred new curricula in social studies and assigned individuals appropriately, maybe everyone would soar.

With respect to specific personality variables that might interact with treatment components, the possibilities are enormous, but there are some clues from the experimental literature. Consider, for example, variables of test anxiety, or of evaluative anxiety more generally. The performance of highly anxious individuals tends to be debilitated under evaluative or otherwise threatening circumstances, whereas the performance of subjects low in anxiety may even be facilitated under such conditions. Programs differing in degree of evaluative stress should thus have differential effects as a function of the characteristic level of anxiety of the student.

There are of course several other possibilities, which admittedly have not been tested experimentally. My general point, however, is that if in reviewing the literature you find 200 examples showing no interactions and only 4 showing interactions, what does that mean? Does it mean that by and large we can ignore consistent individual differences in the educational enterprise? Does it mean that for every educational objective we can hope someday to specify the optimal conditions for learning that would hold for everyone? Or does it mean that we haven't investigated the right variable, or enough variables in the right combinations, with sufficiently powerful methodologies to uncover the educational sources of the great variety of performance dimensions we observe in everyday adult functioning? It seems to me that you are attempting to tally up the score when we haven't yet learned how to play the game.

GLASS: But the evidence is getting awfully unconvincing. I find your illustration about finding the area of a rectangle unconvincing, too. I don't know of a curriculum where, for five minutes a day over six weeks, people find areas of rectangles. Your example is not realistic.

MESSICK: Let me try a somewhat different approach. My point is not only that we should look at interactions of selected measures in assessing treatment effects but that we should look at a broader range of personological and background variables, partly to describe the context of the findings and to monitor possible side effects and partly to be able to investigate the moderating influence of *combinations* of variables. Consider, for example, the possibility of a relationship between family press (or pressure toward achievement) and ultimate school performance. The notion here is that if parents exert pressure in the family situation in the direction of achievement, if they are interested in the child's activities, if they constantly stimulate the child to go on for further education, and if they frequently express concern about his educational performance, then there ought to be an effect upon achievement. If you were to compute a correlation between measures of family press and school achievement, however, it might very well turn out to be zero.

On the other hand, if you were to take into account some other variables, such as socioeconomic status and intelligence, you might find that the impact of family pressure was quite different in the four groups generated by middle class versus lower class and bright versus dull dichotomies. It seems very reasonable, for example, that parental pressure for further achievement on a low-ability child may have quite different results from the same amount of pressure exerted on a high-ability child. And this difference in turn may be a function of the availability of environmental resources. We might find a higher correlation, for instance, between achievement and family press in middle-class homes than in lower-class homes. Middle-class children may not only have more resources to bring to bear than lower-class children, but they may also be able to manipulate them better for their own ends. Parental pressure might thus have a quite different meaning in lower-class homes where the children have very likely not had much opportunity to learn that their environment can indeed be contravened and that a person can have a positive influence on his own destiny. Parental pressure on less bright children or on bright children in lower-class circumstances might result in frustration and feelings of anxiety and futility, thereby possibly decreasing rather than increasing school performance.

Taking into account such variables produces different answers.

GLASS: Does that really make your point? I am not sure. I don't think it said, "Put pressure on some and not on others." It said, "Don't put it on any." We are talking about differential effects (truly disordinal interactions), and this isn't one.

MESSICK: Prescriptive statements aside, it says that if parents put pressure on their children the resulting effect upon achievement will differ as a function of the socioeconomic level of the home and the intelligence level of the child.

GAGNÉ: Two suggestions that have been made along the way, not entirely unrelated to what we are talking about, have the tendency to distract people. I am concerned with keeping people's aim in the right direction.

I am an advocate of what might be called the butter wrapping model in evaluation. I think the main thing that one wants to know, if he has taught somebody to wrap butter, is how many pounds of butter he can wrap. And if one applies this to mathematics, then I want to know whether he can solve a particular kind of mathematics problem.

The two kinds of suggestions that have come up that I feel may tend to get people off this track are, one, that we really ought to be measuring cognitive styles as dependent variables and, two, a question about values.

Now, if I have a butter wrapper or a set of butter wrappers, it is quite true that they may be using a number of different styles. One may use his right thumb and the other use his left thumb. But, as a matter of fact, I'm really concerned about how many pounds of butter they can wrap, because that's my aim and my goal.

Now there's nothing wrong, of course, with asking about interactions or with asking about the effects of cognitives styles as intervening variables. As Sam pointed out, we really know very little about how these might interact with the variables of instruction to produce better butter wrappers.

But I still insist that what we want is better butter wrappers.

SKAGER: What if we have two ways of teaching how to wrap butter, and we want to decide which to use?

GAGNÉ: That's a legitimate question.

Another thing that comes up is the question of value. Suppose we are talking about mathematics. I can see that it may conceivably be a matter of decision as to whether one thinks the major purpose of a course or a curriculum in mathematics is to produce people who can solve algebraic equations rapidly or who can reinstate the logic that goes into the making of equivalent statements; but either of these things can be measured; either of these things can be an outcome. So I don't see that this is a value judgment, unless the evaluator tries to make this judgment himself. I realize that he may have to get some agreement on it by people who have control over the curriculum, but they can make the choice. It is not a value.

Value comes in only when you have two alternative curricula in mathematics with two alternative sets of objectives. Which are you going to choose? That is a matter of value, and we haven't talked about that very much. I don't think the evaluator is capable of making that decision. I don't think even the curriculum designer is capable of making that decision.

I believe these other things distract us from the major point, which is, how do we measure human performance?

MESSICK: Suppose we find that one very efficient butter wrapper has gained his speed and efficiency because he has one little stylistic quirk, namely wetting his thumb with his tongue as he picks up the waxed paper. You might not be too happy with that style of butter wrapping even though he wraps more butter than anyone else. It seems to me that you have to take into account such factors of style and process in order to evaluate the desirability of the outcome.

I also think it would be a little presumptuous of an evaluator, or even of a curriculum maker, to limit attention to a specific set of intended outcomes. The problem is to find out what the student has learned and not just to find out whether he learned what you thought you were teaching him. Focusing on the level of specific performance may thus be getting us off a very important track. We should be concerned not only about producing a large set of specific outcomes, such as skill in solving linear equations but also about preparing the child for effective adult role functioning. And in this case the whole is not just the array of the parts—it matters how the parts are organized and structured. When a student learns something specific, he often also learns something general at the same time, so the learning of a specific element or skill frequently has consequences for other parts of the learning system.

GAGNÉ: I have no disagreement at all. If you want to measure how well someone functions as an adult, that's fine; but I don't see what that has to do with measuring intervening variables.

MESSICK: In teaching him how to solve mathematical equations, you may also incidentally teach him some basic theory about mathematical relations, and . . .

GAGNÉ: That's a different subject. Now you are talking about studying intervening variables. There is nothing wrong with that. That isn't measuring; that is research. It is not evaluation.

MESSICK: That is a point that has been coming through to me over and over again at this conference, and I'm not sure I agree with it—that there is a separate discipline called "evaluation" and a new professional role called "the evaluator." I had always thought that the evaluation of educational programs was an activity engaged in by educational specialists, psychologists, and other behavioral scientists using the methodologies of empirical social science research.

I had thought that there would always be at least some concern in evaluation studies about the source of obtained effects, as well as their size, and about the generalizability of the findings—to other types of students, other time periods, and other settings, if not to other materials embodying similar principles. In this view, indeed, evaluation *is* research.

One final point about cognitive styles is that if we look at the level of adult functioning, we notice some striking consistencies, particularly in the relationships between personality characteristics and occupational preferences. People in similar occupations tend to exhibit analogous patterns of personality and interest, while people in highly dissimilar occupations display quite different personality and interest profiles. If such consistencies appear at the level of adult-role functioning, I suggest that similar consistencies may underlie the differential acquisition of the facilities required for adult-role functioning.

LORTIE: Have you looked at the cognitive style models of teachers?

MESSICK: No, that is one of the things that should be done.

LORTIE: I should think it would be the first occupation you deal with in terms of what you are talking about. Their capacity to teach alternative styles may be quite high.

GAGE: My comment is very pertinent, I think, to Dan's argument. We do have a study under way at our Center on the cognitive preferences of mathematics teachers and of their students for three styles of presenting mathematical ideas: graphic, verbal, and symbolic. Bob Heath and Kenneth Travers are going to be finding out, we hope, whether teachers and students who have the same preferences get along better and whether pupils learn more when styles of that kind are taken into account.

GLASER: In my own thinking, there is a big moderator variable in all this. I think these styles are task specific, revolving around the learning of mathematics, the learning of biology, the learning of art, and the learning of music, for example. In some sense that is why my preference always is to study subject matter learning and then to pull in these kinds of variables in that context.

It seems to me that styles are shaped almost in the way that Thorstein Veblen says: because you are a psychologist or sociologist or economist, you develop certain styles. I guess he calls them "trained inadequacies." So style is shaped in one sense by the kinds of processes you have to use to operate as a scientist or an artist.

Now, overlaid upon these are the kinds of styles you are talking about, but they are very task specific. I may be a convergent thinker when I operate in mathematics; I may be a divergent thinker when I operate in another realm of my life. Insofar as affective variables are concerned, I may be highly anxious in one sort of task but not in another. The whole thing gets narrowed down if you relate these to subject matters or task-specific enterprises.

MESSICK: That is likely to be quite a fruitful approach and would tell us much about the range of differentiation in personality functioning, but I would not discount the possibility of generality as well, for some cognitive preferences and habits almost assume the proportions of a life style. Each of us could probably give examples of this from his own experience, such as the scientist who tends to be a scientist in his stylistic approaches to all other aspects of living, whether watching a play or buying a new car or choosing a wife. Such stylistic single-mindedness does not have to be, and probably would not be, if there were more variety and divergence in learning experiences during the formative years.

GLASER: I would like to study subject matter learning and impose these variables on it, rather than study them in general. I would like to generate these cognitive styles from subject matter learning or investigate them relative to task or performance learning.

MESSICK: I hope you can bring it about.

BLOOM: It seems to me that we are always talking about the elementary and the secondary school, where we may have 100 percent of the students in attendance, and where the students are not really given much choice.

If you look at the work of Pace, and of Pace and Stern, you begin to find that there are ecological differences. When we look at needs versus the environment, some schools seem to get a large number of students of a particular type while other schools get a large number of another type. Both may be equal in SAT. One begins to see the kinds of instructional procedures that some of these students do not like. For example, some students prefer the lecture and have great difficulty with discussion; other students reject the lecture, which results in various kinds of interaction.

I think we may find these personological characteristics far more important where the student has a choice as to institution and kind of instructional treatment, including the particular kinds of subjects that he will choose and reject.

MCDONALD: The problem with what Sam is advocating is that he is leading us into a trap as far as research strategy is concerned. There probably are interactions, and I don't think there is much point in arguing with his response styles, but there is no theory of interaction. When you talk about that triangle or that parallelogram, you can't tell me what cognitive styles might interact with certain kinds of instructional treatments.

If that is true, then the only alternative left is to go again and again and again from one cognitive style to another in the hope that you will find one that will interact. Until there are some rules for relating type of task and type of style, you can't begin to develop a theory of interaction.

MESSICK: I would say that there is a theory of interaction or, rather, there are several developing theories of interaction. Some of them are theories of personality; some are theories of the structure of intellect which can be used to make statements about which kinds of cognitive styles and cognitive aptitudes would interact with certain kinds of teaching methods. You can take Guilford's structure of intellect for example, particularly the operational facet, and develop from it a parallel structure for modes of teaching.

MCDONALD: I agree with you. But you say you are analogizing, and that ain't extrapolating.

MESSICK: Analogizing is one way of developing a theory. I am making a plea that we develop something akin to the sociology of knowledge, only it's the psychology of knowledge. What a person knows and what he cares to know is an indication of what kind of person he is. We ought to take that into account.

TROW: I would like to ask a question. Do the kinds of things you want to study about people bear some relation to the kinds of people you want them to be? I suppose I am really struck here by the assumption that there are certain goals of education quite independent of evaluation; that somebody, "they," make these goals, and then you see the extent to which they are achieved by some mechanisms.

It seems to me these goals are fairly nebulous at present, more than at other times. A great many of the arguments I hear are arguments over what education should be rather than what teaching should be.

MESSICK: Nonetheless there are some overriding values determined by other segments of society, such as the family and the community, that guide and control the formal educational enterprise.

REFERENCES

Bracht, G. H., & Glass, G. V. The external validity of experiments. *American Educational Research Journal*, 1968, *5*, 437–474.

Kress, G. C., & Gropper, G. L. The comparison of two strategies for individualizing fixed-pace programmed instruction. *American Educational Research Journal*, 1966, *3*, 273–280.

CHAPTER 7

Evaluating the Cost-Effectiveness of Instructional Programs

MARVIN C. ALKIN

COST-BENEFIT VERSUS COST-EFFECTIVENESS EVALUATION

What is cost-benefit analysis? What are some of the difficulties encountered in applying the technique to the kind of decision situation that concerns most educators at the individual school or district level? Finally, what kind of evaluation technique might be used instead of cost-benefit analysis for evaluating educational systems?

Techniques such as cost-benefit analysis are designed primarily as aids in making prescriptive decision statements. Consequently, those interested in using such procedures are concerned with providing data about real world situations that will allow decision-makers to act. In this kind of analysis, therefore, we attempt to find the value of alternative courses of action not only in terms of the outcome dimensions or outputs of the treatment but also in terms of the financial costs that are associated with each alternative. Most educators, it seems, have much less difficulty accepting benefits or outcome measures as an indication of value than they do in accepting costs. Despite the educators' disdain for them, costs are also of considerable importance. The only time an individual can safely disregard cost is when he finds himself in the happy situation of having unlimited resources—not only in terms of material goods and services but also in terms of time and energy. To be in a situation in which costs can be disregarded is certainly not the reality of today.

The idea of cost-benefit analysis is deceptively simple. It requires only that we identify the costs and benefits associated with our alternatives. Once

221

we ascertain the costs and benefits of alternatives, we can easily select the alternative that yields the largest benefits for a given cost, or we can select the alternative that will yield the least cost for a given level of benefits. The often-stated idea that cost-benefit analysis attempts to maximize gains or benefits while minimizing costs is not true; however, if it were true, the task would be impossible. It is analogous to asking a geographer to find the deepest lake at the highest elevation. No matter which lake he selected, there would always be a slightly shallower lake at a slightly higher elevation; eventually, he might find himself beside a drop of water on the summit of Mount Everest. However, if we restate this task by limiting either the depth of the lake or the elevation, then the problem can be solved. The same logic applies to cost-benefit analysis. It is impossible to choose a policy that simultaneously maximizes benefits and minimizes costs. There is no such policy. If we compare policies A and B, we might find that occasionally A yields greater benefit yet costs less than B. In this case we might say that A dominates B. A, however, does not minimize cost while maximizing benefits. Maximum benefits are infinitely large, and minimum cost is zero. If we seek a policy that has this outcome, we obviously shall not find it.

In order to use cost-benefit analysis in a fruitful way, we must be able to specify all costs and benefits—our decision criteria. In addition, we must specify those which are variable and those costs or benefits which are limited or constrained. At the very least, limits must be set on the variability that will be allowed to each (costs and benefits) and on the acceptable trade-offs between gains on one dimension and losses on another.

Cost-benefit is primarily an economic analysis. In other words, the method of cost-benefit analysis is a tool of the economist developed primarily to examine economic entities. *One of the main requirements of cost-benefit analysis is that both input and output measures be specified in the same units, namely dollars.* This concept is important if one is to make judgments about specific programs. Thus, in the private sector of the economy, a specific business firm might decide to increase its capitalization in order to expand one of its programs that has a favorable cost-benefit ratio; that is, it is likely to yield a monetary profit.

Applications of cost-benefit analysis in the public sector of the economy primarily have been made in the areas of water resource development and national defense. In each instance the technique demands a specification of the multiple outcome dimensions in terms of dollar benefits. As a result, while the major direct benefit of the construction of a hydroelectric project might be the dollar value of the electrical energy that has been produced, there are indirect benefits—such as relief from losses of home, property, farm crops, and so forth—from potential flooding. Somewhat more intangible benefits, such as the physical and mental well-being of individuals relieved of the fear of floods, are also assigned dollar values (McKean, 1958).

Traditional applications of cost-benefit analyses in education have been primarily at very large levels of educational aggregation, for example, states, regions, nations. This situation is easily understandable, for it is primarily at such levels that data are more readily available on dollar values of educational outcomes. Thus, Becker (1962) focused his attention on the social gain from college education as measured by its effects on national productivity and concluded, among other things, that "private rates of return on college education exceed those on business capital" (Becker, 1962). In another study (Hansen, 1963), the internal money rates of return were calculated for successive stages of education where returns were estimated from cross-section data of the incomes of individuals classified by age and education. Finally, in 1966, Hirsch and Marcus examined the costs and benefits of universal junior-college education as compared to alternative uses of the same financial resources for summer programs in secondary schools.

What is evident in the limited number of examples above is that, in each case, the outcome dimensions have been transformed into dollar benefits utilizing traditional economic indices. But, because school district boundaries are very often not coterminous with other governmental entities, economic indices are not available at the level of individual schools or school districts. Yet, even if economic indices were available, cost-benefit analysis might still prove inappropriate by virtue of the mobility of student populations in school districts, complicated by other difficulties related to identifying long-range economic benefits for educational units as small as individual schools. Moreover, cost-benefit analysis may not address itself to the most relevant question for the kind of unit about which we are concerned. In short, we are concerned not so much with the economic consequences of certain investment decisions in education as with evaluating the system components in terms of the objective dimensions defined.

Unlike cost-benefit analysis, which poses no direct challenge to the general decision-making machinery of the political system, we wish to examine a real-world decision situation in which not all outcomes are definable in economic terms.

In summary, when cost-effectiveness is referred to in the context of this paper, it should bring to mind a model that will enable us to consider relevant elements of educational systems at school or district levels of aggregation in order to (a) compare educational outcomes of different units, (b) assess impact of alternative levels of financial input, and (c) select alternative approaches to the achievement of specified educational outcomes.

COMPONENTS OF A COST-EFFECTIVENESS MODEL

What are the components of a model that allows the decision-maker to evaluate education through a cost-effectiveness evaluation? First, it is necessary to define what we mean by a model.

To put it briefly, a model is simply an attempt at classifying the major elements of an entity or a phenomenon with regard to their functions and interrelationships in order to observe more easily how the elements function within the entity, how they enable the entity to operate, and how they act upon one another. In this way, we can also determine the consequences of modifying the elements. Most models reflect the bias and interests of their developers. This one is no exception; our prime interest is a consideration of administrative and financial variables in education, specifically where a single school or a school district is the unit of analysis. To be sure, an evaluation model, or for that matter any model, is a simplistic statement or representation of sets of complex interrelationships; but such a representation is intended only to help the model builder to structure the universe which concerns him.

What elements comprise our model of evaluation? "Student inputs" are an aspect of our evaluation model. The term refers to the nature and characteristics of the students entering the program to be evaluated. "Educational outputs" are another aspect of the model. By "educational outputs" we mean two things: (a) cognitive and noncognitive changes that take place in students after they are exposed to the instructional program and (b) the impact of the program upon systems external to it (home, community, other programs, and so forth). A third component of the evaluation model is "financial inputs," which refer to the financial resources made available for carrying on the program. "Manipulatable characteristics," a fourth element of the model, are the descriptive characteristics (for example, personnel, school organization and programs, and instructional program) of the way in which financial inputs are utilized within the program in combination with the student inputs. Finally, our evaluation model must consider "external systems," an aspect which is the framework of social, political, legal, economic, and other systems outside the school, formal or informal, which encompass the program, have impact upon it, and are, in turn, modified by the outputs of the program.

In the discussion of manipulatable characteristics, we act under the assumption that they are the only administratively manipulatable set of variables. For the sake of this model, we will assume that (a) external systems are not immediately altered by the outputs of the system and (b) that the school decision-makers have no control over which external systems are allowed to impinge upon the school. If we were to maintain that feedback immediately changes the system, this would imply a dynamic model rather than the static model considered here. The second assumption implies that no attempt will be made to change the nature of the student inputs to the system; that is, we do not usually concern ourselves with the consideration of possible changes in the community that would alter the nature of the student inputs. We act, too, under the assumption that student inputs are relatively nonmanipulatable from outside the system. Thus, we concern ourselves with the manipulatable variables within the system that can be manipulated and altered to maximize student outputs. We recognize that there is a weakness in this assumption and that there are some school-related manipulations that could be instituted which would change the nature of the student input. Instances of this are busing, changing of school boundaries in order to "juggle" student inputs to specific schools, community educational resources (such as educational resource units in disadvantaged areas), and preschool programs (such as Project Headstart). The assumptions of a static model and of nonmanipulatable external systems seem necessary at this early stage of the model development.

With our definition of evaluation and some of the limits we are imposing in mind, it is now possible to discuss the evaluation model.

Student Inputs

We will consider the student input as a description or measure of the student being introduced into the system or, in the case of a larger unit of instructional program, as an aggregated, statistical description of the students being introduced into the system. (See Figure 1.) In the ideal world, when students enter the system, they are given a complete battery of all the traditional kinds of achievement, intelligence, and personality tests, as well as questionnaires and other documentary data describing their homes, status in the community, family background, family memberships in other social systems, and the like. Unfortunately, the ideal world does not exist. We must, therefore, develop a series of proxy measures of student inputs. Very frequently, intelligence scores are available for entering students; also, there is usually a small amount of family data available in the cumulative record folder. Occasionally, achievement tests given in the

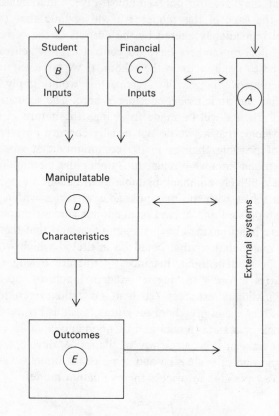

FIGURE 1 *Cost-effectiveness model.*

preceding year or two have been transferred and are available as a measure of the achievement starting-point of the students in the system. A considerable amount of additionally desired data must, consequently, either be collected in the school or, more often, inferred from other more accessible measures. As a result, we often look at the community and the characteristics of the community as an indication of the kind of student input that is being introduced into the system.

Financial Inputs

There is a second class of inputs to the system—financial inputs. If we think of a district as a system, then not only do students enter the system, but finances are provided from local, state, and federal sources and are, in part, a means of implementing different sets of mediating factors within the system. Perhaps it is relevant to determine the portion of the total resources derived from each of the governmental levels. Perhaps it is also important to designate the specific authorizations from federal funds or special state programs to be aware of the "strings attached" and consequent implications for resource utilization within the system.

If we were concerned with evaluating a part of the system, such as the mathematics program or the guidance program, it would be necessary to determine the nature and amount of the financial input to that portion of the system. Unfortunately, present accounting practices in all states provide data only on functions of expenditures rather than on programs of expenditures; that is, data are available on a number of factors such as the amount spent for administration, maintenance, operation, instruction, and fixed charges; but these data are not available on a program basis. Thus, the desire to include financial input data in evaluation studies would require special budget review or new accounting procedures, depending upon the level of aggregation under consideration.

External Systems

The school is placed within the framework of numerous social systems (external social contexts). For example, in the case of the individual school some of the contexts are the community, the district, the nature of the district organization, other governmental systems such as the city and the county, and the patterns of community organizations and of community participation. Each of these external systems, by the nature of the differentiated functions it serves, places sets of demands and restrictions both upon the educational system (school) and upon the individuals within the system. Each of these systems serves specific integrative, adaptive, goal-attaining, and pattern-maintaining functions in the macro-system. Consequently, it is necessary to identify and quantify these external systems' characteristics and relationships that are relevant in terms of the contribution they make towards producing the educational outputs of the system.

In actuality, the external systems interact with the educational system. While each of them may be conceived of as having its own inputs, particular sets of mediating variables, and outputs, each is, in turn, an external system to the educational system and *vice versa*. Thus, each system external to education may be considered as both a source of inputs and a receiver of outputs.

Manipulatable Characteristics

A fourth group of elements of the evaluation model is termed manipulatable characteristics. The financial input to a system can be utilized in a great number of ways. We can decrease the student-to-teacher ratio, establish standards that insure the hiring of teachers with specified characteristics, develop different administrative arrangements within the school, provide more library books, provide more textbooks, introduce different curricula, use different instructional procedures, or provide additional supplies. Thus, these manipulatable characteristics are subject to change or manipulation by educational decision-makers at all levels. We have no definitive evidence, however, indicating which combination of these characteristics is most effective in achieving the objectives of the school—that is, in producing desired educational outputs.

At this point, it is only fair to indicate that we do not mean to imply that all these characteristics that have impact on educational outputs are related to financial input. For example, the cost of implementing certain alterations in the school environment or in the attitudes of teachers may be relatively cost free. Frequently, the instructional procedure used by the teacher in the classroom (the substitution of one procedure for another) has little or no additional cost attached to it. However, some changes in the system such as some of the administrative or organizational arrangements and many instructional procedures that are technologically based are extremely costly. Consequently, the potential output achieved by the change must be examined in terms of the costs involved.

To maintain that more money should be provided for teacher salaries and that in this way, in all likelihood, the educational program will be improved is an easily defensible position. There is evidence that a relationship exists between higher teacher salaries and educational quality. The real question, however, is to what extent a given dollar input, if utilized in an alternate manner, would increase certain educational outputs. This is a cost-effectiveness question and is, after all, one of the elements at the heart of evaluation or, at the very least, one of the reasons why we evaluate.

We have noted that the selection of different sets of mediating factors may lead to the maximization of educational outputs in a system. There is, though, another point to be made: not only are there different sets of manipulatable characteristics applicable for producing given educational outputs; but, significantly, these sets of variables may produce quite different levels of change in the educational ouputs in different systems or for different student input groups. James Coleman observed this point in a study for the Civil Rights Commission entitled *Equality of Educational*

Opportunity. He noted that the "inference might then be made that improving the school of a minority pupil may increase his achievement more than would improving the school of a white child increase his." Similarly, the average minority pupil's achievement may suffer more in a school of low quality than might the average white pupil's. He concluded that "this indicates that it is for the most disadvantaged children that improvements in school quality will make the most difference in achievement" (Coleman, 1966). Appropriate manipulatable characteristics, therefore, are functions not only of the desired educational outputs but of the nature of the student inputs and of the given system as well.

As mentioned earlier, we believe these characteristics to be the only set of variables that can be manipulated. This belief is a simplifying assumption, accepted in part, because it allows us to deal with a static, instead of a more complex dynamic model. Also, the bias implied by this assumption follows from the basic intent of the model we are seeking to construct, which is a decision-making model or, more specifically, a model designed to aid in evaluating schools and the operations of schools.

Outcomes

The first set of outcomes of concern to us in the model is student outcomes that are affected by changes that take place in students from the time they enter the system to the time they leave it. Many of these changes are produced by the nature of the costly manipulatable factors within the system. Here, again, there is a problem, for the outcomes of a school or of a district cannot be measured solely by the scores of students on academic achievement tests.[1] What are the noncognitive aspects of outcome or output? How has the behavior of students changed? What is the relationship between the activities that take place in a district or a school and the eventual success of students in their vocational or future educational endeavors? How does the student's educational experience aid him in dealing with political problems and activities and with cultural affairs? To what extent does the school's social situation, as well as what is learned in classes, affect the student? These are only some of the unanswered questions related to the identification of educational outcomes; and, of course, they can be solved only through further research and investigation.

While there are two prime inputs into the system (student and nonstudent or financial), we will consider that there are no financial outcomes except as we are willing to place financial value on certain behavioral changes or

---

[1] We would readily admit, however, to the chagrin of many reluctant school administrators, that this measure at least would be a feasible starting point.

except as student outcomes yield financial or economic returns, either individual or social.[2]

The second set of outcomes in the model is the nonstudent outputs. The two groups of outcome measures (student and nonstudent) may be thought of as feedback loops in which each modifies, to some extent, the nature of future inputs to the system. The changes in students, for example, have social, political, and economic implications; that is, the very nature of the external systems is altered by changes in student outputs. There are, however, other outcomes of the school (e.g. the impact of educational decisions made as a part of the "manipulatable characteristics" has repercussions in the external systems). Frequently, these outputs are only tangentially related to individual students or to student outputs. For example, the nature of many of the decisions about the proper utilization of resources may produce innumerable educational outcomes not directly student-related. In brief, decisions which influence the number and salaries of teachers, as well as the number and salaries of classified personnel, could, in many ways, modify the nature of some external systems, especially if these employees were to reside in the district. To what extent do teachers paid at different salary levels have the economic ability to forego other earnings and instead participate in community activities and organizations? Furthermore, how is the nature of these external systems modified by the educational decision that determined the particular combination of manipulatable characteristics that allowed greater salaries for the teachers? Also, how do the type and quality of teachers selected affect the changing nature of the community? Another example might be the impact upon the economy of the community brought about by the selection of manipulatable characteristics that include large capital investment or a large amount of supplies and materials locally purchased. How do the educational decisions related to whether school transportation will be provided or the hours of school or the scheduling of student time, in terms not only of regular session classes but with respect to recreational and summer use of school facilities, have implications for parental employment patterns or avocational participation? And, to what extent does the school, as a merchant of facts, knowledge, and ideas, influence community attitudes on political, social, and cultural issues? Finally, although the list could be extended greatly, how does the impact of the selection of manipulatable characteristics upon the social patterns

---

[2] There is evidence that this is a reasonable approach. See Becker; also Miller, "Income and Higher Education: Does Education Pay Off?" S. J. Mushkin (Ed.), *Economics of Higher Education* (Washington, D.C.: U.S. Department of Health, Education, and Welfare, Office of Education, 1962); and Schultz, "Investment in Human Capital," *American Economic Review*, LI (March, 1961), 1–16.

within the school relate to breaking down or reinforcing patterns within the systems external to the school?

We realize that it is not possible to isolate every conceivable element of the total system and to determine its value or its individual, contributory relationship to the educational outputs of the system. Nevertheless, it is requisite in any evaluation scheme to identify and control as many as possible of the factors thought to be significant; for the more we can isolate these factors, the more accurate our analysis can be.

Our next step must be an analysis of how our model might be used in different kinds of evaluation situations.

POTENTIAL APPLICATIONS OF THE COST-EFFECTIVENESS MODEL

As we have already noted, traditional cost-benefit approaches do not provide the necessary data or meet the educational needs to which we have addressed ourselves. In this section, therefore, the cost-effectiveness analysis model we propose is clarified, and its uses in different evaluation situations are described. For purposes of this paper, "program" pertains to a package that encompasses all the agency's efforts to achieve a particular objective or set of allied objectives. In educational terms, programs are defined as secondary education, junior-college education, and so forth. However, it is difficult to assemble and describe a package that would encompass all the efforts to achieve a subobjective like teaching elementary-school children to read; that is, it would be extremely difficult to consider the cost elements and program elements of all aspects of the total school program related to the reading achievement of children.

Thus, "program alternatives" are differing possible approaches towards achieving the same or similar objectives. In education, public schools, and private schools might be program alternatives; if different schools are assumed to be working towards the same objectives, in whole or in part, then the total programs of these schools also may be considered as program alternatives. Different schools have different program alternatives. Consequently, one might evaluate the success of different program alternatives in achieving the specified objectives of the programs. Since there is varying quality in student inputs to programs, one would, of course, expect that the outputs would vary; and in order to evaluate the program alternatives, one must somehow be able to control for differences in student input and external systems.

This notion of alternative programs can be extended. If programs are similar in their uncontrollable characteristics (student inputs and external systems) but different in the levels of financial input, they may be thought of as alternative programs for achieving the same or similar objectives. By taking the "black-box" approach to the problem, one could evaluate the cost-effectiveness of alternative programs where alternative programs are defined as differences in financial inputs to the system, without regard for the manner in which these inputs are utilized.

Consider this evaluation in terms of the model described in Figure 1, where variable set A refers to the external system, variable set B refers to the student inputs, variable set C refers to the financial inputs, variable set D refers to the costly manipulatable characteristics, and variable set E refers to the outcomes. Using this simple diagram and the variable sets as numbered, note that alternative instructional programs (school financial resources) can be evaluated in terms of cost-effectiveness, using variable sets A and B as controls with variable set C financial inputs as the predictor variable set, and variable set E as the criterion (see Figure 2). A question emerges from the model: When student inputs and external systems are held constant statistically, what is the outcome change (on each of a number of dimensions) associated with a dollar increase in financial input?

A second kind of cost-effectiveness evaluation might be concerned with the assessment of specific instructional programs. In this case, we would study specific total instructional programs of schools on the basis of their performance on the outcome dimensions after we have accounted for the effects of specific uncontrollable characteristics of their own system. Thus, if one merely wanted to evaluate schools as institutions, in terms of what kind of job they are doing relative to the resources (human and fiscal) available to them, the model discussed above could be invoked to perform a cost-effectiveness analysis. In short, if financial inputs are considered one of the uncontrollable variables in the system and are, therefore, contained in the model, the degree to which an individual institution achieved success

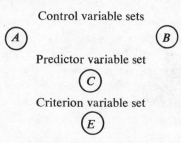

FIGURE 2 *Evaluating cost-effectiveness of alternative instructional programs—school financial resources.*

on the outcome dimensions at the level we would predict is a measure of the cost-effectiveness of the institution's total program. For example, Institution 1 with student inputs (S_1), external-systems characteristics (E_1), and financial inputs (F_1), might be predicted as achieving various criterion dimensions at stipulated levels, $C_{1,1}$, $C_{2,1}$, $C_{3,1}$ $\cdots$ $C_{i,1}$. When the institution matches or exceeds these predictions in terms of outcomes or consequences assumed to be favorable, or at least not deleterious, the institution is being run efficiently, relative to each of the specified outcome dimensions.

Thus, the second type of cost-effectiveness study that might be done is of a particular school. The evaluation of an individual school program would be in terms of the statistically derived expectations for that program in light of its own uncontrollable characteristics (see Figure 3). The cost-effectiveness scores for a school would be determined on the basis of ratios of actual to predicted achievement on each of the criterion dimensions. Therefore, a school whose actual achievement on a criterion measure exceeds its predicted achievement could be said to be cost-effective with respect to the specified criterion dimension.

We may consider the concept of "alternative ways to do a given job" borrowed from PPBS (Planning Programming Budgeting Systems) as a useful means of providing the framework for a third type of cost-effectiveness evaluation. The "given job" notion means that the output to be produced and the program have been predetermined. The question at any phase of the program becomes: Can we alter the production or distribution technique and by doing so (a) improve the timing of the production or delivery (fulfill program objectives in a shorter period of time, thereby consuming less student time), or (b) improve the quantity and quality of the items being produced (educate a greater number of students in the program or achieve a higher level of objectives or fewer undesirable consequences), or (c) modify the unit cost or total cost of the production or

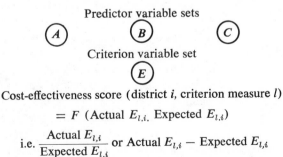

Predictor variable sets

$\textcircled{A}$ $\textcircled{B}$ $\textcircled{C}$

Criterion variable set

$\textcircled{E}$

Cost-effectiveness score (district i, criterion measure l)

$= F$ (Actual $E_{l,i}$, Expected $E_{l,i}$)

i.e. $\dfrac{\text{Actual } E_{l,i}}{\text{Expected } E_{l,i}}$ or Actual $E_{l,i} - $ Expected $E_{l,i}$

FIGURE 3 *Evaluating the cost-effectiveness of individual school programs.*

delivery (which, in education, would refer to fewer financial input dollars to achieve the same objectives)? "Alternative ways to do a given job" takes the program as given or specified and increases the possibilities for changing the mix of input utilization alternatives, thereby modifying the program. This function seems quite appropriate in terms of the problem at hand, for while the question about alternative educational programs provides some answers in terms of the cost-effectiveness of total educational systems, it fails to render insights into the attributes of the system that make a difference in the production of educational outputs.

There are, of course, vast differences from place to place in the quality of resources available for use as alternatives or options. Where the economist thinks of teachers, materials, and so forth, as inputs to the system, he refers to quality differences in inputs. In this model, which is geared to the decision-making of the educational administrator, cost factors such as teachers, textbooks, clerks, and aides are viewed as costly manipulatable characteristics of the system. Each of them represents a potential means of financial input utilization.

A major responsibility of the state is to make available to local districts input uitlization options of high enough quality to insure that the school districts may operate efficiently. States assume this responsibility in a number of ways. In part, the input utilization options are defined by the economy of a state, by alternative employment opportunities, by access to higher education, and so forth. Also, the state government defines the quality of the input utilization options by the state-established legal requirements for education and by state procedures for certifying teachers. Thus, what a financial input will buy in a school district (the purchasing power of a financial input) is determined, in part, by the state government, the geographic region, and even, perhaps, by the nature of the individual community.

We have noted that it is not possible or appropriate to maximize effectiveness while minimizing costs. In terms of the problem posed here, then, it is impossible to consider simultaneously fulfilling program objectives in a shorter period of time, modifying the unit cost of the production of educational outcomes, and providing a higher level of achievement of educational objectives. Several of these must be specified as program constraints with one specifically designated as the purpose of the cost-effectiveness analysis. A consideration of the evaluation of the cost-effectiveness of specific costly manipulatable characteristics of the system (teachers, textbooks, clerks, equipment) has been proposed. This proposal implies a concern for the maximization of outputs that utilizes the options for resource allocation within the system, the total financial input and student inputs, including time, constrained within the model. In terms of our model, this process requires the consideration of variable sets *A, B,* and *C* as control variables, individual variables *D* as predictors, and variable set *E* as criterion measures (see Figure 4).

Another question inevitably arises: When student and financial input characteristics of the external system are held constant statistically, what is the effect of each costly manipulatable characteristic of the system upon increased educational outputs? Such an evaluation requires, in addition to drawing the relationship between the costly manipulatable characteristics and the various outcome dimensions, that one examine the cost functions of the costly manipulatable characteristics.

The procedure, then, is to determine the change in output associated with each incremental unit change in each of the costly manipulatable characteristics. There are at least three major problems that one might anticipate at this stage of an analysis: (a) there would be difficulty in obtaining accurate cost data related to the manipulatable characteristics; (b) there would be difficulties in dealing with cost-effectiveness estimates in the light of systems interrelationships, and (c) there would be difficulties in generalizing to individual cases (if such generalization were desired).

With respect to the first of these problems, actual data would, of course, be preferable. However, accounting systems do not usually provide this information. In instances where actual data is not possible or feasible, costs might be derived by constructing a cost production function; for example, in the analysis of a number of cases, data might be derived relating the presence and extent of various manipulatable characteristics to some cost function, such as current expense of education. In this way, a cost curve could be derived describing the production costs related to those characteristics. Such a production function might be derived using historical or longitudinal data, as was done in a study reported by Adelson, Alkin, Carey, and Helmer (1967); or a production function might be produced using cross-sectional data (Katzman, 1967).

There is no simple solution for the second of these problems, systems interrelationships. One might seek to isolate the individual variable from

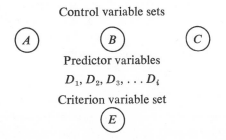

Control variable sets

A B C

Predictor variables

$D_1, D_2, D_3, \ldots D_i$

Criterion variable set

E

FIGURE 4 *Evaluating cost-effectiveness of input utilization options.*

its covariants through appropriate statistical controls. From these statistics on the interrelationships between covariants, one could then determine the expected changes in them that would be associated with an incremental unit change in a given mediating variable. Perhaps systematic use of judgment might be utilized to obtain and isolate the nature of the interrelationships. Then, starting with the statistical data, appropriate cost characteristics could be assigned to elements of the system. Moreover, procedures such as path analysis possibly could be utilized to provide greater insight into the data.

Another possible solution is the use of expert judgment, systematically obtained, for example, the Delphi Method (Gordon and Helmer, 1964; also Adelson, Alkin, Carey, and Helmer, 1967). It could be quite fruitful to assemble a group of knowledgeable, educational decision-makers representing a variety of backgrounds and interests. They could be allowed to consider the nature of the system interrelationships between variables and from these relationships form some judgment of the cost-effectiveness of each of the available manipulatable characteristics of the system. This Delphi process of summarizing findings—allowing for discussion and presentation of deviant views, feedback to participants, and several additional rounds of the same procedure—might lead to consensus or at least to an understanding of the nature of the dissenting opinions.

The third problem posed is related to the difficulties of generalizing to individual cases. One possible solution to this problem rests with the development of a typology of schools to be used as the moderator variable in the prediction of outcomes in the analysis. There are difficulties related to the use of statistics (such as regression coefficients derived from the analysis of a set of data) in predicting criterion measures (outcomes) for individual cases. The accuracy of a predicted outcome for an individual school will depend considerably on the type of school as the school varies its costly manipulatable characteristics. To put it simply, one would not expect the same effect from changing the counselor-student ratio at Beverly Hills High School as he would at a small, rural high school. There is certainly a typology of schools that will act as a moderator variable in the prediction of outcomes. The notion of grouping variables worked on by Klein, Rock, and Evans (1967) at Educational Testing Service might be quite appropriate for use in solving this problem.

Conclusion

In this paper, we drew the distinctions between cost-benefit analysis and cost-effectiveness evaluation. We showed that cost-benefit analysis relies almost exclusively on financial benefits and is, therefore, of limited value in assessing education, where many outcomes cannot be defined economically.

Moreover, we outlined the various components of a model that we believe will enable the decision-maker to perform cost-effectiveness evaluations in education. In the model, we spoke of the need to consider "student inputs"—the characteristics of students entering the system; "educational outputs"—cognitive and noncognitive changes that occur in students after exposure to an instructional program; "financial inputs"—financial resources available to carry on the program; "external systems"—the social, political, legal, and economic structure of society; and, lastly, "manipulatable characteristics"—those aspects of the program which are resource-consuming and which are administratively manipulatable.

Finally, we indicated the potential applications of the cost-effectiveness model in different kinds of evaluation situations and how one model is to be used to evaluate the cost-effectiveness of various financial inputs and of individual school programs. In conclusion, we showed that the cost-effectiveness evaluation model could be used to assess the worth of "alternative ways to do a given job."

REFERENCES

Adelson, M., Alkin, M., Carey, C., & Helmer, O. Planning education for the future: Comments on a pilot study. *American Behavioral Scientist, 10,* April 1967, entire issue.

Becker, J. S. Investment in human capital: Theoretical analysis. *Journal of Political Economy,* October 1962.

Coleman, S. *Equality of educational opportunity.* Washington, D.C.: United States Department of Health, Education, and Welfare, Office of Education, 1966.

Gordon, T. J., & Helmer, O. *Report on a long-range forecasting study.* Santa Monica, Cal.: RAND Corporation, 1964.

Hansen, W. L. Total and private rates of return to investment in schooling. *Journal of Political Economy,* April 1963.

Hirsch, W. Z., & Marcus, M. J. Some benefit-cost considerations of universal junior college education. *National Tax Journal,* June 1966.

Katzman, M. T. Distribution and production in a big city elementary school system. Ann Arbor, Mich.: University Microfilms, 1967.

Klein, S. P., Rock, D. A., & Evans, F. *Using multiple moderators in the prediction of academic success.* Princeton, N.J.: Educational Testing Service, 1967.

McKean, R. N. *Efficiency in government through systems analysis.* New York:
    John Wiley & Sons, Inc., 1958.
Mushkin, S. J. (Ed.). *Economics of higher education.* Washington, D.C.: United
    States Department of Health, Education, and Welfare, Office of Edu-
    cation, 1962.
Schultz, T. Investment in human capital. *American Economic Review,* March
    1961, *51*, 1–16.

Comments on Professor Alkin's Paper

MARVIN HOFFENBERG

The "games discussants play" are many, and I have chosen the "savants game," the presumptuous one of donning the scholar's gown. I prefer this "game" for this Conference since I think it important to relate Professor Alkin's paper to the diverse strains of intellectual thought that underlie the acceptance of methodologies to assist in choosing between alternative actions. Professor Alkin's paper represents one attempt—through cost-effectiveness—to apply such methodologies to decision-making in education.

In reading Professor Alkin's paper, one can discern three recent trends in the applied behavioral and social sciences. First, there is an increasing effort toward rationalization—in the economist's meaning of the term— in the decision process in both the public and private sectors. Over the past two decades various approaches and techniques have been developed as aids (crutches may be a more appropriate term) for a decision-maker to rationalize his decision process. Included here are the programming techniques, extensions of benefit-cost analysis (often referred to as cost-effectiveness or cost-utility analysis), simulation, operations analysis, systems analysis, and program budgeting. Whatever term is used, the common property of them all is that they aid in choosing between alternatives on the basis of relative merit.

In government, we see the developing Federal planning-programming-budgeting system and its imperialistic spread to subnational units, as well as the Department of Defense's cost-effectiveness approach to the analysis of military problems. In industry, it is now commonplace to choose corporate objectives through a systematic search of alternatives and to implement plans based on maximizing the opportunity of goal attainment, at least cost and risk. That complex questions such as Federal budgeting, military effectiveness, and corporate strategy can be attacked through rational processes of analysis no longer seems to be questionable.

There is a difference between attacking a problem and solving a problem. Social problems, and I would include educational problems here, are rarely "solved" (depending on the definition of "solved"); more commonly, they are transformed into more tractable problems. The grand optimum is difficult, if not impossible, to handle in an analytical manner. The problem is broken down into subanalysis, based on lower order criteria that are hopefully consistent with the higher order ones—a suboptimization (Hitch, 1959). Suboptimization is greatly influenced by the hierarchical level at which choice is to be made. (The scope of the decision-making power may be another definition of suboptimization.) Professor Alkin's paper does not clarify just who is the decision-maker, the school administrator, the school board, and so on.

This point needs further elaboration since it is an important one. The methodologies for assisting in rational choice require decision rules. For example, in dealing with a grant program the US Office of Education may well want to choose on the basis of total social costs and total social benefits for a wide geographic area. On the other hand, the local school board is likely to choose on the basis of minimizing local budget costs and to rank programs according to how little money they have to match federal funds. It does make a difference whose ox is being gored.

A second theme reflected in Professor Alkin's paper is the institutionalization of the search for problem areas and for alternative means to handle such problems. Decision-making is concerned only with the future and with alternatives. No decision about past events is necessary; they are "sunk costs," and no decision is necessary if there is no alternative. The "name of the game" in cost-effectiveness is *alternatives*. Such methodologies as cost-effectiveness, systems analysis, and so forth, are no cure-all; at best they are organized methods for conceptualizing multi-dimensional problems and selecting more objectively among open alternatives. They are no better than their simulations, no better than the ingenuity of their designers who must, after all, invent the alternatives to be tested. Incorrect models, unrealistic boundaries, ill-conceived alternatives, and false objectives can lead to choices which may be worse than choosing at random.

At this point we must recognize that in applying rational methodologies and in institutionalizing research in education, we must place these elements into an institutional framework and cease thinking of individuals as individuals making choices. The fact that what we are considering is, in actuality, institutional decision-making leads to a third current intellectual theme: the beginning of a general theory of organizational behavior. (I prefer the term organizational behavior to the more pejorative one, bureaucratic behavior.) A general theory is relevant to large, complex organizations in any field, both in the public and private sectors. I assume from casual empiricism that school systems are large, complex organizations.

The problem posed here by Professor Alkin, since he explicitly recognizes that he is dealing with organizational behavior, is how to combine the "rational" decision process of cost-effectiveness with the behavioral processes of institutional decision-making. I would prefer to look at this problem not as the "rational" versus the "nonrational" but as two "rational" approaches with different decision rules.

If all members of the organization shared the same values, desired the same objectives, and had complete information, if there were no uncertainty, if the school system were relatively closed, and so forth, the two rationalities could yield practically identical choices. But we know that such necessary and sufficient conditions do not exist. There are cognitive limits to rationality as exemplified by the cost-effectiveness approach (March and Simon, 1958). Organizations have no operational goals; their members do. In such cases where resources are scarce and where subunits (individuals) have different preference functions, exchange will take place. This situation leads to a definition of an organization as a coalition bargaining over side payments. A critical role for cost-effectiveness in such a situation is to aid in defining the meaningful boundaries for bargaining or adversary proceedings.

Professor Alkin has posed for us a problem of profound complexity in his following statement:

> The model maintains *that evaluation cannot take place without considering the nature of the instructional parameters in the program being evaluated, without understanding and quantifying the impact of individual and organizational contexts that infringe upon the program, and without considering a multiplicity of outcome measures.*

I infer from this statement that he is looking at education not as a single problem nor as a simple aggregation of problems but rather as an aggregation in which the elements (or subelements) are dynamically integrated because society perceives them as an entity. For example, a characteristic reaction to the Coleman Report was "What the hell. Why give these educational people any more money? Give it to Sargent Shriver"—a direct recognition of the integrative nature of poverty and educational performance. Analytically, I would like to look at Professor Alkin's statement as a trinity whose sacredness should be left to the reader's judgment. First, there is the specific problem area of concern. The stated problem area is the evaluation of instructional programs; and the focal unit is, at the minimum, the individual school. Here, the school is viewed as a system, that is, composed of connected elements. The element of connectiveness should be of major interest. But what is the system definition for the unit, and what is connected?

Professor Alkin correctly implies that he deals with open systems. Open systems operate with continual inputs and outputs, with dynamic functions and everchanging states. Such systems may not be self-regulating, and findings concerning them may not be replicable. Direct intervention at various decision points may be necessary to regulate the system and keep it within tolerable bounds. Difficult methodological problems are raised by such a conceptualization. What I suspect is needed is the subject matter of this conference: a general theory of instructional evaluation in order to unify evaluations.

The first point leads to the second point of my trinity, the methodologies of evaluation. Professor Alkin has "zeroed in" on cost-effectiveness as an evaluation technique. What I assume he means by that term are the various techniques developed for decision-making under conditions of scarcity and uncertainty. By uncertainty, I include both statistical uncertainty (errors of observation and estimation) and, what is more important, the uncertainty of future events.

In dealing with the evaluation of instructional programs, for let us say, the single school, there is the problem of identifying the instructional variables. The school is the "black box" receiving inputs and spewing out outputs which, in turn, lead to certain outcomes. This is a transformation process involving a production function: the relation of inputs of productive services per unit of time to outputs of products per unit of time. To the best of my knowledge, there is considerable controversy over the relevant variables—on both the input and output sides—to be included in the production function for primary and secondary education.

One illustration of our difficulties was an interchange at this session on the question of interactions being an intervening variable. I was following the argument until another comment was made, which struck me from an entirely different point of view. This comment was that the intervening variable had to do with the solution of differential equations to measure how well an individual would perform as an adult in his future life experiences. As the discussion progressed, it became clear to me that the intervening variable was, as used, a proxy variable, although what it was a proxy for remained undefined. I suspect that much of the current uncertainty about the production function hinges on the distinction between a proxy and an intervening variable.

Questions concerning proxy variables often relate to the environment external to the school. I will not say school "system" in the systemic meaning of the term since external elements may be brought into the "system" through the connectiveness of the educational process network. I now have an entry point to mention the third element of my trinity, the environmental matrix. Professor Alkin, in his model formulation, sets the school in an environmental matrix. This step logically follows from the openness of his school "system" in that it constantly interacts with the society around it. I hasten to add that there is both interaction and feedback in this systems network.

There is one striking feature about the environmental matrix for education today—its turbulence. The revolutionary times we live in have introduced increasing uncertainty into our mental projections of future society—uncertainty about its values, its technological requirements, the knowledge that will enable an individual to work and live adequately in it. The openness of the school system is profoundly affected by the turbulent system it interacts with and, more directly related to this conference, by the core of evaluation—the criteria used. As one example, let us be aware of the conflict between the black community and the schools over evaluating the processes and outcomes of our current instructional programs.

The preceding line of thinking leads, in my opinion, to a systemic approach to the evaluation of instructional programs, that is, to what is loosely referred to as systems analysis. What is technically termed cost-effectiveness (benefit-cost, cost utility) is only a part of the systems approach. The backlog of systems studies in physical domains has helped create a new attitude toward dealing with complex questions about complex systems and is being transferred to problems involving people systems. Our experience with this transference is ambiguous, and it is apparent that much more needs to be learned about dealing with people systems. At this point in time, this need is particularly pronounced concerning the educational system and the evaluation of that process and its output. We still need to proceed on a lower level of abstraction with specific elements. However, we can and should begin to work on the systems problems since methodologies need to be developed to integrate the various elements.

Let us remember that social facts are political, in the best sense of the term, and should be so recognized in our evaluations. As an example, one can review the history of the "Moynihan Report" (Subcommittee on Executive Reorganization Hearings, 1966). The very selection of facts and the evaluation of such facts are part of our value systems. They influence how we select, how we evaluate, and how we appreciate the facts. They also mean that, especially in education, we are dealing with multivalued outputs.

In the paper presented here, Professor Alkin has laid out for us a process for evaluating instructional programs; he has left the operations for further research. If my interpretation of what underlies his presentation is correct, then I remain sympathetic. As I have intimated, there are difficult and stimulating problems in making his model operational. The informational requirements are great; the criteria problems, tough setting; the objectives, difficult. But, as an outsider, I must ask what has been going on in research in education over the years.

REFERENCES

Hitch, C. J. Sub-optimization in operations problems. *Journal of the Operations Research Society,* May 1959, 87–99.
March, J. G., & Simon, H. A. *Organizations.* New York: John Wiley & Sons, Inc., 1958.
U.S. Senate, 89th Congress, 2d Session. *Federal role in urban affairs.* Hearings, Subcommittee on Executive Reorganization. Washington, D.C.: U.S. Government Printing Office, 1966.

Comments on Professor Alkin's Paper

JOHN BORMUTH

I think Dr. Alkin takes a very interesting, if not actually daring, position before this group when in his paper he asserts that the evaluation of instruction is not really complete unless it includes some assessment of the costs involved in instruction and is not simply a measure of the behavioral outcomes of that instruction. In other words, to serve sufficiently the purpose of making educational decisions and educational policies, evaluation must also provide us with a description that expresses the benefits of instruction in relation to its costs.

My first reaction to this proposition is to give my hearty endorsement to the general idea, for the reason that to reject it would be approximately equivalent to saying that the values and products achieved through education are somehow exempt from competing with all our other values for their fair share of the public resources. We must realize that education must compete with space projects, war, cosmetics, and dog food for the citizen's dollar.

If the taxpayer has in the past been unwilling to provide education with all the financial support that some of us thought was its due, perhaps his hesitancy is attributable to the natural aversion to buying a pig in a poke. Asking the taxpayer to put out money year after year in ever-increasing amounts for vaguely described products having even more vaguely described costs attached to them places a rather heavy strain on his credibility. Perhaps we should marvel at the fact that the taxpayer is so generous, rather than complain at his seeming parsimony.

If we really believe that public policy should be based upon informed public opinion, if we really believe that people have the right to know the effects that any treatment has upon them, and if we really believe that people have a right to know how their money is being spent, then we must agree with Dr. Alkin that the cost-to-benefit ratio of instruction must somehow be assessed. Hence, Dr. Alkin is asking us to reject the narrower conception of the role of evaluation. He is advocating that evaluation can and must play an important part in the formation of a public policy on education.

I have nothing but applause for Dr. Alkin's contention that evaluation should play a role in the formation of public policy on education. However, I have grave doubts that evaluation is sufficiently developed to play such a role. My argument is that evaluation is based upon the observation of student responses to some sorts of tasks, which I will henceforth call test items, regardless of what their specific form might happen to be; these items are derived by some obscure procedure, and they are then selected for inclusion in a test on the basis of authoritarian judgments of some sort. Hence, a test score necessarily represents what the test-writers and judges choose to measure and cannot be interpreted as a measure of what the instruction actually taught. I further claim that until we are able to specify objectively the population of all possible test items that can be constructed for a given course of instruction, and that until we have developed a set of rules for mechanically deriving these questions directly from the instructional stimuli themselves, evaluation cannot provide us with information which can have sufficient scientific validity to meet the requirements implied by Dr. Alkin's proposal.

No one familiar with test-making procedures would seriously challenge the statement that the items which go into a test are selected solely on the basis of authoritative judgment of their relevance and their importance to the instruction. What seems to have been overlooked frequently is the fact that this method of test item selection makes the information from such tests unacceptable for the serious purpose of making public policy because its result is that the test scores tell us only what the test-makers want us to know. We have no way of determining what all the other things were that could have been taught by the instruction, nor can we even be certain that any performance on the items actually stemmed from the instruction presumably being examined. Therefore, we must regard test items as containing an indeterminate bias. As a result, we can not accept test results as reliable data upon which to base decisions of public policy.

It seems necessary for us to conclude, then, that evaluation techniques can never perform an important role in the making of public policy. Now, is this so? I think not; but before they can do so, new techniques must be developed. These techniques must have the following characteristics:

1. They must permit us to enumerate exhaustively the behaviors that can be acquired as a result of exposure to a course of instruction. The resulting knowledge will allow us to inspect thoroughly the effects of a program and to draw a set of items that will enable us to examine an unbiased sample of those behaviors.

2. Our test construction techniques must permit us to derive the test items in a mechanical and completely reproducible process.

3. If taxonomic classifications are to be used in any way to describe the items so derived, these taxonomic classes must be defined in terms of the transformations by which they were derived from the instructional stimuli.

Although the meeting of these requirements may sound like an impossible task, it seems that the goals can be realized in a fairly adequate way. I suggested one possible solution in a paper I did for the Research and Development Center at UCLA a year ago. I might add that Professor Anderson's transformations the other day seemed to be hitting very much at the same sort of solution.

I began my work with the statement that the knowledge transmitted by a course of instruction may be regarded as a closed system of statements phrased either in natural language or in some other symbolic system governed by syntactic constraints. When the instruction can be cast into this form, many of the test questions that are ordinarily constructed are expressible as transformations of the sentences occurring in the instruction. For example, suppose in the instruction we have a sentence of this sort: "High mountains tend to exhibit rapid hydraulic erosion." From this statement, by a specifiable transformation, we can produce the question, "What kind of mountains tend to exhibit rapid erosion?" Or still another question, by a slightly different set of transformations, would be, "What kind of geologic feature tends to be affected by the destructive forces of runoff?" There are a number of other questions that could be derived from exactly the same sentence, each of which would be derived by a slightly different transformation. These are enumerable in every sense of the word, and they are objectively derived.

The questions derived in this manner are not just those ordinarily judged to be measuring acquisition of explicitly stated facts but also include questions measuring various degrees of generalization and transfer. Further, these classes of questions are objectively definable within the system of transformations used, but in general the questions so derived by the particular set of transformations I have been talking about deal with what we ordinarily classify as explicitly stated facts.

More recently, however, I have begun analyzing the syntactic constraints existing between sentences. These analyses seem to be leading to an ability to deal with questions commonly judged to be testing "knowledge of higher level concepts and more complex processes." Indeed, I seem to be getting the intuitively satisfying result that the traditional essay question has a generic kinship to the mundane short answer completion question. The two types of questions simply represent transformations operating at different levels in the syntactic structure of the discourse.

Many of Anderson's questions appear to fall within the classes derived by these transformations. But some of them also appear to represent transformations of an order that differs from any about which I had yet thought.

What I am arguing, then, is that we need a theory of test writing and that until we have such a theory, the practical use of evaluation for the formation of public policy does not seem to me to be possible.

Open Discussion of Alkin's Paper and of Hoffenberg's and Bormuth's Comments

LINDMAN: We have just learned that present skill in test development is primitive and inadequate and that test results should not be trusted when formulating public policy.

Then, yesterday, you will recall that Art Lumsdaine said, "Granted that we have adequate tests of educational outcomes, we do not know how to convert these to dollar amounts. We can't put a dollar value on them." I conclude that even if the tests were good enough, John, you would still have to overcome Lumsdaine's hurdle of saying, "Even if we had good tests, we have to put a dollar value on them to make use of their results."

And finally, Nate Gage reminds us that the new innovations we heard about yield no significant differences in the outcome.

I would like to ask Marv how the administrator reconciles himself to these three haunting difficulties when making budgeting decisions?

ALKIN: I don't know that I can respond to all three issues simultaneously, but I'll try to take up a chunk of one or more of them.

It seems to me that, in the tentative model I presented, I expressed a concern for cost effectiveness of instructional programs and defined specific kinds of effectiveness evaluation that would be of concern. I deliberately limited myself to considering the use of financial resources already in the public educational sector to maximize educational benefits, without raising the broader question (to which I am sure Marv Hoffenberg would be anxious to address himself) of allocation of financial resources to education as opposed to other sectors of the economy.

While it might be desirable, I am not quite sure that it is necessary to convert outcome measures into dollar figures in this kind of situation. It would seem to me that it is quite possible, quite feasible, simply to look at the nature of the outcomes being produced in terms of dollars and, through some kind of expression of social values, determined perhaps by the community or the various publics involved, arrive at a judgment of the relative worth of these outcomes.

LORTIE: This will get both Marv Alkin and Marv Hoffenberg in the act. As I understood Marv Hoffenberg's paper, you said that in the course of working with these quantitative entities you do what is required; but, if you are a shrewd guy, you say to yourself, "What does this really mean?" That is to say, you don't forsake your wisdom just because you have a bunch of numbers.

However, something worries me. I think it was McClelland who said that in the case of a great deal of data, where one numerical index has some sort of reputation, the tendency of most American investigators is to gravitate toward this numerical index and treat it as primary. Now, when we are dealing with a situation with as many intangibles as in education and where you have problems of internal organizational evaluation, how do you trade off morale against technological gains? Isn't partial quantification dangerous?

HOFFENBERG: Well, let me answer the question this way. If this is the true state of affairs, then one of the evaluations of an educational system would be based on this kind of question: how does one depart from the emphasis you deplore, given the kinds of information you have gathered?

Let me sidestep a little of this by referring to this planning-programming-budgeting system (PPBS) and let me work on the assumption that everyone is familiar with it. Basically, the system handles three kinds of functions. One, it provides a guarantee to the policy-maker that action will follow policy. This is an organizational question; it's an information control question, but a fairly critical one.

The second function is more pertinent to this particular discussion because it focuses on choices between programs. Now, on this particular issue, the relative-merit operations I spoke about before are applicable at various levels. Looking at the decisions that have to be made, let's say at the national level, there is the question of the division of the GNP between the private sector and the public sector. Within the public sector there are questions such as, "How does one allocate resources between defense and education?" "In education, how does one begin to make allocations between primary and secondary schools?" Then another level, "How do you choose one particular program for the primary school?" These steps center on allocative decisions about output trade-offs.

Given the current state of the art our techniques are more applicable to the next stage, of input trade-offs. This is due to the problem of incommensurables (the issue raised by Erick in his question about dollars as a common numéraire). Unless it is feasible to compare alternative programs in commensurable units, I cannot see how a rigorous choice is possible. On the question of input trade-off one can designate certain performance characteristics for a particular program to achieve. He can then look at the various ways of reaching that objective in terms of least-cost, for example.

The problem with this kind of approach, and I think it is going to be the most applicable one in education, brings us to the third function of PPBS program budgeting. With this technique the hope is to get some idea of how to allocate resources between policies. By this, I mean, for example, defense versus education. If one could express everything in a common denominator on the output side, dollars, man years, national wealth, whatever you want, outputs would be commensurable. Then one could begin to choose more rigorously among these wide programs in terms of their worth to the nation. Insofar as we are not able to put our output measures and our performances measures into a common term such as dollars, we have no rigorous way of choosing. In this sense, these rational decision techniques only partially help at this level through providing additional information, and hopefully, more relevant data.

What runs through all these methodologies is an effort to delimit the area of adversary conflict in the public sphere. Quantification within an analytical framework helps here. If you are arguing about unemployment levels, it makes a devil of a lot of difference if you can confine the performance levels sought to 3 or 4 percent rather than having no number at all.

Let me point out one way in which quantification has helped in decision-making. I am thinking of the benefit-cost ratio process in the water-resources field, where it has been public policy through Executive Orders since 1939 that all agencies in the water resources field make benefit-cost analyses. It helps eliminate the "lousy pups" that come up, so that when a Congressman comes and says he has to have this kind of project, you point out that the benefit-cost ratio is much less than one; and it's the beginning of an argument as to why he should reconsider his scheme. Let me make clear, however, that since policy and programmatic choices are multi-valued ones, much more is involved in questions of policy determination. I would dread it if the policy process in the United States depended on a single-evaluation criterion. I hope it doesn't. Basically, what you are after in this kind of choice is somehow to insert a judgmental procedure into the policy process so that you can have consensus on the meaning of these numbers. In this way, you hope to eliminate a certain amount of nonsense.

ANDERSON: I have a simple kind of question. Cost effectiveness has appealed to educators, particularly those involved in programmed instruction, and a rather simple-minded kind of ratio has been applied. You take amount of gain in student achievement as the benefit and student time as the cost. When you apply this simple index, the shortest treatment, the one that takes the least student time, is always the preferred one.

I want to see what cost effectiveness people would say to be the problem in this kind of analysis. I don't want to answer the question myself, but let me point out that the function relating achievement to time is negatively accelerated, so that the last increment in achievement takes a lot more time than the first increment. Another way to say it is that we don't know very much about the units in the achievement scale.

HOFFENBERG: There is a very simple answer to that. One of the cardinal rules is that, unless either the benefits are equal or the costs are equal, you don't use ratios. So it's just a bad application of something logical and systematic, but don't blame me.

ANDERSON: It's not a question of blame.

HOFFENBERG: Frankly, we know very little about the application of these methods except to certain very restricted areas. What has been developed over a period of time—and this has been going on for at least twenty years that I know of—is a much more sophisticated way of what I would call information management. You address yourself to the kinds of information including analytical techniques that may help make a decision, but because some of us misuse the analysis at times don't throw the method away.

GAGNÉ: I was very interested in John Bormuth's observations about the inadequacies of tests as used in cost effectiveness studies, for I, too, am uneasy about some of the uses to which tests are put.

One of the difficulties may be, purely from speculation, that tests are intermediate criteria; and when one undertakes to estimate costs as well as effectiveness he would like to seek, if he could, more nearly ultimate criteria. I am wondering just what possibilities of that kind might exist in evaluation studies.

I have thought of an example that is inadequate in some ways but perhaps illustrates the point. If you were to look at disadvantaged children in a first grade, you could use tests to determine the degree of inadequacy that they have, let us say, in certain language skills, such as reading. That would give you some kind of measure, but there might still be some misgiving that it may not be comprehensive enough or might not include all of the things one really ought to measure.

On the other hand, one could say, "Well now, how much would it cost to get these people to read at the first-grade level?" I would think an empirical study might very well determine that it would take four years to overcome their deficiencies so that they were equivalent to ordinary first graders. Thus, one would have a sounder, more defensible measure.

That is only an example, and I know it's inadequate; isn't there a possibility that we can look to other ways of measuring educational outcomes that don't depend on tests?

BORMUTH: My response is that the kind of test you just suggested is essentially a time-to-criterion test, so you still have the same problem.

Then, secondly, you are still faced with the problem of what is going to be your measure of whether or not the child can read. How well do first-grade children of normal intelligence ordinarily read? This, then, is going to be your criterion.

GAGNÉ: All right. I will have to agree. You are certainly very effectively pointing out the difficulty of that example. Let's throw it away. The question is, can we do other things?

BORMUTH: If we want to make better butter wrappers, should we give them some butter to wrap, perhaps?

GAGNÉ: That's more like it.

BORMUTH: This, of course, pleases me a great deal. I would be most happy with that kind of criterion of learning. At present, we are stuck with the fact that most knowledge transmitted in public schools reaches children through verbal instruction. Moreover, our evidence of performance is usually the verbal emission of the child. This is dictated pretty much by the great economy of being able to use the language. I think if we started talking about actually giving children butter to wrap, or that kind of item, we would find ourselves in a position where our testing would be an exceedingly expensive proposition. That is not to say it might not be worthwhile and be a more effective type of test.

STAKE: A few minutes ago I heard someone say the ratio should be ruled out as a summary statistic in a cost-benefit analysis. I didn't hear you mention the ratio in Figure 4. Marv (Alkin), would you judge this ratio to be useful in the summarizing of the cost-benefit situation?

ALKIN: I believe the ratio was ruled out by Marv Hoffenberg, who was referring in his discussion of ratio to a dollar-to-dollar ratio related to educational items.

I personally would not rule out the ratio but would maintain that the ratio in Figure 4 would be a feasible way of looking at a certain kind of cost effectiveness evaluation. I don't know that I am entirely responding to your question.

STAKE: Ordinarily, we find the ratio to be a benefit over a cost. Here we have an actual outcome over an expected outcome.

ALKIN: It is not a cost-benefit ratio.

STAKE: So, the actual over expected outcome is a useful statistic?

ALKIN: It's a useful summary statistic, right?

STAKE: Let's talk again of the cost-benefit ratio. The question was raised as to converting these things to dollars so that you have the same unit, and the answer was given that you don't want to convert some of the things into dollars. You can analyze quite satisfactorily by looking at an outcome for what it is, the effectiveness of doing a certain task at a certain cost.

But several things are going on at the same time. The students can do a certain job better than they were able to before. You can indicate what the gain, the benefit, has been. But there are side effects, some of them positive and some of them negative. You might call the negative ones cost.

ALKIN: They are guesses.

STAKE: The point I am trying to make is that a ratio may be too simple. There may be three or seventeen or ninety *different* factors that have changed during this period of time. The idea of a single ratio as the summary statistic puzzles me.

ALKIN: How do the other items get included? Is that basically the question?

STAKE: I'm asking for insight as to how, in other than narrative fashion, we can represent the array of costs and benefits that we have measured.

HOFFENBERG: Let me take a crack at that. My comments were on the dollar cost. There are two ways one can approach the problem. One is to look at a very narrow program and do your measuring without looking at the interactions in the system as defined. The more rigorous way is to say, "I have a school that is functioning in a community. Now, if I change one program, what is its effect on the total system?" Then you try to integrate into your analyses the so-called spillovers, the external benefits and costs.

You are perfectly right in saying that you have difficulty in seeing the distinction between benefit and cost, because the only difference is an algebraic sign. A cost is a negative benefit, but, in theory at least, one should integrate all of the spillover costs and benefits and then look at the picture after that.

GAGE: I want to change the subject completely and refer to Marv Alkin's Figure 2. I think the discussion so far has been about what was inside the boxes at *C, B, D,* and *E,* and I want to ask a question about the arrows. As I understand it, the arrow signifies a causal relationship, although later you refer to them as predictor variables. I think you are not concerned with them merely as predictor variables but as causes or determiners, and I was brought up to think that you could feel 100 percent certain that something was causing something else only if you could do a true experiment and assign cases at random to different treatments. Of course, you can't do that with school districts as your units of analysis, typically. How are you ever going to be at all certain that your costly manipulatable characteristics are determining your outcome?

ALKIN: I think one has to enter the assumption of causality in this analysis in order to make it meaningful. I realize that it is dangerous, given the lack of opportunity to apply experimental techniques to schools and school districts; but I believe that there are some recent innovations in statistical procedures that, while not allowing you to assume causality, at least give you some greater insight in the direction of the relationship, although I would be very hesitant to talk too much about that. Perhaps one of the people to your right and elsewhere might be able to do so better than I.

C. HARRIS: We would still clearly distinguish a proposition of cause-and-effect from a proposition of association.

HOFFENBERG: It seems to me there are two questions there; one, what do you mean by *certainty*? I can only think of certainty in probabilistic terms. The other, is what is meant by causality. Causality I rather ignore, because all I can really observe are relative time sequences. If I perform Marv Alkin's black-box operation and observe outcomes over a certain number of trials, regardless of whether I talk about cause or feedback or anything else, all I really know is that I am going through a series of operations that somehow are associated with a series of outcomes and are preferable to another series. Certainty and causation are concepts that I find tricky to handle in operational terms.

TROW: I would like to get outside of the black box and turn to a question asked earlier about the bearing of this on administration.

I am really interested in the connection between what you have talked about and problems of decision-making. I was very struck by Hoffenberg's remark about using cost-benefit analysis to point out to economists what they are talking about. It seems to me that this leads explicitly to quite different functions of this kind of analysis. One of these is the persuasive clarification of the issues and elements in a situation. I think this is what Hoffenberg meant when he referred to a more sophisticated form of data processing.

The second function I have in mind is prescriptive, cost-benefit analysis as a device for generating choices. It seems to me these are quite different kinds of functions. In situations where some administrative machinery begins to generate fairly automatic decisions, or appears to, then the question arises, under what conditions will an institution or individuals accept these prescriptions?

The answer seems to depend on whether men can trust their own judgments. In part this is a question of their own personal security and the extent to which they feel obliged to justify their decisions by reference to some "legitimate," in this case quasi-scientific, process of decision-making. Where men feel themselves to have sound judgment and where they don't have to justify their decisions, it will be very unlikely that the kind of function that results in a fairly automatic process of producing decisions will be accepted. I think that is clear, for example, in resistance to these proceedings in some colleges and universities. One is bound to ask how the quality of intelligence that informs the decisions you generate through cost-benefit analysis compares with the other kinds of intelligence that shape decisions that are made in other ways?

HOFFENBERG: This is why, in my preliminary comments, I tried to put things in an organizational context. We are dealing with large, complex probabilistic types of organizational behavior and, if you observe empirically what has happened over the years, in many cases the analysts become much more humble. Basically what Trow is saying in a sophisticated way is that you think you have a series of operations that will help someone sharpen intuitive judgments to improve the decision-making capacity.

TROW: But is not that exactly the alternative to all the evaluative procedures about which you are talking?

HOFFENBERG: You are asking one man the wrong question. I don't know the answer.

TROW: I'm not asking it directly of you. It's a type of rhetorical question.

GLASER: I think it's appropriate to say, just for the record, even though I'm sure you all know this, that a major danger to educational research and development is the too early application of cost-benefit analysis. I think there is a lack of recognition among the educational community of the fact that initial research and development in schools or any educational development is tremendously expensive and will remain tremendously expensive until eventually we know how to manufacture it.

Industry is very aware of this kind of process; but I find, time and time again, in the design of an experimental school, in the design of any research slanted toward any innovative application in the schools, an almost immediate reaction of either "it's too expensive" or "it's totally inapplicable to our school system because we can't afford it," or an attitude on the part of educational publishers that it is ridiculous because it costs so much. There is an unrealistic reaction to the fact that things are always terribly expensive at the outset, before they begin to get into the realm of cost reality.

PART VI

Methodological Issues

CHAPTER 8

Design and Analysis of Evaluation Studies

DAVID E. WILEY

The original intent which motivated this paper was a desire to say something systematic concerning the design and analysis of evaluation studies. It seemed, however, that before anything explicit could be said on this topic, some clarity would have to come to my mind concerning the definition of evaluation and its important components. As a consequence, and at the risk of infringing on some of my colleagues' territory, I have set down some of my thoughts on this topic also.

The first section of the paper relates some arbitrary distinctions that I impose among the terms evaluation, assessment, and appraisal. In the second, with the help of some previous work, I further narrow the definition of evaluation implied in the first section. The next section outlines and defines four separate components or elements of evaluation that seem to have been confused in some "evaluation" studies. The fourth and fifth sections concern three of these elements and their relations to certain notions about the design, analysis, and measurement aspects of evaluation.

EVALUATION, ASSESSMENT, AND APPRAISAL

The terms evaluation, assessment, and appraisal are often used interchangeably in attempts at gathering information about schools or pupils. This is unfortunate, since the goals of information gathering and the methods used differ so widely. It seems worthwhile to attempt to give some guidelines for the uses of these terms and to explicate some of the similarities and differences implied by these guidelines.

Certainly, it would seem clear that there is some element of judgment either central to these processes or lurking in the background. That is, there is some "valuing" going on somewhere. If we look to one of our strongholds of meaning, the Webster's New Collegiate Dictionary (1953), we find a distinction between evaluation as "ascertainment of value," and assessment or appraisal as "setting of value." From these definitions I would place the judgmental or valuing element further in the background for evaluation, more related to assessment and appraisal. It might be reasonable to place the focus of "evaluation" on the process of ascertaining the levels of particular traits that are viewed as valuable, rather than on establishing which traits are valuable. Certainly the values must be decided upon and structured in some reasonable way before they may be ascertained for a particular object, but we may reasonably separate the two processes.

In this context, then, I would use assessment or appraisal for the general processes of judging what is valuable *and* ascertaining the particular levels of valued traits, while reserving evaluation for the latter.

We can now turn to the problem of what may be evaluated, assessed, or appraised. Harris (1947) makes some useful distinctions in his paper on school appraisal. He designates three aspects of the school that may be appraised: plans, resources, and processes. For Harris, plans consist of the goals of the school; resources are both physical and human, and processes are the activities—both instructional and noninstructional—which go on in the school. In a later paper (1963), he insists that the appraisal becomes evaluation only if the criteria consist of measures of pupil behavior. That is, in the context of the above discussion, the ascertainment of levels of valuable traits must be empirical and behavioral.

A DEFINITION OF EVALUATION

In order to discuss the design and analysis of evaluation studies we must first define evaluation more explicitly. Two papers have been most influential in structuring my thoughts about evaluation. They are those of Harris (1963) and Cronbach (1963). Harris defines evaluation as

. . . the systematic attempt to gather evidence regarding changes in student behavior that accompany planned educational experiences.

Cronbach, however, places some differing emphases:

> . . . collection and use of information to make decisions about an educational program.

We can see that the differences between the two definitions reside in the fact that Cronbach emphasizes the decision aspect of evaluation while Harris emphasizes the behavioral nature of the criterion. Both emphasize the gathering of (empirical) evidence or information about planned educational programs.

In order to focus the content of this paper, I have taken the liberty of combining the two definitions into one which further narrows the concept of evaluation:

> Evaluation consists of the collection and use of information concerning changes in pupil behavior to make decisions about an educational program.

Thus I will be concentrating on behavioral information that is relevant to decisions about educational programs.

In addition to narrowing the evaluation concept to the information gathering or ascertainment process, a further comment is in order about the term "educational programs." In the discussion that follows I will restrict the meaning of "educational programs" to "instructional programs" or "procedures" and their components. This will tend to simplify the terminology in the rest of the paper, even though much of what I say will be relevant to other aspects of the school, for example, the plans and resources of Harris (1947, 1963).

To summarize I will be concentrating on instructional programs or procedures and their components evaluated by means of pupil behavior.

THE ELEMENTS AND TERMINOLOGY OF EVALUATION

In order to help conceptualize the evaluation process it is useful to distinguish certain elements by labeling them with special terms. To these elements I have given the names: Standards, Objects, Vehicles, and Instruments.

The standards of evaluation are a function of valuing or judgment process discussed earlier. The standards consist of the designation of traits that are considered important to evaluate (are valued), and the designation of levels of these traits that are considered desirable. A rough example of standards might consist of the statement that 90 percent of the pupils in a school should be able to read 70 percent of the material in a daily newspaper with 95 percent comprehension. This is incomplete since some of the terms in the sentence are not defined.

The objects of evaluation are the instructional programs or procedures and their components. These might consist of something as complex as a "new math" textbook series or at the other extreme a particular "frame" in an autoinstructional sequence.

The vehicles of evaluation are the carriers of the effects of the objects. That is, the pupils, classes, or schools.

The instruments of evaluation are exhibitors of the behaviors of the vehicles. The selection or construction of these instruments is highly dependent on traits established as important by the standards, the particular objects to be evaluated, and the vehicles that are affected by those objects. In addition, the instruments used in an evaluation may interact with the standards, since the trait levels considered desirable may be differently reflected in different instruments. Examples of instruments run the usual broad gamut of stimuli used for eliciting behavioral responses.

The main problem of evaluation, then, is to establish the *effects* of the *objects* on the *vehicles* by means of the *instruments*. The other element of the process is to compare these *effects* with the *standards*. The latter comparison will not be discussed in this paper.

THE OBJECTS OF EVALUATION AND THEIR DESCRIPTION

In order to evaluate an object (educational program, procedure, or component thereof) we must describe it, or at least be able to distinguish it from other possible objects. In its simplest form this description indicates the presence or absence of the object. Thus in the evaluation of complex educational programs such as textbook series we usually characterize the object by a dichotomous variable indicating its presence (or absence). Studies that involve the characterization of a complex educational program by its presence or absence are called "summative evaluation studies" by Scriven (1965). Two basic types of studies have been proposed by Cronbach (1963) to accomplish the goal of summative evaluation. These types he terms the "horse race" and the "time trial."

The "horse race" is the educational comparative experiment. In this procedure several different objects (educational programs) are compared by randomly assigning relevant vehicles of evaluation to them and then comparing their standing on measures produced by applying relevant instruments to the vehicles. The analytic procedure used for data generated in this fashion is usually the analysis of variance. This procedure transforms the dichotomous variables that indicate presence or absence of the various treatments into contrast variables that differentiate the treatments; then it relates them to the outcome measures.

The "time trial" is a procedure that ascertains the levels of the outcome measures in the presence of the object. It is mainly useful when one is not directly interested in comparison with other objects or when the conditions of the study can be assumed to remain constant. The trouble with the "time trial" study is that one is almost always interested in a comparison with some other objects, for if one were not, a decision would not need to be made. And given that comparison is necessary, the constancy of conditions becomes extremely important and is difficult to guarantee without the important concomitants of a comparative experiment. It is important to acknowledge, however, the pertinence of Cronbach's (1963) point that it is difficult to implement valid comparative experiments.

Another type of evaluation procedure defined by Scriven involves a different class of objects of evaluation. These objects are component parts or procedures of complex educational programs. The general purpose in evaluating them is to gain information that will aid decisions about the modification or deletion of these parts from the overall program. Scriven terms this type of evaluation "formative." It seems generally accepted that the kind of study used in this type of evaluation should be both comparative and experimental. The analytic models used for the analysis of data from these studies are essentially the same as the analysis of variance models described above. An example of this kind of study might be an experiment comparing the effects of varying the sequence of certain instructional units or blocks within a complex instructional treatment. Another might be an optimization study of a particular unit of instruction.

There is a third type of evaluation study that seems to be little discussed. This type might be described by the phrase "making summative evaluation studies formative." This type of study involves making the description of the objects a quantitative characterization of the relevant traits of those objects and then relating that description to the outcomes.

An example of such a quantitative description might be the percentage of time a particular educational program spends with supplementary material as opposed to the basic textbook. This variable might be related to transfer objectives of the instruction.

This procedure may also be used to establish the effects on the vehicles of those characteristics of the instruction that are left free to vary by the program. Note that in this case the emphasis has changed from the educational program (object of evaluation) to variations in the program (objects of evaluation). An example of this type of study was recently conducted by one of Benjamin Bloom's students at the University of Chicago (Anthony, 1967). An appropriate analytic model for this type of study is the standard regression model or appropriate modifications thereof.

VEHICLES AND INSTRUMENTS OF EVALUATION

The appropriate vehicle for evaluation is highly dependent upon a characterization of the object of evaluation. The selection of an appropriate vehicle is equivalent to the selection of a sampling unit for a study.

To make this more concrete, if the object of evaluation is a typical classroom instructional program where the instruction is received simultaneously by all students in the class, then the appropriate vehicle (or sampling unit) is the class and not the individual pupil. This is equivalent to the standard definition of the experimental unit in this case: if two pupils in the same class may not receive different instructional treatments, the classroom is the appropriate unit (Page, 1965). Another way of looking at this is to say that traditional instruction is by nature classroom-based since if it were not it would be tutorial. This concept has been discussed by Wiley (1967).

The other vehicles are, of course, appropriate for objects of evaluation with other characteristics. Thus if one is conducting a formative evaluation study within the context of a computer-assisted instructional system, individual pupils may receive different treatments. The method is essentially tutorial, so the relevant vehicle (sampling unit) is the individual pupil. And if one is studying the effects of administrative policy the vehicle would be the collectivity supervised by the individual policy-maker.

When the appropriate vehicle for evaluation is a collectivity, such as a classroom or school, a number of options open up with respect to instrumentation, the production of measures, and strategies of data analysis.

In the first place the measures produced by the instrument characterize the collectivity and not the individual pupil. This implies that not every pupil need be measured. That is, we may sample pupils from the unit and still be able to measure the status of the relevant unit. We may thus use completely random, or stratified random sampling schemes; and our only concern need be the reliability of the resulting measure with respect to the relevant unit.

It may be useful at this point to sketch a model for the reliability analysis of collectivity data in a simple case. If we are trying to differentiate reliably among classrooms by means of the average scores on a test given to the individuals in that class, an appropriate model might be the following:

$$y_{ij} = \mu + \alpha_i + \epsilon_{ij}, \text{ where } i = 1, \ldots, n$$
$$j = 1, \ldots, m_i$$

n being the number classes and m_i the number of people in each class for which scores are available. The term ϵ_{ij} represents variation among individuals within classes and may be treated as error of measurement with respect to the determination of $\mu + \alpha_1$, the population mean score for the ith class.

The reliability of the measure with respect to differentiating among classes is the proportion of variance in the mean score for each class attributable to true variations among classes. If we let $\sigma_\alpha^2 = \text{Var}(\alpha_i)$, and $\sigma_\epsilon^2 = \text{Var}(\epsilon_{ij})$ then the reliability of the ith class mean is

$$\rho_i = \frac{\sigma_\alpha^2}{\sigma_\alpha^2 + \frac{\sigma_\epsilon^2}{m_i}}$$

This is equivalent to the intra-class correlation stepped up with the Spearman-Brown formula for an increase in test "length" of a factor of m_i.

An appropriate estimate of ρ, when m_i are equal is

$$\hat{\rho} = \frac{\text{MS}_\alpha - \text{MS}_\epsilon}{\text{MS}_\alpha}$$

Bock and Wiley (1968) have determined that in a relatively homogeneous set of suburban school districts approximately 70 percent of the variation in the scores of a group of common standardized achievement tests is due to within-class variation. This would imply that the reliability of these kinds of tests with respect to differentiating classes would be approximately

$$\rho = \frac{.3}{.3 + \frac{.7}{30}} = \frac{.3}{.323} = .93$$

if the classes contain thirty pupils.

In other contexts, it has been my experience that measures of many traits, with respect to classroom means as observations, tend to correlate above .90 with measures of similar traits, implying that the actual reliability of standard achievement instruments for individual differences among classes is somewhat above .90. This would seem to be consistent with the Wiley and Bock data. For many purposes then, it would seem that samples of pupils would be adequate.

Another consequence of the unit being a collectivity is that each pupil does not have to receive the same items if the instrument is a test with more than one item. Procedures for giving different pupils different items are called item sampling procedures and are due to Frederic Lord (1962). They are mentioned in the evaluation context by Cronbach (1963). These procedures may be very useful in that a complex trait, possibly represented by a population of distinct items, may be adequately assessed for units by giving each pupil a small and distinct sample of items.

One such design that seems to have great promise in evaluation studies may be described in the following way. Suppose one has a test consisting of m items. Randomly select m pupils from each of n classes. Randomly assign one of the m items to each pupil under the restriction that every pupil in a class is to receive a different item.

Class	1				2				
Pupil	1	2	....	m	$m+1$	$m+2$	...	$2m$	....
Item	1	2	....	m	1	2	...	m	

n

$(n-1)m+1$	$(n-1)m+2$	...	nm
1	2	...	m

Note that pupils are nested within class and that items cross classes but not pupils. We may formulate the following model for the mn observations.

$$Y_{ij(k)} = \mu + \alpha_i + \beta_j + (\alpha\beta)_{ij} + \epsilon_i(k), i = 1, \ldots, n;$$

$$j = 1, \ldots, m; k = 1, \ldots, nm$$

(where k is completely determined by i and j)

The expectations of the mean *squares* are

$$E(MS\alpha) = n\sigma_\alpha{}^2 + \sigma_{\alpha\beta}{}^2 + \sigma_\epsilon{}^2$$

$$E(MS_\beta) = n\sigma_\beta{}^2 + \sigma_{\alpha\beta}{}^2$$

$$E(MS_{\alpha\beta}) = \sigma_{\alpha\beta}{}^2 + \frac{n}{n-1}\sigma_\epsilon{}^2$$

and the reliability of the mean score for each class is

$$\rho = \frac{\sigma_\alpha{}^2}{\sigma^2}$$

$$\sigma_\alpha{}^2 + \frac{\sigma_{\alpha\beta}{}^2 + \sigma^2}{m}$$

which may be approximately estimated by

$$\hat{\rho} = \frac{MS\alpha - MS\alpha\beta}{MS\alpha}$$

This design is due to Cronbach and others (personal communication, 1967).

Another advantage of a collectivity unit is that single items may be used to characterize the unit in a reliable fashion. And as Cronbach (1963) has mentioned, items are easier to interpret than total scores on tests made up of many items.

Single item scores have other advantages also. It seems apparent (Wiley and Bock, 1967) that a major portion of the variation among *schools* on measures of achievement may be explained by a single source of variation which may be interpreted as social class. It might be expected, then, that if one took the item scores for a small but highly homogeneous set of items (for example, ten items testing the addition of two one-digit integers) most of the covariation among the items could be accounted for by a reliable measure of social class.

A reliable measure of social class could be obtained by using almost any measure of prior achievement or ability, since the collectivity is the unit we are considering. This is so since variation in backgrounds of the pupils within the community associated with the school is error with respect to the determination of the school mean. Thus the mean ability of the pupils in the school is likely to reflect the social class of the community.

It would seem to be a good hypothesis that most of the remaining co-variation after removal of the variation in social class would be due to variation in instruction. This might then imply that the principle component of the matrix of partial covariances (removing social class), would be a revelant criterion measure for the evaluation of instructional methods. One might expect that little covariation would remain after removing both social class and the principle component.

We have explored some of the consequences for instrumentation and measure generation when the relevant unit is a collectivity but there are others. It would seem that the objects of instruction might well affect other characteristics of a unit than the mean level of achievement. They might, in fact, affect the distribution of achievement in the collectivity. If this is true the moments of the achievement distribution might be used as criterion measures. It would seem that the first four moments would be directly interpretable. For example, if one program or object of evaluation tended to produce more homogeneous achievement as indicated by a small variance or logarithm of the variance, this would be directly interpretable.

Another relevant kind of measure that may be produced is a contrast among subpopulations. For example, if one computed the mean score for boys and girls in a classroom and used the difference as a criterion measure, the effects on the difference score may be interpreted as an interaction of the treatments (if any) and sex of pupil with respect to the original criterion measure. It is important, however, to realize that this measure should be looked upon as a characteristic of the class rather than inferring what the effects of the treatments would be if the sexes were segregated.

This treatment of subpopulations may be extended to more than one way of classification. Thus we might create four subpopulations: high ability boys, low ability boys, high ability girls, and low ability girls. The four mean scores would produce three contrasts in addition to the mean: (a) a sex contrast, (b) an ability contrast, and (c) a sex-ability interaction contrast. These contrasts may then be used as separate criterion measures with possibly insightful results.

One might note that in the above example the two ways of creating subpopulations differ in that one was the result of a discrete variable (sex) and the other was a result of a continuous variable (ability). When the contrast is the result of a continuous variable it may be considered to be a rough estimate of the regression coefficient of the original criterion variable with respect to the continuous variable.

This logic might lead one to the use of regression coefficients as new criterion measures for evaluating the differential effect of the treatments on individual pupils.

I hope that some of the ideas and suggestions presented above will be helpful to evaluators and evaluation researchers in clarifying the muddy field of instructional evaluation.

REFERENCES

Anthony, B. M. *The identification and measurement of classroom environmental variables process related to academic achievement.* Unpublished Ph.D. dissertation, University of Chicago, 1967.

Cronbach, L. J. Course improvement through evaluation. *Teacher's College Record*, 1963, *64*, 672–683.

Harris, C. W. The appraisal of a school-problem for study. *Journal of Educational Research*, 1947, *41*, 172–182.

Harris, C. W. Some issues in evaluation. *The Speech Teacher*, 1963, *12*, 191–199.

Lord, F. M. Estimating norms by item-sampling. *Educational and Psychological Measurement*, 1962, *22*, 259–268.

Page, E. B. Recapturing the richness within the classroom. (Paper read at AERA Convention, February, 1965.)

Scriven, M. The methodology of evaluation. February, 1965, pp. 1–58 (dittoed).

Webster's New Collegiate Dictionary. Springfield, Mass.: G. and C. Merriam Company, 1953.

Wiley, D. E. Standard experimental designs and experimentation under school conditions. Paper read at AERA Convention, Chicago, February, 1965.

Wiley, D. E. The design and analysis of experiments. *Highlights of the preconvention institute: Research designs in reading.* Newark, Dela.: International Reading Association, 1967, 9–16.

Wiley, D. E., & Bock, R. D. Quasi-experimentation in educational settings: Comment. *The School Review,* 1968, *75,* 353–366.

Comments on Professor Wiley's Paper

CHESTER HARRIS

We have come into the third day of this conference, and enough things have been said in various contexts to make it possible for me to point out some things that bear in general on Mr. Wiley's paper, but still more generally on the whole set of papers.

I think that the most important contribution that can be made at this point in the conference is to identify and enumerate what I regard as three critical issues in the design and analysis of evaluation studies suggested in these papers and discussions. The area of design and analysis is actively changing and developing, and most of us would be hard pressed to predict the extent to which these issues will be resolved or reformulated in the near future. The measurement problem in evaluation studies involves a situation in which we have an instructional package that is to be used with some group of human subjects, and then evaluated in terms of how good it is. This demands that we adopt some scheme for specifying what we mean by "good."

There appear to be three types of "goodness" for those who take the behavior of students as the relevant evidence. One is goodness defined as a level of performance; a second is goodness defined as change of performance in a specified direction; and a third is goodness defined as change of performance in a specified direction to a specified extent. Buried here are the questions of which behaviors are relevant and whether the observations that are made can become bases for inferences regarding learning as a result of the instructional package. This is an issue that Dr. Gagné posed for us earlier in the session. These three attitudes imply somewhat different measurement operations for any chosen type of performance. Let us leave this with the further acknowledgment that in any study many different types of performance may be regarded as important dependent variables, and that the amount of work required to make preparations for an evaluation study may be extensive.

The reality that there may be relevant dependent variables also suggests that appropriate designs for evaluation probably should be multivariate. This is the first issue that I wish to identify, the issue of univariate versus multivariate dependent variable studies. My strategy is not to resolve the issue but merely to enumerate the factors involved.

Possibly the simplest design for an evaluation study is that which employs only one instructional package and attempts to assess its goodness for two or more categories or types of students. Here we employ stratifying variables: age, sex, intelligence level, residential region, and so forth, to define our groups of students, and then compare and contrast the various student performances. The intent of such a study is primarily descriptive (though tests of significance often are run): to define the goodness of the instructional package with respect to specified groups. This is a fixed-effects model, with the chosen levels of the stratifying variables being the only ones about which information is gained. Here there arises an issue that I will describe by extending the design so that more than one instructional package is used. I assume that we may retain one or more stratifying variables as well, and thus have a reasonably complicated design. I will not, however, complicate it by introducing repeated measurements. Such a design has as its intent a comparison among instructional packages for various groups and subgroups. I repeat that in practice this is a fixed model; for we seem absolutely unable to define a population of instructional packages, and, even if we could, to be quite unwilling to select at random a set of instructional packages to study. Instead, we select the packages arbitrarily and deliberately; this is a fixed effect.

A design such as this has limitations that are inherent in all hypothesis testing. Among them is the familiar problem posed by the reasonable assertion that no sharp hypothesis can possibly be true. Testing such a hypothesis is merely an exercise in testmanship since the outcome depends heavily upon the power of the test.

It is perfectly reasonable to assert that no two instructional packages can possibly have identically the same effect; thus the testing of the hypothesis that two or more such packages have the same mean effect can be viewed as relatively unimportant. This represents my attitude toward the decision theoretic approach which has been mentioned over and over again at this conference.

Those who criticize hypothesis testing urge that we use estimation procedures instead. The question of what kind of estimation procedure is useful here is an important one. Some interest exists in developing an analogue of response surface methodology for evaluation studies. It is an analogue, since the elements of instruction packages that can be identified often exist in only a few discrete rather than continuously ordered forms. This creates some problems with the statistics, but in time these problems may be made manageable.

The response surface design attempts to vary inputs (elements of instruction) to the end of identifying an optimum or maximum output performance. This is quite a different approach to evaluation studies. The choice of this approach as opposed to the more conventional fixed model constitutes a second important issue.

Let me raise a third issue that is often associated with a Bayesian point of view in statistics. The fact that we tend to interpret every study as if it were being done for the first time should make us uneasy, even though we still can not agree on how prior information should be incorporated into our analysis. Actually, there often are relevant prior findings that remain unused.

I am reminded of how we behave in directing dissertations. We always insist on a summary of previous findings in an early chapter, but we would be horrified if the student tried to integrate them numerically with his findings. The issue here is the extent to which, in any evaluation study, the design and analysis will ignore all the possible prior distributions.

A modification in practice—namely, learning to take into account the prior information—might be the one that would most improve the design and analysis of evaluation studies.

Comments on Professor Wiley's Paper

THEODORE HUSEK

I find myself much more interested and stimulated by the latter sections of David Wiley's paper than by the introduction, the definitions, and the refinements of terminology. I know the language framework is necessary, but right now I find, so far as my own work is concerned, I am not as interested as perhaps I should be in the definitional problem.

I see the major task of the methodology in evaluation as being the development of new ways of helping the content specialist construct and evaluate educational products. As part of this task we need to do a better job of data collection and data analysis.

In this context I think the paper brought out some extremely important issues. We should be interested in the distributions of scores on tests as well as the mean. At the same time I think we need to use the traditional item more, and also reexamine the nature of the items that we use in evaluation studies. We have to examine new indices, whether or not they are obtrusive or unobtrusive.

Wiley's point about paying attention to the unit of study is also important. We seldom pay as much attention as we should to whether we are studying students, classes, teachers, or school systems. Many times we really are not interested in the individual student, and in these cases I feel that item sampling may provide an immense break-through in data collection procedures. As a footnote I would like to say that I think it unfortunate that this particular term "item sampling" got started; I do not think it really represents what is happening; there is more involved than sampling just items.

If we do not have to ask every student every question in our study, then it may be possible to begin to obtain data on the multitude of measures that we all seem to think are important. As a simple example, in the classroom situation we can use tests that in part serve to help us grade the students, in part help us to judge the course, and also give us a little data about anything we might be interested in.

With respect to item sampling, I feel that there are at least two important questions for which we do not have answers. The first of them is the context effect. One way to use item sampling is to give each student one item and to give different items to different students, but I have as yet no idea of the physical effect this has on the student. If you give him one item out of context, will he respond differently than if the item were in the context of similar items, or, for that matter, in the context of different items? Ken Sirotnik and I are now performing a study to examine this issue.

My other question about item sampling concerns its optimal use. Given a set of subjects under certain circumstances and items with certain characteristics and various test conditions, what is the optimal number of items to give to how many students? Currently Dr. Sirotnik and I are also planning a computer simulation study to examine this messy issue.

The item sampling research I have been pursuing has reminded me of another dimension that must be considered in evaluation studies. In one of two empirical tryouts of item sampling procedures we obtained an item matrix sample that produced a negative variance for the population from which we were sampling. We finally decided that there was no mistake in the formula and discovered the negative variance would be produced by item matrix samples with negative coefficient outputs.

This led us to some serious thinking about the nature of the collection of items from which we had samples. We were led, for one thing, to see the need for a special kind of homogeneity in the population from which you are taking your items, not necessarily a homogeneity in the coefficient alpha sense, but some other kind. The main conclusion we reached was that we had to pay more attention to the purposes of the test than we had thought necessary, and this is another dimension of extreme importance in evaluation.

Not only is the content of the test important, not only is the unit of study, but also the nature of the test is important. Do we want an achievement test with maximum variance? Do we want a test to measure change? Should the test be course-vocabulary free?

The question here is one of defining criteria for the various purposes. I do not think that we need a new statistics for any of the points I have made up to now; I do not think we need a new test theory. I do think we have to be a lot clearer about what we are trying to do.

As my last point I would like to bring up something I do not know how to handle at all. I will use Dr. Popham as an example, largely because we have talked about his particular issue. He is trying to train product researchers, people who will be near-technicians and who will hopefully produce better instructional programs. It is one thing to say that this can be done by using the rules of the game that we already know, but it would be silly not to try to learn how better products are built. Given that the need to produce a product includes the possibility of performing an interminable series of experiments that examine each variable, how will we be able to collect and use data from the ongoing developmental process to help understand product development and, most of all, improve it?

Open Discussion of Wiley's Paper and of Harris' and Husek's Comments

GLASS: I thought I heard you say that a person could look at a large collection of classrooms, take an average measure, covary out socioeconomic status, and then look at the relationship between the instructional programs they were operating and their output. You said that once the effect of socioeconomic status was removed, you thought that the remaining variation was due to method of instruction. It sounded to me like going out and finding classes being taught in certain ways, removing the socioeconomic level statistically, and concluding that differences in output are due to the fact that they are taught differently. Of course, there is the obvious problem of inferring causation from correlation.

But there is another problem; you probably remove the effects of instruction when you remove socioeconomic status, since it is one of the principal determinants of the way in which classes are taught, through the amount of resources that are brought to bear on instruction.

Were you talking about nonorthogonally arranged data, or were you talking about performing an experiment?

WILEY: I think I was talking about neither, and I really don't know whether I want to view that proposal as a serious proposal so much as something that might provoke your comment.

There are two ways of making inferences. One is based on information, and the other is based on theory.

I think we ought to consider much more seriously how instructional procedures work. The statement you refer to is certainly not true. It is an example of throwing out the baby with the bath water because instructional procedures are related to the social class of the community in which they occur. This poses an inferential problem; but there are two ways we can solve inferential problems: straightforward experimentation, and putting forward a strong theoretical hypothesis and then testing it. I don't think I meant to leave out the residual testing problems. Whether this is a valid procedure depends on how good your theory is. It may be a very bad theory to say that the only things that are operating in the classroom are instructional differences and social-class differences.

But if it's a bad theory, it also has the virtue of being a strong theory, and a strong theory has the virtue of being testable. When one tests the strong theory and finds it's incorrect, one adds and gains and accrues knowledge.

I think that is the major lack in this whole field. I don't view the proposal I made as a serious proposal except in the sense of its being a provocative and tentative step toward making strong theoretical statements that lend themselves more easily to testing.

GLASS: I like that response; and I like the comment that correlation doesn't imply causation, but neither does anything else.

WILEY: It depends upon how you define causation, because I think there are two different definitions.

GLASS: If you had a good theory that socioeconomic status and certain procedures were essentially causal in nature, then your proposal would be inadequate.

ANDERSON: I would like to speak of the matter of giving different sets of items to different students. I think this proposal was made largely to increase the range of items and, therefore, to increase the variety of information that an experiment yields.

If we are going to make conceptual sense of what an instructional treatment does, we are probably going to have to make several different measurements in order to distinguish between learning and transfer of training, for example.

The issue is whether one wants to use a within-subjects or a between-subjects design, a very knotty issue and not merely a matter of the logistics of testing. A colleague at the University of Illinois has written an important paper on this topic that I doubt very many people here have read because the subject matter was classical conditioning. What he shows is that you get different results if you use a within-subject, repeated measurement, repeated treatment design, than when you use a between-subjects, independent group design.

I think that we have to be concerned with the reactive effects of testing. A number of people, for example, Campbell and Stanley, have discussed the reactive effect of taking a pretest. We may have these reactive effects on the posttest side too. So I think we may want to give a common treatment to a group of subjects and then split that group, give some test items to part of the sample, and some to others in the sample in order to get estimates of the quantities needed to make conceptual distinctions among the effects of the treatment.

SCHUTZ: Who is your colleague?

ANDERSON: Robert Grice.

WILEY: If you take the issue of reactivity of testing, it is precisely the same issue involved in the controversy between Sam and me. In a repeated measures design, you may have an interaction between subject characteristics and length of the test. You have an influence of one item on another when a person gets more than one item. This is an effect of item context on the response.

The question about interactions of characterological variables with treatment variables within classroom settings is a question of the effect of pupil context, that is, classroom social context, on response, and I think can not be viewed as a psychological influence because of the very nature of this variable; that is, the difference between giving each subject more than one item is the same as putting different kinds of people in different classes versus putting different kinds of people in the same class.

ANDERSON: Yes. I appreciate the importance of independence of experimental units, the idea that whatever may be going on in that classroom, there is some variance due to the classroom.

WILEY: The essential point here is that the focus of study is different, that is, we need to understand the phenomena of the discrepancy between giving more than one item and giving only one item to a pupil. It's a nuisance variable, but we have to understand it in order to eliminate it.

ANDERSON: Well, it's more than a nuisance variable.

WILEY: I get the impression it's not a focus of study so much as a variable that affects the interpretation of responses. I think that the analogue on the classroom level should be a substantive focus of study for evaluation. The social context and its influence on response in a classroom is not a sociological area because it is not generalized outside of the institution of education, I think. Maybe it is. But it should be a substantive focus of study for evaluation because it is fundamental to our evaluative inferences.

BLOOM: There must be heresy in this some place; I think there is. I am a little concerned that maybe people who are competent in statistics and research design are telling the instructor, the psychologist, and the evaluator, what it is he may or may not do. I think I would like to see it reversed, in the sense that we in education pose the problems.

I have thirty kids. Each of these kids is different in many, many ways. They react differently to a particular teacher, a particular set of materials; they react differently at different times. I think you people are telling us that this isn't really a problem that we can attack, and I am trying to say that maybe we ought to push you to ask, "How can we go about attacking some of these questions?"

I guess I keep going back to some of the personological variables with regard to teachers, with regard to time, with regard to variations in the response of the child to the teacher at different times in life. Maybe we haven't formulated our questions clearly enough. But I feel that we are caught in a particular approach to research and this approach is getting in the way of asking educationally relevant questions.

C. HARRIS: What you want to know, Ben, is whether your instructional package is good.

BLOOM: First of all I want to know, what have I done to this particular child or that particular child? Then I want to go beyond that and know what I can do with this kind of child, teacher, material, purpose. But I want to start with one teacher and one kid and keep working up to thousands of teachers, thousands of kids, and thousands of sets of materials.

WILEY: I think there is an important issue imbedded in your comment, and it is an issue that was raised previously, most explicitly by Sam Messick, and that is the question of roles. Is there a separate role for the evaluator?

When I make my comments, I am not viewing myself as a statistician advising other people about how they should conduct their research. I am saying, "I think we have an area here." I view myself as a substantive person and am just saying how I think people should proceed in this substantive area.

There is a distinction here between how Chet and Gene would view the problem. Maybe I am co-opting Gene to my view. But I think that the issues here are not essentially statistical nor methodological ones of how to proceed but issues about what we should be studying. When I make comments or suggestions, I am not essentially recommending what I think are important substantive phenomena.

C. HARRIS: May I add to that?

I, too, am looking at the issue from this point of view, but I think I go a little bit beyond Dave, because I am also concerned with the fundamental problem of the extent to which one can, with any reasonable certainty, say something as a result of investigation.

Now, I would never want to stop investigation on anybody's part, but I would always want to caution people that if you do this, the conclusion you arrive at may not have any reasonable certainty at all. And at some point I might say, "When you test this hypothesis: *the relation between aptitude and achievement is zero,* you have wasted your time." The conclusion is known in advance, and it's a kind of silly thing to do. Fixed models seem to me to be silly for the same reason.

I am not trying to tell you to be a statistician. I am trying to tell you that the generalizations you want to arrive at ought to be hedged about by some rules of procedure.

GLASER: I thought about pushing Chester on the fixed model, but I will catch him alone.

I find Dave is violating one of Chester Harris' canons: that you ought to pay attention to what has happened in the past. You ignore the existence of a discipline called the experimental psychology of learning.

Your terminology is rather frightening, the attempt to call things *objects* and *vehicles* and *instruments*. Objects really are independent variables. What you called a vehicle is what we occasionally refer to as an organism, and an instrument is a dependent variable. You know, we have been talking this way for a long time. A *standard,* the way you talked about it, was a level or a particular value of a dependent variable that is to be attained. But to avoid this kind of terminology gets us into trouble.

WILEY: I would disagree with you, Bob, because I think that the terms of experimental psychology that are appropriate here are stimulus, organism, and response, and not independent variable, dependent variable. What I am saying is that stimulus, organism, and response are abstract theoretical terms within a theory of experimental psychology, and independent and dependent variables are statistical terms that apply only when you impose an analytic schema on the analysis of data.

The main point I am trying to make is that I think this is a substantive area fundamentally distinct from experimental psychology and that the objects of interest are objects in the sense that I used before. The main thrust and focus of research in the area is not concerned with the same kind of phenomena that experimental psychology is; consequently, we have to have other names than stimulus, organism, and response, for which I substituted objects, vehicles, and instruments.

GLASER: We're miles apart in this respect, because I consider that the process of education involves the design of an environment. This is, essentially, producing an independent variable that has an influence on an organism; this change provides a dependent variable that I have to measure. It is difficult to conceive of it in another way.

WILEY: I think you are expressing exactly the same view that Sam Messick is expressing.

GLASER: Yes.

WILEY: And that is because you are both psychologists.

MESSICK: Sorry about that. (laughter)

WILEY: And, in the context of this reference, I do not consider myself to be a psychologist, and I don't consider that the theoretical terms and objects of study for this field are the same as those of experimental psychology.

GLASER: I think Sam and I agree that the psychology of learning is somehow basic to education.

WILEY: I don't think that means it is identical with evaluation.

MESSICK: The question here is not one of pitting psychology against education but one of specifying the operational references. If you have the same operational references—

GLASER: I was going further to accuse Dave of setting up terms that get us into the danger of ignoring a way of thinking about human behavior that has been going on for some time.

WILEY: I don't think we ought to think about this problem in that way. It's fundamentally wrong.

GLASER: Why?

WILEY: Because I think it's a different problem. I think the study of individuals and the effects of treatments or stimuli on individuals in terms of their responses is a distinct subject matter area that is not the same as the effect of objects on vehicles.

GLASER: You are obliged to suggest why you think they are inappropriate, and so far all you are saying is that it is different. What is so different about it?

WILEY: Because I think the unit of study is the classroom, not the pupil. I think they are fundamentally different things.

LUMSDAINE: I would like to try to make what I think is a fundamental point. We are losing sight of the purposes of this Center, and of the most important meaning of evaluation in reference to this discussion.

I think that the distinction here is partly one between basic and applied science, or between science and technology. I think the evaluative process we are talking about is, as Chet Harris has properly called it, the evaluation of *packages*; and this is not the same as the evaluation of the effects of *variables*. The effects of variables, or the prediction of what characteristics about instruction will ultimately have what kind of effect on what kind of pupils is a problem for basic science. The assessment of particular packages of instructional material or particular procedures is a *technological* problem of product description, the description of the effects of specific products on definable populations of pupils.

We ought to face quite squarely the problem that product evaluation studies do not make very good doctoral dissertations because they don't follow the characteristic analytic paradigm of hypothesis testing. That's too bad. Maybe that means that somebody other than doctoral students ought to do these studies. Nonetheless, the studies have to be done. As Lortie has already pointed out, we have large products, packages costing millions of dollars; we have a tremendous investment and need for ascertaining whether the educational procedures we are using are effective or not. I don't think that we can ignore that problem just because we would like to find out something about the basic dynamics involved.

If this is heresy, make the most of it. Please don't accuse me of running down basic science. I am only saying that the analysis of variables, whether you call this response-surface methodology or whether you cite the type of study that Wiley cited, of which there are many, is not evaluation of products.

I assume that the purpose of the evaluation of product is just as has been stated in the earlier part of this conference. Basically, it has two purposes, one an acceptance-rejection decision, or choice decision, if it's a horse-race kind of thing; and the other is in the formative evaluation situation, the use of data to improve a specific product or program.

Now I'll say again it would be very nice, and it is very nice, whenever we have scientific data about the action of variables to allow us to predict, to allow us to short-circuit and anticipate the process of trial-and-error. But the two are not the same thing. I think there is a great danger that we are being beguiled by our own habits and our scientism into forgetting the need to concentrate a massive effort on the process of product evaluation (for which, because it is certainly an estimation problem and not a hypothesis testing problem, the analysis of variance is not the proper analytic paradigm).

We don't want to know, "Does this product, this course, this instructional package, make a difference?" That's silly. We don't want to know, "Do these two courses differ in effect?" We want to know *how much* they differ, and we want to know how much they differ on specific points. I think the fact that we tend to lapse back into the thinking and the patter of hypothesis testing is symptomatic of a basic tendency we have to fight against: ignoring a crucially important technological problem that isn't perhaps scientifically prestigious; yet it is vital to the educational enterprise.

STAKE: Beautifully said—but I would remind Art that this is not a symposium on the problems of product evaluation, not a symposium for the benefit of the UCLA Center, but a symposium on the problems in the evaluation of instruction.

I find the distinction between formative and summative evaluation not nearly as strong as you do. I like to place instructional research and formative evaluation and summative evaluation on a continuum. The basic difference as you go from one end of the continuum to the other is a matter of how much you can generalize from the results. Summative product evaluation doesn't permit you much in the way of generalizing beyond the community, the environment, the package you have. Formative evaluation is done within the development of an instructional package, but leads to revisions and extensions of the package. It gives you a basis for generalizing, or for limiting generalizations. But these generalizations still pertain to a specific package. Instructional research usually is still more general. The people in the instructional research laboratory at UCLA, or Pittsburgh, or anywhere, are concerned about relationships that will hold for many, many packages.

LUMSDAINE: Sure. I'm perfectly willing to call these in some sense a continuum. My point is simply that we should not slide back in terms of our habit structure so we are working primarily on one end of the continuum, when there is a great deal of at least equally important work on the other end of the continuum that is not, by and large, being done.

C. HARRIS: It may be that there is a real danger in the difference between asking "What is good?" and "What is true?"

SCHUTZ: And in achieving either.

C. HARRIS: That is a separate problem, to achieve it.

ANDERSON: That statement sounded both good and true.

C. HARRIS: I appreciate that.

LUMSDAINE: May I make another comment on an entirely different point, I guess a technical point? This is with respect to Dave Wiley's comment, which in general I don't think I agree with, on the unit of analysis in studies of this kind.

I would like to suggest that the unit of analysis is very simply determined if you just take seriously what R. A. Fisher said many years ago: namely, that the unit of analysis is always the unit of assignment. The business of analysis in an experiment is to conduct the analysis in terms of the operations you actually perform.

There is a little addition to this, however, that I think is quite relevant in the context of evaluation; that is, choosing the unit of assignment, not just the unit of analysis, now becomes important.

I really haven't thought this out fully yet. Let me set myself up for attack by saying off the top of my head that the unit of assignment should be the smallest unit (for economic reasons, which usually apply in evaluating an educational product) that will let us get away from serious reactive effects, serious guinea-pig effects. This can approximate the situation with most of the elements of a true double blind experiment, which of course, Lee Cronbach says is impossible. I don't think I agree with that.

If you are testing the effects of a cultural educational-television program (broadcast, not given on prescribed curricular time), I think the smallest unit of study that you can reasonably use is the community—the range of one broadcasting transmitter—because it is only in this way that you can insure differential exposure without involving serious selection biases or reactive effects.

For the usual introduction of an instructional package in a school, depending on the sociology of the school, it should be either the classroom or the whole school; in a few instances, where a major procedure is involved, I think the unit of assignment has to be the school district. Of course, if this is true, it argues for cooperative studies in which consortia of large numbers of school districts are used.

GLASS: I want to speak of your interpretation of Fisher, not on the latter point.

I looked through Fisher and Cox and half a dozen other references in design, trying to resolve the question of what the true nature of an experimental unit is. I think that they do definitely say that the unit of analysis should be the unit of assignment at which random assignments accomplish the treatment condition; but they were dealing with different materials than we do. We deal with human beings who mutually affect each other; and, even after assignment, conditions can become quite nonindependent in producing outcomes. I think, therefore, we have to expand that definition when we talk about behavioral research to say that the unit of analysis should be the smallest unit of the experimental materials that is randomly assigned to conditions and allowed to react or respond independently for the duration of the experiment.

LUMSDAINE: I think that is exactly in agreement with what I was trying to say in the latter part of my comment.

STAKE: I worry about reductionism. When I think of regression analysis, multivariate analysis, I worry about putting too many "vehicles" together into one composite "vehicle" or too many instruments into one composite instrument. I get scared of losing the meaning of things. I retreat to almost pure narrative, saying that there are these complexes of inputs, these complexes of outputs, and these complexes of values.

Do I see the danger of reductionism improperly here? Are there intermediate steps with these multivariate analyses that still permit us to keep separate the components without reducing them to a single input and a single output?

WILEY: Are you asking the question of me?

STAKE: Of anyone.

WILEY: The interest is one, I think, of how one should view the appropriate unit.

I think if you will look at the historical background, it comes out in terms of what we do with analysis, which I think is a more general problem than one of experimental design for the same concepts apply regardless of particular types of methodology one uses in the study. The question arises, "How do you account for the effects on individuals who may differentially respond to the treatment?"

It seems to me, given the unit context as an appropriate one for my suggestions, that I have to respond to these questions. Looking at characteristics, contrasts, and regression coefficients within classes is an attempt on my part to answer the question of nonreductionism while, at the same time, maintaining the integrity of the unit.

I don't know whether that's responsive to your question.

STAKE: I think you are saying, "Decide all the different things you want to keep separate, and keep them separate."

WILEY: That sounds awfully mechanical.

STAKE: One of the doubts you raised is whether pupil behavior is an adequate criterion to use for evaluation.

WILEY: Your comment, "Is pupil behavior enough?" is really the core of my comment. I think it is not enough. That is, when we talk about the effects of a treatment on the classroom, we are talking about something fundamentally different from the effects of the treatment on the individuals in the classroom.

There is a question here of reductionism in another sense, reduction of social to psychological phenomena, and that is a sticky theoretical issue concerning how one uses the disciplines.

Even if you don't grant that you are measuring completely different levels of phenomena and there is no intrinsic relationship between the two, you can still make the point that pupils react differently in classes than they do by themselves. That is fundamental enough to require discussion of the effect on the collectivity rather than the effect on the individual and to be asking the questions at a different level.

C. HARRIS: I couldn't disagree with you more.

LUMSDAINE: You are asking a question about a particular program used in two different fashions by individuals or in a class situation. I think it a very straightforward question and one that's relevant to our purposes.

C. HARRIS: But how do you distinguish collectivity from the individuals in the collectivity? I think you're way out of bounds on that point. You would still get the data from the individuals. You talk about the distribution of scores, which fundamentally refers to individuals. I think you're in a terrible box at this point.

WILEY: I don't know. It seems to me there are other kinds of data you might collect.

C. HARRIS: What?

WILEY: It's really a question of definition.
Let's say you were talking about trying to move a class in terms of its capacity to interact excitedly about material. This would not in any important sense be a property of the individual. At Point *A*, the class is sullen, threatening, and uninterested. Then, at Point *B*, it is interested, it argues, it discusses, it manifests the quality of enthusiasm. In no meaningful sense is this a property of individuals.

C. HARRIS: But you look at the individuals who do this, I insist.

LORTIE: But you are talking about a different order of reality. You are using the same individuals, but you are using them differently. In the same sense, the psychologist or the physicist can both look at the human being, but this surely does not mean that they are looking at the same order of reality. The social psychologist is using individuals as a source of information, but this does not mean he is talking about the same things in the same way with the same principles.
I think we confuse the fact that we get the data from individuals with the notion that all behavior is individualistic.

WITTROCK: I see advantages to using the class as a unit. But with research in instruction, this unit raises new problems of generalization, especially in longitudinal research.

A given class in a school is a tenuous unit. If one student doesn't attend class one day, we don't have the same unit. The next semester, when the students get assigned to other classes, the original unit ceases to exist. What does this do to my attempts to generalize my results, or to my attempts to do longitudinal research extending over one or more years of time?

If I can talk about individuals in a class and still have some basis for assuming that the errors are independent within that class, I am on a better basis to make generalizations than if I have to work with the class as a unit.

GLASS: A statistician no longer carries around the notion of a population. He did once, but no longer. A population is a notion in the mind of a scientist and researcher who applies the results of a mathematical model (inferential statistics) to real data. In actual fact, no inference of a scientific nature is ever perfectly justified. We sample a thousand people in the population of the United States right now and find out how many are single. We can't generalize that finding to the population tomorrow or next week because someone has died and someone else has been born. So to the extent to which the population you conceive of is like the population you sampled at some time in the past, you can generalize. Inferential statistics does not tell you how much the population at this moment is like the population an hour later, although any scientist will tell you it is different and often how much different.

GLASER: It is still true that no one has ever taught a class. You teach an individual in the context of a class, but no one has ever taught a class. It is impossible to teach a class. You teach individuals whose behavior changes.

LORTIE: If you are trying to explain teacher behavior six weeks after in the middle of October, you have to know certain events that have occurred in that classroom. There is a temporal and jural order that constrains that teacher; there are sets of precedents that are not understandable in terms of any dyadic relationship between that teacher and single individuals.

You may not be interested in explaining teacher behavior, but if you are, you have got to treat it as something *sui generis*.

GLASER: The class is a convenient artifact so that the teacher can reach one student.

LORTIE: Only two million people are constrained by that, two million Americans we call schoolteachers.

GLASER: All right. But they teach to the class only as a manageable way of changing the behavior of a single individual.

LORTIE: That's what you want them to do, but that is not what many of them conceive of as their responsibility.

GLASER: That's the major problem in education today.

MESSICK: I am concerned about several problems in the evaluation of packages or programs, but one of my concerns can be illustrated by a very simple example.

Let's suppose that we are interested in whether or not an educational program given to students in a classroom causes them to learn anything, so we administer a criterion test to them before and after some sequence of instruction. Suppose, in addition, we suspect that there might be some differences based upon sex or sex-role, so we look at the results separately for boys and girls. Let's suppose that in this instance the girls turn out to achieve significant gains on the average, whereas the boys do not. In general, then, it appears that the girls have benefited more from the instruction than did the boys, assuming appropriate controls.

Now, had we attempted to evaluate the effectiveness of the program without taking this interaction with sex into account—say, by following the typical procedure of comparing average gains for all students receiving the treatment with average gains in a control group—we would have reached the wrong conclusion. The point here is that we might think to take interactions with sex into account in the evaluation of educational programs, because it is such a salient characteristic and because there is a variety of empirical and theoretical reasons why it might make a difference, but there are many other student characteristics that might also interact with treatment components to produce differential effects that we might not think to sort out.

To elaborate further, suppose the test scores for the girls are highly correlated with several measures of intellectual ability, but the scores for the boys are not; instead the boys' scores are correlated with measures of interest in the area. Typically, we would not know this because we do not routinely include in evaluation studies a variety of ability and interest tests; however, if different processes are engaged by the treatment and these processes are differentially reflected in the test performance for different kinds of students, then somehow I would like to take this into account in evaluating the effectiveness of the treatment. A failure to be concerned about the processes that are engaged in by the individuals will lead to an incorrect evaluation of the treatment whenever such interactions with student (or background) characteristics are substantial. I guess this means that evaluation studies should be multivariate, since interactions with unmeasured variables are difficult to take into account under any circumstances.

WILEY: Supposing one took just the boys and regressed the criterion variable on interest in that subject.

MESSICK: Of course, but I was assuming that you don't know beforehand about the differential relevance of interest or intellectual abilities. All you know about is—

WILEY: Why do you say that?

MESSICK: That's the problem I was posing to you.

WILEY: In what sense do I not know about it?

MESSICK: Because I was considering an evaluation design, and not an atypical one either, in which meaures of interest and various intellectual abilities had not been given. If you don't include those measures, how would you ever know about this differential relevance?

If you are interested in asking, as part of the evaluation, what processes are engaged in by the individuals, to guard against the possibility that a test may measure different things under different circumstances or for different kinds of students under the same circumstances, then you would include a variety of measures routinely. If you are not concerned about that, you would never put the measures in to find it out, and you may not evaluate the product in the right way.

WILEY: We include measures for different reasons, and I think one should respond to the basic knowledge you might have but still not use the psychological measure, that is, have a different basis of putting different measures in.

MESSICK: In a very real sense, I submit, the treatment may be different for different kinds of people. Therefore, you may not be evaluating one treatment, you may be evaluating several treatments. In setting up methods of evaluating products or packages, we should look to the kinds of developments carried on in other fields where products have been evaluated for some time. I think the drug field is a good example. It is not enough to say, "This drug has the following effects." You should also be concerned about how the drug works and why it produces this effect, so that you will have some guide for looking at certain side effects and for prescribing changes in treatment if circumstances change.

I think we ought to worry not only about the effects of the treatment but also about the processes whereby the treatment works.

C. HARRIS: In a sense, this is the scientific question that is above and beyond the point of view of some people. You don't want it to be above and beyond.

MESSICK: No. And in the drug area, evaluation has not been allowed to let concern for process be above and beyond by federal regulation.

C. HARRIS: You know the wonderful cartoon about the doctor walking into the room of the patient with his student behind him and saying, "We are finding out if this drug has an interesting side effect." As he walks into the room, the nurse is pulling the sheet over the dead body.

CHAPTER 9

Methodological Problems in the Evaluation of Innovation

MARTIN TROW

SOURCES OF INNOVATION IN HIGHER EDUCATION

Currently there is considerable ferment in American higher education arising from widespread discontent with present arrangements and practices. This dissatisfaction has its roots in a set of developments in higher education and in the larger society that are changing the character and functions of our colleges and universities and at the same time changing expectations of what they should be doing.

These forces affect individual institutions in very different or even opposite ways. For example, the steady increase in the percentage of the population that attends college raises the academic quality of entrants to the more selective institutions, while it brings to less selective institutions large numbers of students who are there, at least initially, because there is not much else for them to do. The presence of large numbers of relatively unmotivated students in colleges that have no strong academic traditions poses problems similar to those which gave rise to the transformation in curriculum and in teacher-student relations in our high schools earlier this century. They are the problems, in brief, of generating in the classroom the interest and motivation that one can no longer assume the student brings with him. The concern for relating the curriculum to the lives and interests

289

of the students, rather than to a traditional body of knowledge or the specialized interests of the academic disciplines, underlies many of the current efforts to change the form and content of instruction, especially at the undergraduate and introductory levels.

There are other forces that are making our traditional forms of education less and less satisfying, in the graduate and professional schools as well as in the undergraduate liberal arts colleges. The rapid growth of knowledge makes the traditional syllabus obsolete, while simultaneously weakening the traditional boundaries of the academic disciplines. Closely related are changes in professional education as an increasingly wide range of knowledge becomes directly relevant to effective professional practice; the growing role of the social sciences in the education of physicians, lawyers, engineers, architects, and city planners is a case in point.

Whatever its sources, the ferment has led to a variety of new approaches to higher education. These include the sweeping innovations in the organizational forms of higher education, such as the consortium of institutions in California at Claremont or in New England in the Connecticut valley; the single institutions that embody some distinctive organizational principle, such as Santa Cruz's collegiate structure; the varied means of approaching what used to be called "general education;" and the latest effort any one of us may make to create a new course around a problem, or a cluster of disciplines, a new way of using teaching assistants, or the new technology of electronic instruction.

There are many kinds and degrees of innovation, and the problems of assessment of these varied efforts obviously differ. Though it is difficult, I will try to say something about educational innovations, regardless of how far-reaching in intent they are or where initiative lies. My emphasis will be less on the technical problems of evaluative research—the relative strengths of different modes of investigation or different strategies of analysis—than on the characteristics of the phenomenon being studied and assessed and on the social context in which they are embedded. What forces give rise to an innovation? What are the criteria of its success? Who cares whether or how it is assessed? These are problems for the researcher that often override the knotty difficulties of how to measure change or the influence of a clique of friends.

I would like to address myself to innovations in the curriculum and in the modes of teaching and learning, rather than to innovations in broader organizational forms, which I think involve a somewhat different set of "methodological problems."

SOME FUNCTIONS OF EDUCATIONAL INNOVATIONS

Innovations in instruction in higher education arise most often out of some felt sense of the inadequacy of existing arrangements, and very often from sheer boredom with what one has been doing. We are always tinkering with our courses or with the curriculum, even when they are working reasonably well. And while proposals, whether for a new college or for a new course, are usually justified as promising some improvement on what is being done, very often we know or strongly suspect that what is proposed recommends itself not so much on its promise of betterment as on the certainty of its being different.

An innovation is a break with routine and habit; it disrupts unreflective ways of thinking, feeling, and behaving; it requires a heightened measure of attention and interest in the matters at hand; it forces the participants, and especially the creators, to think in fresh ways about familiar subjects, to reconsider old assumptions. Above all innovation dispels, if only briefly, the fog of boredom that hovers over everything we do in our classrooms. Habit and routine are extremely useful in allowing us to do a great many necessary things without having to think about them, while freeing our minds and energies for other more demanding matters. But when habit and routine begin to encrust educational structures and processes, life, thought, interest, and creative imagination go out of them and they become boring to us and to our students. I think we know intuitively that boredom is a greater enemy of education than ignorance or error or even stupidity, that as an enemy it is rivaled only by dogmatic authority; and if boredom is a chief enemy, innovations and change are our chief weapon against it because they can break through routines and release fresh energy, imagination, and inquiry.

I am suggesting that innovations in education justify themselves by their intrinsic qualities almost without regard to their outcomes. Indeed, innovation goes on constantly. For the most part it does not advertise itself by name, often because the innovator does not need additional resources and because he does not want to become entangled in the cumbersome machinery through which formal changes in the curriculum are made.

Whether advertised or not, it is important that innovation is commonly done for its own sake and only secondarily for its outcomes. Because that fact reduces the relevance of systematic evaluation of innovation, it reduces the significance of the manifest functions of evaluation—to tell the innovator what he has achieved and how successfully—as compared with its chief latent function—to legitimize an innovation and contribute to its continuation and extension. Innovations will be made, with or without evaluations, almost regardless of their nature simply because we enjoy making them. From this perspective, evaluation studies are aimed less at the innovator than at funding agencies or course committees that can support or limit the life or scope of the innovation. Such studies thus are typically directed at expensive innovations or those that have a broader impact on other parts of an institution and thus involve persuading others that the innovation has value and should be supported. Innovations that are inexpensive or are confined within one department or one course usually are not evaluated; they are just enacted.

To emphasize the latent functions of some social pattern or practice like evaluation is implicitly to minimize the significance of its manifest functions. A large part of evaluation in education is best understood as a form of persuasion directed at powerful people who make decisions and control resources. But this is not to say that evaluation studies need be nothing more than devices for legitimation and persuasion. In modest ways evaluation can help shed light on educational practice, and perhaps help us see what an innovation actually consists of as well as what it achieves. But the context and function of such studies affect the way we conduct the studies and how much confidence we can place in the findings, and thus are deeply implicated in methodology.

I would therefore like to discuss three aspects of research and innovation in higher education—first, the political context and significance of evaluation; second, the educational and research problems posed by the diffuseness of the intended outcomes of education, including its innovative forms and the long delay beyond the college years before many of these outcomes manifest themselves; third, the great difficulty, especially in innovative courses, of distinguishing the special circumstances surrounding their creation and adoption from the other characteristics of the innovation that may recommend its institutionalization.

THE POLITICAL CONTEXT OF RESEARCH
IN HIGHER EDUCATION

We see in American higher education a growing sense of the relevance of systematic research procedures along with a considerable hostility to social research and suspicion of the educational implications of its findings. Paradoxically, both the growing need for such research and the wariness of it rise from similar sources. The rapid growth and democratization of higher education—a growth that brings into our colleges an enormous number and variety of students whose values, motives, and purposes are strange to the academic man—leads to the extension of social research in many colleges and universities. Moreover, conditions in the large public colleges and universities make it difficult to establish the old personal relation of student and teacher, and thus for the faculty member to know his anonymous students in any real sense.

Increasingly, and often for much the same kind of practical reasons that prompted the social surveys of the nineteenth century, educators are turning to social science to learn the facts about their students that are no longer directly knowable by the teacher or administrator. But this return is met with the same ambivalence among cultivated men as was the earlier development of social research. It threatens the academic man's role as an intellectual and as an interpreter of his own social experience; it asserts that much that is of importance—not only in the wider society but in his own classroom and in the students' residence halls—no longer can be adequately known and understood by the man of intelligence and sensibility. The suggestion, often made tactlessly by social scientists, that the professor of humanities cannot grasp the social processes going on around him without the aid of the social scientist's special skills and techniques is frequently met with hostility and resentment. The very existence of social research on campus, as some professors have candidly stated, is an insult to their intelligence. Their response, made perhaps with more feeling than logical consistency, is to doubt that social science is more than a pretentious fraud and, at the same time, to fear its manipulative consequences.

But social research threatens not only the intellectual competence of academic men regarding their teaching functions; it is also felt by some to be a threat to liberal education. Colleges where educational practices and arrangements are seen as embodying the values of the institution, instead of merely facilitating their attainment, are likely to be inhospitable to the notion of applying the findings of social research. To the extent that its practices have become highly institutionalized, charged with value in themselves, a college will resist conscious planning based on rationalized procedures and data. Such an institution is likely to rely on committee deliberations as more likely to preserve the primacy of the substantial values. By contrast, a college committed to the achievement of easily measurable goals, and which is prepared to measure and modify its practices against the criterion of the efficient achievement of these goals, is more likely to sponsor and apply social research against whose findings elements of the organization can be evaluated.

Liberal education is a substantial value in itself. It is the practices and relationships and patterns of behavior that enter into it, much more than it is some nebulous "outcome," difficult if not impossible to measure. By contrast, vocational and professional education is to a much greater extent instrumental and goal-oriented—the outcomes are measurable in skills and knowledge acquired, examinations passed, diplomas earned. The colleges and the parts of large universities that are deeply committed to liberal education have been less likely to welcome or apply social research that touches on their core values and activities than have those organizations or parts of organizations whose practices are instrumental to some more clearly defined or measurable goals.

Typically, in American colleges and universities, power is distributed in extremely complicated and obscure ways among the administrators, the faculty, the trustees, and various important constituents, such as alumni, the current body of parents, and, in the case of public institutions, the legislature or other sources of public funds. The question of what is manipulatable and by whom is itself highly uncertain, at least as difficult to know as patterns of student behavior, which may be the nominal subject of investigation. Every organization is to some extent a polity, in which political processes determine who can initiate what events, who can veto them, and whose consent must be gained before policies are put into effect or sabotaged. Some studies of internal organizational processes have been done within formally bureaucratic organizations (for example, business firms) and within formally democratic organizations (for example, trade unions and political parties), but almost nothing has been done by way of studying the political processes within institutions of higher education. These institutions are in part bureaucratic and in part democratic, combining the principles of hierarchy and colleagueship in varying degrees. I am not suggesting a design for the study of colleges and universities as political structures, but rather that the relevance of social science to educational policy cannot be discussed without recognizing that policy recommendations within colleges are quickly transformed into political issues.

A highly rationalistic conception of the relation of research to policy obscures the political character of a college and of recommendations to it; those who hold such conceptions are continually surprised and indignant when the institution does not take the "reasonable" course of action suggested by research. A director of the Bureau of Institutional Research at a large midwestern university has described, with becoming candor, actions taken by faculty committees in two cases in which his bureau conducted research on the issue in question; both actions were at variance with the apparent indications of the research. He observed, with more sadness than anger, that "actions such as these represent one of the frustrations of a person in institutional research. The mere establishment of an institutional research unit does not in itself guarantee that decisions will be made on a more realistic, objective, and reasonable basis. As you can see, even in our institution with its long tradition of faculty-oriented institutional research, faculties and faculty committees have been known to make decisions on other than a purely objective basis."

Without describing these cases in detail, I can report only that the research center's recommendations are "realistic and objective" on the basis of a rather narrow conception of educational efficiency, and that faculty members with other values regarding education might well see such a research report as a political document and oppose it as such. But the claim to objectivity denies the value implications of the research and makes opposition to it mere pigheadedness, or in the words of this research man, "stubborn resistance to change." This in itself tends to excite suspicion of all social research among faculty members whose values are frequently at variance with those implicit in, but denied by, officials and bureaus of research.

The general principle that policy recommendations, whether they are or are not based on social research, are in most cases immediately transformed into political issues alerts us to a number of politically relevant factors intervening between research and implementation. The distribution of power in colleges and universities is more diffuse than in most formal organizations. The principle of bureaucracy tends to centralize formal power and authority at the top of the hierarchy, while the principle of colleagueship tends to spread it more widely among the faculty. There is some evidence of the existence of a long-range trend toward the diffusion of power by means of a strengthening of the principle of colleagueship and of faculty participation in the government of colleges and universities. The AAUP, for example, finds that over the past several decades faculty influence in most of the colleges they have been studying has been growing. There seems little doubt that this tendency is a result of the strong efforts American colleges and universities are making to upgrade themselves to the level of the more distinguished colleges and universities where the principle of colleagueship is most strongly and influentially established. One result of this tendency is for the interests and values of the faculty to become more widely and more directly involved in the application of social research to educational policy. This in turn makes it increasingly difficult for administrators to act with authority, even on the basis of research findings and recommendations.

The interests of the faculty are touched at many points by proposals to modify the structure or content of an educational program. Clearly, areas of investigation vary in the degree to which they visibly impinge upon the interests of the parties concerned. In general colleges will be more receptive to applied research on issues further removed from the interests of those who make the decisions—more hospitable, for example, to research on student life than on faculty authority, to research on the social implications of residence hall architecture than to studies of the distribution of power in college and university departments.

In the United States the bulk of applied research in higher education has been carried out by fact-finding agencies within the colleges and universities, by assistants to the president, by deans or assistant deans, by testing offices, and increasingly by offices of institutional research. The line between social statistics and social science is a fine one and lies in the shift of a passage in a report. Drop-out rates, for example, may be indicators of underlying social and institutional processes; the next step is to study these processes more directly. If this step is taken relatively rarely, it is partly because the people who do this kind of research for colleges and universities rarely are social scientists or have an interest in organizational analysis, and partly because of the suspicion with which research is viewed by important parts of the faculties of many institutions.

Some of this suspicion has a different basis from that which arises from the dispute between humanists and social scientists over the relative power of science and sensibility for interpreting social life, but its effects are similar and reinforcing. The suspicion arises from a profound struggle that goes on within many institutions and takes many different forms, a struggle between those committed to some ideal of liberal education, to the development of the intellectual powers of the individual, of his breadth of vision, independence of mind, and critical faculties, and those primarily interested in education for extrinsic ends, for social and vocational skills. The suspicion of research held by many humanists is that in this struggle, basically a political struggle over the means and ends of education, research is usually on the side of the vocationalists.

It is thought to be so, not only by virtue of the kinds of people who do it but also by virtue of the very kinds of data they collect. For while the indicators of success of a liberal education are likely to be vague, difficult if not impossible to measure, and scarcely distinguishable from the effects of all the other experiences a student has had in his life, the indicators of successful training are the kind of performances that testing offices and offices of institutional research can measure. The recognition of this by those faculty members committed to liberal education, and the suspicion that arises from it, partly explains the mechanisms that surround offices of research to insulate them from the core values and activities of the faculty; for example, their subordinate status and their definition by the institution as technical agencies gathering statistical information primarily for administrative uses, rather than for basic research into the nature and processes of higher education.

The criteria and indicators of "success" of educational practices or innovations that are employed in educational research are elements in the academic-political controversies on many campuses. They affect the forms that research takes and the reception it gets—that is what happens to it.

PROXIMATE AND ULTIMATE GOALS OF EDUCATION

Some "outcomes" of education are easily measured, and for that reason, as well as others, they are commonly measured. Among these are the student's grade-point average, drop-out or transfer rates, achievement of graduate scholarships and higher degrees. These matters are part of almost every research into higher education, not only because they lend themselves to easy and systematic measurement, but also because they are important in themselves. Grades are not merely an "index" (however weak) of what has been learned; they are also an important determinant of the individual's future opportunities and life chances, among them his chances of gaining admission to a good graduate school. Acceptance by a good graduate school is an even more important determinant of a man's chances of making significant contributions to science or scholarship.

But whatever their objective importance, which is very great, grades and higher degrees are inadequate measures of the outcomes of educational experience for many reasons. They do not measure the whole of what some men wish education to do to or for students. They are poor measures, for example, of the success of a liberal education in refining sensibilities, developing capacities for critical and independent thought, or the use of reason and evidence in everyday life, or the enhancement of the individual's capacities for enjoying life and making fruitful contributions to it. Some men want these great goods to flow from a scientific and technical education as well. The difficulties in discovering whether indeed an education has these effects are several.

In large part, these qualities of mind and spirit do not show themselves, during the college years, but may be laid down then as potentialities that bear fruit in later life and career. They are for the most part, exceedingly difficult to measure systematically, however much we pride ourselves on our ability to recognize their presence or absence in others. Moreover, these qualities are not only valued outcomes of formal education, but also the products of the whole of a man's genetic equipment and life experience. Even if we could measure them with some precision and confidence, how are we to distinguish the part played by formal higher education from all the other more enduring and emotionally weightier influences on a man's life and character?

In a word, then, the most important and truly valued outcomes of higher education are extremely difficult, if not impossible, to assess. As a result, many institutions, usually those with the least firm educational purposes and the least distinctive character, fall back in their self-assessments on those presumed outcomes of higher education that are most easily measurable. And, in a familiar translation of necessity into virtue, such an institution may define its aims in terms of what can be measured, and to shape and justify its practice in terms of its success in reducing the drop-out rate, increasing the number of fellowships its graduates earn, and the like.

What are the alternatives for the institution that does not want to reduce its educational aims to the level of the most easily measured of student characteristics? Matters are not quite so hopeless as my remarks above may seem to suggest. There are things that research can do to help an institution assess its success in achieving its most profound and not merely its most proximate aims. For example:

1. We are not confined to the study of the most obvious and easily measurable outcomes of education. There are ways to explore changes in basic values and attitudes of students, and even aspects of their personalities that education aims to modify over the college years; to explore changes in life plans and the conditions and experiences in the institution which give rise to them; to attempt at least to study such subtle matters as creativity and independence of mind and judgment.

2. These are all to a considerable degree a product of the student's life experience before coming to the institution. To some degree we can assess the extent to which they are already present at entrance, so that we can make some assessment of the relative efficacy of different educational practices during the college years in developing (or inhibiting) these qualities.

3. We can do far more than has been done to follow our graduates into their adult careers to see what happens to them there, and to see if we can make even tentative inferences about connections between their adult careers and their college experience.

THE INFLUENCE OF EXPERIMENTAL RESEARCH ON EDUCATIONAL PRACTICE AND ITS OUTCOMES

Different forms of social investigation vary in the extent to which they affect the educational processes that they aim to illuminate. A survey of a college's alumni presumably would have little direct influence on the faculty and students at the institute at the present time. Questionnaires distributed to entering freshmen probably will have relatively little effect on their subsequent behavior, though repeated questioning about a given issue—say, the question of student-faculty relations—might be expected to increase the salience of that issue in the minds of the students. But experimental research-linked changes in the curriculum are likely to have very marked consequences for the teaching-learning process over and above those effects which the alterations are specifically intended to achieve. It may be worthwhile to consider for a moment the problems such experiments pose for research designed to assess their effects and effectiveness.

First, there are the difficulties, already discussed, of measuring the genuinely desired outcomes and of disentangling them from the manifold extraneous influences of life and time outside the experimental classroom. Experiments share this difficulty, as I have suggested, with other forms of research into education.

In addition, experiments in education, like social experiments in general, pose special difficulties for research, in that they introduce into social situations powerful forces over and above those purposefully introduced by the experiment. These "other forces" affect the outcomes of the experiment in ways that are very difficult to separate from the effects of the "intended" experimental procedures, since they so closely resemble them. The general phenomenon to which I am referring has become know as the "Hawthorne effect," after the famous experiment on worker productivity at the Hawthorne plant of the Western Electric Company in the late 1920s. That study showed that the experimental situation itself, independent of the purposeful manipulation of the situation, modified social relations, group morale, and individual motivations among the subjects in ways that affected their performance, in most cases for the better.

This phenomenon has become widely associated with the independent and common observation that in education no experiments fail, so that it has been seriously suggested that one educational strategy would be to "institutionalize the Hawthorne effect" by making "experimental" innovations a regular part of school or college administration. This advice has not been widely adopted because institutions are made as unhappy as individuals are by a steady diet of innovation; it puts a strain on lines of communication and authority, makes the coordination of the different parts of the institution more difficult, and makes life less predictable and thus more unsettling and anxiety-arousing for the individual. The gains of educational innovations may be worth all this, but before recommending a strategy that dissolves the distinction between "action" and "research" by making the research itself the action, it may be worth considering what are the forces involved in such "experiments" to see if indeed they can be made part of the institution's regular procedures without their unsettling side effects. Put another way, what are the sources of their evident power to raise performance?

1. One of the forces generated by a classroom experiment is to make the "subject" students feel somehow distinctive, a "special" group getting special attention. This effect of the experimental situation was noted at Hawthorne, where it presumably generated among workers there the special group morale and commitment to the task that resulted in their higher individual performances.

2. Quite distinct from that process, however, is the fact that experimental courses are customarily instituted and taught by imaginative teachers, who have given an extra measure of thought and effort to the pedagogical problems they face. The innovators themselves, one may guess, are probably better than average teachers. This cannot help but play a part, perhaps the major part, in their customary "success."

3. Not only is the self-selected staff of an experimental class likely to be more gifted than the average but they are also likely to have a strong interest in the success of *their* "experiment," and to communicate that interest through the enthusiasm with which they tackle the course. Enthusiasm for a subject is a well-known characteristic of the successful teacher, even in more routine courses. Coupled with the innovative character of an "experiment," it is a powerful pedagogical force.

4. Typically, if not uniformly, "experimental" courses have been assigned larger amounts of the institution's resources than have comparable "routine" courses. The ratio of teachers to students is higher, and the amount and intensity of student-teacher interaction is commonly greater in "experimental" than in routine courses. This also helps educational "experiments" to succeed, both through the more thorough way in which the course material can be covered with each student and through the higher levels of student motivation that teacher attention can generate.

Much of the success of an "experimental" course is related to the fact that it is a break in routine that forces a higher level of imagination and energy from the staff and excites it in the student. The sheer innovative character of such an "experiment," coupled with its typically rich endowment of resources by the institution, almost ensures its success independent of its purposeful content. But the problem for research that aims at assessing the worth of an educational innovation is clear: how to distinguish the experimental effects from the designed or purposeful effects. It may be argued that the time to assess an innovation is when it is no longer an innovation, when it has become routinized and no longer can call forth the special energies, resources and enthusiasms of an "experiment." The trouble is that an institution usually wants an assessment of an experiment in the curriculum before it has committed major resources, before it has made the necessary organizational adjustments, and before it has persuaded or coerced people who did not initiate it to staff it.

I have emphasized the difficulties for research in assessing the worth of a curriculum experiment, but I do not want to exaggerate them. Research methods of several kinds can be employed to explore the workings and outcomes of an experimental course, and such research may be of real value to the institution so long as the policy-makers recognize the special characteristics of educational experiments that make them so difficult to assess. For one thing, the degree of "success" of such a course, whatever its sources, can be tested at its conclusion by using the ordinary indicators of comparative performance on examinations, or more subtle indicators of intellectual powers and creativity that might be devised. Another approach is to try to identify the pedagogical forces set loose by an innovation by subjecting the experimental course to close and continuous observation, aiming to see what elements in it call forth the greater motivation and effort that are observed. Such observation, of course, should also be accompanied by parallel observation in "ordinary" classes covering the same or comparable materials, to allow something approaching a comparative analysis of the observational data. It may well be that such observation will allow the research to identify aspects of the course— pedagogical devices, organization of the subject, or whatever—which, though not explicitly "intended" by the innovators, appear to be particularly successful, and which might be more widely introduced into the curriculum on a regular basis. In a sense this would be an effort to separate the pedagogical forces associated with innovation from innovation itself. It would be an attempt not to institutionalize innovation but rather to identify those of its elements which are not dependent on the presence of the innovator or extra resources. Knowledge of the genuinely effective aspects of educational practice might liberate institutions from reliance on the specific educational forms in which they manifest themselves, allowing the invention of new forms that embody the effective processes in more effective or less expensive ways. To my knowledge, this kind of observation has not often been done on a systematic basis in educational institutions, and while the value of such observations is heavily conditioned by the skill and sensitivity of the observer, it very much warrants trial.

ILLUMINATIVE VERSUS EVALUATIVE RESEARCH

I have been discussing thus far some of the problems of evaluative research in higher education: difficulties rooted in the suspicions of humanists and the conflicts within faculties; difficulties in the criteria we use to assess educational efforts and in the remoteness of ultimate goals from proximate outcomes; difficulties in disentangling the unique qualities of innovative teaching procedures from their enduring and transferable qualities. But I feel an obligation here to end on a more hopeful note: to suggest that these difficulties are superable and worth the effort needed to deal with them.

The first issue has to do with the institutional context of evaluation: who does the job, to whom does he report his findings, and what is done with his report? Insofar as evaluation is done by a research arm of the administrator, which reports to the administration regarding the value of certain aspects of the curriculum, the research enterprise is likely to face considerable suspicion and hostility from the faculty. As I have suggested, much of the suspicion is merited, since evaluation must be predicated on educational values, however disguised as science, and these values are very often, I might almost say chronically, in dispute. The way for evaluative research to meet this suspicion involves two changes in the character of such research. First, research on innovative efforts must be seen from the beginning as "illuminative" rather than as "evaluative" in the narrow sense. It must recognize that the value of innovation also comprises the rewards gained by the faculty members who create it and are not confined to its easily measured outcomes. Second, researchers must recognize that these outcomes bear only a remote relation to the ultimate impact the faculty member may be hoping to have on the minds, characters, and lives of his students. This means that such researchers must forego the dubious pleasure of awarding gold stars and demerits to academic innovators, but must try instead to serve them. Research on innovation can be enlightening to the innovator and to the whole academic community by clarifying the processes of education and by helping the innovator and interested other parties to identify those procedures, those elements in the educational effort, which seem to have had desirable results. Such research may involve a comparison of proximate results, such as examinations, papers, and so forth, with those produced by other more conventional courses. It may also involve close semiparticipant observation of the course in an effort to identify the operative social and psychological mechanisms that the innovative procedures create (often beyond anyone's intention) that engage the interests and efforts of students and open them to the instructor's attempts to transmit skills, broaden horizons, or deepen understanding. Precise techniques of inquiry are not at issue here; we know pretty well their characteristic strengths and limitations. What is important is that the research be seen to be in the service of the innovative enterprise, and not sitting in judgment on it. And for that, it must accept its own tentativeness and function as a facility of the faculty, not as a part of the administrative apparatus. The formal status of the researcher or the research group, who employs him, to whom he addresses his findings, and how he avoids being drawn into academic controversies, are crucial here, though circumstances differ enough that no set of recommendations on these matters can possibly apply to all institutions.

In considering the gulf between proximate indicators of the results of educational innovation and their long range goals, wisdom resides, I believe, in a decent regard for the limits of research. What are the qualities that make creative engineers, resourceful businessmen, thoughtful and responsible citizens, men of independent mind, moral sensitivity, and aesthetic sensibility? What relation does college performance bear to these qualities? And what influence do specific educational arrangements have on what men do and what they are in their lives? A consideration of the kinds of men who have been exposed to the most varied kinds of higher education, or to none at all, should make us pause before we give any ready answer.

When we return, as does the teacher himself, to the student before him, we may attend to what we see not merely as a most imperfect indicator of future achievement or qualities, but as of intrinsic importance. On one hand it is important that students be able to learn and be able to demonstrate that they have learned assigned material—important for its effect on the range of possibilities that are open to the successful students but closed to the academic failures. On the other hand, it is at least as important whether students are bored or engaged, committing their energies or coolly withholding them, fulfilling obligations or freely involving themselves in learning. And these things as we know can be affected by educational arrangements and procedures—however constrained by deeply set qualities of mind and character that the student brings with him to college and that remain with him unaffected there. We also know with Woodrow Wilson that:

The real intellectual life of a body of undergraduates, if there be any, manifests itself, not in the classroom, but in what they do and talk of and set before themselves as their favorite objects between classes and lectures. You will see the true life of a college—where youths get together and let themselves go upon their favorite themes—in the effect their studies have upon them when no compulsion of any kind is on them and they are not thinking to be called to a reckoning of what they know.

We know also that the life of the student outside of class can be influenced by our efforts. The innovator can see some of this, but he is busy teaching. The researcher can see more, much more. He is trained to see just those things, and he is less constrained to see what he hopes to see. The illumination of educational innovation through systematic research can be in large part the identification of those educational processes that can be linked to the innovation—the processes of learning and growth that go on inside and outside the innovative classroom, laboratory, or residence hall.

Finally, with regard to the uniqueness of innovation and the special resources of talent and imagination frequently available to it, it may be that research should attend precisely to those qualities of abundance, rather than trying to "partial them out" in assessing the effects. It may be that what we should aim for is not so much the routinization and institutionalization of successful experiments as a climate and organizational arrangements that make innovation easy and frequent. If, as I suggested at the outset, innovations recommend themselves for their intrinsic qualities rather than for their putative outcomes, if they are our chief weapon against boredom and routine, then the major research effort should be directed toward the conditions which facilitate their creation rather than toward the effort to "evaluate" them once in being. This posture is completely compatible with the aim of illuminating their processes and proximate gains. We can want to encourage innovation, while recognizing that some experimental efforts will be more successful than others, judged by their own and by broadly accepted criteria. We need not set aside all "academic standards" or notions of craftsmanship and achievement in a wholly unreflective celebration of academic spontaneity. There is enough anti-intellectualism afloat today, both inside and outside the academy, without social research contributing any more. But here we come very near to what is perhaps the central problem for the student of educational innovation. For in innovation we are very often dealing with "enthusiasm" on the part of innovators and sometimes of their students as well. On one hand, this enthusiasm means heightened attention, alertness, involvement, commitment, creativity; on the other, the danger of enthusiasm lies in the passion of the true believer and of his terrible certainties. If our studies of educational innovations can illuminate those forces that are respectively the chief instruments and enemies of education, we can perform a very considerable service to our students and to our innovative colleagues, and to the enterprise of learning.

Comments on Professor Trow's Paper: Toward a Multimodel Theory of Evaluation

EUGENE LITWAK

I should like to make some comments on specific points raised by Professor Trow and then advance a multimodel theory of evaluations with ensuing predictions as to what type of evaluation strategies might be ideal for twenty-four "generic" situations.

OBJECTIVE AND "INTUITIVE" EVALUATION TECHNIQUES

Professor Trow provided a good case in point for Robert Stake's view (stated in his discussion with Glaser) that the degree to which we can provide good measures is not necessarily related to the importance of the objects we are trying to evaluate. As a consequence, when we do not have "objective" measures we may have to utilize crude evaluation techniques. Insisting on more objective measures may mean no evaluation at all or one which is quantifiable but a poorer predictor than quantitative judgments. Thus, Professor Trow points out that it is difficult to operationalize some of the goals of higher education—the notions of good citizenship and liberal education. These are goals that might be achieved ten to fifteen years after a person leaves college and which involve properties that are difficult to measure. The history of evaluation has been one where we have tried to introduce quantification into new areas. On the whole, this has been beneficial. However, as this movement has gained success the dangers mentioned by Stake, and suggested in specific detail by Trow increase. Current evaluation specialists must increasingly ask themselves when to use quantitative techniques for evaluation and when to use more qualitative techniques, rather than assume that invariably quantitative techniques are better. This argument must be differentiated from the one in the past where a hard core group resisted all systematic qualitative evaluation and another insisted on it. In the second part of the paper we will suggest specific evaluation procedures where people can make only a gross estimate of their goals.

DAILY EFFECTIVENESS AND PROGRAM RESULTS— TWO TYPES OF EVALUATION

Another point made by Trow illustrates something discussed by Lortie and Gage in their exchange. Trow points out that it is difficult for people to accept evaluations, especially when their jobs are at stake (for example, when someone in a position superior to theirs is involved). A host of literature (including an article by Lortie) supports this view. In effect, what Trow suggests is that perhaps we should find a way to put evaluation in the hands of the people who are doing the job or in the hands of their colleagues. I think this touches upon the discussion between Gage and Lortie as to where evaluation efforts should be made.

I would suggest that there are two legitimate notions of evaluation that should be accepted. One is the notion of daily job effectiveness. The individual uses the daily information to change his behavior and perform his job more effectively. As mentioned above, there does seem to be some evidence that such kinds of evaluations require a trusted colleague or individuals themselves to do the evaluation. The major problem with this kind of an evaluation is that the evaluator becomes too identified with the individual being evaluated and in situations of ambiguity is likely to orient the evaluation in terms of personal welfare rather than around the goals of the organization. This is commonly recognized in the cry for the "objective" outside evaluator. It is my view that this second type of evaluation is also necessary; I would call it an overall program evaluation. It does involve outside or "impartial" evaluators and the total administrative hierarchy. It is also characterized by the fact that it is not a daily evaluation but yearly or less frequent. This evaluation has all the problems raised by Trow, that people will find it difficult to accept, as well as the virtues of being able to take a hard look at what is being accomplished. It seems to me that we have two important problems with regard to evaluation and each of them requires a different kind of evaluation. I think that Trow has emphasized only one side of the issue. I would suggest that the evaluator must, in any given situation, make a diagnosis of the problem. Is he trying to find methods for getting teachers to improve their daily efforts through some systematic feedback device, or is he interested in overall program evaluation? Both are legitimate goals and at any given stage in an educational institution's development he may want one or the other or both stressed.

HAWTHORNE EFFECT AND SOCIAL ENGINEERING

My next point concerns what Trow referred to as the "Hawthorne" effect. His point is very similar (and paradoxically different) to the remarks made by Gage in his description of Stephen's work. Gage points out that most evaluations show that different school programs make little difference on the students' progress. By contrast, Trow points out that most experiments in education seem to work. These are not necessarily contradictory propositions since one is talking about experiments and the other about established school programs. What is similar about both of these propositions is that both Stephens and Trow suggest that the crucial underlying variable is teacher ability and enthusiasm. These are far more important than program variations. Within a school system teachers with outstanding abilities are randomly distributed among the programs. That presumably is why difference between programs means so little. Among the experimentors and the nonexperimentors they are not randomly distributed. The experimentors are usually highly enthusiastic and able. That is why all experiments work.

I would agree that the Hawthorne effect is an important one and that we should concentrate on ways for maintaining it continuously. However, I think that there are also legitimate problems of social engineering that might explain why successful experiments cannot be translated into successful school programs. It seems to me that often experiments have many hidden complexities aside from ability and enthusiasm of the investigator that the investigator cannot translate to a system-wide basis; sometimes because the investigator is not aware of them, often because there is a lack of knowledge as to how to introduce innovation into a system (both the letter and the spirit of the innovation) and often because the system cannot put the kind of resources used in the experiment into the general application and what emerges is a watered down version of the experiment.

I would be somewhat pessimistic about our educational establishment if indeed all that was involved was a "Hawthorne" effect, because I doubt very much that mass institutions can find sufficient people of the high calibre and degree of enthusiasm suggested by such analysis. I would therefore suggest that we concentrate in addition on the organizational basis for accepting innovation of all kinds rather than how to maintain involvement at the highest pitch.

TOWARDS A GENERAL THEORY OF EVALUATION

I think throughout this conference there has been a questioning as to whether there is one ideal form of evaluation that holds in all situations or whether we have different strategies of evaluation for different situations. Glaser raised this point quite clearly. I would opt for the latter point of view and would now like to review some of the elements that would have to be considered and the differential evaluation techniques they imply. The variables I am suggesting as being generic and their relationships to evaluation strategies are as yet very primitive. However, I do want to go beyond the platitudinous statement that different situations require different evaluation techniques. With this limitation in mind, the following are some of the factors that can be used to differentiate all situations and as a consequence suggest differential evaluation techniques.

Current State of Knowledge

The "classic" evaluation technique is very close to the pure experiment or "classic" planning strategies. The suggestions in all cases tend to be the same. First specify the goal then the alternative strategies (that is, teaching procedures) for reaching this goal. All the evaluator has to do is to measure the children before the new program is introduced, measure them after, and decide which if any of the programs show the most marked difference. Assumed in this analysis is the ability to define one's goal clearly (measure their achievement) as well as to specify the range of alternative means. Professor Trow has pointed out that it is often difficult if not impossible to measure one's goals or even to specify them clearly. He might have also added that it is often difficult if not impossible to specify alternative means. There are various reasons for this (for example, there is not enough time, it costs too much, and so forth). However, in this section I want to stress one reason—the state of knowledge. Is there any theory that systematically suggests what are the best evaluation strategies when we have incomplete knowledge? Most of them start out with the premise that before evaluation can begin we must have excellent states of knowledge. The work of Dahl and Lindbloom and more recently that of Lindbloom on decision making strategies provide some useful alternatives. They suggest in situations where things are going reasonably well in the sense that there are no major calamities, that one use an incremental strategy. This implies introducing innovations that tend to be simply monotonic projections of past historical trends and which are reversible. This often means small innovations. If nothing major happens then one continues this process. Still assuming that one has only a gross specification of goals and little knowledge of alternative means, they suggest that an alternative strategy be used when the situation is bad (as judged by gross qualitative evaluation). Thus, a major depression or the clear sense of the community that the school procedures are not working well in the inner city would be cases in point. In this situation they suggest a "calculated risk" strategy. The main point of this strategy is that one is to depart as radically as possible from past historical trends and pay less attention to the reversibility of the innovation. The reasoning behind this directive is that where things are going very badly, little can be lost and much gained by radical shifts in methods.

The important point to be stressed is that they are suggesting "rational" strategies in situations where we have incomplete knowledge. If their arguments are correct they also suggest criteria for evaluation under incomplete states of knowledge. What they are saying is that the evaluator need make only the grossest qualitative assessments about goals in situations where goals cannot be clearly specified because of lack of knowledge. Thus, the college faculty must make a decision right now as to what constitutes requirements for a liberal arts degree. Yet the goals they seek to achieve (such as good citizenship and the humanitarian man) cannot be measured right now with any degree of accuracy. At this point, Dahl and Lindbloom would be suggesting that the evaluator only has to make, in conjunction with his client, a qualitative judgment as to whether liberal arts programs have failed or not. If he feels that they have not obviously failed in the sense that there is no general complaint or he has some positive general assessment, then he might adopt the incremental approach. This means he should measure any innovation on three criteria—does it fit within the historical trend, is it reversible, does it have any consequence based on the same kind of generalized judgment that can be thought of as definite failure or success? Alternatively, if the initial assessment is that the current situation is very bad then the evaluator uses the "calculated risk" as the basis for setting evaluation criteria. In both cases where historical data are not available the evaluator might utilize as his comparison group other institutions engaged in similar work and in similar circumstances.

To summarize, what is being said is that where one has relatively complete information as to goals and means then one can use the traditional "experimental" before and after evaluation approach. However, where one lacks knowledge, then one uses only gross judgments on goals and turns one's attention to the evaluation of a given approach as being historical on or off the trend line as well as judging the reversibility of the innovation. The more completely one can develop a theory of decision-making under circumstances of differential states of knowledge, the more confident one can be about having a general theory of evaluation that fits the problems that often confront evaluators (for example, how to evaluate with incomplete knowledge).

ECONOMIC MANPOWER SCOPE OF EVALUATION

Another problem that emerges in evaluation is the scope of the evaluation procedures. Should we jump into an evaluation of total systems or should we first evaluate small experimental programs? It seems to me that one might move towards small experimental laboratory evaluation procedures where one has good knowledge (operational measures) of goals and alternative means but little knowledge as to their relationship. A small laboratory based evaluation situation permits the investigator to engage in all kinds of variations with minimal concern for costs. Thus, the general rule would be that where one is suggesting the use of very costly evaluation processes and where one has high states of knowledge on means and goals but not their relationship to each other, the evaluator moves toward a small experimental model. By contrast, where he has low cost processes and either high or low states of knowledge he might want to utilize large scope evaluation procedures (for example, large-field experiments or surveys). This discussion bears directly on the point that Alkin was making. Where a technique was extremely costly the evaluator might either restrict it to small experimental situations or even say it is not worthwhile studying even if it were the most successful. Thus, a teaching method that says that there must be one teacher for every child in the school might be the most successful teaching technique, yet one which we would not bother to evaluate or evaluate in a laboratory-like situation since even with the optimal effectiveness, the costs would be too high for any system to undertake.

CONTROLLABILITY OF INDEPENDENT VARIABLES, AND EXPERIMENTAL VERSUS SURVEY PROCEDURES

Another factor which obviously affects the evaluation procedure is the controllability of the independent variable. Often in the field of education as well as in social sciences in general it is difficult to control our independent variables. We are often in the position of astronomers rather than laboratory experimental physics. For instance, we are often in the position of looking at two schools, one which has a close school-community relationship and the other which does not. We want to see what difference this makes for the child's reading skills. However, we are not in a position to get the schools to alter their procedures systematically. If we are fortunate and can spot these incipient experiments beforehand, we can do some panel analysis. If we are unfortunate, we must do a one-shot comparative survey after the schools have begun their programs. In any case we must seek to match out populations through statistical manipulation or stratified procedures rather than relying on random assignments to experimental and control groups. I think there are at least three points on the continuum of controllability. Where one has maximum controllability then one can approach the classic experimental design. Where one can anticipate changes but not control them, then one can utilize a panel analysis design and highly purposeful samples (for example, natural experiments). When one can neither anticipate nor control independent variables, then one uses a random sample survey and relies on statistical analysis to provide matched groups, and so forth.

COMPLEXITY VERSUS SIMPLE—EXPERIMENTS AND SURVEYS

Unlike some researchers, the evaluator is often called upon to evaluate a stimulus in all of its complexities. By contrast, a researcher faced with a complex stimulus can at his lesiure break it down into its component parts and study each part separately. He can leave to others the problem of how these parts might interact with each other. However, a policy-maker might want to know how a given method of teaching will interact with the various types of teachers he must have in his schools, the various types of intellectual abilities of the students he confronts as well as the various types of motivation they bring to the situation, the various types of social economic groupings of parents he must deal with, and the generalized community support for such a program.

Any time the stimulus is a complex one (that is, consisting of many independent variables with some causal links to each other as well as to the dependent variable) the kind of model that Gagné was suggesting would be difficult to undertake. It would involve an intolerable number of controlled experiments and might yet miss the overall causal links between independent variables. In such situations one might well move to a very large survey or panel study which permitted, in a relatively short period of time, an examination of many different combinations of variables. This might not have the logical eloquence that is suggested by the pure experiment but it has the virtue of providing useful information in a reasonable time.

There is nothing said so far which is very new. However, I would suggest that two things derive from the above analysis that might be viewed as more controversial. First, on the basis of the reasoning I have just gone through, we should forego the notion that there is one ideal mode of evaluation and move towards the concept of a multiple model. In fact, this is what most evaluators are now doing, and what I am suggesting is that rather than viewing this as a departure from an ideal norm we view it as an ideal state. This in turn leads to the second point; is there some theory that states what types of evaluation processes are ideal for the various situations that confront evaluation. Can we show that there are really a limited number of dimensions that characterize most situations we have to evaluate? If so, we have a finite number of models of evaluation procedures rather than an infinite number. The specification of the basic dimensions for classifying situations as well as their evaluation outcome would constitute a multiple model theory of evaluation. What I have done in the above section of this paper is suggest some of the obvious starting points for such a classificatory scheme as well as some of the evaluation outcomes. To make this point quite clear, these dimensions must now be simultaneously considered and the forms of evaluation which ideally emerge from this simultaneous interaction specified.

Table 1 presents in tabular form my first approximates of a multiple model theory of evaluation. This theory is based on all possible combinations of the following simple principles.

1. *Complete knowledge* of ends and means permits true experimental evaluations and the purposeful sampling of individuals where necessary, (for example, a priori matching groups).

Incomplete knowledge of ends and means generally precludes the use of experimental designs—requiring either survey or panel analysis-type instruments and requiring random selections of populations. Where the overall lack of knowledge is coupled with the gross evaluation that the situation is all right then the evaluator seeks comparative data—this is, either historical or not—with the goal in mind of judging any innovation in terms of its continuity and reversibility. Where this lack of knowledge is coupled with a gross evaluation that the current state is very bad then comparative data is examined to see how far the new innovation departs from the old.

2. Where the evaluation process is costly (in terms of time, manpower, or general economic resources) then small laboratory evaluation procedures are desirable. Where the evaluation process is not costly then large scale surveys or field experiments are possible.

3. Where the evaluator has complete control over the stimulus he can

use experimental designs, where he has only partial control he needs to use partial experimental designs like panel analysis, while where he has no control he must use techniques like survey analysis.

4. Where the stimulus to be examined is very simple it provides an ideal situation for small group experiments, whereas if the stimulus is very complex (there are many independent variables and they are related to each other in a causal sequence) then large surveys or panel studies will generally be necessary.

With this in mind, we can look at cell number 1 in our table. According to our multiple-model theory of evaluation this is the situation where the evaluator should use a small experimental laboratory study to do his evaluation because he has fairly good knowledge of the means and ends, the stimuli (means) are very simple, it would be costly to do the evaluation on a large scale, and he is able to control the stimulus. By contrast, if the evaluator is in a situation described by cell 24 he would use large scale surveys with random samples. This is true because he lacks knowledge to operationalize the ends, he cannot control the stimulus, he assumes the stimulus is complex, and he can collect much data inexpensively. These conditions prevent him from setting up an experimental laboratory evaluation or even seeking a natural experiment. At the same time they put a premium on gathering much information (for example, complex stimulus, lack of knowledge, and low costs).

The reader will note that cells 13, 16, 19, and 22 are all considered to be logically impossible. It is argued that in situations where there is incomplete knowledge of ends and means, one cannot (by definition) control the means (stimulus). If we examine cell 12 we find an interesting mixture which in turn suggests a slightly different kind of evaluation method. This is a situation where there is knowledge of ends and means but where the investigator cannot control the stimulus. This is a typical problem of astronomy. In addition, the stimulus is very complex that tends to suggest the use of large survey and this is further reinforced by the low cost of the evaluation. However, this survey can differ from the survey discussed in cell 24 because here the investigator has much more knowledge of the ends and means. He can put this knowledge to use by his sampling procedures. He can either sample to insure that he has incorporated natural experiments or he can stratify his sample to insure that he has relatively equal numbers of cases for all of his major variables. Cell 6 is like cell 12 except we now have a situation where the costs of the evaluation are high. In such circumstances the size of the sample will probably shrink so we now have a medium rather than a large survey. Cell 11 is also like cell 12

Table 1

Relationship of Social Factors to Type of Evaluation

COMPLEXITY OF THE STIMULUS	CONTROL OF THE STIMULUS	KNOWLEDGE OF ENDS AND MEANS VERY GOOD (GOOD OPERATIONAL MEASURES)		KNOWLEDGE OF ENDS AND MEANS VERY POOR (POOR OPERATIONAL MEASURES OF ENDS)	
		COSTLY TO COLLECT DATA	NOT COSTLY TO COLLECT DATA	COSTLY TO COLLECT DATA	NOT COSTLY TO COLLECT DATA
Simple Stimulus (one or two independent variables not causally related)	Complete Control	1. Few small laboratory experiments	7. Small field experiment	13. Logically not possible to have no knowledge and complete control	19. Logically not possible to have no knowledge and complete control
	Partial Control	2. Small panel study with highly stratified sample	8. Medium sized panel study with stratified sample	14. Small, simulated panel, random sample, trend and reversibility analysis	20. Medium simulated panel, random sample, trend analysis reversibility analysis
	No Control	3. Small survey with highly stratified sample	9. Medium sized survey with stratified sample, e.g., around natural experiment	15. Small survey, random sample, reversibility and trend analysis	21. Medium survey, random sample, reversibility and trend analysis

314

COMPLEXITY OF THE STIMULUS	CONTROL OF THE STIMULUS	KNOWLEDGE OF ENDS AND MEANS VERY GOOD (GOOD OPERATIONAL MEASURES)		KNOWLEDGE OF ENDS AND MEANS VERY POOR (POOR OPERATIONAL MEASURES OF ENDS)	
		COSTLY TO COLLECT DATA	NOT COSTLY TO COLLECT DATA	COSTLY TO COLLECT DATA	NOT COSTLY TO COLLECT DATA
Complex Stimulus (many independent variables related in a causal sequence)	Complete Control	4. Many laboratory experiments coupled with survey data (e.g., questionnaires to respondents)	10. Large field experiment coupled with survey analysis of respondents	16. Logically not possible to have no knowledge and complete control	22. Logically not possible to have no knowledge and complete control
	Partial Control	5. Medium panel study with stratified sample	11. Large panel study with stratified sample	17. Medium simulated panel, random sample, trend analysis, reversibility analysis	23. Large simulated panel, random sample, trend analysis, reversibility analysis
	No Control	6. Medium surveys with stratified sample	12. Large survey with stratified sample, e.g., natural experiments	18. Medium survey, random sample, trend analysis reversibility analysis	24. Large survey, random sample, trend analysis, reversibility analysis

but it differs in that the investigator has some control but not complete control over his environment. This suggests that he might be on the scene before a natural experiment is begun and thus he might be able to get before and after measures and do a panel analysis though not have a true experiment. Cell 5 is just like cell 11 but involves a more costly evaluation so we would suggest the chief thing differentiating them would be the size of the panel study. Cell 10 is like cell 12 but here the investigator has control over his environment. This permits an experiment but the large number of variables would suggest that he might not be able to do all possible experiments nor would many single experiments necessarily unravel the interactions between the independent variables. Since this cell also states that we are not dealing with a low cost situation, it would seem to us that a large field experiment coupled with much interview data would be appropriate. The experimental design will permit one to test out some of the variables through experimentation while the use of the survey and consequent panel analysis would permit one to use statistical analysis to deal with the more obscure variables and the more intricate set of interactions. Cell 4 would be like cell 10 but for the increased cost. This may mean smaller field experiments or the use of many laboratory experiments as the chief evaluation procedure. The reader will recall that we said that cell 1 was the ideal situation for a small laboratory experiment. We think that cell 7 would be the ideal situation for a small field experiment. It is exactly like cell 1 but there are little costs in doing the field experiments so it should be done because it often means one less inference for the evaluator (for example, will the laboratory results hold in the field). The reason that this field experiment can be small whereas cell 10, which is very close to cell 7, must involve large field experiments, is because cell 7 has a single or simple stimulus. The reasoning for cells 2 and 8 follow those for 5 and 11 with the difference being in a simple rather than complex stimulus. Similarly, 3 and 9 follow 6 and 12.

If we now examine the opposite side of the table where we have incomplete knowledge, it has already been noted that cell 24 differs from cell 12 (which matches it except there is complete knowledge) in having a random sample rather than a purposeful sample. In addition, this theory suggests that where incomplete knowledge is coupled with a positive gross evaluation of current activities the evaluator will utilize his statistical techniques to look at the method being evaluated historically (through retrospective questions) or comparatively with similar organizations and all assessments will be guided in terms of their "fit" to historical or comparative trends. In addition the methods will be evaluated in terms of their reversibility. In contrast, if the gross evaluation is that the current situation is very bad, then the evaluator, using the same comparative data, will see how far the innovation departs from the historical or comparative standards. Cell 23 is almost the same as cell 24 but here there is some partial state of control over the stimulus. However, it suggests that the control may not be quite as great as cell 11 which is the same except for the knowledge base. Therefore, it is suggested that here we might have some kind of simulated panel study—through use of cohort analysis and possibly two cross-sectional surveys taken at two different periods of time but not with the same people. Using statistical devises one can have a simulated panel design. Cell 18 would be like cell 24 but requires a medium-sized survey because of the cost factor and cell 17 would be the same as cell 23 but smaller in size because of the cost factor. Cell 21 would be like cell 24 but because of the assumed simple stimulus would require a smaller sample size while cell 20 would be a smaller version of cell 23 for the same reasons. Cell 14 would, because of cost, probably be like cell 20 but even smaller while cell 15 would be like 21 but smaller.

This now completes the provisional analysis. We have generated almost 24 different types of evaluation techniques. No attempt is made to argue that this is where an evaluation theory will eventually lead. However, it does illustrate in more detailed terms what we mean when we say there must be a multi-model theory of evaluation. Hopefully, this initial formulation, crude as it may be, will encourage others to pursue this inquiry more deeply.

Comments on Professor Trow's Paper

DAVID NASATIR

The overwhelming sense that I get from this Conference, and in part from Professor Trow's paper, is the punch line of the joke that ends up, "You can't get there from here." In the case of evaluation I am not at all sure where is the "there" that I want to get to, and I am certainly not sure where is the "here" where we are. I do not know what the starting state we have at hand is; and if I cannot adequately describe the context in which I am innovating, I have serious problems about exporting that innovation to some other context. Professor Trow's remarks, although cast in the collegiate vein, are in fact very applicable to the problems of introducing and promoting innovation in general. Value innovation in the educational enterprise may take place at all levels; the problems associated with the politics of innovation are not peculiar to the university. It is necessary to consider explicitly the latent functions of the routines of everyday classroom life.

The need for assessing, evaluating, and describing the present situation in which an experiment will be performed, is a pressing one. It points out very quickly the inappropriateness of the experimental model of research for what is in fact a descriptive task. It is very difficult to make prescriptions for innovation when you cannot adequately define all the relevant conditions.

In addition to describing the starting point for innovation we should, as Professor Trow suggested, also study the side effects. This brings us very quickly to the question of criterion variables, for one man's criterion variables are another man's side effects. An increase in reading scores produced by an experimental technique may be of less importance in determining adoption than problems of classroom behavior generated by adoption of the experimental technique.

A second point raised by Professor Trow with ramifications for the evaluation of educational innovation in the curriculum area has to do with the time perspective. It often appears that educational planners take for granted that the future is quite nebulous, that we do not really know what the world is going to be like, that we are very unsure of the kinds of skills that are going to be needed in the future and consequently become somewhat immobilized. How far away is the future? What is the time perspective that must be brought to bear? If we presume that future society is going to be much like today, I think Martin Trow's comments, while delightful, reveal a personal bias that I personally would not share. It is a strong assumption that the core values of the faculty and the students engaged in education, including higher education in America today, are those of providing and acquiring a liberal education.

This is an empirical question, and it is my feeling that the overwhelming values are not liberal but vocational. While I share the valuation of liberal education, I do not think that it is truly widespread at the moment. Someone should certainly do a study of what constitute the core values of American academic life today. Such a study should be national in scope and include students as well as faculty and administrators. It might not be a bad idea to include legislators and taxpayers as well.

I doubt that many people experience the kind of liberal education about which Professor Trow is talking. Those who do make up the liberal education establishment, and those who control the possibility of change actually appear relatively content. They are not tempted by problems of assessment. I will return to this point, because I think it is suggestive of the importance of broadening the unit being studied in order to include not just the student, but all of the participants in the educational endeavor. You will recall Professor Trow suggesting that many of the innovations that we see are innovations which amuse the innovators and, I suspect, many of us who are engaged in education. Some who are engaged in educational innovation do so only because it is amusing, because it is interesting; were that possibility denied us, we would turn our attention to more diverting things.

Recently in a policy decision dealing with retention of some computer hardware at a research center at Berkeley, the issue was phrased, "If we don't have the toys, we can't keep the programmers." If we do not have the toys with which innovators can amuse themselves, they cannot be kept around.

If we now make the opposite assumption that social patterns of the future are not going to be as they are today, then Professor Trow's concerns are much more germane. We already see a tremendous expansion of formal education toward a point where it becomes coterminous with life itself. This fact is evident when we look at the life style of graduate students at many leading universities. Wives and children of the students are immersed in the educational context; they live on the campus or in its environs; their social, economic, religious, political, military, and vocational experiences are cast in terms of the educational setting. And these conditions may be continuous over periods of three, five, eight, or even fifteen or more years at a time.

It is not at all clear that there is a distinction between educational life and "real" life. As Professor Husek said to me one day when we were bicycling along the coast toward Malibu, "I don't know what you're in training for, but this is the event as far as I'm concerned." Students are not in training. This is the event.

Similarly, because of a concern of social scientists and many others, we see the reaching out of formal education to envelop the young child and to provide in the educational setting almost a total definition of his life. Even at present more than a third of a person's life—this is for the bulk of the population of the United States—is spent in education. Educational enterprise is the setting for life experiences, and I suspect this will be true increasingly, not only in the numbers of people involved but in the scope of their involvement.

Now it may be that organizational differentiation in the future will remove some of the overwhelmingly vocational character of contemporary education. Many of today's problems may be solved by a development of highly specialized educational organizations. As the rate of technological change increases, the length of time that a given skill is useful will diminish. Education, even for the most vocational, will never be finished, and we may expect schools to be reorganized so that dropping out and dropping in is the normal rather than the deviant pattern of attendance. Even the near future is sufficiently vague, the probability of rapid technological and social changes sufficiently great, and the variety of alternative social arrangements so large that those who wish to emphasize the transmission of specific, readily measurable knowledge might wish to hesitate a little bit and consider the merits of what they are doing. If we were to view the future as something different from a continuation of present arrangements, we might redefine the problem of evaluation of instruction to look, instead, at the side effects. We would want to evaluate the quality of the educational experience itself rather than the amount of specific information transmitted. We would want to look at the delight engendered by the participants in the process of learning rather than in what is learned. If education is going to become an all-pervasive element of everyday life and if we are going to be the technocrats who manipulate it, we should concern ourselves with the quality of the educational experience itself in humane terms.

Who are the participants in this endeavor? Professor Trow has pointed out that it is folly even for the most narrow-minded of innovators in the technology of education to confine their considerations only to those things affecting the students. It is folly because the real world does not operate that way. Whatever innovations are to be proposed must be considered in light of their impact on all participants in the enterprise. This consideration determines, in large measure, the likelihood of adoption in the real situation; it also establishes the range of parameters to be considered in evaluating the worth of the innovation. It is necessary for educational researchers to make manifest many of the functions that the school performs. Often, these are in conflict with basic values school administrators hold about the ideal nature of the educational enterprise. It becomes necessary, for example, to make manifest the amusement value of innovation for those involved and to include these considerations in the cost-benefit analysis repertoire Professor Alkin has put forth. It becomes necessary, in order to anticipate the kinds of reactions and degree of recalcitrance that may be displayed by students, faculty, parents, and administrators, to consider the school's role in socializing children to middle-class values when promoting innovations that would tend to undermine this function. Similarly, the innovator must consider its role in the process of social mobility or in courtship, for example.

If we "can't get there from here," where might we go instead? It might be better not to try getting anywhere until we know what it is we are after. So I come back, really, to my original point: instead of studying the evaluation of instructional programs we might better concern ourselves with optimizing the deployment of our scarce educational resources. Central to this task is a consideration of the existential quality of life in the classroom, in addition to any ill-defined, difficult to measure, putative outcomes for which we have little certainty of their future utility.

Thus, in order to evaluate the study of instructional programs you really have to take the instructional program itself as the dependent variable. This does not mean just those things that you choose to manipulate or control because they are easy to manipulate or control, but those things that are actually going on, whether desirable or undesirable. It is important to note the differences between the model program and its actual operation.

In order to rationalize the production of innovations and their evaluation, it is vital that we take into account the interaction of contextual along with the experimental variables. The problem is that we do not have a well-developed theory that allows us to go very far in the quantitative specification of types of contexts. With this shortcoming we unfortunately expend our scarce resources doing that which is somewhat easier to do, simply because we have methods developed for it, not because the proposed innovations lead necessarily to a more desirable end. What must be done, then, is to begin work on the assessment of instructional programs in their totality rather than focusing upon the minor aspects of them that correspond to existing curricular divisions.

Open Discussion of Trow's Paper and of Litwak's and Nasatir's Comments

TROW: I very much like Dave's extended discussion of the point about education being coterminous with life; but that raises a basic question about what it is we are evaluating. It seems to me "evaluation" ordinarily presupposes an instructional outcome rather than an intrinsic good. If, in fact, at a certain point, education becomes coterminous with life, then we are engaged in the criticism of life rather than the evaluation of educational outcomes. Then, perhaps, the model that presents itself is more like the kind of criticism that men indulge in when they say, "What is the effect of the building of a freeway through a city on the quality of urban life?" The answer to that question is somewhat different from the evaluation of some instructional package for a given desired outcome. Here we are making a set of critical judgments, but deeply embedded in those judgments is the problematic quality of the very thing that we are examining. There is very little distinction between the package and the outcome. They are both very much involved with each other, with a variety of values and aesthetic judgments, and also with a different kind of expertise. For example, the evaluator is not content to echo the dilettante's "I don't know whether it's any good or not, but I know what I like." Rather a student of urban life would say, "Well, if you build a freeway here, that is likely to have a set of determinative consequences on a variety of things somewhat independent of whether you like it or not." There is a series of skills that, in practice, research can strengthen. But my point is that research and the quality of judgment and "evaluation" are very much bound up with one another.

Now, it would be very easy for the peace of mind of all of us to say, "Well, this is all very well for higher education and graduate education, but in the lower schools we are really doing something else." I would like to question whether there is such a sharp division. Certainly, there is a difference in emphasis. But is there such a great difference between the kinds of things that you mean by the evaluation of instruction in elementary and secondary schools, and the sorts of things Dave was pointing to when he talked about education becoming coterminous with life, where, I think, he was suggesting a very different model of the criticism of life as an aspect of the evaluation of it?

WITTROCK: The discussion of our final paper will be led by Dr. Alexander Astin, of the American Council on Education. This year he is a Fellow at the Center for the Advanced Study of the Behavioral Sciences. I think he is well known to nearly everybody here for his research in higher education, and he has become well known among the Fellows this year for the many things that he can do, one of which is to lead a discussion.

ASTIN: I wondered what you were going to say there. I'm not sure where Marty stands with respect to the inherent value of innovation. At one point, he suggested that innovation justified itself, and at another point, I think he said he didn't think it did. But whatever his position is, he has suggested another evaluative study. In other words, I am not willing to assume that change or innovation is necessarily beneficial, independent of the substance of the change; but I think it is perfectly legitimate to evaluate it as such. Maybe we can use boredom as one of the dependent variables. I'm serious about this. It clearly exists so I see no reason why we should not be able to incorporate it in an evaluation model.

I want to make a further comment on what Dave said. He is suggesting, I think quite correctly, that a lot of students are interested in the experience of the instructional technique for its own sake and not necessarily in any long-term benefits. Therefore, I think we have another value study here, with maybe enjoyment of the experiences as a dependent variable, although I think we have to distinguish between technique and impact, even if very short-term, on the experience of individuals.

c. HARRIS: This most recent comment bothers me a little bit, because I think instruction necessarily has plans and purposes. If they are played down, then I don't think you can discuss education as being coterminous with life problems or discuss urbanization as an espect of evaluation. Evaluation, it seems to me, follows if, but only if, the construction of the educational enterprise includes plans and purposes that can be formulated.

From this point of view of people who are somehow responsible for instruction and education in this sense, client satisfaction is not an adequate criterion. The quality of life is not adequate. There is this nagging and probably important question, "Did anything important happen and, if so, what?"

NASATIR: I wouldn't disagree with you that there are consequences intended and unintended of all instructional programs. I wouldn't disagree with you that it is vital to pay some attention to what those consequences are likely to be. I think that it is also vital to stress that the educational experience and client satisfaction is of such importance that not only have we seen early evidence but have every reason to believe that there will be more evidence, both on my campus and on yours, that if client satisfaction is not provided there will be no formal educational endeavor at all.

c. HARRIS: My problem with client satisfaction is that, if you had investigated the attitudes of the students in the schools at the time of Hitler's most powerful influence in Nazi Germany you probably would have found a terrific degree of client satisfaction, yet we all know that that was socially terribly expensive, so I am not impressed by client satisfaction as a criterion in this country.

TROW: Part of the confusion here may be in trying to evaluate in terms of one kind of outcome, one set of criteria. Client satisfaction might not be a sufficient condition for you, but maybe it would be for the client. In other words, I don't think you are ever going to get agreement so long as administrators, educators, students, and innovators tell you what the appropriate, relevant criteria are and how they should be weighted.

C. HARRIS: What happens in an enterprise that has certain characteristics? This must be known.

TROW: I think that you are demanding of higher education considerably more of a skeletal framework than it has or is likely to have in the future. Many subjects taught in colleges are functional substitutes for one another, and the people who teach them have very uncertain conceptions of what they want to achieve. They are quite prepared to use an approach the way you use a piece of Kleenex, to change it profoundly from year to year, to give it to other men who would change it more profoundly, or to do away with it completely.

Many of my colleagues in sociology have no belief at all in sociology as a lower-division subject, and others don't believe in it as an undergraduate subject, yet it is taught to large numbers of people. You affirm that they must have plans and intentions. In some sense they do, but the plans and intentions are very much intertwined with the existential problems of filling out a curriculum and earning one's pay rather than being part of a careful plan toward some end or goal.

C. HARRIS: But I want to distinguish between interchange of people and instruction.

ANDERSON: I am a believer in the theory of countervailing force, and I should now like to try to countervail.

The recent observation that education is coterminous with life is a very profound, provocative kind of conception. I want to think about that further. It does make sense to me.

I am impressed by the enormous range of outcomes, intended and unintended, that an instructional program can have. I am also concerned, and have been made to become more concerned, about long-range goals with respect to life and the relation of education to these; but I should like to resist an implication from this that we teach organized bodies of knowledge and measure these outcomes merely because we can, not because this is a significant purpose in its own right.

To my mind, if we can learn something about the conditions under which people will understand an organized body of knowledge and will be led to use and apply this body of knowledge broadly, these are rather significant goals. I wouldn't want to lose sight of these objectives as we consider broader consequences of an educational program.

ASTIN: I think you can justify the use of multiple criteria even though it may upset the educator who has very specialized kinds of objectives in mind, if for no other reason than that I think we need to monitor the side effects of any instruction practice. Consider the drug experiment and its side effects.

C. HARRIS: I agree, because then you get more information that may be relevant. But I think that unless we can define instruction as having definite plans and purposes, I can't talk to you about the problem. You block me off.

ASTIN: I am not worrying about the level. I would say that instruction at the university level, the graduate level, and in seminars has to have plans and purposes, or else I don't know about that which we are talking.

GAGNÉ: We had some discussion about what to evaluate, and I'm a little concerned about that because we were reminded so many times during the conference that procedures, methods, and techniques that have been evaluated have seemed to show very little effects. I think we ought to take that very seriously.

For example, many of the studies done in education have attempted to evaluate some kind of instructional variables, perhaps as simple-mindedly as comparing television lectures with live lectures. We have heard about many others that came up with no differences, so far as any measures are concerned.

I hold the hypothesis that the instructional variables didn't show any effect because their effects were washed out right in the educational setting —where we have something called the class, in which, for obvious reasons, the treatment cannot be applied individually to each person who ultimately is going to be measured. From this hypothesis, I have concluded that the important thing to evaluate in elementary and secondary education is what would happen if you didn't have a class! The same argument would apply to higher education. I suspect that many, many studies in higher education will show very few effects of any instructional treatment.

Martin Trow has reminded us that we must deal with the politics of the situation, that we must somehow arrange to study the kinds of things in a higher education setting that won't be offensive to people with a liberal arts point of view. O.K., but I am tempted to conclude that maybe the important thing to study (if you're looking at higher education) is how good it might be if it got rid of this terrible delusion called liberal education. That would be a good thing to study and evaluate. Otherwise, I think we are going to have more trivia.

STAKE: As an evaluator I don't like to have to choose between interpersonal outcomes and academic outcomes. I don't like to have to choose between client-satisfying outcomes and producer- or instructor-satisfying outcomes. It seems to me that an evaluation study is not an evaluation study until it has included a complex of outcomes, outcomes reflecting the educator's goals and the student's goals, the community's and still other goals.

I don't see the problem as one that can be adequately described as a producer's or a consumer's problem. That is a useful distinction sometimes, but it seems to me that at the end of an evaluation study we must be in a position to say something like, "Too much was spent in providing good sociology classes and not enough in providing good mathematics classes." I think the decision-maker must have information like this from these studies to permit him to allocate his resources better, whether he is a developer or a purchaser of the educational program.

PACE: The way I put some of these things together for myself is something like this. I have often been critical of a number of large-scale evaluations in higher education because, among other things, they have inexcusably ignored the acquisition of broad bodies of knowledge as a significant dependent variable. There have been a lot of major studies that haven't looked at achievement, and while I regard them as interesting and important research studies of personality development during the college years, I can hardly classify them as evaluations, when one of the primary objectives, the acquisition of some organized body of knowledge, is ignored.

The learning of a discipline is always embedded in affective content; consequently, the experience of learning, the commitment to learning, the satisfaction in the task, and the sense of relevance one has about what he is doing, which perhaps is a little bit of what Dave Nasatir had in mind when he talked about the existential experience in its own right, are integral parts, it seems to me, of the plans and purposes of an instructional program.

KEISLAR: I think we ought to recognize that this problem exists at the precollege level. In fact, a feeling is prevalent in society that there are certain values, even at the kindergarten level, that every child should experience quite apart from any future goals.

The expectations of parents and the communities would be an important variable to study for a program like this, because this obviously is not a factor to be ignored in an evaluation enterprise.

While I have the floor, I have another comment to make on something else that Marty Trow brought up. Some of us have been trying to set up carefully controlled program conditions, hoping that we could arrive thereby at what might be considered an evaluation of a sequence that might also hold up when carried out by a hundred different teachers in a hundred different circumstances; but I suspect we haven't really begun to study the effects of what kind of deterioration occurs when the program is taken out in the field.

TROW: I wonder if this problem isn't really a problem of replication. Isn't this really what you are concerned about?

KEISLAR: It is more than replication, because we are asking, "How can we do an evaluation study efficiently and cheaply and then have it work successfully when subjected to what could be very different conditions?"

TROW: So you look at the independent variables and include all of the conditions of the experiment. It is a replication of relevant conditions.

SKAGER: I think the word for it in the field is "Institutionalization." There are many phases of evaluation in the laboratory, but there is a final phase where it is institutionalized. That's what Evan is talking about.

GAGNÉ: Has anyone examined as a model of evaluation the engineering model that deals with component testing, system testing, field testing, and so on? Are there analogous operations here that have some value? I don't know quite whom to ask.

TROW: I am a mechanical engineer, and I can only suggest that a pre-stressed concrete beam in a laboratory is a prestressed concrete beam on a freeway, unlike an educational package that does not always transplant well.

GAGNÉ: Yes, but I was thinking of a weapons system model. There are regulations that prescribe how a system will be tested. To be sure, some of this is component testing, such as one might do with a beam; but then there is the matter of putting the system together and deciding whether it will work in some setting. Then you go on to ask, "Will it work in a larger setting where, in fact, the people are different?"

TROW: I am sure a very clear case in point is when you have replicated what would be the ordinary teacher's experience. What you generally can not replicate is the capacity to get these teachers to accept the package in the way you present it. There may be all kinds of built-in resistances, both by principals and teachers, to the acceptance of an innovation, regardless of the merits of the case. That is something confronting you on an engineering bases that you may not be able to replicate on a lab basis, not that you can't in principle do it but in general you don't think about these things until you are in the field. I am trying to say that there are many field conditions that you don't even think about in the lab experiment. They are just too complicated and too many.

C. HARRIS: Another way of saying all this is that you make a mistake when you think of the teacher as a fixed effect.

LORTIE: I would like to comment empirically on this point, with regard to teachers. I find them to be not too impressed by the notion of disciplined, orderly technique. On the contrary, they like to see themselves as decision-makers who (according to Phil Jackson's close-in observations of perhaps 200 to 250 interpersonal decisions a day) make these decisions in the light of their own conception of what is to be learned.

I gave a questionnaire to 6200 teachers in Dade County, Florida, with the question, "How does the good teacher go about monitoring his or her own performance?" The response that got 63 percent of the vote, I think it was, which is rather high in 6200 cases, was "The good teacher monitors his or her own progress, decides whether he or she is doing a good job, in the light of his or her conception of what the students should learn." So their belief system is that they are acting normatively, acting well, when they make assessments of their own performance based upon personal goals.

I am not saying that these personal goals equal the number of cases, but I sure as hell am saying that they are much, much more differentiated and diverse than any set of stated plans and purposes. It is not a gentlemanly valuing of things for their own sake. Many of them are quite sentimental in a moral sense; they link conventional learning directly to a good moral outcome. Reading or arithmetic in the elementary school is an instrumental act, but it is intrinsically or ultimately good. There are other kinds of conceptions going on on that level that I don't think I want to go into, but teachers certainly do not view themselves as agents of anybody's preplanning.

NASATIR: Is there not somewhere such a thing as a plan or program that somehow could be made optimal for a period longer than an instant? I am reminded of Robert Boguslaw's book about systems of design of social change called THE NEW UTOPIANS, where he discusses the kind of heuristic programs nicely primed to make choices when they run into forecast problems but quite unable to cope with unforeseen problems.

Wouldn't it be characteristic of every evaluation and every program to have a standard component that must itself be involved in change? Furthermore, might it not be true that, in between the time the program is established and the time when observation or anything else begins, what you are after has changed as well?

WILEY: May I make a comment about that? I have done a little bit of data analysis for the SMSG evaluation. If anything is apparent from the study of this very complex educational program, it is that, by the time the data analytical problems are solved and the data analysis done, a program like that will very likely have ceased to exist as a viable program in our society. Ten years have passed and now there is a different curriculum. I think this is essentially what Dave is saying.

TROW: There is another point, too. There is a presumption that the relation between the lab experiment involving innovation on a small scale and its practical implementation is a difference in scale. I think that it's a difference in kind. I might go so far as to say that any two lab programs are more alike than are those lab programs and their extension as engineering or educational programs. They are fundamentally different undertakings, and I think this must have some implications for the use of evaluation on a small scale for the testing of large-scale operations. My own belief is that these are fundamentally different in their entirety.

WITTROCK: Before we close this symposium, I would like to make a few remarks. At this conference I have tried to bring together different groups of educational researchers to discuss new approaches to evaluating instruction. From the methodologists, we have obtained new ideas about important issues, such as the proper units to use in evaluation studies. Gene Glass' comments about units are most helpful, and so are Dave Wiley's comments, although we may not agree that the classroom is the right unit. One still faces the same problem of correlation among units when the classroom is the unit. Each classroom in the school is correlated with each other one. Does that mean the school system should be the unit? I don't think so. The proper unit of analysis is the unit used to assign the treatments to the learners.

We have heard from researchers in learning about what is important to them in an evaluation study. It's very refreshing to hear Bob Gagné say that he is interested in student learning, for example, whether the student can wrap butter. I certainly agree with Bob, and we need his viewpoint in educational evaluation. We also need people such as Anderson, Glaser, and others of our ilk to provide their perspective to evaluation. Consider the help to evaluation Bob Glaser provided several years ago with his article in the *American Psychologist* about criterion referenced tests. As a result of his perspective, we no longer want only to discriminate among students as we once did. We also want to know, "Has or hasn't the student learned something?" An item that all students might fail at the beginning of the semester and that all might pass at the end of the semester is one that most psychometricians would have thrown out of the tests because it did not discriminate among students. But I think Bob Glaser, and I know I, would want such an item in the test if it had content validity, if it sampled concepts important to us.

From differential psychologists and educational administrators, such as Sam Messick and Marvin Alkin, we have also heard about criteria useful in an evaluation study. They have raised issues regarding the multivariate problems in evaluation, where we want to know more than "can the learner wrap butter?" We want to know if he likes to wrap butter, if he likes to go to school to learn how to wrap butter, if he retains his skill at wrapping butter, and if he can transfer his skill at wrapping butter to wrapping oleo-margine. I feel we need multiple criteria to evaluate instruction, including at least learning, retention, transfer, and affectivity.

From the sociologists, including Dan Lortie and Martin Trow, we have had yet another important perspective on evaluation. They suggest we think about our conventional definitions of instructional treatments and instructional variables. Is it most useful for evaluating and for understanding instruction to analyze it into variables, such as reinforcement, which we have studied in the psychological laboratory? Or are we convinced that in addition to the psychological variables we need units to emphasize the sociological and dyadic processes occurring in the classroom. Dave Wiley alluded to this problem by indicating that boys and girls learning to read together in the same classroom represent a variable different from boys and girls learning to read in classes segregated by sex.

And we have heard from nearly all of us about whether or not we "believe in" interactions between instructional treatments and individual differences, such as aptitudes for learning. If we are to become more rigorous and precise about evaluation, we must measure and understand these interactions. I am most concerned with the interaction between the individual's background knowledge, his traits, his aptitudes, and instruction. Unfortunately, relative measures of aptitude and traits haven't been very helpful in studying this interaction. We need absolute measures of individual's knowledge and traits, especially of aptitudes in response to instruction, of aptitude to learn from instruction.

We have heard new and comprehensive approaches to evaluation from Ben Bloom, Robert Glaser, Robert Gagné, and David Wiley. These papers and the other papers at this Conference are the kinds of conceptual activity I had hoped would come from conference.

What other results have come from the interactions of the people at this symposium? I have time to mention only one of them. It is that we have used evaluation differently from the way it has been customarily used. We have frequently talked about evaluation studies that try to relate consequences back to their antecedents. I hope this comprehensive research approach to evaluation of instruction is developed further in coming years. We need to think more about building comprehensive research approaches in education, and I hope evaluation studies will be seen as research tools designed to contribute to knowledge and theory about instruction as well as to practical decisions about teaching and learning.

Open Discussion
of the Symposium

PACE: One type of problem is the evaluation of day-to-day instruction in the school. Evaluating the Los Angeles city schools and evaluating higher education in the United States are other types of problems. The evidence one looks for and the variables that are relevant are related to the magnitude of the unit of analysis. By *magnitude* I don't mean importance in any sense, but simply the scope and size of the problem.

I can't imagine planning a brief instructional sequence, or even a semester course, without a great deal of specific, explicit concern with the intended behavioral outcomes of the instruction. On the other hand, if you are evaluating a large social system you can't, in advance, guess effectively what all its possible consequences might be. For some time I have felt that, when you are evaluating a large-scale social system, the important thing to look for is a variety of effects and consequences, whether anyone had them in mind as objectives or not.

Suppose, in the first decade of this century, somebody had said, "What are the consequences of what Henry Ford is doing?" How many of the current consequences of automotive transportation in our society would have been identified at that time? I suspect probably not more than one or two of any real importance. We had to wait until some effects had an opportunity to manifest themselves. There are appropriately different ways of thinking about objectives, about evidence, and about the role of the evaluator, depending upon the nature of the activity you are trying to evaluate.

332

At this conference there have been comments about the importance of specifically defined, behavioral objectives. I wonder if the people working on problems where behaviorally-defined objectives are important are willing also to entertain the notion that for other kinds of evaluation problems such objectives are impossible and irrelevant.

BLOOM: At the University of Chicago, when we were trying to design the curriculum, we tried to become explicit about how it would be engineered to bring about certain results and certain changes in students. This was a different problem from one where we were asked to evaluate a system in existence over some time, where nobody knew its purposes.

We were trying to produce certain results, to evaluate these results. We wanted to see where the curriculum did or did not succeed. Our problem was how to get the faculty to agree on what their intentions were. We didn't try to use language in all cases. We used all kinds of communication devices to see what they were really trying to produce: how would the student be any different, and how would we know he was any different?

I think this is a different problem from the example you gave.

PACE: Yes, I think that is true. Is this distinction generally agreed upon?

POPHAM: Can you think of any situation, Bob, in the evaluation of an instructional program in which you would find the specification of objectives irrelevant? I can see your example of Henry Ford. Other phenomena you might wish to evaluate post hoc, but I don't see any instructional sequence where the objectives are irrelevant.

PACE: In our Research and Design center, we define an instructional program as anything from a particular learning sequence that a teacher or programmer has planned to a large-scale social enterprise. UCLA is an instructional program. Higher education in the United States of America is an instructional program, with differences from one institution to another.

LORTIE: A film strip is only an instructional program. UCLA is a place where thousands of people earn their livings, where some people rise in social mobility, where some people who like academic politics enjoy administration, where certain well-muscled young men begin professional football careers, and where sculptors can sell nice sculpture. You can list the functions of a university or a school system along so many dimensions that the assessment problem becomes one of basic social philosophy. This is not true of a film strip.

PACE: That's exactly the case.

LORTIE: But to say UCLA is an instructional program is to take only one of many dimensions of UCLA and, perhaps, not the most significant one.

PACE: Among the things we are interested in are functions that neither fit explicitly under the term "instructional program" nor have explicit objectives. A university brings various age groups of people together, many of whom get married. This is not an objective of higher education in the United States. You don't say, "This is a good college because 90 percent of the kids get married before they graduate."

LORTIE: Some women's parents do.

PACE: It's a social phenomenon, but not an objective of the College Board, that tests generate anxiety and that parents spend hundreds of dollars on phony coaching schools to get their kids into college. It is one of the consequences of selectivity. The words *instructional program* do not really effectively convey this kind of breadth.

BLOOM: But we have to restrict it somehow; otherwise, you are going to talk about the language values that have accumulated as a result of UCLA's being here.

SCHUTZ: I am not sure that asking the question, "Should you or shouldn't you?" nets much. I think you can say, "if you do, . . ." Then you have a base for doing some other things, and you can build on that conceptually and operationally.

So long as we mount efforts having some social consequences, we are in the position of saying that, if we do take an approach, it will lead to something. We can specify what we will gain; and that's about as far as we can go.

PACE: Yes.

POPHAM: I would like to respond to the question you raised originally, Bob. Is there a sharp cleavage on this point? It doesn't seem to me there is. We have some people saying that the only thing to be concerned about is the attainment of prespecified instructional objectives. On the other hand, Bob Stake implies that objectives are impractical and unnecessary, and you say there are situations in which they are irrelevant, even to instructional programs. The obvious compromise position is that one should be attentive to prespecified objectives and also to unanticipated consequences. If we take that position, I don't think there should be a controversy.

PACE: Yes, I think that's probably right, but we don't have any rationale for identifying the expected outcomes. They can be looked at only after the fact.

SCHUTZ: This is by definition. If you say something is unanticipated, that defines something you can't prespecify. You say that and then go on.

PACE: But at the beginning you can set up objectives for your particular instructional purposes.

LORTIE: What are you going to know after it happens? Many methods that we have discussed at this conference would not routinely detect side effects or latent effects. Do we really want to say that in every act of evaluation we are open to a wide range of unanticipated consequences?

FESHBACH: Is one reason for so many unanticipated side effects that we have a very narrow base of objectives? As the base becomes broader, including such things as affective variables, many results will become anticipated.

ANDERSON: The question here is not the form in which objectives should be stated. They should be as operational as possible. Nor is the question whether we should be sensitive to unanticipated outcomes. The broader question arises of how to capitalize on rare forms of behavior, such as creativity. By definition, creativity is a rare event. Our inventory of goals should include reinforcing creative behavior when it occurs. Let us assume that in the course of a lesson, based on particular preplanned behavioral objectives, an instance of creative behavior occurs. The rational thing to do at this point would be not to march ahead with the lesson, but to branch out of the lesson to capitalize on the opportunity to promote creativity. We would introduce another goal and seek to promote this objective. These are other kinds of objectives that need not be any less precise in their operationalization to which we branch when the opportunity arises during instruction.

MCNEIL: I wonder if part of the tension that people feel about the objectives doesn't center about the fact that objectives might be unfair or illegitimate. If the objective is clearly stated and, in the course of my fulfilling it, someone sets some other criteria for me, I feel uneasy. New criteria that appear during the course of my instruction or after my instruction should be considered as candidates for future objectives for me to meet. But they will not be used to clobber me now, since they weren't part of my initial agreement in working with you.

PACE: That's a fascinating problem. The people who developed the new physics curricula didn't intend that only half as many people would take physics after they got the new curricula, but that's the fact of the case. So they say, "That wasn't one of our objectives, so don't clobber us with that."

MCNEIL: In the future you may, but not now.

WITTROCK: I think we are talking about a very important problem here, that is, the criteria that should be included in evaluation studies. I would like to take another thrust toward it.

To introduce this problem of selecting criteria for use in evaluation studies, I asked Sam Messick to talk about cognitive style, and Marv Alkin to talk about cost effectiveness. I didn't ask anybody to talk about achievement testing because I thought everybody would agree that we ought to be looking very carefully at achievement.

After Messick had talked about cognitive styles, we heard one reaction for which I had hoped. Bob Gagné said in very clear terms that we ought not to be concerned with cognitive styles but with how well the student learns to do whatever we are trying to teach him. His beautiful little example was of butter wrapping. That is quite a defensible point of view.

I think we need additional criteria. Cost effectiveness scares me. I just can't warm to the idea of using cost effectiveness in evaluation studies because I am still trying to find instructional variables that have any effects at all, much less cheap ones.

We need a theory or a model to guide us in selecting criteria. As a basis for argument, I suggest that we use Bloom's taxonomy to help us select criteria for evaluation studies. I say we ought to use at least one variable in the cognitive area, such as achievement, one in the affective area, and maybe one in the psychomotor area.

GAGNÉ: It seems to me that at some point you have to face the problem of what the ultimate goals are; and you have to get as close to these ultimate goals as you possibly can. I don't believe that any selection of tests or of intermediate intellectual skills of the sort about which Ben Bloom speaks, or about which anyone else speaks, is going to do it.

I think the basic problem is something (I know this sounds terrible) like motherhood. The problem is, how close can you get, in any given situation, to answering the question, "Can I tell whether, as a result of his educational experience, this person (or this group of people) became a more effective, happier, better adjusted, righteous citizen?"

This is the kind of thing you have to face, it seems to me, and I don't believe it comes by using these intermediate criteria. You have to find out the extent to which these things will correlate or will have a causal relationship with these general goals. But I have the feeling that somehow we always skirt the subject.

Certainly, I don't know how to go about determining goals for education. I would suppose that one would have to start with a set of rather simply stated broad goals that almost everyone can agree on. Over a period of about sixty years, various people who have tried to state the goals of education always seem to come out with about three. They are fairly simple and very comprehensive. One has to do with occupations, another has to do with citizenship, and the third one has to do with what is sometimes called self-fulfillment.

Now, you can hardly disagree with these things. But you have to work from these down to the level at which you can begin to define, to give these goals some specificities and, hopefully, some operational meanings. I have a feeling that tests are far from these ultimate goals of education.

GLASER: I would like like to disagree to some extent. It is just not possible at the present stage of the game to measure these long-range goals. The only thing that you can operate on in the present-day educational situation are those goals on which you make a decision whether or not to do or suggest something to a student. When a student leaves a classroom or the university or a certain educational phase, you make a decision on a short-term goal. The assumption is that this short-term goal is in some way related to the long-term goals about which Gagné talked.

At some time, when society gets organized enough, you can relate these short-term goals to the long-term goals by long-term longitudinal studies. For the present, we must assume that the goals on which we make decisions about education are related to the long-term educational values. The only things we make decisions on are short-term goals and short-term values, and those are assessed by tests. I don't care whether they are paper and pencil tests, qualitative tests, or observations; they are assessment. They are the basis on which you must make a decision, hoping that they are related to the distant goals.

GLASS: I have a good illustration of what Bob is saying. Surely a civics course would have as an objective that a person be rational and intelligent in casting a ballot in an election. There is no way to evaluate that outcome. You always do it by means of one that must take the place of an event that cannot be directly observed. You can't invade a man's privacy and peek in the ballot box to see how he cast his ballot. If you had volunteers tell you how they voted after the election, they surely would be systematically different from people who didn't volunteer, and you couldn't infer how people who didn't volunteer would vote.

This example raises the larger issue that there are objectives that are the province of the man's private world, and we will never be able to observe them to evaluate whether he has attained them. We will always have to infer from observation of some proxy event how he will act in the ultimate situation for which he is being educated.

HOFFENBERG: Basically what we are working on in evaluation is a suboptimal level. If you go through all of the suboptimalities, you will never add up to the grand *optim optimorum.*

Can't you set yourself another question in terms of the tests—is your test inconsistent with your longer-range objectives, rather than is the test related to the objectives? At least then you know you are not departing from what you want in the long range.

LORTIE: I have an example of that one. Take an example like team-teaching, which initially in the Boston area was never thought of as a direct or immediate instructional method but as a long-range recruitment strategy. In was a way of getting and holding bright young men in the classroom because you could reward them through the team-leader method.

When Lexington had assessed two years of experience, the evaluator wrote a statement that just sent the superintendent up the wall. He said, "From all the evidence I can gather about the students who have been exposed to team teaching, it has done them no damage."

This was a politically naïve statement, but in terms of relating immediate to long-range action it was extremely sophisticated. What the evaluators were saying was, "you can continue to gamble on this particular step because you are not losing anything, and you may get a long-range gain."

I think what bothers me about what you are saying, Bob, is that there are certain points at which maximizing immediacy results in a long-range gain. If they had used that strategy in Lexington, they would have ruled out team-teaching; and we might never have found out whether team-teaching had the potential for ultimately raising the personnel resources available to public education.

GLASER: Maximizing the short-term gain doesn't preclude your also maximizing the long-term gain.

LORTIE: But if they made the distinction on the basis that they had no demonstrable gain from team-teaching, they would have dropped it right then and there.

GLASER: Oh, yes; but there is always the assumption that the behavior you decide to measure in the short-term gain is related to some distant goal. I know of nobody who doesn't think that "what I am measuring now is good for the future."

HOFFENBERG: But then you ask the question, "Why do you have to think about the problem this way?"

GLASER: Oh, because we are never really interested in short-term gains, but it's the only thing with which the teacher can deal.

HOFFENBERG: That is correct. What you are really evolving is a means-end change over time within an intercausal connection. What I am suggesting is to say, "At least this is not inconsistent with what I want to do in the long run." This gives you a certain amount of flexibility that you may not get in alternatives.

GLASER: Bob Gagné says that if you test in a certain way and don't use a two-stage kind of measurement, you preclude certain kinds of things you really want to measure that have some value for long-term gains. Now I think, Bob, that that's what you meant by nontest. You didn't really mean no test; you meant a bad test.

GAGNÉ: Well, may I say a little bit to clarify that? You know, I don't give up on this easily. I still feel that the more nearly ultimate you can make a measure, the better you are. If you have to depart from this ultimate criterion, of course you choose to construct a situation that you may call a test, in which you do not just assume, but show rationally that it is related to your goals.

We can't just make and measure an inventory of the variety of skills that a person might possess. We have to start with the ultimate goals and work from those down to the point where we decide what measures we can practically use.

GLASER: So the fundamental problem for evaluation is to show that the things that we measure now, the things that we make decisions on now, are somehow related to the behavior we would like to see the individual have twenty or twenty-five years from now.

GAGNÉ: Yes.

GUILFORD: I would like to remind Gagné of something we both know about. During the war we were selecting pilots, and the ultimate payoff for pilots was in combat; but for the first two or three years, all we had for a criterion, and what we used mostly, was whether or not the man could pass flight training in primary school, the first flying experience he had. The correlation was about .5. Later on in the war, we were able to find criteria for men in combat; there was a correlation of about .15 to .2. Had we had only the information as the ultimate payoff, we would have dropped the whole program. We didn't, because we knew that we could predict who could pass the pilot's first hurdle; from then on he was useful, at least for a while. If he didn't pass, he was of no further use as a potential pilot.

So many things happen in between that you can't predict ultimate criteria.

GLASS: But you can count the failures on the ultimate criteria.

GAGNÉ: I am all in favor of that. I don't argue against doing that.

PACE: I wonder if we might turn to another kind of problem now—*interaction.*

SKAGER: Gene Glass took the position that investigating interaction of subvariables comes in the main to nothing.

ANDERSON: He didn't create those data. He reviewed the literature.

MESSICK: In a sense, though, experimental psychologists did create the data. They used certain kinds of criterion tests to evaluate the interaction.

You find, for example, that to a particular kind of teaching, an inductive differential approach, analytic or reflective students would react in a very favorable way. They respond very quickly; they get to the point, and they reach a certain achievement level. They do it quickly. They go home, listen to music, and read literature; they play baseball and they date girls. The poor global kid is having trouble getting the point because he is not reacting to the approach the teacher uses. He spends more time on his homework; he asks more questions, and . . .

ANDERSON: You're talking about the way you think things might be, or about data on how they are?

MESSICK: I am suggesting both—the way I think they might be and the way they are—in an experimental study reporting in terms of a single achievement variable the differential amounts of work cannot be evaluated. In terms of an achievement test at the end of the year, there is no difference between the two performances.

ANDERSON: Are you saying you have a faith that there are these kinds of interactions?

MESSICK: That's what I'm saying. We can never find them if we don't use criteria other than a single achievement test. If we don't ask how much time is spent in homework, if we don't ask how many questions are asked of the teacher or the parents, we will never find out.

FESHBACH: Interactions do occur frequently in studies of individual differences. I want to refer very briefly to the data on sex differences, social-class differences, and birth-order differences, in which there are very striking sex differences in interactions that Art Lumsdaine said were not evident in the literature.

MCDONALD: I think, Norma, you are on the side of the angels because you are in the right literature and the right experimental tradition. You have theoretical and empirical facts to support the kinds of studies you have done, for example, on differences in social class and teacher reinforcement. There is a whole body of theoretical and empirical literature that supports an interactional type of analysis.

When we shift over to the learning of instructional materials, we are in the absolute dark. There is nothing to back us up. When you talk about personality theory, I don't disagree with you. When Bob Pace talks about parallelepipeds and cognitive states, you don't have anything to indicate that you are on the right track except faith.

I think we ought to distinguish between these different theoretical points of view and empirical literature that supports interaction. In the areas where this center is studying instruction, there is no body of literature to support a belief in an interaction hypothesis.

ANDERSON: Lee Cronbach, for a number of years now, has believed that there should be interactions between personological variables and instructional variables. Lee Cronbach has searched existing studies that might demonstrate this, but one finds few references to actual findings of this kind in his papers.

BLOOM: I think there is no doubt about the difficulty of producing this kind of interaction effect, but it seems to me that it's well worth a major effort of this Research and Design Center to try to come up with some of the answers. My own hunch is that most of the things we have been studying in the past have to do with knowledge learning, which seems to be so highly related to verbal abilities that those kids who were high in verbal ability always did better than those who were low, no matter what we did.

It seems to me that our basic problem comes very close to the sort of thing the two Marvs were speaking about today. Suppose we have one method where the high-ability students always do better than the low-ability students. It's a speedy method and gets the high-ability students up to a certain level. If there is another method that costs a great deal more in time and effort, will bring the low-ability student up, but will do no better for the high-ability student, this is not a crossover interaction. This method costs us more. Call it compensatory education or whatever you will; but if you can bring the low-ability student up to a higher level by this second method, although never doing as well as the top-ability students for whom we have a speedier, more efficient, and less costly method for getting to the same place, then it is well worth it.

ANDERSON: I think that we should be looking for the main effects at this point. I think that's the first order of business.

SCHUTZ: But if you do search for the interaction, a simple-minded factorial study is unlikely to isolate it. We had better build a study that gives the best possibility of the interactions occurring.

MESSICK: There is one possibility. Turn the argument upside down; if we are confronted with the fact that there are certain individual differences in adult performance, and if there are multiple, consistent individual differences, might we not be able to define treatments that will capitalize upon these differences? The treatments at present are global, complex, and not producing interactions, but maybe we can create treatments that would produce interactions. We can design specific teaching procedures that will favor one type of student. Then we can demonstrate interactions.

MCDONALD: Let's just debate that for a small moment.

What would you predict on the basis of anything we know in psychology about interactions between affect and mathematics learning, for example?

MESSICK: We do know some things. We know there are certain classes of human beings that react differently to training in mathematics. One major class is females. In general, females do not like math.

SCHUTZ: Where does the interaction come in? Here you are talking about a main effect.

MESSICK: I would say there is an interaction.

ANDERSON: With what?

MESSICK: In terms of females in the process of being trained in mathematics. They also, incidentally, learn to fear it—not to enjoy it, and not to want to pursue it.

SCHUTZ: That is a main effect.

ANDERSON: How is there an interaction?

MESSICK: For females, it is a different matter.

GLASS: You always have two main effects when you compare the groups, one for the males and one for the females.

MESSICK: You have a variable, which is sex, and it's a two-value variable. Males are 1, females are 0. Sex differences interact with training.

ANDERSON: You are using interaction in a different sense, I guess.

WILEY: That's what Gene and everybody else is calling a main effect. It is a sex difference, given constant treatment. That is, you have the males and the females in the same kinds of classes getting the same kind of training, and you have different reactions from males and females to that constant training. That's a main effect.

MESSICK: What I am suggesting is this. I say, given the main effects, which are individual differences . . .

MCDONALD: That would be an interaction.

WILEY: Sam is asserting something, and Fred is asserting something else, and there is a slightly different point of view here. One says that we can arrange various kinds of environmental circumstances in which different kinds of personological characteristics come into full play. That's a psychological question.

Fred's point is that we can't design instructional treatments, that are meaningful educationally, which will capitalize on these abilities, and Sam is saying, "Yes, we can."

Now, I am simply saying we can't demonstrate interactions involving the treatment.

May I make one more point?

Gene's main point this afternoon was that reasonably intelligent people have been trying for years and years to create treatments that would produce interactions, maybe not directly, but they have been making a rather large effort and haven't produced any that are reasonable.

I think they have been looking at the point that you are making, or very similar points, much more intensively than you are willing to grant, and it's an extremely difficult task.

MESSICK: If you want to demonstrate interaction, the way to do it is to look at the differences in terms of people, and then to locate this and capitalize on it.

ANDERSON: Except that when you are trying to improve education, you do it the other way around.

WILEY: The highly significant treatments that will demonstrate these do not tend to be educationally reasonable. I think the kinds of educational treatment that people consider to be educationally reasonable will not, by their very nature, tend to produce interactions.

MESSICK: "Educationally reasonable"—what do you mean by that? Do you mean in terms of applying it to a large, broad school system, to large groups of people in ways that are efficient and cost-beneficial?

LORTIE: In our nursery school, they group the kids and give them an instructor according to a personality test.

WILEY: And it doesn't do a damn thing. When it comes to an actual treatment, using the greatest amount of intelligence and educational know-how one has, one doesn't get results. The only case where one gets results is where the treatments are so artificial that they would never be applied in school.

MESSICK: Nobody has been even trying to do it.

WILEY: The point I am trying to make is that there has been effort, and rather intelligent effort.

FESHBACH: That's what we want to quarrel with, you see.

PACE: Can I interrupt at this point and suggest that we may have identified the problem?
I see there was one other topic to comment on—theory of evaluation.

WILEY: I want to comment on theory in evaluation. If you take evaluation per se and subtract from it methodology, on one hand, and moral ideology or the valuing aspect, on the other, is there anything left?

MESSICK: Statistics.

WILEY: You are subtracting statistics when you subtract methodology.
I would assert that there is a lot left. I would assert that evaluation is in fact a scientific enterprise, that it has a substantive field that is cumulative, in which we gain further knowledge in a cumulative fashion, and that you can formulate relatively abstract terms to deal with the phenomena of educational evaluation.

SCHUTZ: Without methodology?

WILEY: Subtracting out the pure methodological aspects and the purely valuing aspects, there is a scientific problem left.

ANDERSON: I have trouble coming to grips with this subtraction. Could you elaborate a little bit on what's there when we partial out methods and values?

WILEY: I don't know how to phrase it. Look at the last few years of writing in evaluation, such as the Cronbach article in *Teachers College Record* of a few years ago that initiated a new era of looking at evaluation, and the work of Michael Scriven and Bob Stake. We are getting to a point where we have some cumulation of knowledge about evaluation that is neither value nor methodology; but I think we are learning ways of looking at the issues of treatments in large and complex curriculum projects and the effects of such curriculum efforts upon achievement and other behavioral variables; and we are looking at ways of proceeding that are not entirely methodological in the successive modification and development of curricula.

I have a very intense feeling that these are neither entirely methodological nor are they entire value problems. That is, we are gaining substantive knowledge about how to look at educational programs and educational treatment.

So I think there is a residual left in terms of our knowledge after you subtract out the methodological, statistical, or measurement aspects and the philosophical, value, or ideological aspects. I am not exactly sure how one should conceptualize what is left, but I have some kind of idea that there is something left, and I think it is very important.

GORDON: Just a couple of propositions in this area for an illustration, please.

WILEY: Well, let me put it this way. If we look at the structure of education, we find that there are old conceptual units. There is the school district, the school, the classroom, and the pupil.

ANDERSON: *That* is old.

GORDON: What about the conception of the pupil?

WILEY: I don't want to talk about that for the moment.

In the terms that I use to view evaluation, we look at education as the effects of instructional treatments. I view them as being, say, within its original framework on a classroom and not on an individual pupil.

GAGNÉ: That's bad right there.

GORDON: If I can interrupt you, you said this is not methodology. We are talking about a more general conceptual view, but not the management of the variables or even the specification of them. So I accept that, for one.

WILEY: If I may just articulate that a little bit more, methodologically, the problem of the distinction between the pupil, the classroom, the school, and the school district is only a distinction with respect to the relevant unit of analysis. Thinking in terms of how we may formulate variables, criterion variables and other kinds, to look at evaluation problems, the basic principles of variable formulation are tied so closely to the level at which the unit is defined that it can no longer be called a methodological problem. It is a substantive problem.

It's a hard thing to say. For example, the view that the interaction of a personological variable (getting back to the previous point as an example) with an instructional treatment is in fact another dependent variable and not a statistical interaction, I think makes it essentially a substantive issue and not a statistical one. That is, it is my view that when one looks at the discrepancy between males and females in a classroom in terms of their achievement and at how that difference between male and female achievement differs as a function of the educational treatment, you can view it in two very distinct ways. You can view it as a formal statistical interaction between sex and treatment, or you can view it as two different characteristics of the classroom: one being the average achievement level, and the other being the difference between males and females.

MESSICK: Suppose achievement in the two sexes is predictable by different classes of variables? For example, that interest predicts achievement for boys, and aptitudes predict achievement for girls.

WILEY: I would phrase the problem differently. I would say, "What is predictive of the discrepancy between boys and girls?" and "What is predictive of the overall achievement in the classroom?" I would view these two variables as distinct characteristics of the classroom.

MESSICK: I am suggesting there is a qualitative organizational difference between the two sexes that is not a function of the classroom but of the sexes.

WILEY: I think that's exactly the point. I would not be willing to generalize that sex difference to other situations in which one had different groups of boys and girls. I am willing to say that the sex difference is a classroom characteristic. I am not willing to make the other jump to say that we would get exactly the same results if we had boys in one classroom and girls in another classroom.

MESSICK: I would say it is not a matter of taste. It's an empirical question.

WILEY: Right. I am making an empirical prediction. We have different theories. Sam has a psychological theory about what is relevant in these kinds of situations, and it is basically and ultimately a psychological theory. I have an evaluation theory that asks about classroom organization and the impact on how one evaluates instructional treatments.

MESSICK: I would think evaluation procedures would take into account psychological differences.

WILEY: I think they ought to, but I think there is a distinct difference.

Appendix

Causal Inference from Observational Data: A Review of Ends and Means[1]

HERMAN WOLD

CONTENTS

Introduction and Summary

1. A Fourfold Map of Ends and Means in Applied Statistics
    1.1. Description *v.* explanation, a dualism in ends
    1.2. Observation *v.* experimental data, a dualism in means
    1.3. A fourfold map of ends and means
    1.4. Three illustrations from SW sector

2. A Review of Explanatory Approaches, with Particular Regard to the Treatment of Experimental *v.* Observational Data
    2.1. The specification of hypotheses
    2.2. Estimation of parameters and other elements of causal inference
    2.3. Hypothesis testing

3. The Explanatory Analysis of Observational Data: Some Typical Situations
    3.1. Causal patterns
    3.2. Regression analysis
    3.3. Model building on the basis of elementary assumptions
    3.4. Joint treatment of causal and stochastic assumptions

List of References

[1] Read before the Royal Statistical Society, Wednesday, December 21, 1955, the President, Professor E. S. Pearson, C.B.E., in the Chair.

351

INTRODUCTION AND SUMMARY

Intensive development of statistical methods in the last three or four decades has created broad areas of applied statistics whose techniques possess a high degree of exactness and efficiency.

On the other hand, procedures for sampling surveys supply rational techniques for mass observation and for the assessment of frequencies, averages, and other elements of collective description. On the other hand, the rules for the design and analysis of experiments embrace both descriptive and explanatory problems, with emphasis on explanation. Modern methods thus treat three categories of problems: (1) description on the basis of observational (nonexperimental) data, and (2, 3) description and explanation by the use of experimental data.

A fourth broad area remains—explanation on the basis of observational data. In this field, which embraces among other things a large proportion of social science research, progress has been less systematic and spectacular. Current textbooks reveal the stepchild treatment which this sort of problem has received from professional statisticians. Nevertheless a small cadre of statisticians has made basic contributions in this direction, and these developments may be expected to bring the fourth area more into balance with other fields of applied statistics.[2]

The purpose of this paper is to examine the differences in explanatory procedures when dealing with the two types of data: experimental and observational. After introductory comments in section 1 on the areas mentioned, section 2 continues with causal inference. It is argued that the theoretical model on which the statistical analysis is based can be specified with less exactness and detail when passing from experimental to observational data, and that this leads to a partial re-orientation of the statistical techniques. The shifts of emphasis are examined with regard to specification of hypotheses, estimation procedures, and hypothesis testing. The conclusion reached is that with observational data the statistical analysis becomes more dependent on (a) coordination with subject-matter theory, (b) large-sample methods, and (c) checks and tests against other evidence. In section 3 this conclusion is illustrated with reference to four types of approach. The illustrations have been selected so as to bring out the differences in the causal analysis with regard to complexity and aspiration level.

---

[2] In particular I am thinking of the situation in the social and economic sciences. The growing interest in causal models and their study by statistical method is reflected in Unesco (1954). Lazarsfeld, ed. (1954), Kempthorne et al., eds. (1954). The pioneers include Wright (1934) and Tinbergen (1934).

This brief essay treats a large topic and, as my experience and outlook are of necessity limited, the aim is to stimulate interest rather than to stress my own views. Such novelty as the paper may possess lies in the arrangement of material and the integrated picture of statistical method.[3] The examples are simple, many being drawn from my own work on demand analysis, a branch of applied statistics displaying typical problems in the causal analysis of observational data.

1. A FOURFOLD MAP OF ENDS AND MEANS IN APPLIED STATISTICS[4]

1.1. *Description versus Explanation, a Dualism in Ends*

A descriptive approach answers such questions as "How?" or "How much?" An explanatory approach treats the question "Why?", and in some form or other the answer involves an element of causal inference.

A few examples: in agricultural research, the assessment of yield per acre is description, while an investigation of the yield in its dependence on manure falls under the heading of explanation. In medicine we may, on the one hand, refer to the weekly official reports on epidemic disease (description), and on the other, to clinical data on the curative effect of some new antibiotic on a specified disease (explanation). In industrial statistics we may cite the control chart for a certain element of operation along the assembly line (description), and a project of operations analysis which serves to improve the production process by removing the disturbing influence of some nuisance factor (explanation).

A frequent situation is that description serves to maintain some *modus vivendi* (the control of an established production process, the tolerance of a limited number of epidemic cases), whereas explanation serves the purpose of *reform* (raising the agricultural yield, reducing the mortality rates, improving a production process). In other words, description is employed as an aid in the human *adjustment* to given conditions, while explanation is a vehicle for *ascendancy* over the environment.[5]

[3] The paper was planned in consultation with Dr. R. Porter, Fort Walton, Fla., and G. Eklund and K. Medin, Associate Professors at the Univ. Inst. of Statistics, Uppsala. The first draft of the paper has received constructive comments from these colleagues and from Dr. C. A. Anderson, Univ. of Kentucky; Dr. J. G. Bryan and Dr. E. Robinson, Massachusetts Inst. of Technology; Dr. R. Strotz, Chicago; Dr. J. Tukey and Dr. M. Wilk, Princeton; and Dr. P. Whittle, Wellington, New Zealand. To them all I extend my heartfelt thanks.
[4] This introductory section is mainly based on Wold (1954). For the place of causality in the general theory of knowledge, cf. Braithwaite (1953), especially p. 311.
[5] For this last interpretation I am indebted to Dr. R. Porter.

While a statistical investigation may have no purpose other than description, an explanatory investigation always involves an initial phase of description, that is, of orientation and of fact collecting to provide material for the causal analysis. From this point of view a complete research project involves three phases:

(i) Description; including primary measurements, tabular and graphic presentation of facts and the assessment of collective characteristics.

(ii) Explanation; including the specification of causal hypotheses and their testing against the empirical data.

(iii) Application. This final phase includes some element of prediction; that is, the inference drawn from the observed sample is extended to some other sample, different in time or space or otherwise.

1.2. *Observational versus Experimental Data, a Dualism in Means*

Without comment we give as two examples of description: a set of measurements on the specific gravity of chromium (experimental data), and the divorce rate percentage of marriage (observational data).

As regards explanatory analysis, we shall briefly recount a classic in medicine, J. Dietl's experiment on pneumonia (1849). A hundred years ago medicine was still dominated by bleeding and emetics, treatments that had been in general use for all sorts of diseases from mediaeval and earlier times. Dietl made his experiment on three groups of pneumonia patients, 380 cases in all. In accordance with the traditional prescriptions two groups were treated with leeches and tartar emetics, respectively, while (because Dietl was courageous enough to put the established authorities to a test), the third group was given so-called expectative treatment: the patient was not treated at all but placed in bed and given light and nourishing food. The resulting mortality was 20.4 percent for the group treated with leeches, 20.7 percent for the group treated with emetics, and 7.4 percent for the control group. The cures thus were twice as dangerous as the disease itself! Dietl's report was one of the first agents in tearing down the citadel of mediaeval medicine.

The notion of experiment is somewhat fluid, but whether taken in a broad or narrow sense it involves some degree of planning and control from the side of the experimenter. We shall take here the term in a narrow sense which, when a distinct term is required, will be referred to as *controlled experiment,* and which we specify by requiring the following conditions to be fulfilled, more or less rigorously (see Fisher, 1935, esp. Sections 20–21).

(i) The replications of the experiment are made under similar conditions (so as to yield an internal measure of uncontrolled variation).

(ii) The replications are mutually independent. For explanatory experiments the following condition is added:

(iii) The uncontrolled variation in the replications is subject to randomization in the sense of R. A. Fisher.

The causal hypothesis of an explanatory experiment usually takes the form of a relationship in which the variable under investigation, called the effect variable, is expressed as a function of causal variables or factors. Some of the causal factors are controlled in the sense of being subjected to systematic variation, others are uncontrolled. The randomization under (iii) serves to make the controlled variables independent of the uncontrolled factors. Considering, for example, the case of linear regression, let

$$\eta = \alpha + \beta x + \zeta(\epsilon^{(1)}, \cdots, \epsilon^{(s)}); \qquad y = a + bx + z \qquad (1a\text{-}b)$$

be the theoretical and least squares regressions; the randomization makes the controlled variable x independent of the uncontrolled factors $\epsilon^{(i)}$, and if the residual ζ does not depend on x it follows under general conditions that b will be a consistent estimate of β.[6]

Observational or nonexperimental data are those in which one or more of conditions (i)–(iii) are violated. The empirical data are mainly experimental in some sciences, as physics and chemistry, and mainly observational in others, as astronomy, meteorology, economics and the social sciences; but most frequently perhaps the data are drawn both from experimental and observational sources, as in psychology, genetics and medicine. This is to some extent a question of convention, because conditions (i)–(iii) are somewhat vague, and the empirical data will therefore often have features in common with both experiment and observation. Agricultural field experiments are a case in point since the soil variations are not in complete agreement with (i) and (ii).

Assumptions (i)–(ii) are usually adopted in the strict sense of probability theory, the uncontrolled variation being assumed to form a set of independent variables with the same distribution function. The techniques for industrial quality control are a typical case in point. These require that the two assumptions be fulfilled by the control chart of the operation under investigation, and the operation is then said to be under *statistical control* (Shewhart, 1931; Hald, 1952, Ch. 13.2). In many time-series data assumption (ii) is violated by the presence of autocorrelation. This is one reason

---

[6] For a more detailed treatment of the situation, including cases when ζ depends on x, see Wold-Juréen (1952). Exercise IV, 15.

why time-series data will often come under the heading of observational data. Another is that if there are time trends in the uncontrolled variation their correlation with the time variable cannot be removed by randomization, for time is a factor which cannot be subjected to systematic variation.

1.3. *A Fourfold Map of Ends and Means*

The double dichotomy in ends and means briefly commented upon in section 1.1–2 gives us a fourfold map of statistical methods, as shown below. The compass notations serve for easy reference. The classification of methods thus obtained is sufficiently clear-cut for our purpose. The methods of the SW sector being our topic, we shall now prepare the discussion in sections 2–3 by some comments and illustrations.

(i) Description involves simpler problems than explantion, and explana-

Statistical observations:

	Nonexperimental	Experimental

Purpose of statistical inference:

Description:
- Tabular and graphic exposition
- Averages: location measures
- Dispersion measures
- Frequency curves and correlation

} Same methods

Sampling survey techniques for totals, frequencies, averages, variances, etc., and the assessment of confidence intervals for corresponding theoretical values

The assessment of probabilities. Theoretical means, variances, etc., and corresponding confidence interval

Index numbers

| NW | NE |
| SW | SE |

Explanation:
- Specialized branches of applied statistics
- Causal inference from time series
- Econometrics
- Demography
- Genetics

Design of factorial experiment

Randomization methods

Significance tests for differences between frequencies, averages, etc.

Regression analysis

Analysis of variance and covariance

Probit analysis

tory problems are easier to solve with the use of experiments than without. Hence the methods required are on the whole less penetrating in the NW sector of the map than in the SE, and the SE sector in its turn is less difficult than the SW. This situation throws some light on the broad lines of development of statistical method. Up to the beginning of this century statistics was by and large synonymous with the NW sector. Approaches into other sectors were in the picture at an early stage; we note the construction of mortality tables (SW), Gauss's methods for the treatment of observational error (NE and SW), and causal experiments like that carried out by Dietl (SE). The epoch-making contributions of R. A. Fisher brought a powerful expansion in the direction of experimental methods, with emphasis on the SE sector. The exact and efficient methods developed by Fisher and his followers have led to great triumphs in biological sciences, medicine, engineering and other fields where research can be based on controlled experiment, and their range of fruitful application is still expanding. Speaking broadly, classic and modern statistics focus on the NW and SE sectors of our map, respectively. This suggests that the next phase of development will centre on the SW sector, and work in this direction is well in progress, as already noted.

(ii) In the SW sector the statistical methods cannot profitably be set forth in a general formal manner; they split up into a number of specialized topics, such as demography, econometrics, and so forth (Wold, 1954, p. 170). This is because in the absence of experiments the statistical analysis has to be closely coordinated with subject-matter theory both in specifying the causal hypotheses and in testing them against other sources of knowledge. A crucial feature is randomization, which in experimental situations reduces the disturbing effect of uncontrolled variation. This device not being available in observational situations, it is a pertinent problem to what extent the disturbance factors should be taken into explicit account, and at this point strong reliance must fall upon subject-matter arguments.

(iii) As the lines of demarcation in the map are fluid, special attention is called to two zones: (a) between the SE and the SW sectors, (b) between the NW and the SW sectors. Both these zones are important research fronts where the exact methods of the NW and SE sectors are being generalized and adapted so as to cope with some of the problems of the amorphous SE sector.

An important array of intermediate cases between the NW and SW sectors stems from differential statistics: death-rates by sex, rural versus urban marriage rates, etc. An element of explanation lies in the differential factor; since, however, the dependent variable is usually influenced by additional factors, the explanation will only extend beyond the sample in a qualitative and unoperational manner. Emphasis of differential statistics thus lies on the description of the particular sample. Throughout the history of statistics applied work in the social sciences has in this way hovered between description and explanation. In favourable circumstances differential statistics have yielded results that were explanatory in an operational sense and hence definitely belong to the SW sector. The earliest and best example is the computation of death rates by age and the ensuing explanation of mortality as a function of age.

Correlation is another intermediate case. If X, Y are two variables given by observational data, let

$$X \rightarrow Y \qquad X \leftarrow Y \qquad X \leftrightarrow Y \qquad X - Y \qquad \text{(2a–d)}$$

indicate the hypotheses: (a) Y is causally dependent upon X, (b) X is dependent upon Y, (c) X, Y are intercorrelated without any causal explanation being specified, and (d) X and Y are causally independent. If the causal dependence is specified (cases a and b) we assign the case to the SW sector; otherwise (case c) to the NW sector. Regression methods, when used to extract causal relations from the data, belong to the SW sector. Correlation coefficients and other measures of association fall to the NW sector.

1.4. *Three Illustrations from the SW Sector*

It need hardly be stressed that the SW sector is large and important, and its problems are of varying intricacy and difficulty. Innumerable examples could be cited where research has successfully coped with minor aspects but where we are far from having a firm operational grasp of the central factors. We shall return to this problem. One may refer to the notorious difficulties when dealing with clinical data in medicine compared with the treatment of laboratory data. (I think of the selective factors that prevent coordination of experience from different clinics.) The situation is similar in psychology, education, sociology, and so forth; for instance, analysis of causal complexes underlying juvenile delinquency, alcoholism, or divorce. We proceed to discuss three illustrations in more detail.

(i) *Mortality Tables.* The dependence of human mortality upon age is so obvious that it requires an effort to realize that this is in principle a causal explanation as hypothetical as any other. Some time after Halley's mortality table was constructed in 1693, such tables were used in life insurance calculations. The success of the business use demonstrated that mortality could be explained as a function of age, and that the inference from one set of data could be extended with sufficient accuracy to other populations. Two general features in this illustration are important: (a) observational data are used for the numerical assessment of some element of causal inference, (b) the application of the results involves a prediction by which the inference from the observed sample is extended to other samples. Among the many refinements we note Gompertz-Makeham's formula for functional representation of the causal dependence,

$$\mu_x = a + b \cdot c^x$$

where μ_x is the instantaneous death rate; x is age, and a, b, c are parameters.

(ii) *Demand Analysis.* The conception of a demand function was introduced into economic theory by A. Cournot (1838). The representation of demand as a function of price enters into the theoretical model by which he explained the stability of price, together with the balance of production and consumption in a freely competitive market. The same demand function is the basic tool in his theory of monopolistic price. Jevons (1871) stressed the basic role of the demand function and also emphasized the importance of obtaining empirical knowledge concerning demand functions. However, demand functions remained theoretical until the first estimate of a price elasticity was made by R. Benini (1907).[7] After the pioneer work of H. L. Moore (1919–1925) empirical studies multiplied, and were followed in the 1930's by the standard works of Allen and Bowley (1935), who used cross-section data to study demand as a function of income, and of Schultz (1938), who used time series data to study demand as a function of income and prices. These estimates of demand functions utilized least squares regression. In recent contributions we note the following points:

(a) The empirical work has continued and led to a reliable mapping of the basic features of the demand structure.[8] In particular, the results have proved applicable for prediction, as when forecasting the demand for various commodities after a period of shortage or rationing (Wold-Juréen, 1952, Chs. 1.6, 18.2; Fox, 1953, p. 72).

---

[7] Assuming demand for coffee as a function of price to be $d = A \cdot p^{-\alpha}$, Benini estimates the parameter α, or in the terminology of Marshall (1890) the price elasticity of coffee, to be $\alpha = 0.384$. Based on yearly data for Italy 1880–1893, the estimate is obtained in a quite modern fashion as the regression coefficient of log quantity on log price.

[8] Several comprehensive studies have appeared. For the treatment of U.S. data, see Shepherd (1941), Tobin (1950), Fox (1953); U.K. data, Stone (1954); Swedish data, Wold (1940), Malmquist (1948), Wold-Juréen (1952). A multicountry study by Juréen is now in the press (*Econometrica*, 1956).

(b) The empirical studies use cross section data and time series jointly (Wold, 1940; Tobin, 1950; Wold-Juréen, 1952; Stone, 1954).

(c) The existence and certain general properties of demand functions having been established on the basis of the Pareto-Slutsky theory of indifference maps, these theoretical results are exploited for testing the empirical demand analysis. The theoretical results include several general relationships between demand elasticities.[9]

(d) Schultz's work left unsettled the question whether to use the regression of price X on demand Y or that of demand on price for estimating the demand function. Hence, he calculated both regressions and gave two estimates of elasticity. The argument that the two regressions correspond to two different causal hypotheses, as indicated in (2 a–b), and that the notion of demand function implies hypothesis (2 a), leads to the decision to use the regression of demand on price (Wold-Juréen, 1952, Chs. 1.2–3, 14.2). Since this conclusion is a statistical implication of the basic theoretical model, it may be regarded as a special instance of the interplay between theoretical and empirical inference (referred to under c above). The conclusion extends to partial regression, e.g., the simultaneous estimation of the parameters of a demand function with two constant elasticities, say

$$d = \text{const. } \mu^E p^{-e} \tag{3}$$

where d is demand, μ income, p price, E income elasticity, and e price elasticity taken with a negative sign in accordance with Marshall's original definition.

(iii) *Fertility and Reproduction.* The variation of fertility provides a striking instance of a causal complex that has not been mastered operationally. The annual births in Sweden decreased greatly from 1910 to 1934, followed by a 50 percent increase up to 1946 and another decrease thereafter (Fig. 1). It is easy to list causal factors behind the 1934–1946 rise in births: fuller employment, earlier marriages, increased incomes with more even distribution, decreased abortions, paid holidays at pregnancy, maternity grants, housing subsidies, the shortage of commodities during the war,[10] etc.; but opinions are divided as to the relative importance of these several factors. The lack of quantitative knowledge about the causal relationships is illustrated by the divergent forecasts of future fertility.

Forecasts have been made on the basis of mechanical extrapolation of

[9] See Wold-Juréen (1952), also for further references.
[10] It has been pointed out that the expenditures connected with the increase in fertility roughly correspond to the drop in imported cars.

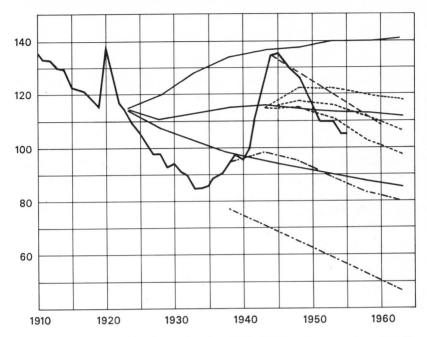

FIGURE 1   *Annual births in Sweden 1910–1934 and recent forecasts.* [11]

death-rates, marriage-rates, fertility-rates combined with high, low and medium estimates for future trends. Since the forecasts rest on no explicit causal analysis of fertility variations it is hardly surprising that they deviate widely from actual developments. Though such forecasts have a certain utility, especially in periods of stable development, they are descriptive rather than explanatory, and typify an intermediate approach between the NW and SW sectors.

2. A REVIEW OF EXPLANATORY APPROACHES, WITH PARTICULAR REGARD TO THE TREATMENT OF EXPERIMENTAL V. OBSERVATIONAL DATA

The material of this section is arranged under three headings, in line with R. A. Fisher's distinction between the consecutive phases of a statistical

[11] Most of the forecasts are reproduced from official publications; for references, see Wold (1956). The graph has been prepared in collaboration with Professor S. Malmquist.

investigation: specification of hypotheses, estimation problems and hypothesis testing.

2.1. *The Specification of Hypotheses*

In explanatory approaches we may in general distinguish between two component parts in the model which forms the basis of the statistical treatment of the data, namely, causal assumptions and stochastic assumptions.

A. *Causal Assumptions.*   These form the main subject-matter content of the explanatory approach. The causal assumptions are usually extracted from prior experience, a frequent case being that they form a special application of a previously established subject-matter theory. In experimental situations the mechanism of the experiment is designed so as to test or demonstrate the causal assumptions.

B. *Stochastic Assumptions.*   These are part of the subject-matter content of the approach inasmuch as they give an interpretation of the deviations between observed and theoretical or expected values. At the same time they supplement the causal assumptions in providing the rationale of the statistical techniques for estimation and hypothesis testing.

Illustrations:

(a) SE sector. An animal experiment with two or more different treatments, each with a fixed dose and the control group with dose zero, the explanatory hypothesis being that the treatments may have different effects. We consider the statistical treatment of such data by the *t*-test or by analysis of variance. The causal assumption is then embodied in the parameter which indicates the varying mean for the different treatments; on the null hypothesis the parameter takes the same value for all treatments. The stochastic assumptions specify the frequency distributions of the various treatment effects: the replications are assumed to be mutually independent and the distributions are taken to be normal with the same variance and with means given by the treatment parameters.

(b) SE sector. A dosage-response experiment with three or more steps of dosage. In the treatment of such data by regression analysis, the causal assumption brings out the variation of response with dosage, by way of a regression curve or a parameter β indicating the slope of a linear regression. The stochastic assumptions specify the deviations from the theoretical regression. The deviations are assumed to be mutually independent, and in a randomized experiment they will, as a rule, be uncorrelated to a good approximation with the dosage. In the ordinary *t*-test deviations are further assumed to be normally distributed with zero mean and constant variance. A typical problem is to estimate the parameter β and to assess the sampling error of the estimate by way of a confidence interval.

(c) SW sector. Demand analysis, say an application of formula (3) to time series data. The causal assumptions are embodied in the relation (3), the interpretation being that an increase of income μ by 1 percent or a decrease of price by 1 percent will, *ceteris paribus,* cause an increase in demand d by E percent or by e percent respectively. Expressing the relation in logarithms,

$$\log d = c + E \log \mu - e \log p + z \qquad (4)$$

where z stands for the deviations between observed and theoretical values, the stochastic assumptions refer to the properties of the residual z. Formally the situation is analogous to a dosage-response experiment. On the assumption that z is uncorrected with $\log \mu$ and $\log p,$ the least square estimates of E and e under general conditions will be consistent. If we add the assumptions that the z-values are independent and normally distributed with constant variance, the sampling error of the estimates can be assessed by the same method as in illustration b.

In the following subsections (i)–(iii) the specification of hypotheses is commented upon from the point of view of experimental v. observational data. The first bears upon the relative importance of the causal and stochastic assumptions in various types of research, the second upon the degree of complexity of the causal assumptions, the third upon the systematic coordination of the two sets of assumptions.

(i) *The Degree to Which Refined Statistical Techniques Are Required.* It happens quite often that the explanatory approach can be carried out by the use of averages, frequency distributions or other elementary devices and that the significance of the results can be judged by common sense without refined techniques. In such cases, of course, the main emphasis lies on the causal assumptions. Experimental situations represent an extreme in the other direction. Generally speaking, the design of the experiment exploits the technical possibilities to bring the uncontrolled variation under statistical control, by randomization and other devices; this control is brought out in the stochastic assumptions (cf. illustrations a and b above), and these form the basis for the exact assessment of confidence intervals for parameter estimates, significance levels in hypothesis testing, and of other elements of the causal inference.

To illustrate the common sense approach, two striking cases may be cited from the recent Presidential Address of R. A. Fisher to this Society

(Fisher, 1953); the geologist Lyell's assessment of the chronological order of fossiliferous strata on the basis of the varying frequency of still surviving species; the biologist Schmidt's observation that the eel differs from other fish in showing no geographic variations in the frequency distribution of the fin-rays, and his ensuing theory that the eels of Europe and the Nile have a common breeding centre in the ocean. In both cases the approach is statistical, but the focus of attention is entirely upon the causal hypothesis. The statistical argument is limited to a comparison between frequencies or frequency distributions which could be performed directly, without the use of any statistical test. Hence it is only natural that the whole credit of the results falls on the subject-matter specialist, whereas the statistical part of the work retires into the background once the causal hypothesis has become established and generally accepted. "The Moor has done his work, the Moor can go," to quote Schiller. The cases of Lyell and Schmidt are rather extreme in this respect, it is true, for, as pointed out by R. A. Fisher, the statistical origin of their theories was almost immediately forgotten.[12]

Most explanatory approaches based on observational data are ranged between the two extremes commented upon above. Illustration (c) is a typical case. Since the data employed for estimating (4) do not come from a randomized experiment in Fisher's sense, income and price may be correlated with other factors that influence demand, and such correlation will in general impair the interpretation of (3) as specified in the causal assumptions. The resulting deviation between estimated and hypothetical parameters is known as an *error of specification*. The presence of a specification error is not indicated by the standard error of a regression coefficient or by its confidence interval. Such probability margins only account for the sampling error. It is also a familiar fact that no routine methods are available for guarding against a specification error. Instead, *ad hoc* methods of various types come to the foreground. This is treated later on; for the moment we sum up the argument symbolically,

$$\text{sampling error} \longrightarrow \text{specification error} \qquad (5)$$

thus indicating a shift of emphasis when passing from experimental to observational data.

---

[12] There are many examples of the same tendency in the literature, and in the scientific workshop any consulting statistician can provide further instances of playing the part of the Moor. This is not meant to discourage consultative work on simple problems. The argument is rather that a statistician with experience in applied work may often render valuable service in the subject field by helping to pose the problems and at the same time making them amenable to statistical treatment. He will then serve both as a statistician and general research consultant, and the conclusion is that his work should be organized in accordance with this double function.

(ii) *The Artichoke Principle of the Experimental Method.* A fundamental and well known advantage of the experimental method is that it can proceed step by step in disentangling a complex causal problem, the technical control of causal factors enabling the experimenter to break down the problems into subproblems, each explored by a separate series of experiments. Thanks to this method or principle, the experiments dealing with the partial problems can work with causal assumptions of a relatively simple structure. There are innumerable ways in which this principle is utilized in experimental research. In the systematic co-ordination of experimental design and statistical technique, which is the keynote of R. A. Fisher's work, the principle is well exploited. The pattern of causal assumptions behind the modern statistical techniques is of a simple standardized type covering the basic situations encountered so frequently in experimental statistical work. I would emphasize that as the causal assumptions become simpler the statistician can concentrate more on the stochastic side of the problem; this feature strengthens the argument behind formula (5).

The simplest experimental devices for the step-wise treatment of causal problems are:[13] (1) Varying one or a few of the controlled causal factors at a time, keeping the other ones constant. (2) Neutralizing the effect of uncontrolled factors by randomization. (3) Arranging for additive and linear effects of the controlled variables. Several devices are available under (3), among these are (a) some appropriate functional transformation of the controlled variables; (b) restricting the variation of a controlled variable to a short interval (so that by Taylor's theorem its influence on the effect variable is approximately additive and linear); (c) restricting the variation of a controlled variable to two values (this restriction is sometimes fulfilled automatically, so-called 0–1 variation), and subjecting the possible non-additivity to a special test of the type known as tests for interaction.

When dealing with observational data the statistician is in a more difficult position. The explanatory approach must then be taken as an entity, and as a consequence the causal assumptions will as a rule be more involved and complicated. As before, it is the absence of randomization that is crucial, for since this device is not available there is no clear-cut distinction between explanatory factors which are explicitly accounted for in the hypothetical model and disturbance factors which are summed up in the residual variation.

The discussion here is closely related to that under (i) and is rather an elaboration of the same general line of argument. As before we state the

---

[13] The various points are more or less explicit in the standard text-books; for an integrated picture of research principles, see Wilson (1952).

conclusion as a shift of emphasis in the analysis of experimental v. observational data:

$$\text{Elements of causal inference} \longrightarrow \text{Integrity in model building} \qquad (6)$$

(iii)   *The Implications of the Stochastic Assumptions for Statistical Technique.* The stochastic assumptions play an essential part in establishing the efficiency of statistical techniques, as regards the accuracy of estimation devices as well as the power of methods for hypothesis testing. Some comment on the common background of estimation and hypothesis testing techniques should now be made.

The standard methods of R. A. Fisher and his followers represent an ideal with regard to the systematic way in which the uncontrolled variation in the experimental replications is exploited for purposes of causal inference. The advantages are manifest both in estimation and hypothesis testing; throughout, the Fisherian methods have a high and even optimal degree of precision and power. This efficiency is the result of a comprehensive specification of the stochastic assumptions. For the simplest cases reference is made to illustrations a–b above. Generally speaking, the optimal accurracy of the modern techniques rests on a fairly complete specification of the distribution of the residual variation. The specification required is not a serious problem in controlled experiments, however, for thanks to the technical design of the replications (the randomization device, etc.) the experimenter can arrange so that the assumptions will be fulfilled in practice, at least approximately. On the other hand, in situations where the explanatory approach is based on observational data there is little or no prior knowledge about the residual variation. Hence its properties cannot usually be specified to the extent required by the modern standard techniques. The consequences of this argument are discussed in detail below.

The modern statistical methods work with stochastic assumptions which are specified with rigour and often in great detail, the basic techniques thus requiring normality, homoscedasticity, etc. Hence it is quite natural that current literature on statistical theory devotes so much space to the task of generalizing and varying the stochastic assumptions behind the standard techniques. The task is so much more important and urgent because of the large array of intermediate cases between observational situations with complete ignorance of the properties of the residual variation and experimental situations where the residual distribution is under sufficient control. The work in this direction has recently been reviewed by J. Tukey (1954) in a stimulating paper. In the present context there are two general arguments of particular interest in Tukey's paper. He points out that the work in question has been almost completely confined to the simple standard situations in regard to the causal hypotheses, with the result that questions referring to systematic *v.* observational errors and other intermediate cases between experimental and observational situations have hardly been touched upon. He also points out that we cannot go far from the simplest types of stochastic assumptions before we are in *terra incognita* with regard to the accuracy and power of the standard techniques and before the exact treatment of the problems becomes troublesome and unwieldy in mathematical and computational respects.

For the future, it is of course important to continue work on the systematic coordination of causal and stochastic assumptions, the goal being an arsenal of accurate statistical techniques from which we may choose for each particular case so that the underlying specification is sufficiently detailed and realistic. Work in this direction has only begun, however, and one must ask whether it can keep pace with the ever-growing number of causal models of varying complexity and their combination with different types of stochastic variation. In any case, the task is enormous if we wish to achieve perfect optimality, since this requires a detailed specification of the distributions entering into the stochastic assumptions. Thus for a long time to come the question, in practice, will be the attainment of an appropriate balance between detailed specification of the stochastic assumptions and accuracy in the resulting technique. Here, a generalization of the assumptions widens the field of potential applications, but this advantage is counteracted by attenuation of the inference. It would seem that large-sample methods of the classic type come near the ideal of such a compromise. Being asymptotically distribution-free they are very flexible, and in ordinary situations they do not diverge far from optimal accuracy. This should be taken as a provisional conclusion, and it will be discussed further in section 2.2–3.

2.2. *Estimation of Paramaters and Other Elements of Causal Inference*

With regard to estimation techniques, the discussion in the previous section may be summed up in the following formula for change of emphasis when passing from experimental to observational situations:

$$\text{Methods of optimal efficiency} \underset{\longleftarrow}{\longrightarrow} \text{Large-sample techniques} \qquad (7)$$

The small arrow in the opposite direction serves to stress the left-hand side as an ideal, even if in practice we are often far from a perfect coordination of causal and stochastic hypotheses and the ensuing optimal efficiency.

For illustration of (7) reference is made to least squares (l.sq.) and maximum likelihood (m.l.) estimation, the principal estimation techniques of classic and modern statistics. The basic facts are well known.[14] The m.l. method is of more universal scope. Under general conditions of regularity both methods give estimates that are asymptotically unbiased. The l.sq. estimates are consistent, i.e. their standard errors tend to zero with increasing sample size, while the m.l. estimates are even of optimal efficiency, i.e. their standard errors are asymptotically the smallest possible. The higher accuracy of the m.l. method rests on a more detailed specification of the stochastic assumptions; generally speaking the l.sq. method is distribution-free, whereas the m.l. method is not. Note that the l.sq. and m.l. estimates coincide in the simplest situations involving normality linearity, independence, etc.; it is only when dealing with degenerate or irregular cases that the loss of accuracy in the l.sq. estimates becomes considerable. The mathematical and computational simplicity of the l.sq. method should also be mentioned. Hence it is no wonder that the l.sq. method has served and still serves satisfactorily over wide fields of applied statistics: astronomy, geodesy, actuarial science, econometrics, etc.

In the recent development of theoretical statistics, with its emphasis on optimal efficiency, the least squares method has unjustly come into disfavour. The above comments are not intended as criticism of the maximum likelihood method; the point is that both methods have their proper spheres of application, and that the l.sq. method has certain distinct advantages when dealing with observational data. It may be added that each method rests on its own distinctive principle or criterion, and that neither method can be regarded as a surrogate for the other. In accordance, herewith, a theory for the two methods can be developed along parallel lines. We note, for example, both are subject to a robustness theorem to the effect that the extremum of the criterion has approximately the same distribution as when the criterion is formed with parameters which extremize the expected value of the criterion.[15]

In symbols, if $f(x, \theta)$ is the criterion defined by the observations x and one or more parameters θ, let $f^*(x)$ be the extremum of $f(x, \theta)$ in respect to θ, occurring, say, for $\theta^* = \theta^*(x)$, so that

$$f^*(x) = \text{extremum} f(x, \theta) = f(x, \theta^*)$$

[14] For the m.l. method, see H. Cramér (1945) and the original works of R. A. Fisher (1950). The statements on the l.sq. method refer primarily to the case of linear relations, but by the use of Taylor developments and other devices they extend to more general cases; see Whittaker-Robinson (1924) and Wilson (1952), also for further references.

[15] For the detailed treatment of a case in point, see Whittle (1954), Ch. 2.9.

Then $f^*(x)$ has approximately the same distribution as $f(x, \bar{\theta})$, where $\bar{\theta}$ is the θ-value extremizing the expected value of $f(x, \theta)$. In fact,

$$f^*(x) = f(x, \theta^*) = f(x, \bar{\theta}) + 0(\theta^* - \bar{\theta})^2 \tag{8}$$

and under general conditions of regularity the term of order of magnitude $(\theta^* - \bar{\theta})^2$ will be small compared with those fluctuations in $f(x, \theta)$ that are directly caused by the fluctuations in the sample values x.

2.3. Hypothesis Testing

Tests for frequencies, averages, etc., by large sample approximations to the normal distribution were in current use in the nineteenth century; early developments of testing techniques included in addition Lexis' divergence coefficient and the ensuing definitions of normal, supernormal and subnormal dispersion together with their interpretation in terms of urn schemes under the names of Bernouilli, Lexis and Poisson.[16] The Fisherian epoch brought rigour in the posing of significance problems, exactness in their treatment, and an intense activity in the construction of tests for various types of hypothesis and (after the impetus given by J. Neyman and E. S. Pearson) in studying the power of the tests to discriminate against counter-hypotheses. The exact assessment of significance levels, power functions, etc., rests on a detailed specification of the stochastic assumptions with regard to the distribution of the residual variation. This is entirely in line with the fact that the modern statistical techniques have been designed in connection with experimental applications, where the residual variation is under sufficient control for the purpose.

With observational data, the modern approach in hypothesis testing is more or less hampered by the scanty knowledge about the properties of the residual variation, and this is particularly true in the treatment of counter-hypotheses. The need for testing the statistical inference is no less than when dealing with experimental data, but with observational data other approaches come to the foreground. The change in the situation has several aspects. J. Tukey has drawn attention to the fact that the modern techniques for hypothesis testing are designed in line with "the tradition of self-contained experiment," the techniques being based solely on the data under investigation (Tukey, 1954, p. 716; Fisher, 1935, esp. p. 69). In the analysis of observational data the treatment of a single sample is more directly tied up with other experience, empirical and theoretical; hence in hypothesis testing various sources of evidence are taken into account by

[16] For a review and development of Lexis' theory, see Charlier (1912).

way of checks and cross-checks. I should like to formulate this tendency as follows:

Testing on the basis of the sample $\longrightarrow$ Testing against other knowledge   (9)
$\longleftarrow$

Hypothesis testing in the right-hand sense is always present in experimental investigations as well. Hence what is stated in (9) is that testing on the basis of the sample is of limited relevance in observational research, and that the checking of causal inference against other sources of knowledge is more indispensable, overt and explicit with observational than with experimental data. The small arrow serves to stress the modern techniques to the left as an ideal, both with regard to the exactness of the methods and to the possibility of assessing, internally, the reliability of the inference from the data.

The testing or checking of statistical inference on the basis of other knowledge is largely a matter of *ad hoc* devices varying from case to case. We may distinguish between three main sources of knowledge available for hypothesis testing in a broad sense; namely, empirical data, theoretical arguments *a priori,* and predictive tests. These will now be briefly discussed; for illustration we shall mainly refer to various aspects of demand analysis.

(i) *Hypothesis Testing by the Use of Other Empirical Data.*   There is, of course, no end of ways in which the conclusions from the sample under investigation can be compared with and tested against similar or related inference from data referring to other geographic regions, other social strata, earlier periods of time, or to whatever sample might be appropriate for the purpose. The broader and more varied the outlook, the better. The causal inference from different sets of empirical data are like pieces in a puzzle; they should combine to display a consistent total picture, and such an integration amounts to a check or test of the inference that is of essential relevance even if it does not, like the modern testing techniques, lead up to a numerical confidence level (Wold-Juréen, 1952, Ch. 2.5 (v)). We have mentioned one sample as checked against other evidence, but usually the investigation at issue is based on several different samples, and these will then in the first place be utilized in the puzzle. This is so in demand analysis, where a comprehensive study may include the estimation of scores or hundreds of demand elasticities referring to different commodities, different family types, and so on. A feature of general scope is that part of the statistical data in demand analysis are time series, part are cross-section data, and the more or less parallel results from these two sources may be employed for testing purposes in various ways.

The rationale of the right-hand approach in (9) is obvious, but it is equally clear that in practice it is hampered by various frictions, some of which are in the realm of organizational and institutional questions. There is the strong impact of the tradition of the self-contained experiment, a force which is felt widely outside the sphere of experimental research. This impact is strengthened by a marked difference between descriptive and explanatory approaches. The inference drawn from a separate sample will always have a descriptive aspect, and in this respect the inference may be both interesting and important, but it is only when it comes to application outside the sample that the need arises to check and test the inference against other evidence. For example, the regression of food expenditure on earnings in a certain group of households has its value as one of the statistics to describe the standard of living in this particular sample, but if interpreted as a causal relation to explain how food expenditure varies with income it must be carefully checked and tested against other data before it can be applied outside the sample, say for forecasting purposes. In the treatment of observational data it is therefore a temptation to rest content with the descriptive results and to slight or avoid the more difficult and committal explanatory problems. This tendency is accentuated as another aggravating force comes in by the institutional features of scientific research. In their work for examination degrees, in research grants, and in many other situations research workers are required to report definite results, and as a consequence limited projects are at a premium. Time-absorbing projects are out of the question or appear as doubtful investments, and this applies particularly to the large-scale projects that would be required to explore the causal complexes if we wished to obtain an operational grasp on the broad problems in the social field, such as those referred to in the beginning of section 1.4.

(ii) *Hypothesis Testing by* a priori *Arguments.* Some theoretical model, more or less elaborate, always enters in the specification of hypotheses behind an explanatory approach. Frequently part of the model enters in the specification, whereas other parts may be employed as auxiliary tools in the empirical analysis, and in particular for purposes of hypothesis testing. This is so in demand analysis, where the Pareto-Slutsky theory of consumer demand provides the existence of the demand functions which in the specification of hypotheses are adopted as a starting point for the empirical analysis. The same theory establishes certain properties of demand functions in the form of general relationships between different demand elasticities, and these relations can be utilized as checks or tests upon the empirical estimates of the elasticities involved. Further comments on this point will be made in section 3.3 (i).

The general features of observational research dealt with under (i) and (ii) place the statistician under a double obligation: to incorporate several types of data in the same investigation, and at the same time to coordinate the statistical techniques with the subject-matter theory of the field of application. In practice these features force the statistician to specialize in one field, or perhaps a few, where he is familiar with the sources of statistical data so as to know their reach and limitation, and where he can acquire a working knowledge of the subject-matter theory. Without such orientation in subject-matter the statistician runs the danger of missing the important problems in applied work, however versatile he may be with the formal aspect of statistical techniques.

(iii) *Predictive Tests.* The ultimate test of the causal inference lies in the question: Are the results useful in practice? In particular, can they be used to obtain realistic and efficient forecasts? Confrontation with fresh evidence is, clearly, the real touchstone for scientific inference in general, and in particular for explanatory approaches based on the observational statistics.

The problems that challenge research in the SW sector of our map vary immensely in complexity and difficulty, and so does the degree to which they are mastered for purposes of prediction. Mortality and fertility here represent two extremes, as stressed above (1.4, illustrations (i) and (iii)). In the first mortality tables, constructed some 250 years ago, the influence of age upon mortality was brought out with an accuracy that was sufficient for the special type of forecasting involved in the running of life insurance companies. The fertility variations are of vital importance to the welfare of a nation, but the failure of forecasts in this field shows that we are far from a quantitative knowledge of even the main features of the causal complex in an operational sense. Demand analysis is an intermediate case both with regard to difficulty and positive results. The work in the last 30 years or so has settled the basic questions of method for measuring the demand structure; the actual features of the structure are now known in broad outline, and some of the results have stood the test of prediction over relatively short periods. On the foundation thus established, research can now proceed to the study of special and more complex problems concerning consumer behaviour.

The comments in (i)–(iii) might seem anti-theoretical at first sight, but this is actually not so. For example, in a research project for explaining the fertility peak in Fig. 1 the coordination between statistical procedures and subject-matter theory would require qualified statistical work. It would be of great practical importance if this could lead to better forecasts, even if the future development far exceeded the tolerance margins set by the sampling errors. However, the difficulties to overcome in such an analysis are radically different from the types of problems specific to the statistical analyses of a self-contained experiment.

3. THE EXPLANATORY ANALYSIS OF OBSERVATIONAL DATA: SOME TYPICAL SITUATIONS

In order to discuss certain general features in the SW sector of our map we shall now take up four types of approach. These are selected to illustrate the differences in complexity and stage of development in various fields of application, from the first groping attempts to trace a causal relationship that may be taken as a basis for a theoretical model, in the streamlined statistical techniques for routine applications of well-established theoretical models. The intention thus is not to describe various stages in one and the same investigation. The main character of the approach is sometimes empirical, sometimes theoretical, sometimes intermediate, but in the SW sector the statistical method is always closely linked with subject-matter theory, and always seeks to copy the experimental method by *ad hoc* devices, utilizing such features in the actual situation as are analogous in some respect to a genuine experiment.

3.1. *Causal Patterns*

The approaches under this heading are concerned with the existence and direction of causal relationships. A typical problem is to distinguish between cause and effect in a complex of interrelated factors, or to distinguish genuine causal dependence from spurious relations due to common influence from other factors. The possible hypotheses in the case of two variables are covered by formulae (2a–d). With the introduction of more variables the possibilities multiply with great speed; among the simplest are:

$$(10a-e)$$

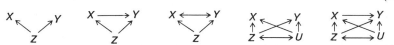

Problems concerning causal patterns are well known from the theory and application of correlation analysis.[17] If X, Y are intercorrelated, the partial correlation of X, Y with respect to Z yields a test criterion for discriminating (10a) from (10b) or (10c), and by considering the partial correlation with respect to a larger set of variables U, V, . . . we can con-

[17] The groundwork is covered by the text-books of Yule and Ezekiel. For a recent review, with special attention to spurious correlation, see H. A. Simon (1954).

tinue to explore the possibility of spurious correlation. In principle this is a general device. A fundamental approach in this direction is Sewall Wright's method of path coefficients for exploring complex causal patterns; this reference belongs partly to the next subsection since the path coefficients give quantitative information on the relationships.[18]

Causal patterns like (2) and (10) can sometimes be explored with advantage by the use of frequency comparisons. An example reported by W. Cochran (1954) deals with the problem of whether there is some hereditary element in the incidence of cancer. Here X and Y are relative frequencies for cancer of the uterus. There are two frequencies X, the first defined for a group A of patients who have the disease, and thus $X = 1$, the second for a group B forming a sample from the total population. Similarly there are two frequencies Y, one defined for a group of specified relatives of A, the other defined for relatives of B. Formulae (2c and d) indicate the hypotheses of presence and absence of hereditary aggregation of the disease, and formulae (10c and a) corresponding hypotheses if the data are stratified with respect to some disturbing variable Z; in the present case Z distinguishes between an older and a younger generation of relatives. The difference between the frequencies Y forms a test criterion for discriminating between the two hypotheses, and Cochran shows how this test can be performed by an application of the χ^2-method. It turns out that there is an association of type (2c), but on stratification this vanishes in the sense of (10a); the conclusion thus is that the data do not support the hypothesis of hereditary aggregation.

The method employed by Cochran extends to patterns with more stratification. The approach is of further general interest as an instructive design of sampling for purposes of causal inference. Current text-books on the theory and application of sampling deal almost exclusively with sampling techniques that are designed for some descriptive purpose. The optimal allocation of sampling units will, however, be radically different if the data are to serve an explanatory analysis. For example, if we wish to estimate the number of smokers in the total population it may be appropriate to use proportional sampling, say after stratification according to income, but if the problem is whether smoking is influenced by income, we should rather select the same number of individuals, in each income stratum.[19] The increase of work in this direction is one of the indications that the SW

[18] See Wright (1934) and his contribution in the volume edited by Kempthorne *et al.* (1954), also for further references. Tukey's paper in the same volume re-formulates and develops Wright's approach in terms of regression coefficients.
[19] The problem has been treated from this point of view by Frankel and Stock (1939). Cf. the uniform allocation of sampling units in contingency tables employed in the Kinsey report (1948).

sector is becoming of more immediate concern to professional statisticians.

If the circumstances are favourable it is possible not only to give evidence about the absence of causal connections, but also to establish the presence and the direction of such relationships. A classic instance is the use of observations on twins for discriminating between hereditary and milieu influences; owing to the close similarity between one-egg twins, they approach the ideal of the replicated experiment under constant conditions (see Dahlberg (1926)). For another case in point, reference is made to a recent study of denture diseases by E. Welander (1955). Caries, tartar incrustations (calculus), soft coatings, pocket formations, mouth hygiene, positional factors in the denture, diet habits, etc. form a causal complex that is hard to disentangle by *a priori* arguments. However, thanks to a coincidence in favourable features, certain aspects of the complex can be studied by statistical methods. The symmetry of the mouth allows us to eliminate the positional factor in the comparisons between different teeth; also, each tooth has 4 or 5 different surfaces, and by taking into account the points of contact of these, their position relative to places of affinity for the various denture diseases, etc., it is possible to specify certain plausible hypotheses on the causal complex. By utilizing and enlarging upon the available Swedish records of the requisite detailed type, Welander found, among other things, that there is inter-individual correlation between caries and calculus, and also between caries and pocket formations; the first correlation vanishes when formed for teeth with symmetric position, but the second does not. This result agrees with the plausible argument that caries and calculus have no local interaction, whereas caries and pocket formations should have.

3.2. *Regression Analysis*

Next we turn to situations where the existence and direction of a causal relation has been established (perhaps tentatively) and we wish to quantify the relation. The problem is thus to estimate the effect variable as a function of the explanatory variables. As regards the causal and statistical interpretation of such a function we note: (a) the relation indicates how the effect will vary as one explanatory variable is allowed to vary while the others remain constant; in general the relation further involves a residual and this accounts for the effect of disturbance factors which have not been explicitly introduced as explanatory; (b) the explanation brings back the variations of the effect variable upon variations in the other variables; in general the explanation is partial, the residual variance being a measure of the variation not explained.

The least squares regression of the effect variable upon the explanatory variables yields an estimate of the causal relation, and under general conditions the estimate is consistent. One or two aspects of the situation have been illustrated and commented upon above (sections 1.4 (ii); 2.1, illustration c; and 2.2). Regression methods being of fundamental importance in the SW sector, we shall now discuss the approach in some detail.

(i) *The Least Squares Principle.* As is clear from (a) and (b) above this principle constitutes an obvious rationale of least squares regression when the problem is to estimate a causal relationship. In fact, when applied to the given sample, no other estimate of the relation will give such small residual variance. For a linear regression, as is well known, this minimum property of the residual is equivalent to its property of having (in the given sample) zero correlation with each of the explanatory variables (e.g. Wold-Juréen, 1952; theorem 12.1.1–2). Referring to (a) above, this feature allows us to formulate the rationale of the regression in another way, namely, as being unbiased on the assumption that the joint influence of the unspecified factors is uncorrelated with the explanatory variables.

(ii) *Specification Error.* The estimation of a causal relation by regression analysis on the basis of observational data is formally the same procedure as in the case of experimental data, but as stressed in formula (5) there is an increased risk of specification errors, since the uncontrolled factors cannot be neutralized by randomization. Let

$$y = f(x^{(1)}, \cdots, x^{(h)}) + z \tag{11a}$$

or in the linear case

$$y = b_1 x^{(1)} + \cdots + b_h x^{(h)} + z \tag{11b}$$

be the hypothetical relation, and suppose that we are primarily interested in how y is influenced by $x^{(1)}$ and $x^{(2)}$. How many and which further explanatory variables $x^{(3)}$, $x^{(4)}$, . . . should be introduced is essentially a subject-matter question. This is a most important question, for the neglect of a relevant factor which is correlated with $x^{(1)}$ or $x^{(2)}$ will result in a specification error which will not tend to zero with increased size of the sample; on the contrary, it will remain of the same order of magnitude as the regression coefficient to be estimated. The dilemma is that the factors of potential influence are often numerous, whereas in practice the regression analysis must be confined to a limited number of explanatory variables. The traditional compromise is to include as explanatory those variables which, according to experience and *a priori* theory, are believed to be the main causal factors, the resulting regression being tested for sampling error by a significance formula of ordinary type, and for specification error by one or more *ad hoc* devices, (in line with the comment in section 2.3, (i)–(iii)).

A formal analysis of what can happen when another explanatory variable $x^{(h+1)}$ is introduced in the linear regression (11b) elucidates the dilemma at issue. We note:[20]

A. In principle, $x^{(h+1)}$ may upset the regression picture entirely, for there exist variables $x^{(h+1)}$ with unit variance such that a given coefficient, say b_1, will change to an arbitrarily prescribed value b between $-\infty$ and $+\infty$.

B. All coefficients b_1 will remain the same if $x^{(h+1)}$ is uncorrelated with every $x^{(1)}, \ldots, x^{(h)}$. More generally, b_1 will remain the same if $x^{(h+1)}$ is uncorrelated with the residual in the regression of $x^{(1)}$ on $x^{(2)}, \ldots, x^{(h)}$.

C. Suppose that y allows the representation

$$y = \beta_1 x^{(1)} + \cdots + \beta_h x^{(h)} + z^* \qquad (12)$$

with a disturbance term z^* which (a) has small standard deviation, say $\sigma(z^*) \lesssim \theta_1$, and (b) has small correlation coefficients with $x^{(1)}, \ldots, x^{(h)}$, say $r(z^*, x^{(i)}) \lesssim \theta_2 \cdot \sigma(z^*) \sigma(x^{(i)})$. Then the regression coefficients in (11b) approximate the true values β_i in (12) within margins that are small of order $\theta_1 \theta_2$,

$$|b_i - \beta_i| < c \cdot \theta_1 \theta_2 \qquad (i = 1, \cdots, h) \qquad (13)$$

where c does not depend upon z^*.

In C we have a proximity or robustness theorem for least squares regression which lends partial support to the traditional compromise. Stated in words, if the residual is small and the additional variable has no more than a slight correlation with the other explanatory variables, the two conditions strengthen each other so as to keep the specification error within limits of a smaller order.

(iii) *Sampling Error.* For regression coefficients, just as for most statistical estimates, the sampling error is of the order $O(1\sqrt{/n})$, if n is the size of the sample. Thus in large samples it tends to be of a smaller order of magnitude than the specification error. There is always the danger of specification error in a regression relation based on observational data, so when assessing its sampling error in the form of a standard error or a confidence interval, the results will make only a partial test of the validity of the regression. This is by no means a recommendation to ignore the sam-

[20] For proofs and further comment on the theorems, see Wold-Juréen (1952), Theorems 12.1.3 and 2.3.2–4. See also Ezekiel (1930), p. 347.

pling errors in applied work in the SW sector of our map; what I wish to stress is that they must be supplemented by validity tests of the type discussed in 2.3, (i)–(iii).

The many regression variants and the corresponding tests of significance provide a typical illustration of a general feature commented upon in 2.3, namely that the exact test techniques require a detailed specification of the stochastic assumptions. The situation was briefly discussed in connection with formula (4). In the standard tests it is assumed that the residual variation is homogeneous in the sense of forming sample values from one and the same distribution and that these sample values are independent (see Cramér, 1945, Chs. 29.8, 29.12, 37.2–3). This type of assumption is well suited for experimental situations, independence and homogeneity of the replications being essential aims in the experimental design. With observational data, on the other hand, these assumptions are often impaired by tendencies to patchiness and cluster, a characteristic feature of social and economic material. One source of such interrelation lies in the slow diffusion of behaviour patterns, which give rise to similarities between sampling units that are neighbouring in space or time, to group effects within different social strata, etc. Here we have entered the danger zone between sampling error and specification error. At the same time we note that, provided the interrelations follow some regular pattern, they need not in themselves imply a specification error or a change in the order of magnitude of the sampling error. Reference may here be made to the regression based on time-series data of the stationary type. The interrelation then takes the form of autocorrelation in the residual series, and this feature can be accounted for in assessing the sampling error. Thus in a linear regression (4) with one explanatory variable the standard error of the regression coefficient has to be corrected by the multiplicative factor

$$\sqrt{(1 + 2r_1\rho_1 + 2r_2\rho_2 + \cdots)} \tag{14}$$

where

$$r_1, r_2, \cdots \quad \text{and} \quad \rho_1, \rho_2, \cdots$$

are the autocorrelation coefficients of the explanatory variable and the residual, respectively.[21] We see that the large sample standard error remains of the order $0(1\sqrt{/n})$.

---

[21] For the proof of this and more general results, see Wold (1950) and, also for applied work, Wold-Juréen (1952), Chs. 13.4, 15.2 and 17.2–7. Further results in this direction are due to Grenander (1954), who shows, *i.a.*, that there are cases where a least squares estimate has optimal efficiency, asymptotically, in spite of the autocorrelation.

(iv) *Observational Error.*   A complication arises if the explanatory variables are subject to inaccuracy in measurement. Corrections for such error have been worked out in the assumptions that the errors are independent of the error-free variables and that the error variances are known *a priori* (e.g. Wold, 1940, §16). In general the correction is of the same order as the regression coefficient itself; thus, like the specification error, it is of a larger order of magnitude than the sampling error. The disadvantage in such correction methods is that in practice we have little or no information about the observational errors, neither of their presence nor of their distributional properties. Hence if it is felt that the data contain observational errors that are not negligible (negligible relative to the influences upon the effect variable that are due to unspecified causal factors), it is dangerous to employ the data for more than a tentative orientation.

A problem sometimes dealt with in statistical literature refers to the situation in which the relationship to be estimated is exact in the mathematical sense, so that the residual deviation is entirely due to the presence of observational errors.[22] This type of situation is well known from astronomy, geodesy, and related sciences. For example, when determining a comet's orbit on the celestial globe the latitude-longitude observations are subject to error, and the orbit is treated as an exact relation between the error-free observations. For such applications an adjustment technique is available, based on the least-squares principle. Within their limited field of application these techniques are indispensable; on the other hand it can be said that the statistical aspect of these matters is of secondary importance, for in practice the main concern in regard to observational errors is to reduce them by improved methods of measurement, and especially to reduce systematic errors.

(v) *Simultaneous Regressions.*   A regression relation which has been obtained as an estimate for a hypothetical causal relation may in principle be employed just as if it were the theoretical relation itself, for any purpose within the limits posed by general logic and special subject-matter theory. Thus it can be combined with any other knowledge, theoretical or empirical, and in particular it can be put together with other regressions to make models in the form of simultaneous relationships. For pioneering applications of such models reference is made to the work of J. Tinbergen (1939) on the statistical testing of business cycle theories. Because his approach is instructive from the point of view of ends and means in causal inference it will be considered in some detail. The systems of Tinbergen are built so as to allow a clear-cut causal interpretation. Each relation

[22] For a recent review, see Durbin (1955). Cf. also Wold-Juréen (1952), Ch. 2.4.

refers to a specified *economic unit* and serves to explain its actions or behaviour with regard to a specified variable; for example, a demand relation shows how the group of consumers change or adjust their demand according to changes in price, income and other explanatory variables. The variables thus explained by the system are called *endogenous*; other variables appearing in the system are called *exogenous*. The economic units and their behaviour patterns are *autonomous* in the sense that any unit may modify or alter its behaviour pattern without affecting the behaviour patterns of the other economic units. Finally, the relations are specified as a dynamic system in which the causal relations link together so as to form a *causal chain*; that is, on the basis of the past history of the system, its relations enable us to predict the future path of the effect variables recursively, one by one, and period by period. Systems of this type are known as recursive systems or *causal chain systems*.

The following simple system is a theoretical demand-supply model of causal chain type,[23]

$$d_t = D(p_t); \quad s_t = S(p_{t-1}); \quad p_t = p_{t-1} + \gamma(d_{t-1} - s_{t-1}) \text{ with } \gamma > 0 \quad (15\text{a–c})$$

The economic units are the consumers for the demand relation, the producers for the supply relation, and the merchants, who in a free market serve the function of bringing demand into contact with supply and of regulating the price mechanism, for the price formation relation. In (16) the causal chain is illustrated by an *arrow scheme* of the type introduced by Tinbergen; it indicates, for example, that supply at period t is assumed to be a function of price at period $t - 1$. The causal chain as pictured by an arrow scheme forms a dynamic generalization of the causal patterns in (2) and (10). Two stipulations that general logic imposes on the arrow scheme are (a) it must not be ambiguous or self-contradictory in the sense that there are two or more different causal relations for one and the same variable, and (b) a variable that occurs as causal with a certain lag must not appear later on in the chain as effect variable with the same lag. If such a causal circle were admissible, some endogenous variable via one or more intermediate causal links would form part of its own cause, thus defeating the general purpose of a causal model, namely to express a given variable

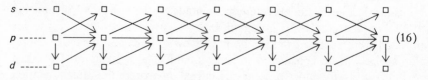

$$(16)$$

23 See Wold-Juréen (1952), Chapters 1.4 and 3.2, also for comments and references.

in terms of others. Generally speaking, the model will be a causal chain system if the relations can be arranged in such manner that all arrows in the scheme point either from left to right or vertically in one direction, say downwards.

The analogy between economic models and physical feed-back systems has recently been developed by A. Tustin (1953). A crucial point is that the physical systems work with feed-backs that are so rapid that they can be treated as instantaneous, whereas in causal chain systems the feed-back reaction (the lagged dependence of a variable upon itself) cannot be expressed for a shorter time than the unit of observation. Over large sectors of economics the reactions take place slowly, and then the causal chain systems will be appropriate; in other cases the reactions are rapid and may as a consequence require instantaneous feed-back models.

As regards the statistical treatment of causal chain systems we have already stated that they can be estimated by forming the least squares regression for each relation in the system. In fact, the bias in this regression is a matter of intercorrelation between the theoretical residuals and the explanatory variables, and the situation is the same whether the relation is single or belongs to a system. Naturally, since a system contains several relations, the risk of specification error multiplies, but a specification error in one relation need not affect the others. For example, the price formation in a free market being a complicated mechanism, relation (15c) may at best be taken as a first crude approximation, but a specification error here is of no consequence in the demand and supply relations of the system.

In estimating causal relations by regression analysis the logical necessity to avoid causal circles makes a clear-cut departure from regression analysis as used for descriptive purposes. Thus if we form a system (17a) of least square regressions,

$$x^{(1)} = b_{12}x^{(2)} + b_{13}x^{(3)} + z^{(1)}$$

$$x^{(2)} = b_{21}x^{(1)} + b_{23}x^{(3)} + z^{(2)}$$

$$x^{(3)} = b_{31}x^{(1)} + b_{32}x^{(2)} + z^{(3)} \tag{17a}$$

$$x^{(1)} = u^{(1)}$$

$$x^{(2)} = c_{21}x^{(1)} + u^{(2)}$$

$$x^{(3)} = c_{31}x^{(1)} + c_{32}x^{(2)} + u^{(3)} \tag{17b}$$

these so-called elementary regressions may always serve to describe the sample on which they are based. For example, the first relation shows how $x^{(1)}$ varies, on the average within the sample, if $x^{(2)}$ and $x^{(3)}$ are allowed to vary, and in the variance of the residual $z^{(1)}$ we have a measure for the accuracy of the description. On the other hand, a regression system of type (17b) is in the form of a causal model; in fact, for causal circles to be absent, irrespective of the number of relations and variables involved, it is clearly a necessary and sufficient condition that the relations can be arranged so as to make the coefficient matrix triangular. One way to characterize the situation is that in systems of type (17b) the residual variances are brought down to a minimum of what a causal explanation can achieve with the variables considered. If a system (17a) were adopted as a causal model, the residuals would be smaller, but the reduction would be due to a causal circle, the variations in a variable being partly explained in terms of themselves. In this quantitative sense, systems of type (17a) would, as causal models, "explain too much."

Some fifteen years ago the method of least squares regression was vigorously attacked in connection with a study of theoretical models in the form of simultaneous relations, and it was shown that for a general category of models—later to be known as systems of interdependent relations—the l.sq. method is not applicable without bias (Haavelmo, 1943).[24] The situation was reviewed in a joint paper by R. Bentzel and Wold (1946); we found that for causal chain models with normal and mutually independent residuals the l.sq. method is equivalent to the maximum likelihood method. In a later paper I have pointed out that the general conditions for the l.sq. estimates to be unbiased remain the same and can be satisfied if the estimated relation belongs to a causal chain system (Wold, 1951). In regard to the rationale of interdependent systems I should now like to comment from the point of view of description v. explanation. A special case, a demand-supply model borrowed from Girshick and Haavelmo (1947), will be cited. With a slight change in arrangement for easier comparison with (15) the model is

$$d_t = \alpha p_t + \beta + u_t$$

$$s_t = h_1 p_t + k_1 + v_t$$

$$d_t = s_t = x_t \qquad (18a)$$

$$x_t - \alpha p_t = \beta + u_t$$

$$x_t - h_1 p_t = k_1 + v_t \qquad (18b)$$

Both the causal chain model (15) and the interdependent system (18a) are attempts towards the dynamization of Cournot's static model for

[24] For later contributions see Hood-Koopmans, eds. (1953).

demand-supply equilibrium. Whereas (15) aims at a complete dynamization, a causal relation being specified for each of the variables involved, the dynamization in (18) is partial, the demand and supply relations being specified while price is dealt with as an equilibrating variable. Hence model (18) stands in close relation to the approach known as *comparative statics*. This is an attractive aspect, inasmuch as the problems of comparative statics are of great practical importance, and the model focuses upon these without entering into the price formation process with its notoriously complicated mechanism. Another interesting feature of interdependent models is that they involve identities which are introduced by way of assumptions, definitional relations, or otherwise, such as $d_t = s_t = x_t$ in (18) or, to give another example, total income = consumption + investment. The identities form a constraint for the effect variables, and this implies that the relations are not autonomous in the sense of causal chain systems (hence the term interdependent systems). Another possible interpretation of the identities is that they represent instantaneous feed-backs in the model. The properties mentioned have no doubt combined to arouse interest in the interdependent systems, particularly with regard to the use of total categories in economic models.

Against these attractive features there is, however, some obscurity in the approach of interdependent relations, especially with regard to the operational significance of the model. Once its parameters have been estimated, what applications can be made of the model? Can a relation in the system be used for estimating one variable in terms of the other ones? According to my understanding this approach may lead into the pitfall of "explaining too much," although the situation is more sophisticated than in the elementary regressions (17a). The regressions (17a) refer to the total distribution of the variables involved, whereas in interdependent relations of type (18b) the left-hand expressions usually refer to the conditional distribution defined by regarding the predetermined variables appearing in the right-hand members as fixed. Further, the left-hand expressions are not defined as elementary regressions of the conditional distribution, but as having residuals with certain specified correlation properties. The number of parameters to the left in (18b) is, however, the same as in a set of elementary regressions, and this feature gives rise to the risk that the relations "explain too much" if interpreted in a causal sense. In the applications of interdependent systems this risk has actually materialized, inasmuch as some of the reported models have given residuals with smaller variance than is compatible with a causal interpretation of the relations (Wold, 1955). When this happens it implies that the parameters of the interdependent system are, on the whole, larger in absolute size than in a causal model for the same phenomena.[25]

(vi) *The Subject-matter Background.* As a tool for causal inference from observational data regression analysis is by no means a routine affair, and above all it is important for the regression to have a sound theoretical background. In experimental situations the design of the experiment indicates how to specify the regression, and in particular it is clear which variables are effects and which are causes. With observational data the specification of hypotheses is in essence a subject-matter question. This is, however, only one aspect of the coordination between statistical analysis and subject-matter theory; we shall now proceed to a more general discussion.

3.3. *Model Building on the Basis of Elementary Assumptions*

Causal inference is an interplay between empirical and theoretical analysis, and in this mixed procedure the lead is sometimes taken by the empirical, and sometimes by the theoretical approach. Earlier in this section we have been concerned with only one aspect or function of the theoretical element in the interplay; namely, to pose an articulate question to the data under investigation or, otherwise expressed, to specify the causal hypothesis behind the statistical analysis. Following up the comment in 2.3 (ii) we shall now turn to situations where a theoretical model is available which is only partially exploited in the specification of hypotheses, leaving other parts as ancillary information that can be utilized for supporting and testing the statistical inference. There are several ways in which the statistical analysis can profit in such situations, notably:

(a) Several types of data can be treated on the basis of the same theoretical model.

(b) The empirical results can be tested for agreement with theoretical relationships, asymptotic properties, etc., that are indicated by the ancillary information.

(c) The rationale of the statistical procedure can be examined by subjecting the empirical results to tests of type (b).

If the statistical hypotheses in this way form part of a more embracing theoretical model, a general feature in the situation is that the model is

---

[25] In agreement with this argument, some applications of interdependent systems have resulted in demand elasticities which are larger than those obtained by least squares methods; see Bergstrom (1955), p. 265, and Hildreth-Jarrett (1955), p. 115.

based on more fundamental and elementary hypotheses. The more firm and rich in substance the theoretical model, the more favourable is the situation for judging the validity of the statistical results at issue. The best examples of well-established models belong to the experimental sciences, as in genetics or statistical mechanics. Such reliable and comprehensive models are an ideal also in the social sciences, but unfortunately difficult if not impossible to attain. Here the models are far less exact, and are usually fragmentary, covering only a limited sector of the field of application. To illustrate the points (a)–(c) above, two models will be cited from the social sciences.

(i) *The Pareto-Slutsky Theory of Consumer Demand.*   The fundamental assumption is that the consumer has a consistent pattern of preferences with regard to the commodities under consideration. Under general conditions of regularity this simple assumption suffices to establish the existence of the consumer's demand functions; these indicate how his demand for the various commodities is causally influenced by the commodity prices and by his disposable income.[26] This basic result gives a common theoretical model for the statistical treatment of cross section data (demand as a function of income) and time-series data (demand as a function of prices and income); we have here an application of type (a). To mention one advantage of this, an elasticity estimated from one category of data may, in principle, be used as a known entity when treating another category of data (so-called conditional regression) (Wold, 1940, §10; Wold-Juréen, 1952, Ch. 2.6).[27] Furthermore the Pareto-Slutsky theory leads to a number of relationships between demand functions, demand elasticities, etc., propositions that allow applications of type (b). Hereunder we note Slutsky-Schulz' relation involving all elasticities for one commodity; Hicks-Allen's relation involving one type of elasticity for all commodities; Hotelling-Juréen's relation involving a pair of cross elasticities; the theorem of Törnqvist, confirming and extending an empirical conjecture by the author, that for necessities the income elasticity is smaller than the price elasticity, and conversely for luxuries. Finally, we note an application of type (c). The income elasticity for an aggregate commodity should theoretically be a weighted average of the elasticities for the separate commodities; the same relation should hold for the estimated elasticities, and so it does for estimates obtained by least squares regression but not for those obtained by

---

[26] For an exposition of the Pareto-Slutsky theory covering the statements here and in the following, see Wold-Juréen (1952), Chs. 4.5, 6.1–5, 14.2 and 17.2–3.
[27] For an extension of the approach, see Durbin (1953).

orthogonal or diagonal regression; thus, the l.sq. regression has passed the test without bias, but not the two other estimation methods.

(ii) *Migration Models.*   In the study of internal migration it is a natural approach to represent the frequency of migration between two places as a function of their distance, say a power of their distance; in symbols

$$f = M(d) \qquad f = A \cdot d^{-a} \tag{19a-b}$$

For data on the migration to a district in Northern Sweden, formula (19b) has given a fairly good fit.[28] The parameter α turned out to be remarkably stable, 4 different communities during 8 different decades giving 32 values ranging between $\alpha = 1.72$ and $\alpha = 2.87$. These results are pleasing, but, on the other hand, the model (19) is rather formal, an approach intermediate between formal description and causal explanation. A model penetrating deeper into the causal mechanism of the migration movements has recently been presented by R. Porter. The driving force behind the migration is here assumed to be economic, unemployed people seeking the nearest vacant job and employers seeking the nearest people for their vacant jobs. Briefly stated, the migration is thus interpreted as a *matching process.* The mathematical analysis of the process leads to a representation of the distance function in terms of regional integrals over the population density. The resulting formula gives a good fit to the same data, especially in view of the radical reduction in the number of parameters employed; these are 2, against 64 when applying formula (19b). A beautiful feature of Porter's model is that it gives an interpretation of the parameter α in (19b). If we imagine a homogeneous country in the shape of a long line (as Chile) the asymptotic value for the parameter would be $\alpha = 2$, whereas a large circular country (as pre-war Germany) would give $\alpha = 4$. The empirical α-values obtained for Sweden have $\alpha = 2.3$ for mean value, and this corresponds quite well to the oblong shape of the country. For another thing, the basic assumptions of the model can be varied so as to explore other hypotheses about the causal mechanism. We may, for example, assume that employees seek the nearest job, while employers seek over the whole country when filling vacancies; this would lead to another expression for the distance function. Moreover, on the introduction of auxiliary hypotheses Porter's migration model can be used for the analysis of several types of data, e.g. the percentage of people who live in the same district where they were born.

---

[28] The applications of (19b) are quoted by Mr. Lövgren. I am indebted to Mr. Lövgren and Dr. Porter for placing their as yet unpublished work on migration at my disposal.

3.4. *Joint Treatment of Causal and Stochastic Assumptions by Exact Methods*

The models dealt with in section 3.3 are constructed with exclusive regard to the causal aspects, the deviations from reality being left aside simply as an unexplained residual. We shall now turn to models which have a higher aspiration level, that is, models which are complete in the sense that they specify both the causal and the stochastic assumptions. The two types of models will be referred to here as I and II. Examples of type II are the birth and death process, various epidemic models, models for the learning process, to cite only a few instances from the current literature.[29]

These two lines of approach represent two important fronts in contemporary research. Speaking broadly, type I emphasizes application, synthesizing several sources of data into an integrated approach, and the aim is to achieve operational results, even though the approximations are crude. In type II the emphasis is on pure research, the approach is more analytic, more exact, and the statistical tests follow the principles of the self-contained experiment. In practice the degree of difficulty determines the aspiration level, and this varies widely, depending upon the field of application. For example, in the complex problems of the social sciences operational results are frequently not available, and therefore a model of type I that actually works will represent a significant advance, even if the residuals are large. In other fields, and here examples could be cited from industrial, biological and medical applications, work on models of type II has already given results of practical use. On the other hand there is a wide gap between the problems solved in the birth and death process and the problems encountered in population forecasts (cf. Fig. 1), and there are also other obvious instances of the same type of shortcoming.

It would seem that these two research fronts display differences in institutional background. The work on models of type I has its main roots in the NW sector of our map, and accordingly is carried on in keeping with the attitudes and traditions of the NW sector. Research of type II is largely inspired by the exact methods of the SE sector, the purpose being to perform a systematic coordination between the causal and stochastic elements of the model. At the present time progress in the amorphous SW sector seems to be hampered by the lack of contact between the two lines of approach. From the foregoing it may be seen how each of the approaches has something to learn from the other. Research carried out with the standards of the SE sector will benefit from the broader outlook towards problems which is customary in the NW sector, and in particular it is desirable

---

[29] For a recent treatment of this subject, see Bartlett (1955).

to cover several types of data by the same model. Approaches originating in the NW sector will profit from posing the problems more vigorously in causal terms, and from more determined efforts to subject the inference to predictional and other decisive tests. The plea for such a mutual exchange has been an underlying incentive for this paper, and my purpose will be fulfilled if the suggestions here presented can contribute to a clearer understanding of the ends and means of present-day statistics.

REFERENCES

Allen, R. G. D., and A. L. Bowley (1935), *Family Expenditure.* London: Staples.

Bartlett, M. S. (1955), *An Introduction to Stochastic Processes with Special References to Methods and Applications.* Cambridge: Univ. Press.

Benini, R. (1907), *Giorn. Econ., 35,* 1053.

Bentzel, R., and H. Wold (1946), *Skand. AktuarTidskr., 29,* 95.

Bergstrom, A. R. (1955), *Econometrica, 23,* 258.

Braithwaite, R. B. (1953), *Scientific Explanation.* Cambridge: Univ. Press.

Charlier, C. (1912), *Ark. Mat. Astr. Fys., 7,* no. 17.

Cochran, W. (1954), *Biometrics, 10,* 417.

Cramér, H. (1945), *Mathematical Methods of Statistics.* Stockholm: Geber. Princeton: Univ. Press, 1946.

Dahlberg, G. (1926), *Twin Births and Twins from a Hereditary Point of View.* Stockholm: Tiden.

Dietl, J. (1849), *Der Aderlass in der Lungenentzündung.* Vienna: Kaulfuss & Prandel.

Durbin, J. (1953), *J. Amer. Statist. Assn., 48,* 799.

_____ (1955), *Rev. Inst. Int. Statist., 22* (1954), 23.

Ezekiel, M. (1930), *Methods of Correlation Analysis.* 2nd ed. 1941. New York: Wiley.

Fisher, R. A. (1935), *The Design of Experiments.* 7th ed. 1949. Edinburgh: Oliver & Boyd.

_____ (1950), *Contributions to Mathematical Statistics.* New York: Wiley.

_____ (1953), *J. R. Statist. Soc.,* A, *116,* 1.

Fox, K. A. (1953), *The Analysis of Demand for Farm Products.* U.S. Dept. of Agriculture, Technical Bull. no. 1081.

Frankel, L. R., and J. S. Stock (1939), *Ann. Math. Statist., 10,* 288.

Girshick, M. A., and T. Haavelmo (1947), *Econometrica, 15,* 79.

Grenander, U. (1954), *Ann. Math. Statist., 25,* 252.

Haavelmo, T. (1943), *Econometrica, 11,* 1.

Hald, A. (1952), *Statistical Theory with Engineering Applications.* New York: Wiley.

Hildreth, C., and F. G. Jarrett (1955), *A Statistical Study of Livestock Production and Marketing*. New York: Wiley.

Hood, Wm. C., and Tj. C. Koopmans, Eds. (1953), *Studies in Econometric Method*. New York: Wiley.

Kempthorne, O., *et al.*, Eds. (1954), *Statistics and Mathematics in Biology*. Ames, Iowa: Iowa State Coll. Press.

Kinsey, A. C., W. B. Pomeroy, and C. E. Martin (1948), *Sexual Behavior in the Human Male*. Philadelphia: Saunders.

Lazarsfeld, P. F., Ed. (1954), *Mathematical Thinking in the Social Sciences*. Glencoe, Ill.: The Free Press.

Lövgren, E., *Migration and the Mobility of Labour. Geografiska Annaler*. To appear.

Malmquist, S. (1948), *A Statistical Analysis of the Demand for Liquor in Sweden. A Study of the Demand for a Rational Commodity.* (Doctoral thesis.) Uppsala.

Marshall, A. (1890), *Principles of Economics*. London: Macmillan.

Moore, H. L. (1919), *Pol. Sci. Quart., 34,* 546.

———— (1925), *Quart. J. Econ., 39,* 357.

Porter, R., Approach to Migration through its Mechanism. *Geografiska Annaler*. To appear.

Shepherd, G. S. (1941), *Agricultural Price Analysis*. 3rd ed. 1950. Ames, Iowa: Iowa State Coll. Press.

Shewhart, W. A. (1931), *Economic Control of Quality of Manufactured Product*. New York: van Nostrand.

Schultz, H. (1938), *The Theory and Measurement of Demand*. Chicago: Univ. Press.

Simon, H. A. (1954), *J. Amer. Statist. Assn., 49,* 467.

Stone, R. (1954), *The Measurement of Consumers' Expenditure and Behaviour in the United Kingdom 1920–1938*, I. Cambridge: Univ. Press.

Tinbergen, J. (1939), *Statistical Testing of Business Cycle Theories, II. Business Cycles in the United States of America 1919–32*. Geneva: League of Nations.

Tobin, J. (1950), *J. R. Statist. Soc. A, 113,* 113.

Tukey, J. (1954), *J. Amer. Statist. Assn., 49,* 706.

Tustin, A. (1953), *The Mechanism of Economic Systems*. Cambridge, Mass.: Harvard Univ. Press.

Unesco (1954), "Mathematics and the Social Sciences." *Int. Soc. Sci. Bull.,* 6, no. 4.

Welander, E. (1955), *The Occurrence of Dental Caries in the Permanent Dentition*. Stockholm: Odentological Inst.; and Uppsala: Univ. Inst. of Statistics.

Whittaker, E. T., and G. Robinson (1924), *The Calculus of Observation*. 4th ed. 1944. London: Blackie.

Whittle, P. (1954), Appendix 2 in H. Wodl, *A Study in the Analysis of Stationary Time Series*. 2nd ed. Stockholm: Geber.

Wilson, E. B. (1952), *An Introduction to Scientific Research*. New York: McGraw-Hill.

Wold, H. (1940), *The Demand for Agricultural Products and Its Sensitivity to Price and Income Changes* (Swedish). Stockholm (Statens Offentliga Utredningar, 1940: 16).

——— (1950), *Bull. Inst. Int. Statist., 32*, I, 145 and II, 277.

——— (1951), *Sankhyā, 11*, 205.

——— (1954), *Econometrica, 22*, 162.

——— (1955), *Cahiers Séminaire d'Econométrie de R. Roy., 3*, 81.

——— (1956), *Nordisk Statistisk Skriftserie*, No. *3* (1955) 95.

Wold, H., in association with L. Juréen (1952), *Demand Analysis: A Study in Econometrics*. Stockholm: Geber; and New York: Wiley, 1953.

Wright, S. (1934), *Ann. Math. Statist., 5*, 161.

Yule, G. U. (1911), *An Introduction to the Theory of Statistics*. 8th ed. 1927. London: Griffin.

Reprinted by permission from pages 1–38, "Model Building in the Human Sciences," edited by R. Peltier and H. Wold, *Entretiens de Monaco en Sciences Humaines, Session 1964,* Centre International d'Etude des Problèmes Humains, Monaco, 1966.

The Approach of Model Building: Crossroads of Probability Theory, Statistics, and Theory of Knowledge

HERMAN WOLD

The paper takes up some aspects of model building that I believe are of particular relevance for being discussed at the *Monaco entretiens* as scheduled for 1964. As a scientific paper the treatment is expository; what is new lies mainly in the arrangement of the material.[1]

1. SCIENTIFIC MODEL BUILDING IN EXPERIMENTAL VS. NONEXPERIMENTAL SITUATIONS

In the techniques of model building it makes a fundamental difference whether controlled experiments are or are not possible. For a start we shall consider two cases which are typical as well as simple. The ensuing comments draw to a large extent from Ref. 85.

---

[1] When drafting the paper in 1961 for purposes of planning the 1964 meeting, I incorporated fresh research material in a few passages, notably the reinterpretation in (3.23) of the primary form of interdependent systems in terms of *eo ipso* predictors, the matrices (3.11) and (3.17) that illustrate the difficulties that arise when the parameter estimation of multirelation models is based on their reduced form, the general argument in Remark 1.61, and the two last illustrations in Remark 1.62. Some of the new material has been used in more recent publications, as indicated by references.

391

1.1. *Two Unirelation Models*

(i) A model based on controlled experiments. With reference to Fig. 1.10, corn yield y is studied as a function of two fertilizers, viz. phosphate x_1 and nitrate x_2, say

(1) $$y = f(x_1, x_2)$$

The graph shows how y varies with phosphate quantity x_1 at three levels of the nitrate quantity x_2, viz. $x_2 = 0$, $x_2 = 160$ and $x_2 = 320$, respectively (all quantities are measured per acre). The data from the individual harvest plots are shown in the graph, and the curves refer to the following nonlinear functions in x_1, x_2 as fitted to the data according to the principle of least squares:

(2) $$y = -5.68 - 0.417x_1 - 0.316x_2 + 8.5155x_1^{1/2} + 6.3512x_2^{1/2} + 0.3410x_1^{1/2}x_2^{1/2}$$

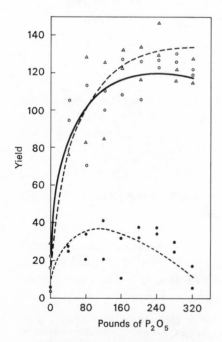

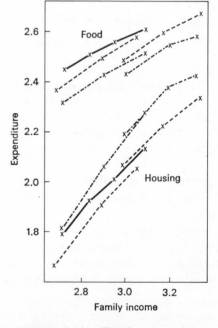

FIGURE 1.10 *Total yield with P$_2$O$_5$ (phosphate) variable and N (nitrogen) fixed at three levels. Ref. (no. 32): Heady and Dillon, 1961.*

FIGURE 1.11 *Engel curves for food and housing in families at different income levels. Logarithmic data. Refs. 78 and 95.*

Model (1.1) does not take into explicit account the deviations between the curve and the actual observations. This is done in the stochastic model

(3) $$y = f(x_1, x_2) + v$$

with

(4) $$E(y/x_1, x_2) = f(x_1, x_2)$$

In (1.3)–(1.4) the corn yield y is assumed to be a random variable, and $f(x_1, x_2)$ represents the *average value* or *conditional expectation* of yield y for a specified combination x_1, x_2 of fertilizers. The residual v is a random variable that represents the difference between the actual corn yield y and its expected value $f(x_1, x_2)$. In general the distributions of y and v will depend upon the fertilizer combination x_1, x_2.

(ii) A model based on nonexperimental data. Fig. 1.11 refers to a model based on household statistics. The families have been grouped in income classes, and in each class the average expenditure on food (and, respectively, housing) has been calculated and plotted.

The great pioneer in the use of household data is the French sociologist Le Play (Ref. 46). The curves shown in Fig. 1.11 are known as *Engel* curves after the German statistician E. Engel (Ref. 20). The data behind Fig. 1.11 are from three Swedish household surveys in 1913, 1923 and 1933.

The approach as illustrated in Fig. 1.11 can be summed up in the model

(5) $$y = f(x_1, x_2, x_3, x_4)$$

where y is expenditure, x_1 family income, x_2 an indicator variable for the budget item (food or housing), x_3 an indicator for social stratum (the curves to the left: workers' and low grade employees' families; the curves to the right: middle class families), and x_4 indicates the time of the survey (1913, 1923 or 1933).

Further we note the stochastic form of the model,

(6) $$y = f(x_1, x_2, x_3, x_4) + v$$

with

(7) $$E(y/x_1, x_2, x_3, x_4) = f(x_1, x_2, x_3, x_4)$$

As in (1.3)–(1.4), the variable y and the residual v are assumed to be stochastic, and f represents the conditional expectation of y for given x_1, x_2, x_3, x_4.

Remark 1.20. Models (1.3)–(1.4) and (1.6)–(1.7) will serve as background for several comments. Subsections 1.2–1.6 set the stage for the rest of the paper. Readers who have a working knowledge of econometrics or statistics can rapidly skip over to section 2, checking perhaps with Theorems 1.50–1.51, and the three illustrations in the beginning of section 1.6.

1.2. *Experimental versus Nonexperimental Data (Refs. 85, 90, 94)*

The models (3)–(4) and (6)–(7) have been chosen so as to bring into relief the similarity as well as the deepgoing difference between experimental and nonexperimental data. In the fertilizer experiment the different observations are comparable in the sense that other factors than the fertilizers x_1, x_2 are kept constant, or as constant as possible, in accordance with the principle that experiments should be repeated under constant conditions. In the household data the different observations are comparable in the sense that other factors than the income x_1 and the item x_2 under analysis are, if possible, kept constant by suitable stratification or restriction of the survey, and suitable classification of the material; in the present case such variables are in the first place the family size x_3 and the year x_4 of the survey.

The fundamental difference between the two situations is the following: In the fertilizer experiment the variables x_1, x_2 are controlled by the experimenter in the sense of being *steered*, regulated so as to attain values in accordance with the design of the experiment. In the household data the income variable x_1 is not steered in this sense; the experimenter just observes the income of the various families in the sample. We note that this difference implies that the design of a controlled experiment can be randomized; see Remark 1.60 below.

1.3. *Predictors (Refs. 87–91, 92a, 93)*

A stochastic relation

(8) $$y = f(x_1, \cdots, x_n) + v$$

with

(9) $$E(y/x_1, \cdots, x_n) = f(x_1, \cdots, x_n)$$

is called an *eo ipso predictor,* or briefly a *predictor*. While the term is recent (Refs. 90, 92a), the notion of predictor is as old as the concept of conditional expectation.

Predictors provide a tool for unified treatment of experimental and nonexperimental models, as is clear from the simple models (1.3)–(1.4) and (1.6)–(1.7). In nonexperimental situations the variables $x_1, \cdots, x_n$ are ruled by a joint probability distribution. In experimental situations the variables $x_1, \cdots, x_n$ are controlled (steered) by the experimenter, the joint distribution of $x_1, \cdots, x_n$ may then be called a *controlled distribution*.

1.4. Theoretical Model vs. Empirical Data (Ref. 33)

In essence, scientific model building is a systematic coordination of theoretical and empirical elements of knowledge into a joint construct.

In scientific model construction it is important to discern on the one hand between the hypothetical assumptions that constitute the theoretical part of the model, on the other the empirical observations that the model serves to interpret. Empirical observations enter in different ways in the model construction: at an early stage when observations and experience are accumulated, be it that a tentative model has or has not been formed; in assessing the parameters of the model on the basis of the observations; in testing the theoretical model against the empirical evidence.

It is customary to use different symbols to keep the theoretical concepts distinct from the empirical observations. Thus in model (1.2) we write the theoretical relation with Greek letters, say

$$y = \alpha_0 + \alpha_1 x_1 + \alpha_2 x_2 + \alpha_{11} x_1^{1/2} + \alpha_{12} x_1^{1/2} x_2^{1/2} + \alpha_{22} x_2^{1/2} + v$$

and use Latin letters for the parameters that refer to or have been obtained from the empirical data, say

$$y = a_0 + a_1 x_1 + a_2 x_2 + a_{11} x_1^{1/2} + a_{12} x_1^{1/2} x_2^{1/2} + a_{22} x_2^{1/2} + u$$

Remark 1.40. Econometrics is a pioneering area of nonexperimental model building in the human sciences. It was however rather late that a genuine coordination of theoretical and empirical material came into the picture; the 1910s and 1920s mark the first beginnings.[2] By a remarkable coincidence the same period was one of pathbreaking but much more rapid developments in a related area, the statistical methods for the design and analysis of controlled experiments, to a large extent solo work by Sir R. A. Fisher, Refs. 23–24. In econometrics the developments have been slowed up by two problems of method, known as "the choice of regression" and "simultaneous equations." Being fundamental for nonexperimental building in general, these problems will be key themes in the present paper.

---

[2] Analysis of consumer demand is the pioneering area in these developments; compare Ref. 64.

Remark 1.41.　Theoretical and empirical research are to some extent independent vehicles for scientific progress. For example, reference is made to theoretical physics and experimental physics. This reference also illustrates that in some areas theoretical model building is far ahead of what has been explored and verified empirically, in other areas the converse is true. To put it otherwise, and contrary to what is sometimes vindicated, it is not so that theoretical approaches have some kind of general priority or advantage over empirical approaches. It is quite another matter that when it comes to the reporting of fresh research results, or to expository treatments in articles and textbooks, it is often appropriate and convenient to present first the theoretical model and then its empirical aspects.

1.5. *Statistical Techniques of Parameter Estimation*

The approach of model building is broad and flexible, and a host of models of different types have been constructed for a variety of purposes. To some extent the technique of parameter estimation varies with the type of the model, to some extent general estimation techniques are available that can be adapted to specific models. The general techniques include the method of *least squares* (Legendre 1806, Gauss 1809; see Ref. 76 for details) and the method of *maximum likelihood* (R. A. Fisher 1925, Ref. 23, foreshadowed by Gauss 1809), to mention the two best known and most developed methods.

The classical method of regress analysis (Galton 1886, K. Pearson 1896, Yule 1897; for detailed references, see Ref. 100) is an estimation technique that belongs to the general category of least squares methods. To emphasize the broad applicability of least squares regression we shall recall some elements of the approach by way of two theorems.

Theorem 1.50.　Considering an *eo ipso* predictor (1.8)–(1.9), let

$$\bar{y}(x_1, \cdots, x_n)$$

denote the conditional mean of y for given $x_1, \cdots, x_n$. If the sample size is allowed to increase indefinitely, $\bar{y}(x_1, \cdots, x_n)$ will, according to the law of large numbers, and thus under very general assumptions, tend stochastically to the corresponding conditional expectation, in symbols

$$(10) \qquad \text{prob} \lim \bar{y}(x_1, \cdots, x_n) = E(y/x_1, \cdots, x_n)$$

In other words: In the sense of the law of large numbers, and under the conditions of this law, an observed conditional mean will be a consistent estimate of the corresponding conditional mean in the theoretical model; (Ref. 41).

The conditional mean $\bar{y}(x_1, \cdots, x_n)$ is sometimes called the (empirical) *mean value regression* of y on $x_1, \cdots, x_n$. The conditional expectation $E(y/x_1, \cdots, x_n)$, correspondingly, is called the (theoretical) mean value regression.

In Figs. 1.10 and 1.11 the curves and broken lines are the (empirical) mean value regression of y on x, or rather two variants of the mean value regression.

Theorem 1.51. *Linear regression.* Let a linear *eo ipso* predictor be given by

$$(11) \qquad y = \beta_0 + \beta_1 x_1 + \beta_2 x_2 + \cdots + \beta_n x_n + v$$

with

$$(12) \qquad E(y/x_1, \cdots, x_n) = \beta_0 + \beta_1 x_1 + \beta_2 x_2 + \cdots + \beta_n x_n$$

Then under very general conditions the least squares regression of y on $x_1, \cdots, x_n$, say

$$(13) \qquad y = b_0 + b_1 x_1 + b_2 x_2 + \cdots + b_n x_n + u$$

will provide consistent estimates for the parameters $\beta_0, \beta_1, \cdots, \beta_n$.

For a detailed proof, see Ref. 91. We specify the conditions of validity of the theorem:

(a) The *ergodicity* assumption:

$$(14) \qquad \text{prob lim } m_i = \mu_i; \qquad \text{prob lim } m_{ik} = \mu_{ik} \qquad (i, k = 0, 1, \cdots, n)$$

or in words: the observed first and second order moments have the corresponding theoretical moments as stochastic limits as the sample increases indefinitely.

(b) The *definiteness* assumption

$$(15) \qquad \det[\mu_{ik}] > 0 \qquad (i, k = 1, \cdots, n)$$

or equivalently, the joint distribution of $x_1, \cdots, x_n$ is linearly nonsingular.

Remark 1.50. In more or less general form Theorem 1.51 is standard material in statistical textbooks (Refs. 17, 56). The proof given in Ref. 91 differs from the customary treatment in two respects. For one thing, the theoretical normal equations are derived from the assumption that the theoretical relation (1.11) constitutes a conditional expectation plus a residual, whereas the normal equations of the sample are derived from the criterion that the observed residual should have the smallest possible variance. In this way assumption (1.14) becomes the salient point of the theorem. As is well known this assumption is fulfilled in a variety of situations, notably (a) the case of independent replications of an experiment, and (b) the case when the variables $y, x_1, \cdots, x_n$ are given as time series, and the variables as well as the residual may be autocorrelated. For another thing, the residual properties

(16a–b) $\qquad E(v) = 0; \qquad r(v, x_i) = 0; \qquad i = 1, \cdots, n$

usually are adopted as assumptions, while they are here obtained as implications of the basic assumption (1.12), a twist that emphasises the predictive aspect of the regression (Ref. 88; cf. also Ref. 35 for an early definition of regression in terms of predictors).

Remark 1.51. Ever since the beginnings of correlation theory (K. Pearson 1896, Yule 1897; see Ref. 100) it has been emphasized as a crucial feature of regression that in a scatter diagram of two variables x, y the regression of y on x is not the same line as the regression of x on y. The pluralism, which increases with the number of variables, makes what is known as "the choice of regression"; see Refs. 25, 51, 62, 64, 96.

For later reference, Fig. 1.50 illustrates this fundamental fact. The fulldrawn line is the linear regression of length on weight in a sample of 200 Swedish military recruits; if the weight x is known this line gives a prediction of the average or expected length y. The broken line is the regression of weight on length in the same sample; for given length y this line predicts the average weight x. As already stated, the two lines do not coincide.

The same dualism or pluralism extends to mean value regression. In Figs. 1.10 and 1.11 the curves are estimates of the mean value regressions of y and x, while the mean value regressions of x on y have not been assessed. Thus in Fig. 1.10 the fulldrawn curve gives the expected corn yield y for known phosphate quantity x_1 (and constant nitrate quantity $x_2 = 160$). In Fig. 1.11 the mean value regressions show the average expenditure on food (or housing, respectively) for known level of consumer income.

1.6. *Causal Inference*

To repeat, Figs. 1.10–1.11 and 1.50 show three variants of regression of y on x, and these variants are closely similar in interpretations as conditional means. The reverse regression of x on y (shown only in Fig. 1.50)

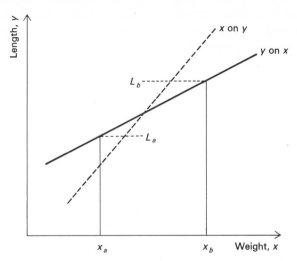

FIGURE 1.50   *Correlation between length* (y) *and*
weight (x) *of Swedish recruits 1960.*
Regression of y *on* x: ——————
Regression of x *on* y: - - - - - - - - - -

has the corresponding reverse interpretation. Turning now to regression
analysis as a tool for causal inference this order of ideas lies deeper than
the purely technical procedure behind the different regression variants in
Figs. 1.10–1.11 and 1.50. The illustrations have been selected so that
there are fundamental differences in the causal interpretation in the three
situations.

At this point some readers may wonder what is the precise meaning of
the causal terms used here and in the following. This theme is subject to
a special study in this volume, Ref. 94. We shall stop for a clarification on
the basis of the three graphs.

To start with Fig. 1.10, the causal inference from the fertilizer experiment is that the expected corn yield of one and the same agricultural plot
will change with the quantity of fertilizer and that the expected yield will
follow the fulldrawn curve if the quantity of phosphate shifts, say from
$x_1 = a$ to $x_1 = b$ (while nitrate is kept fixed at level $x_2 = 160$ and other
relevant factors remain the same). This inference is causal in the sense of
stimulus-response, with phosphate for stimulus and corn yield for response,
not the other way round; and it is the very purpose of the experiment to
demonstrate this causal relationship.

In Fig. 1.11 the situation is similar, the causal inference being that if the income of an individual consumer changes, say from $x_1 = a$ to $x_1 = b$, while other relevant factors remain constant, his expenditure for food will shift in accordance with the mean value regression. Thus income is interpreted as stimulus and demand for food as response, not the other way round. To paraphrase, both of the models (1.3)–(1.4) and (1.6)–(1.7) behind Figs. 1.10 and 1.11 are causal in the sense that the relations are directed from x to y (not from y to x) and that they are designed not only to group response but also to individual response. On the other hand there is the difference that in Fig. 1.10 the causal inference is based on experimental data, in Fig. 1.11 on nonexperimental data. We shall come back to this difference in Remark 1.61.

Turning now to Fig. 1.60, the regression of length on weight is not causal in the above sense. In fact, suppose that a slim recruit with weight $x = x_1$ begins to put on weight; then his length will remain practically constant (level L_a) and not go up along the linear regression y on x. Similarly, if a heavy-weighter at $x = x_b$ begins to reduce, his length will remain at level L_b, and not go down following the regression y on x.

For a more elaborate discussion of causal analysis, with special regard to experimental vs. nonexperimental model building, see Refs. 83, 85, 86, 90, 91. The distinction between a purely descriptive and a causal interpretation of regression is fundamental (variation in group averages vs. individual response to variation in the hypothetical causal factor), for example in the treatment of the problem of the choice of regression. Nonetheless, in the statistical treatment of nonexperimental data the purely descriptive interpretation dominated the picture until the beginning of the 1940s. This is in particular so in demand analysis (cf. Refs. 2, 26, 62), but it is also in the econometric area that the causal interpretation first came to the fore (cf. Refs. 71, 72, 78, 79, 81, 94; see also Refs. 98, 99).

Remark 1.60. *Random sampling and randomization.* It is important to discern between these two devices. In taking out a sample at random from a larger population—or from a substratum in the population—the purpose is, broadly speaking, that the conclusion from the sample should extend to the population or the stratum (Ref. 63). Random sampling so defined applies both in experimental and nonexperimental situations.

Randomization is an experimental device, one of the great innovations by R. A. Fisher (Ref. 24). In an experiment with a treatment group and a control group, or in the case of a stimulus-response experiment with several stimulus levels, the device is to allocate the individual units at random on the various experiment groups. Speaking broadly, the purpose of randomization is to neutralize the disturbing influence of other factors than the variables that are steered in the experiment. Thus in Fig. 1.10 if the experiment were not randomized there would be the risk that the harvest plots with the best soil had happened to be treated by the largest quantities of the fertilizer, and this would distort the causal inference from the experiment.

As to nonexperimental situations, let us again use Fig. 1.11 for illustration. There is now always the risk that the causal inference is distorted, since income can be correlated with other factors that influence demand. For example, family size may on the average be smallest at medium levels of income, and such a tendency would imply a bias if the Engel curves were assumed to display the influence of income, and only of income. Such bias is known as a *specification error* in the model (Ref. 85). Randomization not being available, the answer to the risk for specification error is to take the variables of potential relevance into explicit account in the model, using (a) multiple regression, and/or (b) to stratify the sample and pool the regressions of the substrata by a weighting procedure.

Remark 1.61.   *Time series vs. cross section data as a basis for causal inference.*

The combined use of time series and cross section data is an important device for causal inference in model building. For illustration, let

$$(17) \qquad d_t = \alpha_0 + \beta\mu_1 + \gamma_1 x_1 + \gamma_2 x_2 + v$$

be a demand relation as specified applied to time series data, and

$$(18) \qquad d_c = \alpha_1 + \beta\mu_1 + \lambda_1 z_1 + \lambda_2 z_2 + \omega$$

a demand relation as specified for the analysis of cross section data, say data of the type known as household statistics. In (1.17) the demand d for the commodity considered is assumed to depend on income μ and on two other variables x_1, x_2 that vary with time, say the price x_1 of the commodity and the price x_2 of some competitive commodity. In (1.18) demand d is specified as being dependent upon income μ and upon two variables z_1, z_2 that vary in the cross section, such as family size and social stratum (in practice the regression then is formed not as a multiple regression but as an aggregate of the separate regressions of d on μ for the various strata; see Refs. 78, 95). The point of the specification is that the income variable μ has the same coefficient, β, in both relations. Otherwise expressed, our model is

$$(19) \qquad d = L(\mu, x_1, x_2, z_1, z_2) + \epsilon$$

where L is a linear function with

$$(20) \qquad E(d/\mu, x_1, x_2, z_1, z_2) = L(\mu, x_1, x_2, z_1, z_2)$$

and x_1, x_2 vary in time but not between the households, z_1, z_2 vary between the households but not in time, whereas μ varies both in time and between the households.

As always with causal relations—disturbed or nondisturbed—their application is guarded by a *ceteris paribus* clause, and it is such a clause that lies behind the assumption that β is the same in (1.17) and (1.18). When (1.17) and (1.18) are applied to data from the same country and the same period, the assumption at issue is made in order to obtain logical consistency in the model. The salient point is that the two relations describe the economic behaviour of one and the same group of consumers, and μ measures their reaction to income changes, whether these are observed over time or between the households. In practice, the equality between the two β's is—at best—approximate. The realism of this assumption is a matter of an adequate choice of coinfluencing variables x_i and z_i, and there is here always a risk of more or less troublesome specification errors (see Remark 1.60).

The importance of the approach (1.17)–(1.18) is that it allows us to use cross section inference for purposes of time series analysis, and conversely (Refs. 78, 85, 95). For example, an income elasticity β derived from cross section data can replace an income elasticity β as used in time series analysis. This is a general device that can be exploited to remove collinearities in the time series data and the ensuing indeterminacy of the time series estimation of β; alternatively, if there is no such collinearity, the comparison of the two estimates for β will make a test on the logical consistency of the two relations.

The approach (1.17)–(1.18) is of general scope. For example, L may be nonlinear, and there may be several variables x_1, x_2, $\cdots$; y_1, y_2, $\cdots$; μ_1, μ_2, ... in each of the three categories. It must be remembered, however, that the risk for specification errors sets limits for the approach in practice. As mentioned, the approach has proved useful in the analysis of economic demand. Variations in birth rates may be referred to as an area which in practice is outside of the scope of the approach. In fact, to judge from empirical investigations, the factor catalogue behind fertility variations over time seem to be essentially different from the catalogue behind the cross section variations of the fertility.

Remark 1.62.   *The direction of causal relationships.* We have seen that the models illustrated by Figs. 1.10 and 1.11 are causal, the hypothesis being that y is influenced by the variable x. Since the causal relation is subject to disturbance, the disturbance is treated as random, the causal relation is assessed as the regression of y on x. This argument provides a general solution to the problem of "choice of regression." To put it otherwise, the dualism or pluralism of regression relations (see Remark 1.51) makes it necessary to specify the direction of the relation, that is, whether x influences y or y influences x. (Compare Refs. 78, 85, 95, 98, 99.)

In controlled experiments it is no problem to specify the direction, for it lies in the very design of the experiment which variable is stimulus and which is response.

In nonexperimental situations the specification of causal relations, and in particular of their direction, is usually treated as a nonstatistical problem, as a matter for the subject-matter theory of the field of application at issue. This is for example so in Fig. 1.11: According to Pareto's classic theory of indifference maps consumer demand depends upon consumer income, not the other way round. In the specification of causal directions, needless to say, there is a risk of specification error, just as in the selection of influencing variables.

As to the specification of causal relations in nonexperimental situations it is a standard argument that in a scatter diagram like Fig. 1.60 there is complete formal symmetry between the regression of y on x and of x on y, and that the specification of the causal direction therefore must be a non-statistical matter (compare Refs. 25, 26, 51). H. Working (1934, Ref. 97) has revealed a flaw in this argument, inasmuch as the introduction of a third variable may give rise to asymmetries between x and y that can be exploited for causal inference. Working's approach was ignored for a long time. It has recently been reviewed and developed by the present author, Ref. 90, but more research is required before the new technique can be regarded as established.[3] When applied to household statistics (see Fig. 1.11) the results of the new technique supports the hypothesis that the causal influence goes from income to demand. Further results are on the way; thus it turns out that in the length-weight data behind Fig. 1.50 this purely statistical technique indicates rather clearly that the influence goes from length to weight, not from weight to length.

2. THE TRANSITION FROM TACIT TO EXPLICIT ALLOWANCE FOR ERRORS IN THE MODEL

2.1. *Three Steps in the Transition*

Starting with exact models, we shall characterize and briefly illustrate the three steps. (For a more detailed treatment, see Refs. 87, 90, 92a.)

[3] For fresh results in this direction, see E. Lyttkens, Ref. 50b.

(i) The empirical observations can with sufficient accuracy be covered by a model that is deterministic (exact) in the sense that no disturbances are involved. In the natural sciences many models are of this type, for example the law of Boyle and Gay-Lussac

(1) $$PV = cT$$

where P is pressure, V volume and T absolute temperature. Logarithmic transformation throws (2.1) on linear form, say

(2) $$\log P = \log c + \log T - \log V$$

or in general notations,

(3) $$y = \alpha + \beta_1 x_1 + \beta_2 x_2$$

with

(4) $$\alpha = \log c; \qquad \beta_1 = 1; \qquad \beta_2 = -1$$

(ii) The model is designed as approximate, but formally presented as being deterministic, and it is tacitly understood that there are deviations between the theoretical model and the actual observations. In model building in the socioeconomic sciences this approach has a long historical tradition. Up to the present day it is the dominating mode of exposition even in quite advanced textbooks (compare Refs. 1, 6, 60). A few typical cases in point will be quoted from classic economic theory.

(a) *Malthus' law* (1798): The population tends to increase exponentially, while the food supply can at best increase only linearly, with result that the standard of living for the bulk of the population is pressed down to an existence minimum. (For a modern review, see Ref. 61.)

(b) *Cournot's model* (1838; *Ref.* 16) *for the equilibrium between demand and supply in a free market:*

$$d = D(p) \qquad \text{demand relation}$$
(5) $$s = S(p) \qquad \text{supply relation}$$
$$D(p^*) = S(p^*) \qquad \text{equilibrium condition}$$

The model explains how it is that price on the whole is stable, say at level p^*, and that demand and supply are in balance at this price level. The argument is illustrated in Fig. 2.10. If market price is below p^*, say at p_0, demand will be higher than supply, and the market forces will press price upwards. Conversely, a price p_1 above p^* will be pressed downwards. At p^* price will be stable, and demand will equal supply.

Cournot's model (2.5) is one of the milestones in the development of

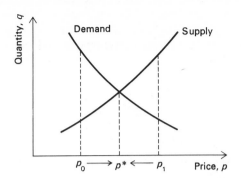

FIGURE 2.10 *Cournot's model for demand-supply equilibrium in a free market.*

economic model building. For one thing, the notions of demand and supply functions were here used for the first time. As a formal system (2.5), Cournot's model is static, but in his verbal explanation there is a dynamic element.

For a later reference we shall write down Cournot's model in the case of linear relations, say

(6a) $\qquad\qquad d = \alpha_1 - \beta_1 p \qquad$ demand relation

(6b) $\qquad\qquad s = \alpha_2 + \beta_2 p \qquad$ supply relation

(6c) $\qquad\qquad d = s \qquad\qquad$ equilibrium condition

(c) *The cobweb theory* (J. Tinbergen, Ref. 70, and other authors around 1930; compare also M. Ezekiel, 1938, Ref. 21). This is an attempt to dynamize Cournot's model (2.5). We quote the following simple case of a cobweb model, say for the wheat market,

(7a) $\quad d_t = \alpha_1 - \beta_1 p_t \qquad$ demand relation

(7b) $\quad s_t = \alpha_2 + \beta_2 p_{t-1} \qquad$ supply relation

(7c) $\quad d_t = s_t \qquad\qquad$ assumption of instantaneous equilibrium

The close similarity to the Cournot model (2.6) will be noted. There are two differences. One is that the variables in (2.7) are specified in time t, with t referring to consecutive time periods, and say, with the year for time unit. The other is that current supply is assumed to be influenced by lagged price p_{t-1}, on the argument that current price determines the acreage and thereby next year's crop.

Demand and supply being assumed to be equal, we write

(8) $$q_t = d_t = s_t$$

System (2.7) allows us to express current price and quantity in terms of lagged variables, giving

(9a) $$p_t = \frac{\alpha_1 - \alpha_2}{\beta_1} - \frac{\beta_2}{\beta_1} p_{t-1}$$

(9b) $$q_t = \alpha_2 + \beta_2 p_{t-1}$$

Given an initial price, say $p_{t-1} = p$, system (2.9) allows us to calculate, by iterated substitutions,

(10) $$p, q_t, p_t, q_{t+1}, p_{t+1}, \cdots.$$

The initial price $p_{t-1} = p$ thus determines how the variables of the model will develop in the future.

Remark 2.10.   In (2.10) we see a case of stepwise forecasting, each forecast generating the next. This device will be referred to as the *chain principle,* other current terms being *recursive* or *iterated* forecasting. The chain principle is of old standing, notably in the forecast techniques for population developments (see section 3.1 below). The chain principle is a key topic in the present paper; for a more detailed exposition, see Ref. 92a.

(iii) Stochastic models. In model building under (ii) the model is mainly a theoretical construct, and the confrontation with reality consists in *ad hoc* comparisons between theoretical model and empirical evidence. At stage (iii), disturbances (residuals) in the form of stochastic error terms are introduced in the model to allow for deviations between theoretical relations and actual observations. Stage (iii) involves a bold raise in the aspiration level, the model making for systematic coordination between theoretical approaches on the one hand and empirical observations on the other. There are several more or less independent approaches that here might be referred to as relevant for the development of stochastic model building. It will suffice for our purpose to give three examples, chosen so as to make typical and simple illustrations for the subsequent review.

First a demand relation, say

(11) $$d = \alpha - e \cdot p + v$$

where demand d and price p are taken to be logarithmic, so that e is the price elasticity as defined by Marshall (1890; Ref. 53). Benini (1907;

Ref. 7) obtained $e = 0.384$ for the price elasticity of coffee, the first price elasticity on record to have been estimated from statistical data. For the early developments in empirical demand analysis, see the brilliant review by G. Stigler, Ref. 64.

Second, reference is made to *pure causal chain models,* the approach used by Jan Tinbergen in his pioneering construction of macroeconomic models in the 1930s (Refs. 71–74; see Remark 1.60). Tinbergen's models were large systems with up to 50 relations and 70 variables, too large to be quoted here. To illustrate the characteristic features of pure causal chains we shall instead consider a small model with only three relations,

(12a) $d_t = \alpha_1 - \beta_1 p_t + \omega_t$ demand relation

(12b) $s_t = \alpha_2 + \beta_2 p_{t-1} + \omega_t^*$ supply relation

(12c) $p_t = p_{t-1} + \lambda(d_{t-1} - s_t) + \omega_t^{**}$ price mechanism

Model (2.12) was originally designed to provide a simple illustration of the characteristic features of the pure causal chain approach (see Ref. 81). It is here quoted with a slight change first given in a paper (Ref. 86) where a three-relation model almost as simple as (2.12) was found to give good fit to empirical data, and in particular so the price mechanism. For further results of the same type, see Ref. 65.

Third, reference is made to *interdependent systems,* the approach initiated by T. Haavelmo in 1943 and developed under the auspices of Cowles Foundation (Refs. 28, 30, 34, 43). The following simple model, the cobweb system (2.7) subject to disturbance, belongs to the early illustration material of the approach,

(13a) $d_t = \alpha_1 - \beta_1 p_t + \nu_t$ demand relation

(13b) $s_t = \alpha_2 + \beta_2 p_{t-1} + \nu_t^*$ supply relation

(13c) $d_t = s_t = q_t$ assumption of instantaneous equilibrium

From a mathematical point of view the transition from (2.6a) to (2.11) and from (2.7) to (2.13) involves a radical generalization. The generalization has confronted the model builders with many novel types of problems. Two of these have been veritable stumbling blocks on the road of stochastization.

The first is "the choice of regression." In the 1920s and 1930s this problem or group of problems was subject to an intense debate; among the most important contributions we note Refs. 25, 26, 47, 51, 62, 96. Most of the debate had an econometric setting, and more specifically it centered on the statistical assessment of demand relations. The debate was mainly concerned with unirelation models. Before it had been carried through to universal agreement on the central issues the second problem came to the fore, T. Haavelmo in 1943 opening up to the debate on "simultaneous equations," Ref. 30. In the 1940s and 1950s the debate focussed on the rationale and relative merits of "interdependent systems" and "pure causal chains," that is, the two types of multirelation models illustrated by (2.12) and (2.13); see Refs. 8, 9, 28, 34, 43, 67, 81, 83–90, 92, 95.

To repeat, "the choice of regression" and "simultaneous equations" are problems of fundamental importance for the rationale of model building in nonexperimental situations. In section 2.2 the debate on these problems will be reviewed from the point of view of stochastic models that are specified in terms of predictors. Briefly stated, the confused and partly controversial debate on "choice of regression" and "interdependent systems" has a common source in the mathematical fact that predictor relations do not follow the same operation rules as relations that are deterministic (exact; disturbance-free).

Remark 2.10.   In stochastic model building there is a parting of the ways known as "errors in equations" versus "errors in variables." Models (2.11)–(2.13) belong under "errors in equations." As to "errors in variables" this approach has important applications in geodetics, astronomy and other areas where it is realistic to assume that the error-free variables satisfy a deterministic relationship; Refs. 18, 19, 25, 26, 42, 54. In the human sciences, however, this assumption is of limited applicability. Hence we shall focus our attention on the approach of "errors in equations."

2.2.   *Operative Rules for* eo ipso *Predictors*

The transition from deterministic (disturbance free) to stochastic models is a radical generalization. But generalization is not an unmixed blessing. The other side of the coin is that generalization is accompanied by attenuation in the inference from the model, an attenuation that takes a variety of forms, and may be more or less severe. First of all, prediction from the model is no longer deterministic; at best we can hope that it is valid in the sense of unbiased predictors, that is, that the prediction holds good on the average. Hence it is a fundamental question whether and to what extent the model allows inference in the sense of *eo ipso* predictors. We proceed to some general comments on this question (compare Refs. 87–92).

Speaking generally, some relations in a model are intended to be used for prediction, others are not. Whenever a relation in a stochastic model is intended for prediction, it has a double advantage to specify the relation as an *eo ipso* predictor, if this is possible, for then (a) the predictions given by the relation will be unbiased, that is, correct on the average, and (b) the relation can (see section 1.5) be estimated by the simple method of least squares regression.

In commenting upon the operative rules for *eo ipso* predictors, it will suffice for our purpose to deal with linear relations. For a deterministic relationship we shall write

(14) $$y = \beta_0 + \beta_1 x_1 + \cdots + \beta_h x_h$$

and for a corresponding stochastic relationship

(15) $$y = \beta_0 + \beta_1 x_1 + \cdots + \beta_h x_h + v$$

where the predictor specification takes the form

(16) $$E(y/x_1, \cdots, x_h) = \beta_0 + \beta_1 x_1 + \cdots + \beta_h x_h$$

For operative procedures that are valid for exact relations there are three possibilities:

G. The procedure can always be extended to *eo ipso* predictors.

Y. The procedure can be extended to *eo ipso* prediction under supplementary conditions.

R. The procedure can never be extended to *eo ipso* predictors.

The notation *G* associates with green light, *Y* with yellow and *R* with red. Fig. 2.20 gives a symbolic illustration. The inner circle is the class of exact models, the outer circle the more general class of *eo ipso* predictors. Operative procedures are represented by dotted lines from the center; in sector *G* the lines extend the outer ring; in sector *Y* the requisite supplementary assumptions are indicated by the line extending only through a part of the outer ring; in sector *R* the lines do not extend into the outer ring.

We shall now consider a few basic procedures, beginning with two cases in category *G* or *Y*.

(i) Aggregation (cf. Refs. 69, 78, 79, 95).

Given the *n* linear relations

(17) $$y_i = \beta_{i0} + \beta_{i1} x_1 + \cdots + \beta_{ih} x_h \qquad i = 1, \cdots, n$$

the aggregate variable $y = \Sigma y_i$ is given by

(18) $$y = \Sigma \beta_{i0} + x_1 \Sigma \beta_{i1} + \cdots + x_h \Sigma \beta_{ih}$$

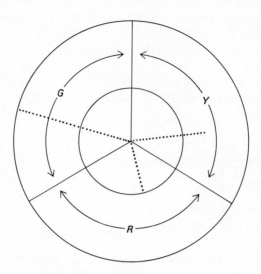

FIGURE 2.20 *Symbolic graph of the three
categories G, Y, R of operative procedures.*

the summations being over $i = 1, \cdots, n$. Similarly, aggregation of the
eo ipso predictors

$$(19) \qquad y_i = \beta_{i0} + \beta_{i1}x_1 + \cdots + \beta_{ih}x_h + v_i \qquad i = 1, \cdots, n$$

with

$$(20) \qquad E(y_i/x_1, \cdots, x_h) = \beta_{i0} + \beta_{i1}x_1 + \cdots + \beta_{ih}x_h$$

gives

$$(21) \qquad y = \Sigma\beta_{i0} + x_1\Sigma\beta_{i1} + \cdots + x_h\Sigma\beta_{ih} + \Sigma v_1$$

with

$$(22) \qquad E(y/x_1, \cdots, x_h) = \Sigma\beta_{i0} + x_1\Sigma\beta_{i1} + \cdots + x_h\Sigma\beta_{ih}$$

Remark 2.20. For the validity of (2.22)—and thus for the aggregation
to belong under *G*—it is essential that all expectations to the left in (2.20)
involve the same set $x_1, \cdots, x_h$ of conditional variables. Thus in a more
general class than (2.21) of exact aggregates, the procedure of aggregation
belongs under *Y*.

(ii) Substitution (Ref. 90; cf. also Refs. 87–89).

Let (2.14) with (2.15) and

(23) $$x_1 = \alpha_0 + \alpha_2 x_2 + \cdots + \alpha_h x_h + \omega$$

with

(24) $$E(x_1/x_2, \cdots, x_n) = \alpha_0 + \alpha_2 x_2 + \cdots + \alpha_h x_h$$

make two *eo ipso* predictors. Then (2.23) can be substituted into (2.14), and y gives an *eo ipso* predictor, just as for the exact relations that correspond to (2.14) and (2.23). Explicitly,

(25) $$y = \beta_0 + \alpha_0 \beta_1 + (\beta_2 + \alpha_2 \beta_1) x_2 + \cdots + (\beta_h + \alpha_h \beta_1) x_h + v + \beta_1 \omega$$

with

(26) $$E(y/x_2, \cdots, x_h) = \beta_0 + \alpha_0 \beta_1 + (\beta_2 + \alpha_2 \beta_1) x_2 + \cdots + (\beta_h + \alpha_h \beta_1) x_h$$

Remark 2.21.   For the validity of (2.26)—and thus for substitution to belong under G—it is essential that the conditional variables $x_2, \cdots, x_n$ in (2.24) include all conditional variables in (2.15) except the variable x_1 that is eliminated by the substitution. Thus in a more general class than (2.23) of substitutions, the procedure belongs under Y.

The argument (23)–(26) illustrates that the transition from exact to stochastic models is a recent affair. In fact, it was not until 1933 that the mathematical foundations of probability theory were established in a satisfactory fashion (Kolmogorov, Ref. 41), and before that date a general and rigorous treatment of the substitution theorem (23)–(26) could not be given.

We shall now turn to two procedures that have been the source of much confusion in "the choice of regression" and "simultaneous equations." The root of the trouble is in both cases that the model in disturbance free form is used for two different purposes, each requiring a procedure of its own, but only one of the two procedures extends to *eo ipso* predictors. In "the choice of regression" the two procedures are prediction from a relation as initially specified and from its reverse; in "simultaneous equations" it is prediction from an equation system in implicit and explicit form.

(iii)   Reversion (Refs. 88–90).

Considering an exact relation

(27) $$y = \alpha + \beta_x$$

with $\beta \neq 0$, the relation can be reversed, giving

(28) $$x = \frac{1}{\beta}(y - \alpha)$$

In a disturbance free model, both relations (2.27–28) can be used to predict one variable when the other is known. This dualism does not extend to *eo ipso* predictors, a classic fact (see e.g. Ref. 100) which we restate:

Theorem 2.20.   Given an *eo ipso* predictor

$$(29) \qquad y = \alpha + \beta x + v$$

with

$$(30a\text{–}b) \qquad E(y/x) = \alpha + \beta x \quad \text{and} \quad \text{Prob } (v \neq 0) \neq 0$$

then

$$(31) \qquad E(x/y) \neq \frac{1}{\beta} (y - \alpha)$$

Remark 2.22.   It is important to discern between (a) reversion of the direction of an *eo ipso* predictor, and (b) reversion of the direction of inference from an *eo ipso* predictor. According to Theorem 2.20, reversion in the sense (a) is never allowed, and therefore belongs under category R. On the other hand it is readily seen that reversion in the sense (b) is allowed. In fact, considering the predictor (2.29)–(2.30), let $y = y_0$ be given. Then if we ask for what value x the (expected) value of y will equal y_0, the answer is obtained from the reverse relation (2.28), viz.

$$(32) \qquad x = \frac{1}{\beta} (y_0 - \alpha)$$

For a more elaborate treatment, see Ref. 90; cf. also Ref. 95.

(iv) Prediction from equation systems in implicit vs. explicit form (Ref. 90; cf. also Refs. 87–89).

Beginning with the case of disturbance free systems, we shall consider a linear system

$$(33) \qquad \begin{aligned} \alpha_1 + \alpha_{11}y_1 + \cdots + \alpha_{1h}y_h + \gamma_{11}z_1 + \cdots + \gamma_{1m}z_m &= 0 \\ &\vdots \\ \alpha_h + \alpha_{h1}y_1 + \cdots + \alpha_{hh}y_h + \gamma_{h1}z_1 + \cdots + \gamma_{hm}z_m &= 0 \end{aligned}$$

or in matrix form

$$(34) \qquad \alpha + Ay + \Gamma z = 0$$

We assume that the matrix $A = [\alpha_{ik}]$ is nonsingular,

(35) $$\det A \neq 0$$

Then the system can be solved to give the y's explicitly, say

(36)
$$y_1 = \lambda_1 + \lambda_{11}z_1 + \cdots + \lambda_{1m}z_m$$
$$\vdots$$
$$y_h = \lambda_h + \lambda_{h1}z_1 + \cdots + \lambda_{hm}z_m$$

or in matrix form

(37) $$y = \lambda + \Lambda z$$

where

(38a–b) $$\lambda = -A^{-1}\alpha; \quad \Lambda = -A^{-1}\Gamma$$

In the operative use of the model, some or all of the relations of the implicit system (2.33) and of the explicit system (2.36) may be exploited. The dualism between (2.33) and (2.36) involves no problem, for the two forms are mathematically equivalent. If stochastic residuals are introduced in the models, however, the equivalence disappears, and in particular it is an important problem whether all relations in (2.33) and (2.36) can be specified by predictors. A partial answer to this last question will now be quoted from Ref. 90.

Theorem 2.21.   Given the system

(39)
$$y_1 = \alpha_1 + \qquad\qquad \gamma_{11}z_1 + \cdots + \gamma_{1m}z_m + v_1$$
$$y_2 = \alpha_2 + \beta_{21}y_1 + \qquad \gamma_{21}z_1 + \cdots + \gamma_{2m}z_m + v_2$$
$$y_3 = \alpha_3 + \beta_{31}y_1 + \beta_{32}y_2 + \gamma_{31}z_1 + \cdots + \gamma_{3m}z_m + v_3$$
$$\vdots$$
$$y_h = \alpha_h + \beta_{h1}y_1 + \cdots + \beta_{hh}y_h + \gamma_{h1}z_1 + \cdots + \gamma_{hm}z_m + v_h$$

or in matrix form

(40) $$y = \alpha + By + \Gamma z + v$$

let B be subdiagonal in the sense that all elements in and above the main diagonal are zero. Further suppose that all relations in the system make *eo ipso* predictors, that is,

(41) $E(y_1/y_1, \cdots, y_{i-1}, z_1, \cdots, z_m)$
$$= \alpha_i + \beta_{i1}y_1 + \cdots + \beta_{i,i-1}y_{i-1} + \gamma_{i1}z_1 + \cdots + \gamma_{im}z_m \qquad (i = 1, \cdots, h)$$

Let (2.39) be solved so as to obtain the y's in explicit form, say

(42)
$$y_1 = \lambda_1 + \lambda_{11}z_1 + \cdots + \lambda_{1m}z_m + \omega_1$$
$$\vdots$$
$$y_h = \lambda_h + \lambda_{h1}z_1 + \cdots + \lambda_{hm}z_m + \omega_h$$

or in matrix form

(43)
$$y = \lambda + \Lambda z + \omega$$

where

(44a–c) $\quad \lambda = (I - B)^{-1} \cdot \alpha; \qquad \Lambda = (I - B)^{-1} \cdot \Gamma \qquad \omega = (I - B)^{-1}v$

Then all relations (2.42) will make *eo ipso* predictors, that is,

(45) $\qquad E(y_1/z_1, \cdots, z_m) = \lambda_i + \lambda_{i1}z_1 + \cdots + \lambda_{im}z_m \qquad (i = 1, \cdots, h)$

In a system (2.41) of *eo ipso* predictors such that the variables y_1, $\cdots$, y_h cannot be ordered so as to make B subdiagonal, supplementary assumptions are required if (2.45) is to hold true.

To verify (2.45) we note (a) since B is subdiagonal, the passage from (2.39) to (2.42) can be performed by iterated substitutions; (b) the argument (2.23)–(2.26) applies to each of the substitutions. The last part of Theorem 2.20 states that the explicit system (2.42) in general will not make *eo ipso* predictors if the implicit system is not of the subdiagonal form (2.39). The truth of this last statement is clear from special cases. In the three-relation model (2.13), for example, it is only for special values of the parameters that both the implicit and explicit forms can be specified as *eo ipso* predictors (for details, see Ref. 87). Thus with reference to Fig. 2.20, twofold inference from a system in implicit and explicit form is a procedure which belongs to sector G, provided the implicit system is of the subdiagonal form (2.39); for more general systems the twofold procedure belongs to R (or Y, with restriction to special sets of parameter values).

3. FOUR TYPES OF MULTIRELATION MODELS

In the large department store of scientific models, most of the approaches have their origin in the natural sciences. This is in particular so for models that use the basic methods of calculus and algebra. Reference is made to models built in the form of a system of differential equations, say

(1)
$$\frac{dy_i}{dt} = F_i(y_1, y_2, \cdots, y_h) \qquad i = 1, \cdots, h$$

We remember Laplace's famous dictum (Ref. 44) that the entire future could be forecast in every detail if we could solve a sufficiently large system of differential equations. The dictum does not have the status of an established truth, but it does illustrate the flexibility and wide scope of model (3.1).

Model building by the techniques of probability theory—and in particular so by the theory of stochastic processes—is a recent development, which belongs mainly to this century (cf. Refs. 5, 41, 57, 58, 77). Here the socioeconomic sciences come into the picture by genuine innovations in the model building. This is particularly so for causal chains and interdependent systems, the models briefly referred to in 2.1 (iii). The subsequent review will emphasize these two types of models as being of general scope for purposes of model building in nonexperimental situations.

3.1. Prediction by the Chain Principle in Its Simplest Form: Vector Regression

We shall take model (3.1) for starting point. In (3.1) time t is treated as a continuous variable; in the following models t is discrete, since the socioeconomic data usually refer to consecutive periods of years, quarters, days, or other time units. Hence (3.1) is modified into a difference equation,

$$\Delta y_{i,t} = F_i(y_{1t}, \cdots, y_{ht}) \qquad i = 1, \cdots, h$$

which is the same as

(2) $$y_{it} = y_{i,t-1} + F_i(y_{1,t-1}, \cdots, y_{h,t-1})$$

More generally, we form

(3a) $$y_{it} = F_i(y_{1,t-1}, \cdots, y_{h,t-1}; \quad x_{1t}, \cdots, x_{mt}) + v_{it}$$

Along with the endogenous variables $y_{1t}, \cdots, y_{ht}$, which the model has for purpose to explain or forecast, we have here introduced the *exogenous* variables $x_{1t}, \cdots, x_{mt}$, which are ancillary in the explanation or forecasting. Further we stochasticize the model by adding the residuals $v_{1t}, \cdots, v_{mt}$ and assuming that relations (3.3) are *eo ipso* predictors,

(3b) $$E(y_{it}/y_{1,t-1}, \cdots, y_{h,t-1}; x_{1t}, \cdots, x_{mt})$$
$$= F_i(y_{1,t-1}, \cdots, y_{h,t-1}; x_{1t}, \cdots, x_{mt}) \qquad (i = 1, \cdots, h)$$

A few comments to clarify the approach:

(i) The functions F_i are assessed on the basic of theoretical considerations and/or empirical material.

(ii) The forecasting follows the chain principle: The forecasts for y_{1t}, $\cdots$, y_{ht} are obtained from the right-hand member of (3.3) on the basis of $y_{1, t-1}$, $\cdots$, $y_{h, t-1}$ and x_{1t}, $\cdots$, x_{mt}; the resulting forecasts for y_{1t}, $\cdots$, y_{ht} are used in calculating forecasts for $y_{1, t+1}$, $\cdots$, $y_{h, t+1}$ by the same formula, and so on for $t + 2, t + 3, \cdots$.

(iii) For the exogenous variables x_{1t}, $\cdots$, x_{mt} the requisite forecasts at periods $t, t + 1, t + 2, \cdots$ are obtained by ancillary devices.

(iv) If the functions F_i are linear, the argument (2.23)–(2.26) applies, showing that the forecasts referring to $t + 2, t + 3, \cdots$ are unbiased.

(v) Comment (iv) is in accordance with Theorem 2.21, inasmuch as model (3.3) gives the variables $y_{1t}, \cdots, y_{ht}$ explicitly, which implies that the subdiagonal matrix B in (2.40) is in this special case formed by mere zeros.

Illustration. The techniques of population forecasting (see Ref. 61 for a broad review) provide typical examples of the approach (3.3). The following model is simple, yet sufficiently close to current techniques to indicate the essential features of the approach,

$$(4a) \quad d_x(t) = L_{x-1}(t - 1) \cdot \mu_x(t) + v_x(t); \qquad x = 1, 2, \cdots$$

$$(4b) \quad L_x(t) = L_{x-1}(t - 1) - d_x(t); \qquad x = 1, 2, \cdots$$

$$(4c) \quad L_0(t) = \sum_x L_{x-1}(t - 1)\phi_x(t)\left(1 - \frac{1}{2} \cdot \mu_0(t)\right) + \omega(t)$$

The model involves two sets of *endogenous* variables:

$L_x(t)$ is the number of persons of age x (i.e. between x and $x + 1$ years) at the end of calendar year t.

$d_x(t)$ is the number of persons in the group $L_{x-1}(t - 1)$ who die during year t.

We used capitals for L_x and small letters for d_x to indicate that L's are "stock variables" while the d's are "flow" variables (counting a group of statistical units at a specified instant and, respectively, a stream of events during a specified period).

Further the model involves two sets of *exogenous* variables:

$\mu_0(t)$ is the yearly mortality rate for newborn during year t.

$\mu_x(t)$ is the yearly mortality rate for persons who are at age $x - 1$ in the beginning of year t.

$\phi_x(t)$ is the yearly fertility rate for the same group of persons. For the sake of simplicity, model (3.4) does not deal separately with men and women.

Relations (3.4a) and (3.4c) are assumed to be *eo ipso* predictors. Hence the residuals v and ω are ignored when the model is used for prediction. Relation (3.4b) is deterministic by its very definition.

In using model (3.4) for prediction, ancillary forecasts are required for $\mu_x(t)$ and $\phi_x(t)$ for periods $t, t + 1, t + 2, \cdots$. Model (3.4) is written so that the forecasting proceeds recursively, period by period, on the basis of the forecasts obtained for the previous period. To repeat, the system (3.4) is explicit in the variables to be forecast for each period, and therefore the difficulty dealt with in Theorem 2.21 does not arise.

Remark 3.20. *Vector Regression.* If (3.1) were a system of differential equations of order k, the corresponding model (3.3a–b) would involve the lagged variables $y_{i,t-1}, \cdots, y_{i,t-k}$. Using the vector notation $y_t = (y_{1t}, \cdots, y_{ht})$ the resulting model may be written

$$(5a) \qquad y_t = F(y_{t-1}, \cdots, y_{t-k}; x_{1t}, \cdots, x_{mt}) + v_t$$

with

$$(5b) \quad E(y_t/y_{t-1}, \cdots, y_{t-k}; x_{1t}, \cdots, x_{mt}) = F(y_{t-1}, \cdots, y_{t-k}; x_{1t}, \cdots, x_{mt})$$

Known as *vector regression,* we see that model (5a–b) covers (3a–b) as a special case.

3.2. *The Approach of Pure Causal Chain Systems (Cf. Refs. 71–74, 84, 90, 92)*

(i) Comparison with the approaches (3.1)–(3.3) and (3.5). We shall first give a graphical illustration to link up pure causal chains with the system of differential equations (3.1), difference equations (3.2)–(3.3) and vector regression (3.5).

System (3.1) and its solution may be interpreted as a model for recursive forecasting over infinitesimal time periods, the variables at t generating those at $t + dt$, these in their turn generating those at $t + 2\,dt$, and so on. This device is illustrated in Fig. 3.20 for a system with three endogenous variables y_i. In each period there is one arrow for each relation in the systems, and in accordance with the time scale at the top the arrows indicate how the forecasting proceeds over infinitesimal periods of time.

Fig. 3.20 also covers models of type (3.2), the only difference being that the periods are no longer infinitesimal. As indicated at the bottom of the graph, the period is usually taken for time unit. Moreover, Fig. 3.20 can be elaborated so as to cover models like (3.3) and vector regression (3.5) which involve both endogenous and exogenous variables. For example, the exogenous variables can be represented by as many dot sequences

Model (3.1): $t - dt$ t $t + dt$ $t + 2\,dt$

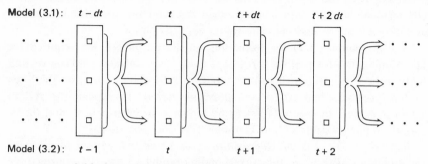

Model (3.2): $t - 1$ t $t + 1$ $t + 2$

FIGURE 3.20   *Graphical illustration of models* (3.1)–(3.3) *and* (3.5).

at the top, but without arrows in between since their future path is assumed to be known (by ancillary forecasts).

Fig. 3.21 gives two illustrations of the simple system (2.12). The first graph, where there is one arrow for each relation, emphasizes that if the relations are rearranged in the order s_t, p_t, d_t the forecasting proceeds recursively both with regard to time and variables; that is, the forecasts are obtained stepwise period by period and within each period stepwise variable by variable. Fig. 3.21 (right) is of the type known as Tinbergen's arrow scheme, Ref. 73. The arrows that point to one and the same variable specify the explanatory variables for that variable. For example, in the relation for p_t the explanatory variables are p_{t-1}, d_{t-1} and s_t.

System (2.12) gives the following explicit relations for the variables,

(6a) $s_t = \alpha_2 + \beta_2 p_{t-1} + v_t'$

(6b) $p_t = \lambda(\alpha_1 - \alpha_2) + (1 - \lambda\beta_1 - \lambda\beta_2)p_{t-1} + v_t^*$

(6c) $d_t = \alpha_1 - \beta_1\lambda \cdot (\alpha_1 - \alpha_2) - \beta_1(1 - \lambda\beta_1 - \lambda\beta_2)p_{t-1} + v_t^{**}$

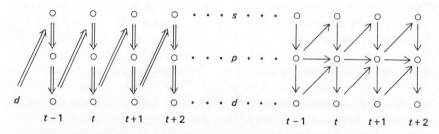

FIGURE 3.21   *The pure causal chain* (2.12) *illustrated by two types of graphs: (left) One arrow for each relation; (right) Tinbergen's arrow scheme: one arrow for interconnection between variables.*

where the residuals $v_t{}^*$, $v_t{}^{**}$ are linear expressions in ω_t, $\omega_t{}'$, $\omega_t{}''$. Clearly, system (3.6) has the form of the vector regression (3.5), and can be illustrated by a graph of the type shown in Fig. 3.20.

(ii) The general design of pure causal chain models (Refs. 73, 84, 90). The model specifies a set of *behaviour relations* for the endogenous variables, say

$$(7) \quad y_i(t) = \alpha_i + \sum_{j=1}^{i-1} \beta_{ij}y_j(t) + \sum_{j=1}^{h}\sum_{k=1}^{q} \beta_{ijk}y_j(t-k)$$

$$+ \sum_{j=1}^{m}\sum_{k=1}^{q} \gamma_{ijk}x_j(t-k) + v_i(t) \qquad i = 1, \cdots, h$$

where the x's are exogenous variables. Relations (3.7) are called the *primary* (or *structural*) form of the model.

The characteristic feature of the approach is that the current endogenous variables $y_1(t), \cdots, y_h(t)$ can be solved explicitly by iterated substitutions in (7), giving the *reduced form* of the model, say

$$(8) \qquad y_i(t) = \lambda_i + \sum_{j=1}^{r}\sum_{k=1}^{q} \lambda_{ijk}z_j(t-k) + \omega_i(t) \qquad i = 1, \cdots, h$$

where the $z_j(t-k)$, called the *predetermined variables,* are either lagged endogenous variables or lagged or nonlagged exogenous variables. We see that the reduced form of a causal chain system takes the form of vector regression (3.5).

The primary form (3.7) can be illustrated by graphs of the two types shown in Fig. 3.21. In graphs of type Fig. 3.21 (left) the flow of arrows allows a double interpretation: as a flow of unbiased prediction, and as a flow of causation. As to the illustration of the reduced form, the first type of graph (Fig. 3.21, left) will be of the simple type shown in Fig. 3.20.

(iii) Inference from the model in primary form and/or reduced form (Refs. 72, 73, 84, 90). The behaviour relations, and thereby the primary form, constitute the basic hypotheses of the model. Speaking generally, a behaviour relation refers to a group of individuals and indicates how the group reacts to specified changes in the explanatory variables of the relation. The reduced form indicates how the current endogenous variables are influenced by the predetermined variables.

Both the primary form and the reduced form are important as potential sources of inference from the model. The behaviour relations serve purposes of forecasting from separate relations of the model. For example, if a demand relation specifies demand as a function of price and income, an ancillary forecast for price and income will provide a separate forecast for demand. The reduced form comes into operation when the entire model is used for forecasting according to the chain principle.

Pure causal chain systems have the fundamental property that all relations of the primary form as well as of the reduced form are eo ipso *predictors.* It need not be elaborated that this property is invaluable both in theoretical and applied work with the model. At first sight it may seem that the twofold specification in terms of predictors will to some extent make for overidentification of the parameters, and that the approach therefore is of limited scope in applied work. It is not so, however, for it can be shown that any given set of time series can, to any prescribed accuracy, be covered by a pure causal chain system that fulfills the twofold specification; Refs. 80, 90. The twofold specification thus involves no limitation of the potential field of application of pure causal chain systems.

Remark 3.20. In differential equation systems (3.1) the distinction between the model in primary form and reduced form disappears since the time periods are dealt with as infinitesimal. The situation is the same if (3.1) is stochasticized; cf. Ref. 55.

We see that for linear models where time is dealt with as a discrete parameter it is a distinctive property of vector regression (3.5) that the structural form is from the beginning in reduced form; the dualism between the two forms does not arise.

(iv) The statistical estimation of parameters. Once the stochastic structure of a model is specified, the parameter estimation is a problem which is purely technical and therefore in principal noncontroversial. In pure causal chain systems the parameter estimation is very simple: Since all relations of the model are *eo ipso* predictors, Theorems 1.50–51 apply, and it follows that consistent estimates for the parameters can be obtained by the method of least squares regression, estimating each relation separately (Refs. 87, 88, 91; cf. also Refs. 9, 50a, 82, 91).

Knowing that all relations are *eo ipso* predictors both in the primary form and in the reduced form, the question arises which of the two forms should be taken as a basis for the parameter estimation. It is easy to see that the estimation should be based on the primary form; otherwise the parameter estimation will usually be marred by indeterminacies. The following pure causal chain system has been designed to illustrate this last argument.

The system in primary form is defined by

$$(9) \qquad y_i(t) = \beta_i y_{i-1}(t) + \gamma_{ii} x_i(t) + v_t \qquad (i = 1, \cdots, h)$$

with $\beta_0 = 0$, or in matrix form

(10) $$y(t) = By(t) + \Gamma x(t) + v$$

where

(11a–b) $$B = \begin{bmatrix} 0 & 0 & 0 & \cdots & 0 & 0 \\ \beta_2 & 0 & 0 & \cdots & 0 & 0 \\ 0 & \beta_3 & 0 & \cdots & 0 & 0 \\ \multicolumn{6}{c}{\dotfill} \\ 0 & 0 & 0 & \cdots & \beta_h & 0 \end{bmatrix}, \quad \Gamma = \begin{bmatrix} \gamma_{11} & 0 & 0 & \cdots & 0 \\ 0 & \gamma_{22} & 0 & \cdots & 0 \\ 0 & 0 & \gamma_{33} & \cdots & 0 \\ \multicolumn{5}{c}{\dotfill} \\ 0 & 0 & 0 & \cdots & \gamma_{hh} \end{bmatrix}$$

showing that the model involves $h - 1$ parameters β and h parameters γ.

The reduced form is readily obtained,

(12) $$y_i(t) = \lambda_{i1}x_1(t) + \cdots + \lambda_{ii}x_i(t) + \omega_t \quad (i = 1, \cdots, h)$$

where the λ's are simple expressions in the β's and γ's, while the ω's are linear in the v's, or in matrix form

(13) $$y(t) = \Lambda \cdot x(t) + \omega$$

with

(14) $$\Lambda = \begin{bmatrix} \lambda_{11} & 0 & \cdots & 0 \\ \lambda_{21} & \lambda_{22} & \cdots & 0 \\ \multicolumn{4}{c}{\dotfill} \\ \lambda_{h1} & \lambda_{h2} & \cdots & \lambda_{hh} \end{bmatrix}$$

Least squares regression when applied to the primary form gives us consistent estimates for the $2h - 1$ parameters to be estimated, each regression giving one β and one γ, except the first where there is no β. Least squares regression when applied to the reduced form (3.12) gives us estimates for the coefficients λ, in all $\frac{1}{2} h (h + 1)$ in number. This device involves two difficulties; namely (a) in transforming back from the λ's to the β's and γ's, the β's and γ's will be overdetermined, and (b) there is a drastic increase in the risk for collinearities and for ensuing indeterminacy in the parameter estimation, for instead of two parameters there are now i coefficients to be determined from the relation for $y_i(t)$.

Remark 3.21. The difficulties under (a) and (b) are not specific for the illustration (3.9). Except for very special cases the typical situation is that the reduced form will involve more coefficients than the primary form, and the larger the system the more drastic the difficulties would be in basing the parameter and estimation on the reduced form.

3.3. *The Approach of Interdependent Systems*

Interdependent systems are designed for forecasting on the basis of the reduced form in accordance with the chain principle. Refs. 34 and 42 give general accounts of the theory of the approach, with full references to earlier work. Among the major contributions on the applied side we note Refs. 3, 4, 39, 40, 68.

(i) Illustrations. We shall first consider the simple system (2.13), Ref. 28. A graphic illustration corresponding to Fig. 3.21, left (that is, with one arrow for each relation in the primary form) gives the picture shown in Fig. 3.30. The ordered flow in Fig. 3.21 breaks down, inasmuch as there are two relations for q_t and none for p_t. This shows that the design of the primary form is more general than in pure causal chains. With reference to the general form (3.10–11) for pure causal chains, the matrix B need not be subdiagonal in interdependent systems, nor need there be one and only one behavioural relation for each endogenous variable.

For further comment on interdependent systems we shall give two illustrations that link up with (3.11).

First, an interdependent system with primary form given by

$$(15) \qquad y_i = \alpha_i y_{i-1} + \beta_i y_{i+1} + \gamma_{ii} x_i(t) + v_i \qquad (i = 1, \cdots, h)$$

with $\alpha_0 = \beta_h = 0$, or in matrix form

$$(16) \qquad\qquad\qquad y = Ay(t) + \Gamma x(t) + v$$

where Γ is the same as in (3.11b), and

$$(17) \qquad A = \begin{bmatrix} 0 & \beta_1 & 0 & \cdots & & 0 & 0 \\ \alpha_2 & 0 & \beta_2 & \cdots & & 0 & 0 \\ 0 & \alpha_3 & 0 & \cdots & & 0 & 0 \\ \multicolumn{7}{c}{\cdots\cdots\cdots\cdots\cdots\cdots\cdots\cdots} \\ 0 & 0 & 0 & \cdots & \alpha_{h-1} & 0 & \beta_{h-1} \\ 0 & 0 & 0 & \cdots & 0 & \alpha_h & 0 \end{bmatrix}$$

Second, an interdependent system with primary form

$$y_1(t) = \beta_2 y_2(t) + \beta_3 y_3(t) + \cdots + \beta_h y_h(t) + \gamma_{11} x_1(t) + v_1(t)$$
$$(18) \quad y_i(t) = \alpha_i y_{i-1}(t) + \gamma_{ii} x_i(t) + v_1(t), \qquad (i = 2, \cdots, h)$$

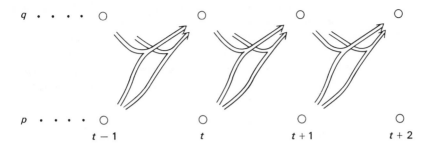

FIGURE 3.30   *Graphic illustration of the interdependent system* (2.13).

or in matrix form

(19) $$y(t) = Cy(t) + \Gamma x(t) + v$$

where Γ is the same as in (3.11b) and (3.16), while

(20) $$C = \begin{bmatrix} 0 & \beta_2 & \beta_3 & \cdots & \beta_{h-1} & \beta_h \\ \alpha_2 & 0 & 0 & \cdots & 0 & 0 \\ 0 & \alpha_3 & 0 & \cdots & 0 & 0 \\ \cdots\cdots\cdots\cdots\cdots\cdots\cdots \\ 0 & 0 & 0 & \cdots & 0 & 0 \\ 0 & 0 & 0 & \cdots & \alpha_h & 0 \end{bmatrix}$$

Turning now to the reduced form of interdependent systems, the formal representation will be the same as for vector regression (3.5), and the same as for the reduced form (3.8) of pure causal chair systems. Hence the graphic illustration in Fig. 3.20 extends to the reduced form of interdependent systems.

(ii) Basic difference between interdependent systems and pure causal chains. (Refs. 87–92, cf. also Refs. 8, 9, 28, 30, 34, 43, 67, 80, 81, 83–86, 95.) The basic difference relative to pure causal chains is that the twofold specification of the primary form and the reduced form in terms of predictors breaks down for interdependent systems. In line with the purpose of interdependent systems, only the reduced form is specified so as to constitute *eo ipso* predictors. The relations of the primary form, and in particular the behaviour relations of the model, in general will not constitute *eo ipso* predictors.

Ever since its beginnings, it has been characteristic for the approach of interdependent systems that the behaviour relations are not designed for being used separately for forecasting (cf. Refs. 28, 30). A typical example is provided by the simple model with primary form (2.13). The reduced form is the same as in (2.9), except that the relations now involve residuals. The reduced form is specified so as to make its residuals uncorrelated with p_{t-1}, and as is easy to see this implies that in the demand relation (2.13a) the residual v_t will be correlated with p_t (except possibly for special values of the parameters); hence the demand relation cannot constitute a predictor.

(iii) The primary form of interdependent systems and its interpretation. Granted that the relations in the primary form of interdependent systems are not designed for separate use in forecasting, what is then the meaning of the primary form, and what is in particular the interpretation of the behaviour relations of the model?

Considering once more the simple model (2.13), we repeat its demand relation

$$(21) \qquad (d_t =)q_t = \alpha_1 - \beta_1 p_t + v_t$$

Since v_t in general is correlated with p_t, we infer

$$(22) \qquad E(q_t/p_t) \neq \alpha_1 - \beta_1 p_t$$

except possibly for special values of the parameters. In the same model we now form

$$(23) \qquad (d_t =)q_t = \alpha_1 - \beta_1 p_t^* + v_t^*$$

where q_1, α_1, β_1 are the same as in (3.21), while p_t^* is defined by

$$(24) \qquad p_t^* = E(p_t/p_{t-1}) = \frac{\alpha_1 - \alpha_2}{\beta_1} - \frac{\beta_2}{\beta_1} p_{t-1}$$

and the new residual v_t^* is defined in accordance with (3.23–24). Then it can be shown that (3.23) is an *eo ipso* predictor, i.e.

$$(25) \qquad E(q_t/p_t^*) = \alpha_1 - \beta_1 p_t^*$$

To paraphrase in terms of elasticities, suppose that all variables are given as logarithms. Then β_1 is the elasticity of quantity q_t with respect to *expected* price p_t^*, not with respect to *observed* price p_t.

This result is of general scope (Refs. 92a and 93; compare also Ref. 90). Thus in interdependent systems any behaviour relation can be interpreted as an *eo ipso* predictor, *provided those explanatory variables that are current endogenous variables are replaced by their expected values (in accordance with the reduced form).* Well to note, the shift in the current endogenous variables does not affect the numerical values of the parameters of the system.

In the pure causal chain (2.12) the demand relation (2.12a) is specified as an *eo ipso* predictor, that is, as the theoretical regression of d_t on p_t, say

(26) $$d_t = \alpha_1{}^* - \beta_1{}^* p_t + \omega_t{}^{**}$$

with

(27) $$E(d_t/p_t) = \alpha_1{}^* - \beta_1{}^* p_t$$

In the small model under consideration there is quite a drastic difference between the parameters in (3.27) on the one hand and (3.21) and (3.23) on the other, and in particular β_1 and $\beta_1{}^*$ may be very different. In a simple case we have $\beta_1{}^* = 0.8$ and $\beta_1 = 0.6/p$, where ρ may be any number in the interval $0 < \rho < 0.96$ (for details, see Ref. 87, where the various models are interpreted as stochastic processes).

The same striking difference is borne out by empirical investigations. From a comparative study (Ref. 86) where a pure causal chain model has been fitted to a statistical material that had earlier (Ref. 68) been used for the construction of an interdependent system, we quote

(28a–b) $$\beta_1 = 0.907 \qquad \beta_1{}^* = 0.207$$

for a price elasticity as estimated (a) in the interdependent system, and (b) in the pure causal chain. Interpreting these numerical results in accordance with (3.25) and (3.26) we see that the first value is demand elasticity with respect to expected price, while the second elasticity refers to observed price.

In the long debate on interdependent systems, a key topic has been the causal interpretation of their behavioural relations (3.16), and in particular of the individual parameters α of these relations (Refs. 8, 34, 43). The argument (3.21)–(3.27) and the ensuing distinction between elasticities with respect to *expected* variables vs. *observed* values provides a clearcut answer to the questions at issue. We see that the argument is based on the notion of conditional expectation, and thus belongs to mathematics and probability theory.[4]

---

[4] In earlier contributions to the debate, the author has argued in terms of general causal notions, with related but less sharp conclusions (Refs. 83–86, 95). Specific reference is made to a paper written jointly with R. Strotz (Ref. 67), where an attempt is made to give a causal interpretation of interdependent systems as written in the customary form (3.21), not in the form (3.23) specified in terms of expected values.

In conclusion, the behaviour relations in interdependent systems do not allow the same causal and stochastic interpretation as in pure causal chains. The root of the trouble can be seen as a pitfall in the transition from disturbance free to stochastic models: The primary form and the reduced form are mathematically equivalent as sources of inference in deterministic models. In stochastic models this equivalence may or may not extend to inference by way of *eo ipso* predictors; it does in pure causal chains, but in general it does not in interdependent systems.

(iv) Parameter estimation in interdependent systems. From the very beginning of the approach it has been emphasized that special procedures are required for the statistical estimation of the parameters of interdependent systems (Refs. 28, 30, 43). Several techniques have been developed for the purpose (see, also for further references, Refs. 3, 34, 43, 69). Just as for pure causal chains there is no need in this review to enter in detail upon the techniques of parameter estimation, for the differences are secondary to the basic difference between the models as reviewed under (ii)–(iii) above. Thus with reference to (3.28) both coefficients are, in principle, technically correct estimates for the corresponding parameters of the two models. The fact that the two coefficients are drastically different although they refer to one and the same demand (for watermelons in USA 1932–51. Refs. 68, 86) is explained by what we have seen under (ii) above, namely that the parameters do not have the same operative meaning in the two models. The point we wish to make in the present context is that the discrepancy in (3.28) is a matter of model specification, and cannot be removed by a change in the estimation technique.

Quite apart from the difference in the meaning of the parameters, the parameter estimation in interdependent systems is technically much more difficult than in pure causal chains. Speaking broadly, this is so because the methods for the estimation of *eo ipso* predictors are here available for estimating the reduced form but not for estimating the primary form, and when estimating the reduced form the difficulties touched upon in section 3.2 (iii) are now even more pronounced than in the case of pure causal chains. For example, let us consider the two interdependent systems (3.16) and (3.19). In each system there are $3\ h - 2$ parameters, but the reduced form will in general involve no less than h^2 parameters. In comparison with the pure causal chain (3.10) this shows that the overidentification as well as the risk for collinearities has become even more serious.[5]

[5] Added when the manuscript is submitted to the printer: Quite recently a new estimation method has been established, Ref. 93, which operates only with the primary form, not the reduced form, and thereby avoids the difficulties at issue.

3.4. *Conditional Causal Chains*

This type of model is a kind of parallel to interdependent system, designed primarily for didactic purposes (Refs. 87–90). As we know from (3.22), the primary form of an interdependent system in general does not constitute *eo ipso* predictors. Now if (3.21) were part of a conditional causal chain system it would be specified so as to make

(29) $$E(q_t/p_t) = \alpha_1 - \beta_1 p_t$$

It would then in general be impossible to satisfy (3.24); that is, (3.29) implies

(30) $$E(p_t/p_{t-1}) \neq \frac{\alpha_1 - \alpha_2}{\beta_1} - \frac{\beta_2}{\beta_1} p_{t-1}$$

The dualism between (3.21)–(3.22) on the one hand and (3.29)–(3.30) on the other brings in relief, once more, that the parameters of the behavioural relations do not have the same operational meaning in interdependent systems as in (pure or conditional) causal chains. Now we have seen that the respecification (3.24) provides a clearcut meaning to the parameters of the behaviour relations of interdependent systems, a third interpretation that dissolves the somewhat paradoxical dualism.

3.5. *Input-Output Models*

Introduced by W. Leontief in 1941 (Refs. 48–49), input-output analysis is perhaps the most widely known approach in macroeconomic model building. For brief illustration of the basic ideas we quote the following summary of an input-output table for Norway 1948 (the original table, Ref. 14, has 34 x 34 sectors).

Let us consider the building industry. The second column gives the gross product of this industry, 3083 mcrs, and the second row its net product, 2852 mcrs. The balance, 231 mcrs, is the inputs of the building industry into the five receiving industries, of which 22 mcrs are delivered to the consumption goods production, 26 mcrs are transfers within the building sector, and so on. The table thus shows how the total supply of goods and services, 19,263 millions crowns = gross national product 14,092 mcrs + imports 5,171) emerges as a production net after division into six production sectors. The oblique figures give the transfers between the production sectors as percentages of the gross product in the receiving sector. For example, the transfers from "Other industries" into the building sector make

Input-output table for Norway 1948. (Refs. 14, 89.)
Values in million Norwegian crowns (mcrs). Ratios in percent.

DELIVERING PRODUCTION SECTOR	RECEIVING PRODUCTION SECTOR					PROD. NET
	I	II	III	IV	V	VI
I. Consumption products	1322	51	80	16	34	5606
	18.6	1.7	1.6	0.5	0.4	(y_1)
II. Building industry	22	26	64	9	111	2852
	0.3	0.8	1.3	0.2	1.2	(y_2)
III. Other industries	202	848	560	67	142	3302
	2.9	27.5	11.0	1.9	1.6	(y_3)
IV. Transport	56	45	28	18	689	2681
	0.8	1.5	0.6	0.5	7.8	(y_4)
V. Trade and services	2137	336	1453	379	1147	3421
	30.0	10.9	28.4	10.7	12.9	(y_5)
VI. General sector: Household- ing; capital; foreign trade	3370	1776	2936	3028	6750	1401
	47.4	57.6	57.1	86.1	76.1	
I-VI. Gross product	7109	3083	5122	3517	8873	19263
	(X_1)	(X_2)	(X_3)	(X_4)	(X_5)	

27.5 percent of the gross product of the building industry. The percentages are called *technical coefficients*.

The key assumption of Leontief's approach is that the technical coefficients are stable in the receiving sectors. Hence the coefficients can be used to assess what gross products X_i are required in the various sectors to yield a prescribed set of *final demands* y_i, that is, of net products in the sectors. Writing the approach in mathematical form, we obtain

$$(31) \qquad a_{i1}X_1 + \cdots + a_{in}X_n + y_i = X_i \qquad (i = 1, \cdots, n)$$

a_{ij} being the technical coefficients,

$$(32) \qquad a_{ij} = X_{ij}/X_j \qquad (i, j = 1, \cdots, n)$$

where X_{ij} are the transfers between the n sectors. Conversely (3.29) may be solved to give the gross products X_i in terms of the final demands y_i, say

$$(33) \qquad X_i = b_{i1}y_1 + \cdots + b_{in}y_n \qquad (i = 1, \cdots, n)$$

A few comments: Input-output relations (3.29) are in current theory specified as *deterministic*. When stochasticized they take the form of an interdependent system. In (3.31) we then regard the X_i's as endogenous and the y_i's as exogenous variables, assume the technical coefficients to be constant over time, and interpret (3.33) as the reduced form of (3.31). The stochastization however involves the incompatibility which is mentioned in the last sentence of Theorem 2.21 and in a special case illustrated by (3.22). Hence in the stochasticized input-output system we meet again the same pluralism with regard to specification in terms of predictors that has been discussed in sections 3.3 (iii) and 3.4.

3.6. *The Potential Applications of Multirelation Models*

In sections 3.2–5 the theoretical rationale of four multirelation models has been briefly reviewed, and we shall now round off by some comments on their actual and potential applications. Above all we shall emphasize their general scope. The models have their origin in econometrics, but their potential applications extend over the entire socioeconomic area; still wider, they are of general scope in nonexperimental situations (Refs. 85, 90, 92a).

Model building by multirelation models is an approach that combines flexibility with specialization, for example static vs. dynamic analysis. In consequence—as emphasized in section 3.3 (ii) above—the approach has raised the aspiration levels both with regard to scope and precision if compared with other current techniques for economic analysis and forecasting.

The theory of multirelation model building is more developed than the applied work, although on the whole both are in their beginnings. Hence it is an important task to take up the various types of multirelation models for unprejudiced comparison and scrutiny, for better understanding of the theoretical issues, and for better guidance in the applied work. The systematic comparison of applied work is so much the more important as multirelation models usually are large and very costly undertakings.

(i) Description vs. causal explanation. Reference is made to the fundamental distinction between descriptive vs. explanatory models. The models under review are explanatory in the sense that (the variations in) one or more variables are represented in terms of (variations in) other variables. Forecasting is sometimes based on descriptive techniques, such as graduation by polynomials or exponential functions of time; at higher aspiration levels, forecasting is based on explanatory models.

Here and in the following it is instructive to compare meteorology and economics with regard to forecasting (cf. Ref. 52). It is an argument of old standing that forecasting on the basis of model building is possible in meteorology, but is of limited scope or impossible in economics, because public forecasts have repercussions on enterprisers, consumers, and other behaving units in the economic sphere, repercussions that are liable to upset forecasts that otherwise might be valid. The rejoinder to this argument is that such repercussions in principle can be taken into account in the model, just as any other economic behaviour, an approach that is well known from the engineering techniques of servomechanisms.

The line of demarcation is floating between descriptive and explanatory approaches. An intermediate case is anticipation data, such as the statistics compiled by the IFO-institute at Munich on enterprisers' anticipations of the economic developments during the next quarter or six months (see Ref. 36, an early program paper).

(ii) Static vs. dynamic approaches. Input-output models are essentially static, inasmuch as they involve assumptions of equilibrium (unspecified in time) between demand and supply transfers between the various economic sectors; as to practical use they are primarily intended for inference by way of comparative statics (Refs. 48, 49). At the other extreme are the pure causal chains; this approach is purely dynamic in the sense that no equilibrium assumptions whatever are included in the basic assumptions of the model. For example, the discrepancies between demand and supply give rise to changes in orders and stocks, and thereby they are essential as driving forces in the causal chain. It is quite another matter that propositions about long run equilibrium between demand and supply can on appropriate assumptions be obtained from the model by way of deductive theorems (Refs. 84, 87, 90).

Interdependent systems are an intermediate case, inasmuch as assumptions of instantaneous equilibrium and other static elements are typical for the basic hypotheses of the model construction (Refs. 34, 43). From this point of view the approach is a generalization of pure causal chains, since more types of relationships are used, but the generalization is bought at the price of the incompatibility which is illustrated by (3.22).

(iii) Forecasting vs. planning. By way of a first crude dichotomy, we may discern between situations of control in the sense of controlled experiments and nonexperimental situations (cf. Ref. 85). Speaking broadly, *forecasting* is primarily of relevance in nonexperimental situations, whereas *planning* is the guide for action in situations of complete control of the strategic factors.

In the socioeconomic area most situations are intermediate, some factors being under control while others are not. In such cases forecasting models have an important function as planning instruments. For example, a large scale enterprise has a more or less complete control over its production apparatus and marketing organization, while it has little or no control over such macroeconomic factors as the price level and total purchasing power. At the government level there is a similar distinction between controlled and noncontrolled factors. The more the macroeconomic factors are under control, the more pronounced are the repercussions on the forecasting that were referred to under (i), and the more the forecasting will shift into planning. For a general treatment of planning problems at the government level, reference is made to Jan Tinbergen's pioneering work; Ref. 75.

(iv) Short term vs. long term forecasting. The problems pose themselves very differently in forecasting over short and long time spans, and they call for a fargoing specialization in the model building. Both meteorology and economics provide typical illustrations of this point.

In meteorology the short term forecasts are fairly reliable over 24 to 48 hours. The principal basis of the short term forecasting techniques is Bjerknes' thermodynamic theory of cyclones (Refs. 10, 12). The successful development of this model can be read off in the gradual increase in the reliability of the forecasts from 1920 or thereabout.

Meteorological forecasts over the "long range" of 4 or 6 weeks is a more recent development. Here the forecasting has to be based on other phenomena than individual cyclones. The technique is still in its beginnings, and the reliability much lower than for the short range forecasting.

In economic forecasting, "short term" means ranges from 3 or 6 months up to 6 or 8 quarters, whereas "long range" usually means something like 5 or 10 years. On the whole—to paraphrase a recent statement by T. Haavelmo (Ref. 31)—the theory of forecasting models is more developed than the actual field work, and the applied results thus far make a case for the German proverb of "Viel Geschrei und wenig Wolle." There is a widespread feeling, however, that the stage is being set for substantial progress, in particular so for short range forecasting.

Of special interest are dynamic forecasting models based on the chain principle. Tinbergen's pioneering work in the 1930s with pure causal chain models was not primarily concerned with forecasting, but rather with economic analysis and with the problem of damping the business cycles. The applied work with interdependent systems has primarily been focussed on forecasting, and in particular so the models constructed by L. Klein and his associates (Refs. 3, 4, 39, 40). In a first phase the models were based on annual data. The transfer to using quarterly data (Ref. 4) is no doubt a great step forward towards the goal of reliable short range forecasts. The interdependent systems dominated the scene from 1945 through the 1950s, but less so in the most recent developments (Refs. 15, 65, 67, 86). The approach of causal chains has come more to the fore in applied work (Refs. 65, 86), with promising results, but thus far only in partial or highly aggregated models.

4. MODEL BUILDING AND THE THEORY OF KNOWLEDGE

The techniques of model building form a central chapter of scientific method, and thereby of the general theory of knowledge (epistemology, or the philosophy of science). This is so with regard to the foundations of model building in the theory of knowledge as well as to the specialized tools of model building. At both of these levels the techniques of model building provide ample material for discussion at the *Monaco entretiens* 1964, so much indeed that there is the question whether it might be appropriate to continue the discussion and devote the whole of a later symposium to this area.

As to the epistomological foundations of model building, each science can be seen as a *collection of models*. The emphasis is here on the pluralism of model building: Science does not aim at constructing an all embracing model for the entire body of scientific knowledge. An early reference to science as model building is H. Herz (1894, Ref. 33), whose term "image" (German: Bild) may be taken as a synonym for scientific model, and who emphasized the dualism between the theoretical model and its empirical aspects. Other important references are the grand attempt of Russell and Whitehead (1910–1913) to construct an axiomatic theory that embraces all mathematics, and the famous "indecision theorem" by K. Gödel (1931). Theorems can be constructed that cannot be proved in the axiom system, but which nonetheless are recognized as intuitively obvious. Gödel's result implies, for one thing, that all-embracing theories of the Whitehead-Russell type are doomed to failure. In line herewith, Laplace's all-calculating gnomon is no longer the ideal in the scientific workshop. The actual product of scientific research is a stream of models at different aspiration levels, models that are partly overlapping, partly disconnected and sometimes deliberately even in mutual conflict. (Cf. Refs. 11, 13, 22, 38, 45, 94, also for further references.)

The basic texts of the theory of knowledge emphasize as its general program to assess and examine the procedures by which scientific results are actually established. According to this program—which, alas, is not always adhered to in practice—the general object for study in the theory of knowledge is *human knowledge as a body in steady growth*. Model building as commented upon in the previous paragraph then evidently is a main chapter in the theory of knowledge: Human knowledge as a system of models that provide a systematic coordination of theory and empirical observation. But this is not all. In the assessment, ordering and steady growth of knowledge there is also a human-institutional element, and this aspect also belongs under the general program of the theory of knowledge as quoted above. In this second chapter of the theory of knowledge the emphasis is on the one hand on the *creative* element of scientific progress: The assessment of new results is not a matter of scientific routine, neither in pure mathematics nor in applied model building. On the other hand the emphasis is on the assessment of human knowledge as a matter of *group decision:* Science is an institutional system with the strength and weaknesses of all human organizations. For a new result to be accepted in the body of human knowledge it does not suffice that it is correctly derived— be it a logical proposition that fulfils the appropriate truth table, or an applied model that satisfies the customary test criteria—it must also reach an established status. The road of a new scientific truth is often thorny— it has to be accepted in a circle of friends and collaborators, to pass one or more referees and editors on its way to the pages of a book or learned journal, and finally it must attract the attention of reviewers and readers if it is to come to life and be a valid element in the growing human knowledge.

REFERENCES

1. Allen, R. G. D. (1956). *Mathematical economics*. London: Macmillan.
2. Allen and A. L. Bowley (1935). *Family expenditure*. London: Staples.
3. Ball, R., J. A. Hazlewood and L. R. Klein (1959). "Econometric forecasts for 1959." *Bulletin of the Oxford University Institute of Statistics, 21*, pp. 3–16.
4. Barger, H. and L. R. Klein (1954). "A quarterly model for the US economy." *Journal of the American Statistical Association, 49*, pp. 413–437.
5. Bartlett, M. S. (1955). *An introduction to stochastic processes with special reference to methods and applications*. Cambridge: Univ. Press.
6. Baumol, W. J. (1951). *Economic dynamics. An introduction*. New York: Macmillan. 2nd ed. 1959.
7. Benini, R. (1907). "Sull'uso delle formule empiriche nell'economia applicata." *Giornale degli Economisti, 35*, pp. 1053–1063.
8. Bentzel, R. and B. Hansen (1954). "On recursiveness and interdependency in economic models." *Review of Economic Studies, 22*, pp. 153–168.
9. Bentzel and H. Wold (1946). "On statistical demand analysis from the viewpoint of simultaneous equations." *Skandinavisk Aktuarietidskrift, 29*, pp. 95–114.
10. Bergeron, T. (1959). "Methods in scientific weather analysis and forecasting. An outline in the history of ideas and hints of a program. "Paper in *The atmosphere and sea in motion*, pp. 440–474. New York: Rockefeller Inst. Press.

11. Bergmann, G. (1943). "Outline of an empiricist philosophy of physics." *American Journal of Physics, 11*. Also in *Ref. 22*, pp. 262–287.

12. Bjerknes, J. (1919). "On the structure of moving cyclones." *Geofysiske Publikationer, 1*, no. 2. Oslo.

13. Braithwaite, R. B. (1953). *Scientific explanation*. Cambridge: Univ. Press.

14. Central Bureau of Statistics, Norway (1952). *National accounts 1930–1939 and 1946–1951*. Norges Officielle Statistikk XI, no. 109. Oslo: Aschehoug.

15. Clark, C. (1960). "Contribution (pp. 287–288) to "The present position of econometrics; A discussion." *Journal of the Royal Statistical Society, Ser. A, 123*, pp. 274–296.

16. Cournot, A. (1838). *Recherches sur les principes mathématiques de la théorie des richesses*. Amer. ed. 1927, New York: Macmillan.

17. Cramér, H. (1945–46). *Mathematical methods of statistics*. Uppsala: Almqvist & Wiksells. Princeton, N.J.: Univ. Press.

18. Czuber, E. (1891). *Theorie der Beobachtungsfehler*. Leipzig: Teubner.

19. Durbin, J. (1954). "Errors in variables." *Review of the International Statistical Institute, 22*, pp. 23–32.

20. Engel, E. (1895). "Die Lebenshaltung belgischer Arbeiter-Familien früher und jetzt." *Bulletin Inst. Intern. Statist. 9*, 1–124; with an Appendix, pp. 1–54.

21. Ezekiel, M. (1938). "The cobweb theorem." *Quarterly Journal of Economics, 52*, pp. 255–280.

22. Feigl, H. and May Brodbeck, eds. (1953). *Readings in the philosophy of science*. New York: Appleton-Century-Crofts.

23. Fisher, R. A. (1925). *Statistical methods for research workers*. Edinburgh: Oliver and Boyd. 14th ed. 1954.

24. _____ (1935). *The design of experiments*. Edinburgh: Oliver and Boyd. 7th ed. 1949.

25. Frisch, R. (1928). "Correlation and scatter in statistical variables." *Nordisk Statistisk Tidskrift, 8*, 36–102.

26. Frisch, R. (1934). "Statistical confluence analysis by means of complete regression systems." *Univ. Inst. of Economics, Oslo, Pub. No. 5*.

27. Gini, C. (1921). "Sull'interpolazione di una retta quando i valori della variabile indipendente sono affetti da errori accidentali." *Metron, 1*, no. 3, pp. 63–82.

28. Girshick, M. A. and T. Haavelmo (1947). "Statistical analysis of the demand for food." *Econometrica, 15*, pp. 79–110. Reprinted, in revised form, in *Ref. 34*.

29. Gödel, K. (1931). "Ueber formal unentscheidbare Sätze der Principia Mathematica und vetwandter Systeme, I." *Monatschefte für Mathematik und Physik, 38*, pp. 173–198.

30. Haavelmo, T. (1943). "The statistical implications of a system of simultaneous equations." *Econometrica, 11*, pp. 1–12.

31. _____ (1958). "The role of the econometrician in the advancement of economic theory." *Econometrica, 26,* pp. 351–357.

32. Heady, E. O. and J. L. Dillon (1961). *Agricultural production functions.* Ames, Iowa: State Univ. Press.

33. Herz, H. (1894). *Die Prinzipien der Mechanik.* Leipzig: Barth.

34. Hood, W. C. and T. C. Koopmans, eds. (1953). *Studies in econometric method.* New York: Wiley and Sons.

35. Hurwicz, L. (1950). "Prediction and least squares." Paper in *Ref. 43,* pp. 266–300.

36. IFO Institute (1953). *Auswertungsmöglichkeiten des Konjunkturtestverfahrens für die theoretische und angewandte Nationalökonomie.* IFO-Institut für Wirtschaftsforschung, Munich: Merkblatt IV/6.

37. Jeffreys H. (1931). *Scientific inference.* Cambridge: Univ. Press. 2nd ed. 1937.

38. Jörgensen, J. (1948). *The development of logical empiricism.* (Danish.) Copenhagen: Luno.

39. Klein, L. R. (1950). *Economic fluctuations in the United States 1921–1941.* New York: Wiley and Sons.

40. Klein, L. R. and A. Goldberger (1955). *An econometric model of the United States 1929–1952.* Amsterdam: North-Holland.

41. Kolmogorov, A. (1933). "Grundbegriffe der Wahrscheinlichkeitsrechnung." *Ergebnisse der Mathematik und ihrer Grenzgebiete, 2,* nr. 3.

42. Koopmans, T. C. (1936). *Linear regression analysis of economic time series.* Thesis (Leiden); also separately at Haarlem: Bohn.

43. _____, ed. (1950). *Statistical inference in dynamic economic models.* New York: Wiley and Sons.

44. Laplace, P. S. (1812). *Théorie analytique des probabilités.* Paris. 3rd ed. 1820.

45. Lazarsfeld, P. F., ed. (1954). *Mathematical thinking in the social sciences.* Glencoe, Ill.: The Free Press.

46. Le Play, F. (1855). *Les ouvriers Européens.* Paris: Imperiale.

47. Lehfeldt, R. (1915). "Review of 'Economic cycles' by H. Moore." *Economic Journal, 25,* pp. 409–411.

48. Leontief, W. W. (1941). *The structure of American economy,* 1919–39. Cambridge, Mass.: Harvard Univ. Press.

49. Leontief, W. W., ed. (1953). *Studies in the structure of the American economy.* New York: Oxford Univ. Press.

50a. Lyttkens, E. (1964). "Standard errors of regression coefficients by autocorrelated residuals." Paper in *Ref. 92,* pp. 169–228.

50b. _____ (1964). "A large sample χ^2-difference test for regression coefficients." Paper in *Ref. 92,* pp. 236–278.

51. Mackeprang, E. P. (1906). *Pristeorier.* Copenhagen: Bagge.

52. Marschak, J. and W. H. Andrews, Jr. (1944). "Random simultaneous

equations and the theory of production." *Econometrica, 12,* pp. 143–205.

53. Marshall, A. (1890). *Principles of economics.* London: Macmillan. 8th ed. 1946.

54. Pearson, K. (1901). "On lines and planes of closest fit to systems of points in space." *Philosophical Magazine* (6), *2,* 559–572.

55. Phillips, A. (1959). "The estimation of parameters in systems of stochastic differential equations." *Biometrika, 46,* pp. 67–76.

56. Plackett, R. L. (1960). *Principles of regression analysis.* Oxford, Clarendon.

57. Robinson, E. A. (1959). *Infinitely many variates.* London: Griffin.

58. _____ (1961). *Random wavelets and cybernetic systems.* London: Griffin.

59. Russell, B. and A. N. Whitehead (1910–1913). *Principia Mathematica,* I-III. Cambridge: Univ. Press.

60. Samuelson, P. A. (1947). *Foundations of economic analysis.* Cambridge, Mass.: Harvard Univ. Press.

61. Sauvy, A. (1952–54). *Théorie générale de la population,* I-II. Paris: Presses Univ. de France.

62. Schultz, H. (1938). *The theory and measurement of demand.* Chicago, Ill.: Univ. Press.

63. Stephan, F. F. (1947). History of the uses of modern sampling procedures. *Bulletin of the International Statistical Institute, 31,* III A, pp. 81–112.

64. Stigler, G. J. (1954). "The early history of empirical studies of consumer behaviour." *Journal of Political Economy, 62,* pp. 95–113.

65. Stojkovic, G. (1961). "Market models for agricultural products." Paper in *Ref. 92,* pp. 386–419.

66. Stojkovic and H. Wold (1961). "Un effet de biais dans les modèles à équilibre instantané." Paper in *Money, growth and methodology,* ed. H. Hegeland, pp. 425–433. Lund: Gleerup.

67. Strotz, H. and H. Wold (1960). "Recursive vs. nonrecursive systems: An attempt at synthesis." *Econometrica, 28,* pp. 417–427.

68. Suits, D. (1955). "An econometric model of the watermelon market." *Journal of Farm Economics, 37,* pp. 237–251.

69. Theil, H. (1954). *Linear aggregation of economic relations.* Amsterdam: North-Holland.

70. Tinbergen, J. (1930). "Bestimmung und Deutung von Angebotskurven. Ein Beispiel." *Zeitschrift für Nationalökonomie, 1,* pp. 669–679.

71. _____ (1937). *An econometric approach to business cycle problems.* Paris: Hermann et Cie.

72. _____ (1939). *Statistical testing of business cycle theories.* I: *A method and its application to investment activity.* II. *Business cycles in the United States of America,* 1919–1932. Geneva: League of Nations.

73. _____ (1940). "Econometric business cycle research." *Review of Economic Studies, 7*, pp. 73–90.

74. _____ (1951). *Business cycles in the United Kingdom,* 1870–1914. Amsterdam: North-Holland. 2nd ed. 1956.

75. _____ (1956). *Economic policy: Principles and design.* Amsterdam: North-Holland.

76. Whittaker, E. T. and G. Robinson (1924). *The calculus of observations.* London: Blackie. 4th ed. 1944.

77. Wold, H. (1938). *A study in the analysis of stationary time series.* Uppsala: Almqvist & Wiksells. 2nd ed. 1954.

78. _____ (1940). *The demand for agricultural products and its sensitivity to price and income changes.* (Swedish.) Statens Offentliga Utredningar 1940: 16.

79. _____ (1943–44). "A synthesis of pure demand analysis, I-III." *Skandinavisk Aktuarietidskrift, 26,* pp. 85–118 and 220–263; *27,* pp. 69–120.

80. _____ (1948). "On prediction in stationary time series." *The Annals of Mathematical Statistics, 19,* pp. 558–567.

81. _____ (1949). "Statistical estimation of economic relationships." *Econometrica, 17,* Supplement, pp. 1–22.

82. _____ (1950). "On least squares regression with autocorrelated variables and residuals." *Bulletin of the International Institute of Statistics, 32, II,* pp. 277–289. Oral discussion: Same *Bulletin, 32, I,* (1952), pp. 145–147.

83. _____ (1954). "Causality and econometrics." *Econometrica, 22,* pp. 162–177.

84. _____ (1955). "Possibilités et limitations des systèmes à chaîne causale." Paper in *Cahiers du séminaire d'économétrie de R. Roy,* No. 3 (pp. 81–101). Paris: Centre National de la Recherche Scientifique.

85. _____ (1956). "Causal inference from observational data. A review of ends and means." *Journal of the Royal Statistical Society (A), 119,* pp. 28–61.

86. _____ (1959). "A case study of interdependent versus causal chain systems." *Review of the International Statistical Institute, 26,* pp. 5–25.

87. _____ (1959–1960). "Ends and means in econometric model building. Basic considerations reviewed." Paper in *Probability and Statistics. The Harald Cramér volume,* ed. U. Grenander, pp. 355–434. Stockholm: Almqvist & Wiksells. New York: Wiley and Sons.

88. _____ (1960). "A generalization of causal chain models." *Econometrica, 28,* pp. 344–463.

89. _____ (1961). "Construction principles of simultaneous equations models in econometrics." In *Bulletin of the International Statistical Institute, 38,* no. 4, pp. 111–138.

90. _____ (1961). "Unbiased predictors." *Fourth Berkeley Symposium of Mathematical Statistics and Probability Theory*, Vol. *1*, pp. 719–761. Berkeley, Cal.: Univ. Press.

91. _____ (1963). "On the consistency of least squares regression." *Sankhya, 25*, no. 2, pp. 211–215.

92. _____, ed. (1964). *Econometric model building. Essays on the causal chain approach.* Amsterdam: North-Holland Publ. Co.

92a. _____ (1964). "Forecasting by the chain principle." Paper in *Ref. 92*, pp. 5–36.

93. _____ (1965). "A fix-point theorem with econometric background. I-II." *Arkiv för Matematik, 6*, no. 12–13, pp. 209–240.

94. _____ (1966). "On the definition and meaning of causal concepts." Paper in this volume, pp. 255–285.

95. Wold, H. and L. Juréen (1952–1953). *Demand analysis. A study in econometrics.* Stockholm: Almqvist and Wiksells. New York: Wiley and Sons.

96. Working, E. J. (1927). "What do statistical demand curves show?" *Quarterly Journal of Economics, 41*, pp. 212–235.

97. Working, H. (1934). "Price relations between May and new-crop wheat futures at Chicago since 1885." *Wheat Studies, 10*, pp. 183–230. Stanford: Food Research Institute.

98. Wright, S. (1921). "Correlation and causation." *J. Agricultural Research, 20*, pp. 557–585.

99. _____ (1934). "The method of path coefficients." *Annals of Math. Stat., 5*, pp. 161–215.

100. Yule, G. U. (1910). *An introduction to the theory of statistics.* London: Griffin. 8th ed. 1927.

Path Analysis: Sociological Examples[1]

OTIS DUDLEY DUNCAN

Linear causal models are conveniently developed by the method of path coefficients proposed by Sewall Wright. Path analysis is useful in making explicit the rationale of conventional regression calculations. It may also have special usefulness in sociology in problems involving the decomposition of a dependent variable or those in which successive experiences of a cohort are measured. Path analysis focuses on the problem of interpretation and does not purport to be a method for discovering causes. It may, nevertheless, be invaluable in rendering interpretations explicit, self-consistent, and susceptible to rejection by subsequent research.

The long-standing interest of sociologists in causal interpretation of statistical relationships has been quickened by discussions focusing on linear causal models. The basic work of bringing such models to the attention of the discipline was done by Blalock,[2] drawing upon the writings of Simon[3] and Wold[4] in particular. The rationale of this approach was strengthened

[1] Prepared in connection with a project on "Socioeconomic Background and Occupational Achievement," supported by contract OE-5-85-072 with the U.S. Office of Education. Useful suggestions were made by H. M. Blalock, Jr., Beverly Duncan, Robert W. Hodge, Hal H. Winsborough, and Sewall Wright, but none of them is responsible for the use made of his suggestions or for any errors in the paper.
[2] Hubert M. Blalock, Jr., *Causal Inferences in Nonexperimental Research* (Chapel Hill: University of North Carolina Press, 1964).
[3] Herbert A. Simon, *Models of Man* (New York: John Wiley & Sons, 1957), chap. ii.
[4] Herman Wold and Lars Juréen, *Demand Analysis* (New York: John Wiley & Sons, 1953).

when Costner and Leik[5] showed that "asymmetric causal models" of the kind proposed by Blalock afford a natural and operational explication of the notion of "axiomatic deductive theory," which had been developed primarily by sociologists working with verbal formulations. Most recently, Boudon[6] pointed out that the Simon-Blalock type of model is a "special case" or "weak form" of path analysis (or "dependence analysis," as Boudon prefers to call it). At the same time, he noted that "convincing empirical illustrations are missing," since "moderately complicated causal structures with corresponding data are rather scarce in the sociological literature." This paper presents some examples (in the form of reanalyses of published work) which may be interesting, if not "convincing." It includes an exposition of some aspects of path technique, developing it in a way that may make it a little more accessible than some of the previous writings.

Path coefficients were used by the geneticist Sewall Wright as early as 1918, and the technique was expounded formally by him in a series of articles dating from the early 1920s. References to this literature, along with useful restatements and illustrations, will be found in Wright's papers of 1934, 1954, and 1960.[7] The main application of path analysis has been in population genetics, where the method has proved to be a powerful aid to "axiomatic deductions." The assumptions are those of Mendelian inheritance, combined with path schemes representing specified systems of mating. The method allows the geneticist to ascertain the "coefficient of inbreeding," a quantity on which various statistical properties of a Mendelian population depend. It also yields a theoretical calculation of the genetic correlations among relatives of stated degrees of relationship. Most of Wright's expositions of this *direct* use of path coefficients are heavily mathematical;[8] an elementary treatment is given in the text by Li.[9]

Apart from a few examples in Wright's own work, little use has been made of path coefficients in connection with the *inverse* problem of esti-

[5] Herbert L. Costner and Robert K. Leik, "Deductions from 'Axiomatic Theory,'" *American Sociological Review,* XXIX (December, 1964), 819–835.

[6] Raymond Boudon, "A Method of Linear Causal Analysis: Dependence Analysis," *American Sociological Review,* XXX (June, 1965), 365–374.

[7] Sewall Wright, "The Method of Path Coefficients," *Annals of Mathematical Statistics,* V (September, 1934), 161–215; "The Interpretation of Multivariate Systems," in O. Kempthorne *et al.* (eds.), *Statistics and Mathematics in Biology* (Ames: Iowa State College Press, 1954), chap. ii; "Path Coefficients and Path Regressions: Alternative or Complementary Concepts?" *Biometrics,* XVI (June, 1960), 189–202.

[8] Sewall Wright, "The Genetical Structure of Populations," *Annals of Eugenics,* XV (March, 1951), 323–354.

[9] C. C. Li, *Population Genetics* (Chicago: University of Chicago Press, 1955), chap. xii–xiv. See also C. C. Li, "The Concept of Path Coefficient and Its Impact on Population Genetics," *Biometrics,* XII (June, 1956), 190–210.

mating the paths which may account for a set of observed correlations on the assumption of a particular formal or causal ordering of the variables involved. Of greatest substantive interest to sociologists may be an example relating to heredity and environment in the determination of intelligence.[10] Another highly suggestive study was a pioneer but neglected exercise in econometrics concerning prices and production of corn and hogs.[11] Although the subject matter is remote from sociological concerns, examples from studies in animal biology are instructive on methodological grounds.[12] If research workers have been slow to follow Wright's lead, the statisticians have done little better. There are only a few expositions in the statistical literature,[13] some of which raise questions to which Wright has replied.[14]

PATH DIAGRAMS AND THE BASIC THEOREM

We are concerned with linear, additive, asymmetric relationships among a set of variables which are conceived as being measurable on an interval scale, although some of them may not actually be measured or may even be purely hypothetical—for example, the "true" variables in measurement theory or the "factors" in factor analysis. In such a system, certain of the variables are represented to be dependent on others as linear functions. The remaining variables are assumed, for the analysis at hand, to be given. They may be correlated among themselves, but the explanation of their

[10] Sewall Wright, "Statistical Methods in Biology," *Journal of the American Statistical Association,* XXVI (March, 1931, suppl.), 155–163.

[11] Sewall Wright, *Corn and Hog Correlations,* U.S. Department of Agriculture Bulletin 1300 (Washington: Government Printing Office, 1925); also, "The Method of Path Coefficients," pp. 192–204.

[12] Sewall Wright, "The Genetics of Vital Characters of the Guinea Pig," *Journal of Cellular and Comparative Physiology,* LVI (suppl. 1, November, 1960), 123–151; F. A. Davidson *et al.,* "Factors Influencing the Upstream Migration of the Pink Salmon (*Oncorhynchus gorbuscha*)," *Ecology,* XXIV (April, 1943), 149–168.

[13] J. W. Tukey, "Causation, Regression and Path Analysis," in O. Kempthorne *et al., op. cit.,* chap. iii; Oscar Kempthorne, *An Introduction to Genetic Statistics* (New York: John Wiley & Sons, Inc., 1957), chap. xiv; Malcolm E. Turner and Charles D. Stevens, "The Regression Analysis of Causal Paths," *Biometrics,* XV (June, 1959), 236–258; Eleanor D. Campbell, Malcolm E. Turner, and Mary Frances Wright, with the editorial collaboration of Charles D. Stevens. *A Handbook of Path Regression Analysis,* Part I: *Estimators for Simple Completely Identified Systems* (Preliminary Ed.; Richmond: Medical College of Virginia, Department of Biophysics and Biometry, 1960); Henri Louis Le Roy, *Statistische Methoden der Populationsgenetik* (Basel: Birkhäuser, 1960), chap. i; P. A. P. Moran, "Path Coefficients Reconsidered," *Australian Journal of Statistics,* III (November, 1961), 87–93.

[14] "Path Coefficients and Path Regressions."

intercorrelation is not taken as problematical. Each "dependent" variable must be regarded explicitly as *completely* determined by some combination of variables in the system. In problems where complete determination by measured variables does not hold, a residual variable uncorrelated with other determining variables must be introduced.

Although it is not intrinsic to the method, the diagrammatic representation of such a system is of great value in thinking about its properties. A word of caution is necessary, however. Causal diagrams are appearing with increasing frequency in sociological publications. Most often, these have some kind of pictorial or mnemonic function without being isomorphic with the algebraic and statistical properties of the postulated system of variables —or, indeed, without having a counterpart in any clearly specified system of variables at all. Sometimes an investigator will post values of zero order or partial correlations, association coefficients, or other indications of the "strength" of relationship on such a diagram, without following any clearly defined and logically justified rules for entering such quantities into the analysis and its diagrammatic representation. In Blalock's work, by contrast, diagrams are employed in accordance with explicit rules for the representation of a system of equations. In general, however, he limits himself to the indication of the sign (positive or negative) of postulated or inferred direct relationships. In at least one instance[15] he inserts zero-order correlations into a diagram which looks very much like a causal diagram, although it is not intended to be such. This misleading practice should not be encouraged.

In path diagrams, we use one-way arrows leading from each determining variable to each variable dependent on it. Unanalyzed correlations between variables not dependent upon others in the system are shown by two-headed arrows, and the connecting line is drawn curved, rather than straight, to call attention to its distinction from the paths relating dependent to determining variables. The quantities entered on the diagram are symbolic or numerical values of *path coefficients,* or, in the case of the bidirectional correlations, the simple correlation coefficients.

Several of the properties of a path diagram are illustrated in Figure 1. The original data, in the form of ten zero-order correlations, are from Turner's study of determinants of aspirations.[16] The author does not provide a completely unequivocal formulation of the entire causal model shown here, but Figure 1 appears to correspond to the model that he quite tentatively proposes. At one point he states, "background affects ambition and

[15] Blalock, *op. cit.,* p. 77.
[16] Ralph H. Turner, *The Social Context of Ambition* (San Francisco: Chandler Publishing Co., 1964), pp. 49 and 52, Tables 11, 17, and 20.

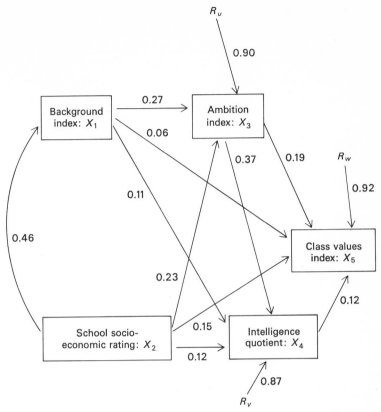

FIGURE 1 *Causal model from Turner,* op. cit., *with path coefficients estimated for male sample.*

ambition affects both IQ and class values; in addition . . . there is a lesser influence directly from background to class values, directly from background to IQ, and directly between IQ and class values."[17] Elsewhere,[18] he indicates that school rating operates in much the same fashion as (family) background. As for the relationship between the two, Turner notes, on the one hand, that "families may choose their place of residence," but also that "by introducing neighborhood, we may only be measuring family background more precisely."[19] Hence, it seems that there is no firm assumption about the causal ordering within this pair of variables; but since these two

[17] *Ibid.,* p. 107.
[18] *Ibid.,* pp. 54–61.
[19] *Ibid.,* p. 61.

precede the remaining ones, it suffices to represent the link between X_1 and X_2 as merely a bidirectional correlation.

Allowing Turner to take responsibility for the causal ordering of the variables (assuming his statements are understood correctly) and deferring the question of how the path coefficients were estimated, let us see what the system represented by Figure 1 is like. Each variable is taken to be in standard form; that is, if V_i is the ith variable as measured, then $X_i = (V_i - \bar{V}_i)/\sigma_{Vi}$. The same convention holds for the residuals, R_u, R_v, and R_w, to which a literal subscript is attached to indicate that these variables are not directly measured. The system represented in Figure 1 can now be written:

$$X_3 = p_{32}X_2 + p_{31}X_1 + p_{3u}R_u,$$

$$X_4 = p_{43}X_3 + p_{42}X_2 + p_{41}X_1 + p_{4v}R_v,$$

$$X_5 = p_{54}X_4 + p_{53}X_3 + p_{52}X_2 + p_{51}X_1 + p_{5w}R_w \qquad (1)$$

The use of the symbol p for the path coefficient is perhaps obvious. Note that the order of the subscripts is significant, the convention being the same as that used for regression coefficients: the first subscript identifies the dependent variable, the second the variable whose direct effect on the dependent variable is measured by the path coefficient. The order of subscripts is immaterial for correlations. But note that while $r_{42} = r_{24}$ and $r_{42.123} = r_{24.123}$, $p_{42} \neq p_{24}$; indeed p_{42} and p_{24} would never appear in the same system, given the restriction to recursive systems mentioned subsequently. Contrary to the practice in the case of partial regression and correlation coefficients, symbols for paths carry no secondary subscripts to identify the other variables assumed to affect the dependent variable. These will ordinarily be evident from the diagram or the equation system.

In one respect, the equation system (1) is less explicit than the diagram because the latter indicates what assumptions are made about residual factors. Each such factor is assumed by definition to be uncorrelated with any of the immediate determinants of the dependent variable to which it pertains. In Figure 1, the residuals are also uncorrelated with each other, as in the Simon-Blalock development.[20] We shall see later, however, that there are uses for models in which some residuals are intercorrelated, or in which a residual is correlated with variables antecedent to, but not immediate determinants of, the particular dependent variable to which it is attached. Where the assumption of uncorrelated residuals is made, deductions reached by the Simon-Blalock technique of expanding the product of two error variables agree with the results obtained by the formulas men-

[20] Blalock, *op. cit.*, p. 64; Boudon, *op. cit.*, p. 369.

tioned below, although path analysis involves relatively little use of the partial correlations which are a feature of their technique.

Equation system (1), as Blalock points out, is a recursive system. This discussion explicitly excludes non-recursive systems, involving instantaneous reciprocal action of variables, although Wright has indicated ways of handling them in a path framework.[21] Thus we shall not consider diagrams showing a direct or indirect feedback loop.

The principle that follows from equations in the form of (1) is that the correlation between any pair of variables can be written in terms of the paths leading from common antecedent variables. Consider r_{35}. Since

$$X_3 = (V_3 - \bar{V}_3)/\sigma_3$$

and

$$X_5 = (V_5 - \bar{V}_5)/\sigma_5$$

we have

$$r_{35} = \Sigma(V_3 - \bar{V}_3)(V_5 - \bar{V}_5)/N\sigma_3\sigma_5 = \Sigma X_3 X_5/N$$

We may expand this expression in either of two ways by substituting from (1) the expression for X_3 or the one for X_5. It is more convenient to expand the variable which appears later in the causal sequence:

$$r_{35} = \Sigma X_3 X_5/N$$

$$= \frac{1}{N}\Sigma X_3(p_{54}X_4 + p_{53}X_3 + p_{52}X_2 + p_{51}X_1 + p_{5w}R_w)$$

$$= p_{54}r_{34} + p_{53} + p_{52}r_{23} + p_{51}r_{13} \qquad (2)$$

making use of the fact that $\Sigma X_3 X_3/N = 1$ and the assumption that $r_{3w} = 0$, since X_3 is a factor of X_5. But the correlations on the right-hand side of (2) can be further analyzed by the same procedure; for example,

$$r_{34} = \frac{1}{N}\Sigma X_3 X_4 = \frac{1}{N}\Sigma X_3(p_{43}X_3 + p_{42}X_2 + p_{41}X_1 + p_{4v}R_v)$$

$$= p_{43} + p_{42}r_{23} + p_{41}r_{13} \qquad (3)$$

and

$$r_{32} = \frac{1}{N}\Sigma X_2 X_3 = \frac{1}{N}\Sigma X_2(p_{32}X_2 + p_{31}X_1 + p_{3u}R_u)$$

$$= p_{32} + p_{31}r_{12} \qquad (4)$$

[21] Sewall Wright, "The Treatment of Reciprocal Interaction, with or without Lag, in Path Analysis," Biometrics, XVI (September, 1960), 423–445.

Note that r_{12}, assumed as a datum, cannot be further analyzed as long as we retain the particular diagram of Figure 1.

These manipulations illustrate the basic theorem of path analysis, which may be written in the general form:

$$r_{ij} = \sum_q p_{iq} r_{jq} \tag{5}$$

where i and j denote two variables in the system and the index q runs over all variables from which paths lead directly to X_i. Alternatively, we may expand (5) by successive applications of the formula itself to the r_{jq}. Thus, from (2), (3), (4), and a similar expansion of r_{13}, we obtain

$$r_{53} = p_{53} + p_{51}p_{31} + p_{51}r_{12}p_{32} + p_{52}p_{32} + p_{52}r_{12}p_{31} + p_{54}p_{42}p_{32}$$
$$+ p_{54}p_{42}r_{12}p_{31} + p_{54}p_{43} + p_{54}p_{41}p_{32}r_{12} + p_{54}p_{41}p_{31} \tag{6}$$

Such expressions can be read directly from the diagram according to the following rule. Read *back* from variable i, *then forward* to variable j, forming the product of all paths along the traverse; then sum these products for all possible traverses. The same variable cannot be intersected more than once in a single traverse. In no case can one trace back having once started forward. The bidirectional correlation is used in tracing either forward or back, but if more than one bidirectional correlation appears in the diagram, only one can be used in a single traverse. The resulting expression, such as (6), may consist of a single direct path plus the sum of several compound paths representing all the indirect connections allowed by the diagram. The general formula (5) is likely to be the more useful in algebraic manipulation and calculation, the expansion on the pattern of (6) in appreciating the properties of the causal scheme. It is safer to depend on the algebra than on the verbal algorithm, at least until one has mastered the art of reading path diagrams.

An important special case of (5) is the formula for complete determination of X_i, obtained by setting $i = j$:

$$r_{ii} = 1 = \sum_q p_{iq} r_{iq} \tag{7}$$

or, upon expansion,

$$r_{ii} = \sum_q p_{iq}^2 + 2 \sum_{q,q'} p_{iq} r_{qq'} p_{iq'} \tag{8}$$

where the range of q and q' ($q' > q$) includes all variables, measured and unmeasured. A major use for (8) is the calculation of the residual path.

Thus we obtain p_{3u} in the system (1) from

$$p_{3u}^2 = 1 - p_{32}^2 - p_{31}^2 - 2p_{32}r_{12}p_{31} \qquad (9)$$

The causal model shown in Figure 1 represents a special case of path analysis: one in which there are no unmeasured variables (other than residual factors), the residuals are uncorrelated, and each of the dependent variables is directly related to all the variables preceding it in the assumed causal sequence. In this case, path analysis amounts to a sequence of conventional regression analyses, and the basic theorem (5) becomes merely a compact statement of the normal equations of regression theory for variables in standard form. The path coefficients are then nothing other than the "beta coefficients" in a regression setup, and the usual apparatus for regression calculations may be employed.[22] Thus, the paths in Figure 1 are obtained from the regression of X_3 on X_2 and X_1, setting $p_{32} = \beta_{32.1}$ and $p_{31} = \beta_{31.2}$; the regression of X_4 on X_3, X_2, and X_1, setting $p_{43} = \beta_{43.12}$, $p_{42} = \beta_{42.13}$, and $p_{41} = \beta_{41.23}$; and the regression of X_5 on the other four variables, setting $p_{54} = \beta_{54.123}$, $p_{53} = \beta_{53.124}$, and so on. Following the computing routine which inverts the matrix of intercorrelations of the independent variables, one obtains automatically the standard errors of the β coefficients (or b^*-coefficients, in the notation of Walker and Lev). In the present problem, with sample size exceeding 1,000, the standard errors are small, varying between .027 and .032. All the β's are at least twice their standard errors and thus statistically significant.

In problems of this kind, Blalock[23] has been preoccupied with the question of whether one or more path coefficients may be deleted without loss of information. As compared with his rather tedious search procedure, the procedure followed here seems more straightforward. Had some of the β's turned out both nonsignificant and negligible in magnitude, one could have erased the corresponding paths from the diagram and run the regressions over, retaining only those independent variables found to be statistically and substantively significant.

As statistical techniques, therefore, neither path analysis nor the Blalock-Simon procedure adds anything to conventional regression analysis as applied recursively to generate a system of equations, rather than a single equation. As a *pattern of interpretation,* however, path analysis is invaluable in making explicit the rationale for a set of regression calculations. One may not be wholly satisfied, for example, with the theoretical assump-

[22] Helen M. Walker and Joseph Lev, *Statistical Inference* (New York: Holt, Rinehart & Winston, 1953), chap. xiii.
[23] *Op. cit.,* chap. iii.

tions underlying the causal interpretation of Turner's data provided by Figure 1, and perhaps Turner himself would not be prepared to defend it in detail. The point is, however, that *any* causal interpretation of these data must rest on assumptions—at a minimum, the assumption as to ordering of the variables, but also assumptions about the unmeasured variables here represented as uncorrelated residual factors.[24] The great merit of the path scheme, then, is that it makes the assumptions explicit and tends to force the discussion to be at least internally consistent, so that mutually incompatible assumptions are not introduced surreptitiously into different parts of an argument extending over scores of pages. With the causal scheme made explicit, moreover, it is in a form that enables criticism to be sharply focused and hence potentially relevant not only to the interpretation at hand but also, perchance, to the conduct of future inquiry.

Another useful contribution of path analysis, even in the conventional regression framework, is that it provides a calculus for indirect effects, when the basic equations are expanded along the lines of (6). It is evident from the regression coefficients, for example, that the direct effect of school on class values is greater than that of background, but the opposite is true of the indirect effects. The pattern of indirect effects is hardly obvious without the aid of an explicit representation of the causal scheme. If one wishes a single summary measure of indirect effect, however, it is obtained as follows: indirect effect of X_2 on $X_5 = r_{52} - p_{52} = .28 - .15 = .13$; similarly, indirect effect of X_1 is $r_{51} - p_{51} = .24 - .06 = .18$. These summations of indirect effects include, in each case, the effects of one variable via its correlation with the other; hence the two are not additive. Without commenting further on the substantive implications of the direct and indirect effects suggested by Turner's material, it may simply be noted that the investigator will usually want to scrutinize them carefully in terms of his theory.

DECOMPOSITION OF A DEPENDENT VARIABLE

Many of the variables studied in social research are (or may be regarded as) composite. Thus, population growth is the sum of natural increase and net migration; each of the latter may be further decomposed, natural increase being births minus deaths and net migration the difference between in- and out-migration. Where such a decomposition is available, it is of interest (1) to compute the relative contributions of the components to

[24] *Ibid.,* pp. 46–47.

variation in the composite variable and (2) to ascertain how causes affecting the composite variable are transmitted via the respective components.

An example taken from work of Winsborough[25] illustrates the case of a variable with multiplicative components, rendered additive by taking logarithms. Studying variation in population density over the seventy-four community areas (omitting the central business district) of Chicago in 1940, Winsborough noted that density, defined as the ratio of population to area, can be written:

$$\frac{\text{Population}}{\text{Area}} = \frac{\text{Population}}{\text{Dwelling Units}} \times \frac{\text{Dwelling Units}}{\text{Structures}} \times \frac{\text{Structures}}{\text{Area}}$$

Let $V_0 = \log(\text{Population/Area})$, $V_1 = \log(\text{Population/Dwelling Units})$, $V_2 = \log(\text{Dwelling Units/Structures})$, and $V_3 = \log(\text{Structures/Area})$; then

$$V_0 = V_1 + V_2 + V_3$$

If each variable is expressed in standard form, we obtain,

$$\frac{V_0 - \bar{V}_0}{\sigma_0} = \frac{V_1 - \bar{V}_1}{\sigma_1} \cdot \frac{\sigma_1}{\sigma_0} + \frac{V_2 - \bar{V}_2}{\sigma_2} \cdot \frac{\sigma_2}{\sigma_0} + \frac{V_3 - \bar{V}_3}{\sigma_3} \cdot \frac{\sigma_3}{\sigma_0}$$

or

$$X_0 = p_{01}X_1 + p_{02}X_2 + p_{03}X_3$$

where $X_0, \cdots, X_3$ are the variables in standard form and p_{01}, p_{02}, p_{03} are the path coefficients involved in the determination of X_0 by X_1, X_2, and X_3. Observe that the path coefficients can be computed in this kind of problem, where complete determination by measured variables holds as a consequence of definitions, without prior calculation of correlations:[26]

$$p_{01} = \sigma_1/\sigma_0 = .132 \qquad \sigma_0 = .491 \qquad \sigma_1 = .065$$

$$p_{02} = \sigma_2/\sigma_0 = .468 \qquad\qquad\qquad \sigma_2 = .230$$

$$p_{03} = \sigma_3/\sigma_0 = .821 \qquad\qquad\qquad \sigma_3 = .403$$

The intercorrelations of the components, shown in Table 1, are used to complete the diagram, Figure 2, *a*. The correlations of the dependent variable with its components may now be computed from the basic theorem, equation (5).

[25] Hal H. Winsborough, "City Growth and City Structure," *Journal of Regional Science*, IV (Winter, 1962), 35–49.
[26] Based on data kindly supplied by Winsborough.

Table 1

Correlation Matrix for Logarithms of Density and Its Components and Two Independent Variables: Chicago Community Areas, 1940

VARIABLE	X_1	X_2	X_3	W	Z
X_0 density (log)	−.419	.636	.923	−.663	−.390
X_1 persons per dwelling unit (log)		−.625	−.315	.296	.099
X_2 dwelling units per structure (log)			.305	−.594	−.466
X_3 structures per acre (log)				−.517	−.226
W distance from center					.549
Z recency of growth					

Source: Winsborough, *op. cit.*, and unpublished data kindly supplied by the author.

$$r_{01} = p_{01} + p_{02}r_{12} + p_{03}r_{13} = -.419$$

$$r_{02} = p_{01}r_{12} + p_{02} + p_{03}r_{23} = .636$$

and

$$r_{03} = p_{01}r_{13} + p_{02}r_{23} + p_{03} = .923$$

The analysis has not only turned up a clear ordering of the three components in terms of relative importance, as given by the path coefficients, it has also shown that one of the components is actually correlated negatively with the composite variable, owing to its negative correlations with the other two components.

Winsborough considered two independent variables as factors producing variation in density: distance from the city center and recency of growth (percentage of dwelling units built in 1920 or later). The diagram can be elaborated to indicate how these factors operate via the components of log density (see Fig.2, *b*).

The first step is to compute the path coefficients for the relationships of each component to the two independent variables. (The requisite information is given in Table 1.) For example, the equations,

$$r_{1W} = p_{1W} + p_{1Z}r_{ZW}$$

$$r_{1Z} = p_{1W}r_{ZW} + p_{1Z}$$

may be used to solve for p_{1Z} and p_{1W}. (This is, of course, equivalent to computing the multiple regression of X_1 on W and Z, with all variables in standard form.) Substantively, it is interesting that distance, W, has somewhat larger effects on each component of density than does recency of growth, Z, while the pattern of signs of the path coefficients is different for W and Z.

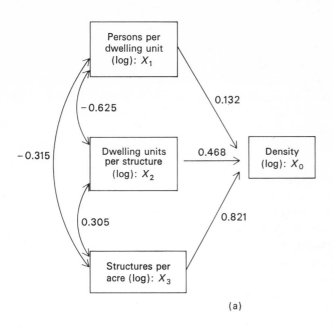

(a)

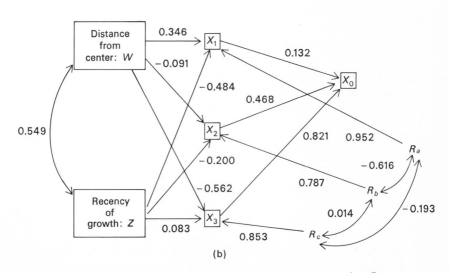

(b)

FIGURE 2 a, *decomposition of log density* (X_0) *into components;* b, *effects of distance and recency of growth on log density via components. (Source: Winsborough,* op. cit., *and unpublished calculations kindly supplied by the author.)*

The two independent variables by no means account for all the variation in any of the components, as may be seen from the size of the residuals, p_{1a}, p_{2b}, and p_{2c}, these being computed from the formula (7) for complete determination. It is possible, nevertheless, for the independent variables to account for the intercorrelations of the components and, ideally, one would like to discover independent variables which would do just that. The relevant calculations concern the correlations between residuals. These are obtained from the basic theorem, equation (5), by writing, for example,

$$r_{23} = p_{2W}r_{3W} + p_{2Z}r_{3Z} + p_{2b}p_{3c}r_{bc}$$

which may be solved for $r_{bc} = .014$. In this setup, the correlations between residuals are merely the conventional second-order partial correlations; thus $r_{ab} = r_{12.WZ}$, $r_{ac} = r_{13.WZ}$, and $r_{bc} = r_{23.WZ}$. Partial correlations, which otherwise have little utility in path analysis, turn out to be appropriate when the question at issue is whether a set of independent variables "explains" the correlation between two dependent variables. In the present example, while $r_{23} = .305$, we find $r_{bc} = r_{23.WZ} = .014$. Thus the correlation between the logarithms of dwelling units per structure (X_2) and structures per acre (X_3) is satisfactorily explained by the respective relationships of these two components to distance and recency of growth. The same is not true of the correlations involving persons per dwelling unit (X_1), but fortunately this is by far the least important component of density.

Although the correlations between residuals are required to complete the diagram and, in a sense, to evaluate the adequacy of the explanatory variables, they do not enter as such into the calculations bearing upon the final question: How are the effects of the independent variables transmitted to the dependent variable via its components? The most compact answer to this question is given by the equations,

$$r_{0W} = p_{01}r_{1W} + p_{02}r_{2W} + p_{03}r_{3W}$$
$$= .039 - .278 - .424 = -.663$$

and

$$r_{0Z} = p_{01}r_{1Z} + p_{02}r_{2Z} + p_{03}r_{3Z}$$
$$= .013 - .218 - .185 = -.391$$

Density is negatively related to both distance and recency of growth, but the effects transmitted via the first component of density are positive (albeit quite small). Distance diminishes density primarily via its intermediate effect on structures per acre (X_3), secondarily via dwelling units per structure (X_2). The comparison is reversed for recency of growth, the less important of the two factors. More detailed interpretations can be obtained, as explained earlier, by expanding the correlations r_{1W}, r_{2W}, and so forth, using the basic theorem (5). For further substantive interpretation, the reader is referred to the source publication, which also offers an alternative derivation of the compound paths.

The density problem may well exemplify a general strategy too seldom employed in research: breaking a complex variable down into its components before initiating a search for its causes. One egregious error must, however, be avoided: that of treating components and causes on the same footing. By this route, one can arrive at the meaningless result that net migration is a more important "cause" of population growth than is change in manufacturing output. One must take strong exception to a causal scheme constructed on the premise, "If both demographic and economic variables help explain metropolitan growth, then we may gain understanding of growth processes by lumping the two together."[27] On the contrary, "understanding" would seem to require a clear distinction between demographic *components* of growth and economic *causes* which may affect growth via one or another of its components.

A CHAIN MODEL

Data reported by Hodge, Siegel, and Rossi[28] seem to fit well the model of a *simple causal chain* (see Fig. 3, *a*). These authors give correlations between the occupational prestige ratings of four studies completed at widely separated dates: Counts (1925), Smith (1940), National Opinion Research Center (1947), and NORC replication (1963). In a simple causal chain, the correlations between temporally adjacent variables are the path coefficients (this is an immediate consequence of the definition of path coefficient). Using these three correlations as reported by Hodge *et al.*, we may infer that the correlation between NORC (1963) and Smith is $(.990)(.982) = .972$; between NORC (1963) and Counts is $(.990)(.982)$ $(.968) = .942$; and between NORC (1947) and Counts is $(.982)(.968)$ $= .951$. The observed values of these correlations (with differences from the inferred values in parentheses) are $r_{YS} = .971$ ($-.001$), $r_{YC} = .934$ ($-.008$), and $r_{XC} = .955$ (.004). Acceptance of this causal chain model

[27] George L. Wilber, "Growth of Metropolitan Areas in the South," *Social Forces,* XLII (May, 1964), 491.
[28] Robert W. Hodge, Paul M. Siegel, and Peter H. Rossi, "Occupational Prestige in the United States, 1925–1963," *American Journal of Sociology,* LXX (November, 1964), 286–302.

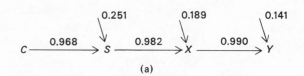

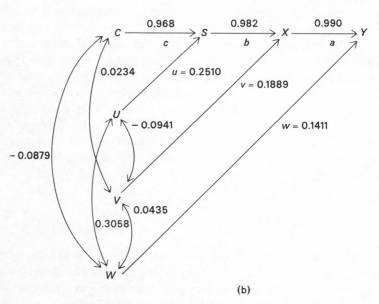

FIGURE 3   *Causal chain: a, correlations taken from Hodge* et al., *op. cit.*
*(C = Counts, 1925; S = Smith, 1940; X = NORC, 1947; Y = NORC,
1963); b, interrelations of residuals implied by acceptance of chain hypothesis for the data in* a.

is consistent with the conclusion of Hodge *et al.* that the amount of change
in the relative positions of occupations in a prestige hierarchy is a direct
function of elapsed time.

Although the discrepancies between inferred and observed correlations
seem trivial, it is worth noting that acceptance of the estimates shown in
Figure 3, *a,* along with the assumption of a simple causal chain, requires
us to postulate a complex pattern of correlations (most of them negligible
in size) among the residuals or errors. This pattern is shown in Figure 3, *b.*
In obtaining this solution, we assume that each residual is uncorrelated
with the immediately preceding variable in the chain but not necessarily
with the variables two or more links behind it. In the present example, then,

the crucial assumptions are that $r_{VS} = r_{WX} = 0$. We can then, using equation (5) or the verbal algorithm, write the number of equations required to solve for the quantities to be entered on the diagram (for convenience, lower-case letters designate paths):

$$r_{YX} = a = .990$$

$$r_{XS} = b = .982$$

$$r_{SC} = c = .968$$

$$r_{YY} = 1 = a^2 + w^2$$

$$r_{XX} = 1 = b^2 + v^2$$

$$r_{SS} = 1 = c^2 + u^2$$

$$r_{XC} = .955 = bc + vr_{VC}$$

$$r_{YC} = .934 = abc + avr_{VC} + wr_{CW}$$

$$r_{YS} = .971 = ab + cwr_{CW} + uwr_{UW}$$

$$r_{VS} = 0 = ur_{UV} + cr_{CV}$$

$$r_{WX} = 0 = vr_{VW} + br_{SW}$$

$$(\text{where } r_{SW} = cr_{CW} + ur_{UW}) \qquad (11)$$

In general, if we are considernig a k-variable causal chain, we shall have to estimate $k - 1$ residual paths, $(k - 1)(k - 2)/2$ correlations between residuals, $k - 1$ paths for the links in the chain, and $k - 2$ correlations between the initial variable and residuals 2, 3, $\cdots$, k in the chain. This is a total of $(k^2 + 3k - 6)/2$ quantities to be estimated. We shall have at our disposal $k(k - 1)/2$ equations expressing known correlations in terms of paths, $k - 1$ equations of complete determination (for all variables in the chain except the initial one), and $k - 2$ equations in which the correlation of a residual with the immediately preceding variable in the chain is set equal to zero. This amounts to $(k^2 + 3k - 6)/2$ equations, exactly the number required for a solution. The solution may, of course, include meaningless results (for example, $r > 1.0$), or results that strain one's credulity. In this event, the chain hypothesis had best be abandoned or the estimated paths modified.

In the present illustration, the results are plausible enough. Both the Counts and the Smith studies differed from the two NORC studies and from each other in their techniques of rating and sampling. A further complication is that the studies used different lists of occupations, and the observed correlations are based on differing numbers of occupations. There is ample opportunity, therefore, for correlations of errors to turn up in a variety of patterns, even though the chain hypothesis may be basically sound. We should observe, too, that the residual factors here include not only extrinsic disturbances but also real though temporary fluctuations in prestige, if there be such.

What should one say, substantively, on the basis of such an analysis of the prestige ratings? Certainly, the temporal ordering of the variables is unambiguous. But whether one wants to assert that an aspect of social structure (prestige hierarchy) at one date "causes" its counterpart at a later date is perhaps questionable. The data suggest there is a high order of persistence over time, coupled with a detectable, if rather glacial, drift in the structure. The calculation of numerical values for the model hardly resolves the question of ultimate "reasons" for either the pattern of persistence or the tempo of change. These are, instead, questions raised by the model in a clear way for further discussion and, perhaps, investigation.

THE SYNTHETIC COHORT AS A PATTERN OF INTERPRETATION

Although, as the example from Turner indicates, it is often difficult in sociological analysis to find unequivocal bases for causal ordering, there is one happy exception to this awkward state of affairs. In the life cycles of individuals and families, certain events and decisions commonly if not universally precede others. Despite the well-known fallibility of retrospective data, the investigator is not at the mercy of respondents' recall in deciding to accept the completion of schooling as an antecedent to the pursuit of an occupational career (exceptions granted) or in assuming that marriage precedes divorce. Some observations, moreover, may be made and recorded in temporal sequence, so that the status observed at the termination of a period of observation may logically be taken to depend on the initial status (among other things). Path analysis may well prove to be most useful to sociologists studying actual historical processes from records and reports of the experience of real cohorts whose experiences are traced over time, such as a student population followed by the investigator through the first stages of post-graduation achievement.[29]

The final example, however, concerns not real cohorts but the usefulness of a hypothetical synthesis of data from several cohorts. As demographers have learned, synthetic cohort analysis incurs some specific hazards;[30] yet

[29] For example, Bruce K. Eckland, "Academic Ability, Higher Education, and Occupational Mobility," *American Sociological Review*, XXX (October, 1965), 735–746.
[30] P. K. Whelpton, "Reproduction Rates Adjusted for Age, Parity, Fecundity, and Marriage," *Journal of the American Statistical Association*, XLI (December, 1946), 501–516.

the technique has proved invaluable for heuristic purposes. Pending the execution of full-blown longitudinal studies on real cohorts, the synthetic cohort is, at least, a way of making explicit one's hypotheses about the sequential determination of experiences cumulating over the life cycle.[31]

In a study of the social mobility of a sample of Chicago white men with nonfarm backgrounds surveyed in 1951, Duncan and Hodge,[32] used data on father's occupational status, respondent's educational attainment, and respondent's occupational status in 1940 and 1950 for four cohorts: men 25–34, 35–44, 45–54, and 55–64 years old on the survey date. Their main results, somewhat awkwardly presented in the source publication, are compactly summarized by the first four diagrams in Figure 4. (The superfluous squared term in their equations has been eliminated in the present calculations. The amount of curvilinearity was found to be trivial, and curvilinear relations cannot be fitted directly into a causal chain by the procedure employed here.)

These data involve partial records of the occupational careers of the four cohorts and thus depict only segments of a continuous life history. In the original analysis, it was possible to gain some insights from the interperiod and intercohort comparisons on which that analysis was focused. Here, attention is given to a different use of the same information. Suppose we thought of the four sets of data as pertaining to a single cohort, studied at four successive points in time, at decade intervals. Then, all the data should fit into a single causal or processual sequence.

It is obvious that one cannot achieve perfect consistency on this point of view. The initial correlation, r_{UX}, varies among cohorts, for example. Moreover, age-constant intercohort comparisons of the other correlations (the Y's with X and U) suggest that some variations result from genuine differences between the conditions of 1940 and 1950. But if one is willing to suppress this information for the sake of a necessarily hypothetical synthesis, it is possible to put all the data together in a single model of occupational careers as influenced by socioeconomic origins.

The four correlations r_{UX} were averaged. The remaining correlations for adjacent cohorts were likewise averaged; for example, r_{1U} based on 1950 data for men 25–34 years old was averaged with r_{1U} based on 1940 data for men 35–44 in 1951, and so on. Only r_{4X}, r_{4U}, and the three intertemporal correlations, r_{21}, r_{32}, and r_{43}, had to be based on the experience of just one cohort. (In deriving this compromise one does, of course, lose the

---

[31] See, for example, A. J. Jaffe and R. O. Carleton, *Occupational Mobility in the United States: 1930–1960* (New York: King's Crown Press, 1954), p. 53 (n. 6) and Table 13.

[32] Otis Dudley Duncan and Robert W. Hodge, "Education and Occupational Mobility," *American Journal of Sociology,* LXVIII (May, 1963), 629–644.

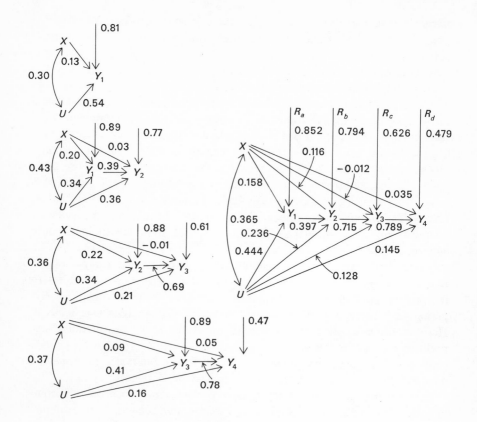

FIGURE 4 *Respondent's occupational status* (Y) *at successive ages, in relation to father's occupational status* (X) *and respondent's educational attainment* (U). *Occupational status at age 25–34* = Y_1; *at 35–44* = Y_2; *at 45–54* = Y_3; *at 55–64* = Y_4. (*Source: Duncan and Hodge, op. cit., and unpublished calculations kindly supplied by the authors.*)

temporal specificity of the data by smoothing out apparently real historical fluctuations.) When the correlations had been averaged, the results shown in the "composite" model on the right of Figure 4 were obtained. The estimates of path coefficients here are simply the partial regression coefficients, in standard form, of Y_1 on X and U; Y_2 on Y_1, X, and U; Y_3 on Y_2, X, and U; and Y_4 on Y_3, X, and U.

The results for the synthetic cohort make explicit the following interpretations: (1) The background factors, father's education (X) and respondent's education (U), have an important direct impact during early stages of a cohort's life cycle; after age 35–44 their direct effects become small or negligible, although they exert indirect effects via preceding achieved statuses (Y_1 and Y_2). (2) Careers tend to stabilize after age 35–44, as indicated by the sharp rise in the path coefficients representing persistence of status over a decade (compare p_{21} with p_{32} and p_{43}) and by the decreasing magnitudes of the residual paths from $R_a, \cdots, R_d$. (3) During the life cycle, many circumstances essentially independent of background factors affect occupational mobility, so that achievement in the later stages of the career becomes more and more dependent upon intervening contingencies while continuing to reflect the indirect influence of conditions determinate at the outset. Thus, for example, r_{4c}—the correlation of occupational status at age 55–64 with residual for age 45–54—may be computed as $(.789)(.626) = .494$, and the residual path to Y_4 itself is $P_{4d} = .479$. These are comparable in size with the correlations $r_{4X} = .301$ and $r_{4U} = .525$. The residuals are, by definition, uncorrelated with X and U and represent, therefore, the influence of factors quite unrelated to social origins and schooling. The prevailing impression that the United States enjoys a rather "loose" stratification system is thus quantified by a model such as this one. (4) While the data include observed interannual correlations of occupational statuses separated by a decade (r_{43}, r_{32}, and r_{21}), the synthetic cohort model also implies such correlations for statuses separated by two or three decades. These may be computed from the following formulas based on equation (5):

$$r_{42} = p_{4X}r_{2X} + p_{43}r_{32} + p_{4U}r_{2U}$$

$$r_{31} = p_{3X}r_{1X} + p_{32}r_{21} + p_{3U}r_{1U}$$

$$r_{41} = p_{4X}r_{1X} + p_{43}r_{31} + p_{4U}r_{1U}$$

inserting the value of r_{31} obtained from the second equation into the third. The observed and implied correlations are assembled in Table 2. The latter

Table 2

Observed and Implied (*) Correlations for Synthetic Cohort Model of Occupational Achievement

VARIABLE (AGE AND OCCUPATIONAL STATUS)	VARIABLE		
	Y_2	Y_3	Y_4
25–34 (Y_1)	.552	.455*	.443*
35–44 (Y_2)		.722	.690*
45–54 (Y_3)			.866
55–64 (Y_4)			

Source: Duncan and Hodge, *op. cit.*, and calculations from model in Figure 4.

represent, in effect, hypotheses to be checked whenever data spanning twenty or thirty years of the occupational experience of a cohort become available. In the meantime, they stand as reasonable estimates, should anyone have use for such estimates. If forthcoming evidence casts doubt on these estimates, the model will, of course, be called into question. It is no small virtue of a model that it is capable of being rejected on the basis of evidence.

This last example, since it rests on an explicit fiction—that of a synthetic cohort—perhaps makes clearer than previous examples the point that the role of path analysis is to *render an interpretation* and not merely to provide a format for presenting conventional calculations. In all the examples the intention has been to adhere to the purpose of path analysis as Wright formulated it:

> . . . the method of path coefficients is not intended to accomplish the impossible task of deducing causal relations from the values of the correlation coefficients.[33] . . . The method depends on the combination of knowledge of the degrees of correlation among the variables in a system with such knowledge as may be possessed of the causal relations. In cases in which the causal relations are uncertain, the method can be used to find the logical consequences of any particular hypothesis in regard to them.[34] . . . Path analysis is an extension of the usual verbal interpretation of statistics not of the statistics themselves. It is usually easy to give a plausible interpretation of any significant statistic taken by itself. The purpose of path analysis is to determine whether a proposed set of interpretations is consistent throughout.[35]

NEGLECTED TOPICS

This paper, for the lack of space and especially for lack of "convincing" examples, could not treat several potentially important applications of path analysis: (1) Models incorporating feedback were explicitly excluded. Whether our present techniques of social measurement are adequate to the development of such models is perhaps questionable. (2) The problem of two-wave, two-variable panel analysis, recently discussed by Pelz and Andrews,[36] might well be formulated in terms of path coefficients. The

[33] "The Method of Path Coefficients," p. 193.
[34] "Correlation and Causation," *Journal of Agricultural Research,* XX (1921), 557–585 (quotation from p. 557).
[35] "The Treatment of Reciprocal Interaction, with or without Lag, in Path Analysis," p. 444.
[36] Donald C. Pelz and Frank M. Andrews, "Detecting Causal Priorities in Panel Study Data," *American Sociological Review,* XXIX (December, 1964), 836–854.

present writer, however, has made little progress in attempts to clarify the panel problem by means of path analysis. (3) The pressing problem of the disposition of measurement errors[37] may perhaps be advanced toward solution by explicit representation in path diagrams. The well-known "correction for attenuation," where measurement errors are assumed to be uncorrelated, is easily derived on this approach.[38] It seems possible that under very special conditions a solution may also be obtained on certain assumptions about correlated errors. (4) Wright has shown[39] how certain ecological models of the interaction of populations can be stated in terms of path coefficients. The inverse method of using path analysis for studies of multiple time series[40] merits consideration by sociologists. (5) Where the investigation involves unmeasured variables, path analysis may be helpful in deciding what deductions, if any, can be made from the observed data. Such unmeasured variables may, in principle, be observable; in this case, path analysis may lead to hypotheses for testing on some future occasion when measurements can be made. If the unmeasured variable is a theoretical construct, its explicit introduction into a path diagram[41] may well point up the nature of rival hypotheses. Ideally, what are sometimes called "validity coefficients" should appear explicitly in the causal model so that the latter accounts for both the "true causes" under study and the ways in which "indicator variables" are thought to represent "underlying variables." A particular case is that of factor analysis. As Wright's work demonstrates,[42] a factor analysis is prone to yield meaningless results unless its execution is controlled by explicit assumptions which reflect the theoretical structure of the problem. An indoctrination in path analysis makes one skeptical of the claim that "modern factor analysis" allows us to leave all the work to the computer.

[37] H. M. Blalock, Jr., "Some Implications of Random Measurement Error for Causal Inferences," *American Journal of Sociology,* LXXI (July, 1965), 37–47; Donald J. Bogue and Edmund M. Murphy, "The Effect of Classification Errors upon Statistical Inference: A Case Analysis with Census Data," *Demography,* I (1964), 42–55.

[38] Wright, "The Method of Path Coefficients" and "Path Coefficients and Path Regressions."

[39] "The Treatment of Reciprocal Interaction."

[40] *Ibid.*

[41] H. M. Blalock, Jr., "Making Causal Inferences for Unmeasured Variables from Correlations among Indicators," *American Journal of Sociology,* LXIX (July, 1963), 53–62.

[42] "The Interpretation of Multivariate Systems."

Reprinted with the permission of the authors and the American Psychological Association from the *Psychological Bulletin,* volume 70, number 2, 1968, pp. 115–126.

Techniques for Estimating the Source and Direction of Causal Influence in Panel Data[1]

A. H. YEE

N. L. GAGE

Techniques for estimating the source and direction of causal influence in panel data are described and applied to illustrative data on teachers' and pupils' interpersonal attitudes. The techniques are Lazarsfeld's 16-fold table, Campbell's cross-lagged panel correlation, and the present authors' frequency-of-shift-across-median and frequency-of-change-in-product-moment. The latter method seems preferable because it permits treatment of continuous data, analysis of all cases, and a necessary distinction between the source and direction of causal influence.

Contemporary scientists seem uncertain as to the value of causal anaysis, especially in the social sciences. Explicit discussions of causality rarely

[1] The research reported in this paper was supported (*a*) by contract (OE-6-10-077) with the United States Department of Health, Education and Welfare, Office of Education, under the provisions of the Cooperative Research Program; (*b*) by the Research and Development Center in Teacher Education, University of Texas; (*c*) by the Stanford Center for Research and Development in Teaching; and (*d*) by the Research Committee, the Graduate School of the University of Wisconsin, Madison. The University of Oregon's School of Education and Center for Advanced Study of Educational Administration facilitated this work by providing the first writer with the freedom and cooperation he enjoyed during his USOE-sponsored postdoctoral research training fellowship there in 1966–1967. The Center for Advanced Study in the Behavioral Sciences and a special fellowship of the National Institute of Mental Health gave the second writer freedom to work on this paper in 1965–1966. The authors thank Donald T. Campbell, Donald C. Pelz, Philip J. Runkel, Joan E. Sieber, Julian Stanley, and M. C. Wittrock for advice and encouragement on preliminary drafts, but absolve them of responsibility for any shortcomings of the present version.

occur. But, as Nagel (1965) observed, "though the *term* may be absent, the *idea* for which it stands continues to have wide currency," as "when scientists distinguish in various inquiries between spurious and genuine correlations [p. 12]." Simon (1957) also noted the common reference to causality in scientific writing, despite its "generally unsavory epistemological status [p. 11]."

In the natural sciences causal connections may be perceived in the tangible or visible mechanisms underlying the connections. Natural scientists also have the advantage of freedom to control and manipulate the matter they investigate: they can burn, catalyze, hybridize, electrolyze, break apart, boil, vivisect, bombard, and subject to acid tests almost as they please. Lacking such freedom, social scientists must place greater reliance upon statistical treatments than upon direct manipulation.

Recent statements by social psychologists indicate increasing concern with causal relationships. For example, Gerard and Miller (1967) noted in their review that "The study of the determinants and consequences of mutual attraction is a focus for a good deal of research in social psychology [p. 294]." Terms implying causality—such as, determine, influence, produce, affect, effect, modify, and attract—occur frequently in the literature. Occasionally, a direct reference to causality may be found; for example, Andrews (1967) studied the business organization as the "causal link" between a nation's achievement concern and its economic development. Causal connections must be exploited, of course, when social-psychological research findings are used in efforts to improve individuals and society, as in the programs of the "Great Society" and investigations into the causes of civil disorders. Greater precision in connecting theory and methods has led to more explicit use of causal inference in the social sciences (Lerner, 1965).

In recent years sociologists (e.g., Blalock, 1964), political scientists (e.g., Alker, 1966), and psychologists (e.g., Runkel, 1961), among others, have given increased attention to statistical methods for investigating causal relationships. Faris (1964) noted that

the research equipment of sociology contains a rich and rapidly growing body of techniques for the extraction of causal generalizations from the data . . . most important . . . is the fund of statistical methods, which can uncover regularities in masses of data too bewildering in their complexity to give up their secrets to any kind of personal skill or intuition. . . . These statistical, and related formal logical methods, employed in connection with modern high-speed computers, promise exponential progress in scientific knowledge of human and social behavior [p. 23].

Similarly, McGuire (1967) recommended that courses in experimental design and statistics for social psychologists "give more attention to techniques that allow us to tease out causal directions among covariants in situations where we do not have the resources to manipulate one of the factors [p. 134]."

One category of techniques for causal analysis consists of those that can be applied to panel data, that is, data collected on the same two or more variables on the same individuals at two or more points in time. This paper reviews two techniques of this kind—the 16-fold table (Lazarsfeld, 1948) and Campbell's cross-lagged panel correlation technique (Campbell and Stanley, 1963)—presents two new ones, and applies all four to the same data on relationships between teachers' and pupils' attitudes.

CAUSAL RELATIONSHIPS IN SOCIAL INTERACTION

Social psychology is largely the study of social interaction, in which the action of one person is a response to that of a second person, whose next response is in turn influenced by that of the first. "The actions of each are at once a *result* of and a *cause* of the actions of the other [Krech, Crutchfield, & Ballachey, 1962, p. 4]." Thus, influence flows in both directions as interacting individuals mutually determine the nature and outcome of the interpersonal behavior event.

In this framework, the "warmth" of a teacher toward his class may be regarded as at once a cause and an effect of the liking of the pupils for their teacher. The following questions can then be raised: Does teacher warmth tend to make the pupils like their teacher better? Or does teacher warmth make the pupils *less* favorably disposed toward their teacher? Or does the influence actually flow in the opposite direction, so that pupils' liking of their teacher increases teacher warmth? Or, finally, does the pupils' favorable attitude toward their teacher *decrease* teacher warmth?

These are four possible combinations of the source and direction of influence between persons in social interaction. These possibilities can characterize any human relationship. For example, Bell (1968) questioned the assumption that influence always flows from parent to child and presented evidence that children's characteristics influence parent behavior. The methods considered in this paper make possible the testing of alternative hypotheses concerning the source and direction of influence between characteristics and behaviors of interacting persons in any relationship. The methods are also useful in determining the relative strength of two influences *within* a set of persons, as the illustrative data for Lazarsfeld's (1948) method, discussed in a following section, indicate. Finally, the methods may be considered applicable to variables of any kind—economic, political, demographic, etc.—where the source and direction of causal influence are to be estimated.

Given paired measurements of two variables that may be causally related, one can compute correlations. With repeated measures, or panel data, one can compute test-retest and same-occasion correlations. These correlations may suggest the operation of causal influence in some direction when (*a*) the correlations between the variables increase (or decrease!) over time; and (*b*) there is marked stability in one variable and marked instability in the other. But, suggestive as such results may be, inferences of causal direction from such correlational results alone are suspect; other independent variables may be influencing the relationship. Suppose it is assumed, however, that no other independent variable is as potent as the two interacting variables in producing what Zeisel (1957) has designated as "true" correlations "which reflect a direct causal connection [p. 205]." Then the four previous questions may be raised: Does one variable affect the other more than it is affected by the other? Or less? Does an increase in the value of one variable increase the value of the other? Or decrease it?

THE DATA ON TEACHER-PUPIL RELATIONSHIPS

These questions can be illustrated with data from a recent study (Yee, 1966) of teachers' attitudes toward pupils (*T*) and pupils' attitudes toward their teacher (*P*). Here it is possible that *T* is determining *P*, or that *P* is determining *T*. In many studies of teacher-pupil interaction (e.g., Della Piana & Gage, 1955; Flanders, 1965, p. 65; Ryans, 1963, p. 432; Withall & Lewis, 1963), it has been suggested that the direction of influence is an open question.

In Yee's study, teachers' attitudes toward children and teacher-pupil relationships were measured with the Minnesota Teacher Attitude Inventory (MTAI); pupils' attitudes toward their teacher were measured with the 100-item "About My Teacher" inventory developed by Beck (1964). Pretests of these attitudes were made as early in the school year as administrators would allow, mostly during the second week of school. Posttests were made about 5 months later, after considerable interaction between teachers and pupils. Thus, the posttest measures represented teachers' and pupils' interpersonal attitudes that had evolved from initial attitudes. Corrected split-half and Horst (1949) coefficients in the high .80's indicated substantial reliability of the teachers' scores and pupils' class means, respectively.

Results were obtained not only for the total group but also for various subgroups based on classifications of teachers by years of teaching experience and of pupils by social class background. In addition to total scores, subscores based on factor analyses of the teacher and pupil attitude measures were analyzed. Hence, 720 correlations between T and P for all classifications were obtained. This report, however, deals only with results for (a) the total group of 212 teacher-class pairs and the two subgroups based on whether the modal pupils' social class background was lower class or middle class, and (b) total MTAI and "About My Teacher" scores.

First, Lazarsfeld's 16-fold table technique is described in terms of the intrapersonal opinion data to which he applied it. Then Campbell's cross-lagged panel correlation technique is described, applied to the authors' own data, and referred to problems with that technique noted by Campbell and also by the authors. Finally, two methods developed by the authors —the frequency-of-shift-across-median technique and the frequency-of-change-in-product-moment technique—are described. In each section, the merits of the various techniques are examined.

LAZARSFELD'S 16-FOLD TABLE TECHNIQUE

The 16-fold table technique was described in two writings (Lazarsfeld, 1948; Lipset, Lazarsfeld, Barton, & Linz, 1954). Unfortunately, the published treatment of 1954 omitted and glossed over crucial features which may be found in the earlier mimeographed paper. In 1948 Lazarsfeld wrote:

> Now let us consider for a moment what we mean by saying that the attitude A has an "effect" on, or is the "cause" of the attitude B. We mean two things: First of all, the attitude A will tend to *generate* the attitude B; that is, if a person has the attitude A but not the attitude B, he will tend to acquire the attitude B: the attitude pattern $A\bar{B}$ (where $\bar{B}$ denotes the lack of B, or non-B) will tend to change to AB, and conversely, the pattern $\bar{A}B$ will tend to change to $\bar{A}\bar{B}$; secondly, the attitude A will tend to *preserve* the attitude B; that is, there will be fewer changes from AB to $A\bar{B}$ than we would expect from chance variations in the attitude B, that is, the attitude pattern AB will tend to be stable, and conversely, the attitude pattern $\bar{A}\bar{B}$ will also tend to be stable [p. 4].

In this passage, Lazarsfeld described four possibilities—two that do not change, AB → $\bar{A}\bar{B}$, $\bar{A}\bar{B}$ → AB, and two that change in the "congruent" direction, that is, that raise the correlation between the attitudes, so that $A\bar{B}$ → AB, $\bar{A}B$ → $\bar{A}\bar{B}$. But, given A as cause and B as effect, there are two additional possibilities, AB → $\bar{A}$B and AB → A$\bar{B}$, which represent possible change in the "incongruent" direction, that is, change that lowers the correlation between attitudes; these possibilities are not mentioned. Let us employ Lazarsfeld's own analogy to illustrate these possible causal relationships; in this analogy, A = consumption of vitamins and B = good health. One can find logical grounds for asserting that vitamin consumption while enjoying good health (AB) can change incongruently to the situation when vitamins may not be consumed but good health continues ($\bar{A}$B). Also, the AB situation can change incongruently to the situation where vitamin consumption continues but good health does not (A$\bar{B}$), especially when the wrong kind of vitamins or too many vitamins are consumed.

Although his illustration could be misleading, his method (Lazarsfeld, 1948) did not overlook the possibilities of incongruent influence. Lazarsfeld wanted to see which variable, party allegiance or attitude toward Willkie, was "cause" and which was "effect" in the 1940 presidential campaign. The two variables correlated highly at the time of the first interview ($r = .53$) and even higher at the time of the second ($r = .67$); data for the study are summarized in Table 1.

In Table 1, we see that Lazarsfeld took account of what he called "divergent" cases, namely, those where $(++) \rightarrow (+-)$ or $(-+)$, and those where $(--) \rightarrow (+-)$ or $(-+)$, which we have termed incongruent cases. Nevertheless, Lipset *et al.* (1954) concentrated only on the response patterns of people who "harmonized" their attitudes between the two interviews, that is, those where $(+-) \rightarrow (++)$ or $(--)$ and those where $(-+) \rightarrow (++)$ or $(--)$. In our terminology, these would be

Table 1

Concurrent Change in Vote Intention and Personal Liking for Willkie

INTERVIEW	SECOND INTERVIEW					TOTAL
		++	+−	−+	−−	
	Republican (+) for Willkie (+)	129	3	1	2	135
First	Republican (+) against Willkie (−)	11	23	0	1	35
interview	Democrat (−) for Willkie (+)	1	0	12	11	24
	Democrat (−) against Willkie (−)	1	1	2	68	72
	Total	142	27	15	82	266

Note.—From Lipset *et al.* (1954, p. 1161). All entries represent the first and second sets of responses from the same Ss; for example, 3 in Row 1. Column 2 represents the same Ss who were Republican (+) for Willkie (+) in the first interview but Republican (+) against Willkie (−) in the second interview.

instances of congruent intrapersonal influence. Having only the 1954 description of the technique before him, a reader could easily be misled to consider only cases of congruent change.

In his 1948 paper, Lazarsfeld described a method of analyzing his data as follows: "A good measure of the relative strength of the two attitudes, then, will be the number of adjustments toward 'vote intention' beyond the expected chance value, plus the excess beyond the expected chance value of losses of adjustment away from 'Willkie opinion' [p. 6]." He offered the following index for the relative strength of two variables:

$$I_{A,B} = \frac{8\left(\dfrac{\Delta_H}{N_H} + \dfrac{\Delta_V}{N_V}\right)}{N}$$

Where, as restated by us, with more concise notation:

$I_{A,B}$ is an index for the relative strength of two variables A and and B, in causal relationship

$$\Delta_H = N_{(-+\to--)}N_{(+-\to++)} - N_{(-+\to++)}N_{(+-\to--)}$$

or net change toward congruence, where the first variable is the cause

$$N_H = N_{(-+\to--)} + N_{(+-\to++)} + N_{(-+\to++)} + N_{(+-\to--)}$$

or the sum of the four Ns in the Δ_H elements

$$\Delta_V = -\left[N_{(--\to+-)}N_{(++\to-+)} - N_{(--\to-+)}N_{(++\to+-)}\right]$$

or negative amount of net change toward incongruence where the second variable is the cause

$$N_V = N_{(--\to+-)} + N_{(++\to-+)} + N_{(--\to-+)} + N_{(++\to+-)}$$

or the sum of the four Ns in the Δ_V elements,

$$N = \text{total cases in study}$$

As Lazarsfeld (1948) explained this method:

In the ideal case, $\dfrac{\Delta_H}{N_H}$ and $\dfrac{\Delta_V}{N_V}$ will have the same sign: they will both be positive if the first variable (in the present example "vote intention") is stronger, and both negative if the second variable (in the present example "Willkie opinion") is stronger. Their relative magnitude will depend on the comparative frequency of adjustment and maladjustment cases, that is, on whether the correlation between the two variables has been increasing or decreasing in the interval between the two interviews [pp. 6–7].

Unfortunately, the 1954 publication merely stated that "The details of this index will be omitted here; suffice it to say that the index takes into account the stability of each variable separately and that the more change in one variable is influenced by change in another, the larger the index will be [Lipset *et al.*, 1954, p. 1161]." Lazarsfeld's method takes into account both "adjustment," or congruent, cases (Δ_H), and "nonadjustment," or incongruent, cases (Δ_V).

In an appendix by William L. Robinson, Lazarsfeld (1948, p. vi) presented a significance test which requires computation of the variance of Δ/N and the mean deviation of $I_{A,B}$. Chi-square appears to offer greater power and to be simpler to compute and interpret. Applying chi-square tests to Lazarsfeld's data in Table 1 shows that party allegiance caused "Willkie opinion" to change; that is,

$$27 > 4$$

or

$$N_{(+ + \rightarrow + -)} + N_{(+ - \rightarrow + +)} + N_{(- + \rightarrow - -)} + N_{(- - \rightarrow - +)} > N_{(+ + \rightarrow - +)}$$
$$+ N_{(+ - \rightarrow - -)} + N_{(- + \rightarrow + +)} + N_{(- - \rightarrow + -)}$$
$$(\chi^2 = 15.6, \quad p < .0001)$$

Furthermore, party allegiance caused "Willkie opinion" to change toward congruity; that is,

$$22 > 2$$

or

$$N_{(+ - \rightarrow + +)} + N_{(- + \rightarrow - -)} > N_{(+ - \rightarrow - -)} + N_{(- + \rightarrow + +)}$$
$$(\chi^2 = 15.04, \quad p < .0001)$$

Finally, party allegiance did not cause "Willkie opinion" to change significantly toward incongruity; that is,

$$5 > 2$$
$$N_{(+ + \rightarrow + -)} + N_{(- - \rightarrow - +)} > N_{(+ + \rightarrow - +)} + N_{(- - \rightarrow + -)}$$
$$(\chi^2 = .57, \quad p, \quad \text{nonsignificant})$$

Despite its ingenuity, the 16-fold table technique has limitations. First, it is applicable only to dichotomous variables. Second, it has no readily understood metric, such as the value of *r*. And, as Campbell (1963) has pointed out, "regression becomes a plausible rival hypothesis when the item marginals are extreme and differ for the two variables [p. 241]."

CAMPBELL'S CROSS-LAGGED PANEL CORRELATION TECHNIQUE

In an attempt to extend Lazarsfeld's reasoning to continuous data, Campbell (Campbell and Stanley, 1963) offered the "cross-lagged panel correlation technique." The method was later discussed in greater detail by Campbell (1963) and has been noted by Blalock (1964, pp. 191–192), Pelz and Andrews (1964), and McGuire (1967).

Campbell (1963) argued that cross-lagged series can differentiate between opposing interpretations of the causal relationship between two variables:

> Where two data series correlate, . . . the direction of causation may be equivocal. . . . In such a situation, $r_{C_n E_{n+1}}$ should be greater than $r_{C_{n+1} E_n}$, where C stands for cause, E for effect. These cross-lagged series correlations can frequently differentiate the relative plausibilities of competing causal interpretations. When both variables are on both sides of the comparison, i.e., when relative correlation magnitude is used rather than the absolute level of $r_{C_n E_n}$, secular trends of long-term cycles are controlled. . . . Our criterion becomes $r_{C_1 E_2} > r_{C_2 E_1}$ [pp. 235–236].

Campbell cited the following illustrative question: "Does lack of parental love cause children to be behavior problems, or does a difficult child cause parents to love less [p. 236]?" In Yee's (1966) data, the comparable question is: Do unsympathetic and unfavorable attitudes of the teacher toward pupils cause her pupils to develop a dislike for their teacher, or do hostile, aggressive pupils cause the teacher to develop unfavorable and unsympathetic attitudes toward pupils?

Using the cross-lagged technique, one would infer that pupils' attitudes P tend to influence teachers' attitudes T if $r_{P_1 T_2} > r_{T_1 P_2}$. One would infer that teachers' attitudes influence pupil attitude if $r_{T_1 P_2} > r_{T_2 P_1}$. But these two inferences are not the only possible ones. The first finding could result not only from greater pupil influence toward raising the correlation between teachers' and pupils' attitudes (which we term influence toward *congruity*), but also from greater teacher influence toward *incongruity* (i.e., toward lowering the correlation between teachers' and pupils' attitudes). In that event, teachers' influence may be greater than pupils' but in an incongruent direction. But it is impossible to ascertain this possibility from the cross-lagged r's because the latter confound, or prevent us from distinguishing between, the source and direction of influence of the two correlated variables.

This unexpected problem in the use of the cross-lagged technique was also found independently by Rozelle (1965), who noted that there were *four* competing hypotheses, namely, A increases B, B increases A, A decreases B, and B decreases A. Later, Rozelle and Campbell (1966) concluded that "The apparent power of the technique is now seen as much less than in previous estimates, even though under some conditions the confounded pair can be separately examined [p. 12]."

FREQUENCY-OF-SHIFT-ACROSS-MEDIAN (FSM) TECHNIQUE

Prior to our study of Lazarsfeld's 16-fold table technique, we developed one of our own that turned out to be highly similar, except that it entailed trichotomizing rather than dichotomizing each variable. The trichotomies consist of scores (*a*) above the median, (*b*) at the median, and (*c*) below the median. The matrix shown in Figure 1 provides for all possible types of shifts in paired trichotomous measures from pre- to posttest. This matrix forms the basis for what we termed the frequency-of-shift-across-median technique. In applying this technique, we determined the frequencies of teacher-class pairs that shifted between first and second testings in the various ways shown in Figure 1. Such shifts could be interpreted as (*a*) raising or lowering (i.e., shifting toward congruity or incongruity, respectively) the correlation between teachers' and pupils' attitudes, and (*b*) indicating whether the teacher or the pupils exerted the influence toward change. Table 2 presents interpretations of the 81 possible shifts between pre- and posttest.

As is shown in Table 2, the source of influence operating in each of the 81 resolutions was judged to be the teacher (T) or the pupils (P) on the basis of which participant in social interaction changed less in relation to the pre- and posttest medians. For example, if the teacher remained stable and pupils changed from below-the-pupils'-median to above-the-pupils'-median, then teachers' influence would be considered the cause of pupils' change. Cells in which it could not be determined whether teachers' or pupils' influence was operating were considered "uncertain"; such a case would be one where both teachers and pupils remained in the H-H cell on both testing occasions.

Table 2 also indicates whether the teachers' and pupils' attitudes shift toward congruent (C) or incongruent (I) states. If a cell showed teachers and pupils moving to or remaining in resolutions where their attitudes were similar (both above or both below the median), then that cell was considered "congruent." If a cell showed teachers' and pupils' attitudes moving to or remaining in resolutions where their attitudes were dissimilar (one

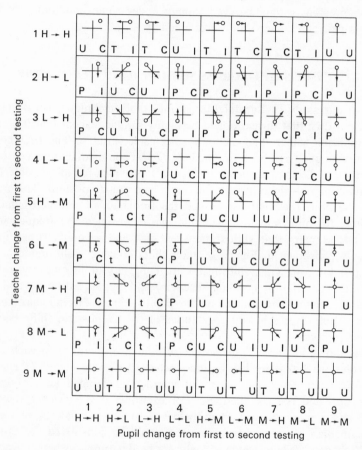

FIGURE 1 *Possible resolutions and nature of influence in the relationship of teachers' and pupils' attitudes. (Arrows both in the margins and in the cells denote direction of change in relationship to the medians of teachers' and pupils' measures; lack of arrow denotes no change. H = above median; L = below median; M = on median; T = teacher is dominant influence; P = pupils are dominant influence; U = uncertain influence; t = teacher causes pupils to change more than pupils cause teacher to change; p = pupils cause teacher to change more than teacher causes pupils to change; C = continuation in or change toward state of congruity; and I = continuation in or change toward state of incongruity. Whether cells in Row 9 and Column 9 are states of congruity or incongruity cannot be determined.)*

Table 2

Nature of Influence in 81 Possible Resolutions in the Cause-Effect Relationship of Teachers' and Pupils' Attitudes

CATEGORY TYPE	NATURE OF INFLUENCE	CELLS[a]
TC	Teacher influence to increase correlation (Teacher stays high, pupils move higher. Teacher stays low, pupils move lower.)	1.3, 1.6, 1.7, 4.2, 4.5 4.8, 5.2, 6.3, 7.3, 8.2
TI	Teacher influence to lower correlation (Teacher stays high, pupils move lower. Teacher stays low, pupils move higher.)	1.2, 1.5, 1.8, 4.3, 4.6 4.7, 5.3, 6.2, 7.2, 8.3
PC	Pupil influence to increase correlation (Pupils stay high, teacher moves higher. Pupils stay low, teacher moves lower.)	2.4, 2.5, 2.8, 3.1, 3.6 3.7, 5.4, 6.1, 7.1, 8.4
PI	Pupil influence to lower correlation (Pupils stay high, teacher moves lower. Pupils stay low, teacher moves higher.)	2.1, 2.6, 2.7, 3.4, 3.5 3.8, 5.1, 6.4, 7.4, 8.1
UC	Uncertain influence, no change from pretest to posttest; teacher and pupils continue in state of congruity. Uncertain influence, teacher and pupils change in same direction, that is, staying in state of congruity.	1.1, 4.4 2.2, 3.3, 5.5, 5.8, 6.6 6.7, 7.6, 7.7, 8.5, 8.8
UI	Uncertain influence, no change from pretest to posttest; teacher and pupils continue in state of congruity. Uncertain influence, teacher and pupils change in opposite directions, that is, staying in state of incongruity.	1.4, 4.1 2.3, 3.2, 5.6, 5.7, 6.5 6.8, 7.5, 7.8, 8.6, 8.7
TU	Uncertain teacher influence causing pupils to change.	9.2, 9.3, 9.5, 9.6, 9.7, 9.8
PU	Uncertain pupil influence causing teacher to change.	2.9, 3.9, 5.9, 6.9, 7.9, 8.9
UU	Uncertain influence, no change from pretest to posttest; teacher and pupils continue in uncertain state.	1.9, 4.9, 9.1, 9.4, 9.9

[a] Cell designations from Figure 1: first numbers represent teachers' row and second numbers represent pupils' column.

above and the other below the median), then that cell was considered "incongruent." Whether some teacher-class pairs, such as those falling exactly on pre- and posttest medians (Row 9 and Column 9), shifted in congruent or incongruent directions could not be determined; these were judged "uncertain."

To summarize, the 9×9 table of 81 possible resolutions is based on the relationships of the teachers' and pupils' pre- and posttest attitudes to their medians, and two logical interpretations are made for each resolution: (a) whether it is caused by the teacher, the pupils, or an uncertain influence, and (b) whether it leads to a state of congruity, incongruity, or an uncertain attitude adjustment. Frequencies in each cell of the 9×9 table are tabulated and then summarized in the 3×3 schema shown in Table 3.[2]

The following hypotheses refer to the frequencies of teacher-class pairs reflecting the various sources and directions of influence indicated in Table 3.

H_1: Teacher-class pairs showing teacher influence toward either congruity or incongruity are more frequent than those showing pupil influence toward either congruity or incongruity. That is,

Teacher Influence (TC + TI + TU)
> Pupil Influence (PC + PI + PU)

H_2: Teacher-class pairs showing teacher influence toward congruity are more frequent than those showing pupil influence toward congruity. That is,

Teacher Influence toward Congruity (TC)
> Pupil Influence toward Congruity (PC)

H_3: Teacher-class pairs showing teacher influence toward incongruity are more frequent than those showing pupil influence toward incongruity.

Table 3

Schema for Summarizing Frequencies in Table 2

	DIRECTION OF INFLUENCE		
SOURCE OF INFLUENCE	CONGRUITY	INCONGRUITY	UNCERTAIN
Teacher	TC	TI	TU
Pupil	PC	PI	PU
Uncertain	UC	UI	UU

[2] Descriptions and listings of the Fortran programs (CDC 1604 computer) for the FSM and FCP techniques may be obtained by request from the first author. H. Albert Napier, William Geeslin, and Leslie Shroyer provided programming and data-processing assistance.

That is,

Teacher Influence toward Incongruity (TI)
> Pupil Influence toward Incongruity (PI)

These hypotheses can be tested with chi-square, adjusted with Yates' correction for continuity, one-tailed with $df = 1$ (Guilford, 1965, pp. 228–230, 237–239).

FREQUENCY-OF-CHANGE-IN-PRODUCT-MOMENT (FCP) TECHNIQUE

In depending on shifts in relation to the medians, the FSM technique requires disregarding the many cases (about 60% in the present study) that do not change in relation to the medians from pre- to posttest. The frequency-of-change-in-product-moment (FCP) technique was developed in part to overcome this problem. It entails putting every teacher-class unit into one of the four categories of influence—TC, TI, PC, or PI—by the following procedure:

1. Convert the raw scores for teachers' and pupils' pre- and posttest attitudes to standard scores on the basis of their respective means and standard deviations. That is, determine $z = (x - \bar{x})/s$ for every score.

2. For each class, ascertain whether the cross-product of its posttest z scores is more positive or negative than the cross-product of its pretest z scores. If the cross-product of posttest z's, $z_{T_2}z_{P_2}$, is algebraically greater than $z_{T_1}z_{P_1}$, the direction of change is considered to be congruent; that is, the interaction between the teacher and her class makes the overall correlation more positive. If the cross-product of posttest z's is algebraically lower than that of pretest z's, the direction of change is considered to be incongruent; that is, the interaction between the teacher and her class makes the overall correlation more negative. This manner of assessing direction of influence is, of course, based on the defining formula for the product-moment correlation coefficient:

$$r = \frac{\Sigma z_x z_y}{N - 1}$$

In short,

If $z_{T_1}z_{P_1} < z_{T_2}z_{P_2}$, classify as an instance of congruent change.

If $z_{T_1}z_{P_1} > z_{T_2}z_{P_2}$, classify as an instance of incongruent change.

3. For each class, examine the cross-lagged z products, $z_{T_1}z_{P_2}$, and $z_{P_1}z_{T_2}$. When direction of change is congruent, the variable whose pre-

measure is part of the more positive product is considered to be the source of the influence. When direction of influence is incongruent, the variable whose premeasure is part of the more negative product is considered to be the source of the influence. That is,

If change is toward congruency, and

if $z_{T_1}z_{P_2} > z_{T_2}z_{P_1}$, then T is source of influence;

if $z_{T_1}z_{P_2} < z_{T_2}z_{P_1}$, then P is source of influence.

If change is toward incongruency, and

if $z_{T_1}z_{P_2} > z_{T_2}z_{P_1}$, then P is source of influence;

if $z_{T_1}z_{P_2} < z_{T_2}z_{P_1}$, then T is source of influence.

RESULTS

Table 4 presents the results obtained with the cross-lagged, FSM, and FCP techniques. Findings with the 16-fold table technique will be discussed with results from the FSM technique.

Results with the Cross-Lagged Panel Correlation Technique

All three pairs of cross-lagged r's indicated greater pupil influence than teacher influence; that is, $r_{P_1 T_2} > r_{T_1 P_2}$. The greatest difference between cross-lagged r's occurred in the subgroup with lower-class pupils. Although none of the differences was statistically significant, according to the formula developed by Olkin (1967), the predominant source of causal influence, judged on the basis of the cross-lagged technique, was the pupils.

But the question now arises: Did pupil attitude influence teacher attitude in the congruent direction? Or did teacher attitude influence pupil attitude in the incongruent direction?

According to Campbell's earlier view (1963, pp. 239–240), if r's between teachers' and pupils' second measures ($r_{T_2 P_2}$) are higher than those between the first measures ($r_{T_1 P_1}$), then it may be inferred that there is some causal connection of unspecified direction. Thus, a partial answer may be found in the following same-occasion correlations: for the total sample, $r_{T_1 P_1} = .19$, $r_{T_2 P_2} = .17$; for the lower-class subsample, $r_{T_1 P_1} = .23$, $r_{T_2 P_2} = .21$; and for the middle-class subsample, $r_{T_1 P_1} = .04$, $r_{T_2 P_2} = .05$. Thus, the same-occasion r's did not increase from pre- to posttest.

Table 4

Summary of Results from the Three Techniques

TEACHER-CLASS GROUP		TOTAL $n = 212$ LOWER CLASS $n = 110$ MIDDLE CLASS $n = 102$		
	T_1T_2	.79	.76	.80
	P_1P_2	.69	.62	.71
r's	T_1P_1	.19	.23	.04
	T_2P_2	.17	.21	.05
	T_1P_2	.10	.08	.02
	P_1T_2	.20	.25	.06
	TC	29	12	8
	TI	22	16	14
Frequency-of-shift-across- median frequencies[a]	PC	27	8	12
	PI	20	5	6
	UC	66	40	29
	UI	48	29	33
	H_1	.09	4.78*	.23
Chi-squares[b]	H_2	.02	.45	.45
	H_3	.02	4.76*	2.45
	TC	56	33	28
Frequency-of-change in-product- moment frequencies	TI	65	38	25
	PC	45	21	24
	PI	46	18	25
	H_1	3.97*	8.74*	.09
Chi-squares	H_2	.99	2.24	.17
	H_3	2.92*	6.45*	.02

[a] No cases found for TU, PU, or UU.
[b] H_1: (TC + TI) > (PC + PI); H_2: TC > PC; H_3: TI > PI.
* $p < .05$.

Hence, the possibility arises that pupil influence causing congruent teacher change is weaker than the alternative of teacher influence causing incongruent pupil change.

We are assuming from past evidence that the interaction of teachers and pupils in hundreds of classroom encounters significantly influences their attitudes. Such interaction can either raise or lower the correlation between the teachers' and pupils' attitude measures. And the results of applying the cross-lagged technique are inadequate to portray such possibilities.

Results with the Frequency-of-Shift-across-Median Technique

In Table 4, we see that the test of H_1 with the FSM technique yielded significant results favoring teacher influence in the lower-class subsample ($\chi^2 = 4.78$, $p < .02$). The difference between the results on H_1 for the lower-class and middle-class subsamples is striking. For the lower-class pupils, the frequencies for (TC + TI) and (PC + PI) are 28 and 13, respectively; for the middle-class pupils, they are 22 and 18.

The results for H_2 and H_3 show that the teachers' significant influence on lower-class pupils is in the direction of incongruence; that is, for H_3, TI $>$ PI, or $16 > 5$ ($\chi^2 = 4.76$, $p < .02$). When it is recalled that the largest difference between cross-lagged r's shown in Table 4 was that for the lower-class subgroup, where $r_{P_1 T_2} > r_{T_1 P_2}$, or $.25 > .08$, it is evident that the FSM results indicate the *source* as well as the *direction* of influence for those teacher-class pairs that shift position in relation to the median attitude.

The FSM technique is very similar to Lazarsfeld's 16-fold table technique. If one compares the 16-fold table (Table 1) with the 81-cell table of the FSM method (Figure 1), it can be seen that the 16 cells in the upper-left corner of Figure 1 resemble those of the 16-fold table. Since most of the FSM frequencies were found in these 16 cells and few were tabulated in the other 65 cells in Figure 1, results of the two techniques should be equivalent.

Results with the 16-Fold Table Technique

When the 16-fold table technique is applied to the illustrative problem

$$\Delta c, \text{ or change toward congruity} = N_a N_b - N_c N_d$$

Where,

N_a = number of classes where teachers exert congruent influence, or TC, and pupils shift from + to −

N_b = number of classes where teachers exert congruent influence, or TC, and pupils shift from − to +

N_c = number of classes where pupils exert congruent influence, or PC, and teachers shift from + to −

N_d = number of classes where pupils exert congruent influence, or PC, and teachers shift from − to +

$$\Delta_I \text{ or change toward incongruity} = -[N_e N_f - N_g N_h]$$

Where,

N_e = number of classes where pupils exert incongruent influence, or PI, and teachers shift from + to −

N_f = number of classes where pupils exert incongruent influence, or PI, and teachers shift from − to +

N_g = number of classes where teachers exert incongruent influence, or TI, and pupils shift from + to −

N_h = number of classes where teachers exert incongruent influence, or TI, and pupils shift from − to +

In the subgroup with lower-class pupils, the frequencies are:

$$N_a = 6, N_b = 6, N_c = 4, N_d = 4, N_e = 2, N_f = 3, N_g = 9, N_h = 7$$

$$\Delta_C = (6)(6) - (4)(4) = 20$$

$$\Delta_I = -[(2)(3) - (9)(7)] = 57$$

Both Δ_C and Δ_I show teachers' influence to be stronger, especially in Δ_I. This finding accords with the FSM and FCP results given in Table 4.

Results from the Frequency-of-Change-in-Product-Moment Technique

Frequencies from the FCP technique for all three hypotheses, as shown in Table 4, indicate that teacher influence occurred more often than pupil influence. Significant chi-square results support H_1 and H_3 for the total group and the lower-class subgroup, but not for the middle-class group. The results for the middle-class subgroup are consistent with those obtained by the cross-lagged method, inasmuch as the near-zero r's for this subgroup could have resulted from the finding that influences of opposite direction and source were approximately equal in frequency. Also consistent are the FSM results showing statistically insignificant differences between competing frequencies.

Although the H_2 results for the total group and lower-class subgroup are not significant, the frequencies for TC are greater than those for PC. The significant H_1 results for the lower-class subgroup ($\chi^2 = 8.74$, $p < .001$) reflect the combined effect of greater teacher-congruent frequencies in H_2 and the strikingly greater teacher-incongruent frequencies in H_3 (TI $= 38$, PI $= 18$, $\chi^2 = 6.45$, $p < .01$). But all the results for the middle-class subgroup are nonsignificant. Similar results were obtained from the FSM technique, and both sets of results are consistent with those obtained with the cross-lagged technique for the lower-class subgroup. Significant H_1 and H_3 results for the total sample reflect the combination of both subgroups' frequencies. Refer to Yee (1968) for greater discussion of FCP results.

DISCUSSION

First, some interpretation of incongruent teacher influence of the kind revealed in these data should be attempted. Such influence means that teachers with relatively high initial MTAI scores tended to make their pupils have less favorable attitudes later in the school year, and vice versa. Perhaps high MTAI-scoring teachers tried to substitute "warmth" for instructional effectiveness, and their pupils eventually resented their ineffectiveness, while the opposite trends occurred in the classes of low MTAI-scoring teachers. But, of course, additional data on other variables would be needed to test this interpretation.

At any rate, the results obtained with the cross-lagged technique support the contention of Rozelle and Campbell (1966) that analyses of causal influence in panel data must consider incongruent as well as congruent outcomes. While results with the cross-lagged panel correlation technique are equivocal, the 16-fold table, FSM, and FCP techniques appear to be consistent in the objective estimates of source and direction of influence which they yield.

The FSM technique resembles the 16-fold table technique, for the majority of frequencies found by both methods in the illustrative problem were tabulated and interpreted similarly. By providing for the consideration of more types of shift, however, the FSM technique offers the potential advantage of handling a wider range of outcomes than is possible with the 16-fold table technique. The FSM method relies upon those cases that shift relative to the arbitrary criterion of the median; its results indicate causal source and direction for the cases that shift most.

The FCP method, in using all cases, has an advantage over the FSM method; in being applicable to continuous data, it has an advantage over both the FSM and 16-fold table methods; and in revealing both source and direction of influence it has an advantage over the cross-lagged panel correlation method. Analyses of other panel data, in which measures of two correlated variables are obtained on two or more occasions, should be made to explore the utility of the FCP method in testing causal hypotheses. Pending further experience with and analysis of this technique, the authors recommend its use in preference to the others.

REFERENCES

Alker, H. R., Jr. Causal inference and political analysis. In J. Bernel (Ed.), *Mathematical applications in political science, II*. Dallas, Texas: The Arnold Foundation, Southern Methodist University, 1966.

Andrews, J. D. W. The achievement motive and advancement in two types of organizations. *Journal of Personality and Social Psychology*, 1967, *6*, 163–168.

Beck, W. H. Pupils' perceptions of teacher merit: A factor analysis of five hypothesized dimensions. Unpublished doctoral dissertation, Stanford University, 1964.

Bell, R. Q. A reinterpretation of the direction of effects in studies of socialization. *Psychological Review*, 1968, *75*, 81–95.

Blalock, H. M., Jr. *Causal inferences in nonexperimental research*. Chapel Hill: University of North Carolina Press, 1964.

Campbell, D. T. From description to experimentation: Interpreting trends as quasi-experiments. In C. W. Harris (Ed.), *Problems in measuring change*. Madison: University of Wisconsin Press, 1963.

Campbell, D. T., and J. C. Stanley. Experimental and quasi-experimental designs for research on teaching. In N. L. Gage (Ed.), *Handbook of research on teaching*. Chicago: Rand McNally, 1963. (Also published as a separate: *Experimental and quasi-experimental designs for research*. Chicago: Rand McNally, 1966.)

Della Piana, G. M., and N. L. Gage. Pupils' values and the validity of the Minnesota Teacher Attitude Inventory. *Journal of Educational Psychology*, 1955, *45*, 167–178.

Faris, R. E. L. The discipline of sociology. In R. E. L. Faris (Ed.), *Handbook of modern sociology*. Chicago: Rand McNally, 1964.

Flanders, N. A. *Teacher influence, pupil attitudes, and achievement*. Document No. OE-25040, 1965, Washington, D.C.: United States Government Printing Office.

Gerard, H. B. and N. Miller. Group dynamics. *Annual review of psychology,* 1967, *18,* 287–332.

Guilford, J. P. *Fundamental statistics in psychology and education.* (4th ed.) New York: McGraw-Hill, 1965.

Horst, P. A. A generalized expression of the reliability of measures. *Psychometrika,* 1949, *14,* 21–32.

Krech, D., R. S. Crutchfield, and E. L. Ballachey. *Individual in society.* New York: McGraw-Hill, 1962.

Lazarsfeld, P. F. Mutual effects of statistical variables. New York: Columbia University, Bureau of Applied Social Research, 1948. (Mimeo)

Lerner, D. (Ed.) *Cause and effect.* New York: Free Press, 1965.

Lipset, S. M., P. F. Lazarsfeld, A. H. Barton, and J. Linz. The psychology of voting: An analysis of political behavior. In G. Lindzey (Ed.), *Handbook of social psychology.* Vol. 2. Cambridge, Mass.: Addison-Wesley, 1954.

McGuire, W. J. Some impending reorientations in social psychology: Some thoughts provoked by Kenneth Ring. *Journal of Experimental Social Psychology,* 1967, *3,* 124–139.

Nagel, E. Types of causal explanation in science. In D. Lerner (Ed.), *Cause and effect.* New York: Free Press, 1965.

Olkin, I. Correlations revisited. In J. C. Stanley (Ed.), *Improving experimental design and statistical analysis.* Chicago: Rand McNally, 1967.

Pelz, D. C., and F. M. Andrews. Detecting causal priorities in panel study data. *American Sociological Review,* 1964, *29,* 836–848.

Rozelle, R. M. An exploration of two quasi-experimental designs: The cross-lagged panel correlation and the multiple time series. Unpublished master's thesis, Northwestern University, 1965.

Rozelle, R. M., and D. T. Campbell. More plausible rival hypotheses in the cross-lagged panel correlation technique. Evanston: Northwestern University, Department of Psychology, 1966. (Mimeo)

Runkel, P. J. Appendix Q: An index of influence by one individual on another for multiple-item, nonhomogeneous instruments. In J. T. Hastings, P. J. Runkel, and D. E. Damrin, *Effects on use of tests by teachers trained in a summer institute.* Vol. 2. Cooperative Research Project No. 702, 1961, University of Illinois, Urbana, United States Department of Health, Education and Welfare, Office of Education.

Ryans, D. G. Assessment of teacher behavior and instruction. *Review of Educational Research,* 1963, *33,* 415–441.

Simon, H. A. *Models of man: Social and rational.* New York: Wiley, 1957.

Withall, J., and W. W. Lewis. Social interaction in the classroom. In N. L. Gage (Ed.), *Handbook of research on teaching.* Chicago: Rand McNally, 1963.

Yee, A. H. *Factors involved in determining the relationship between teachers' and pupils' attitudes.* Cooperative Research Project No. 5-8346, 1966,

University of Texas, Contract OE-6-10-077, United States Department of Health, Education and Welfare, Office of Education.

Yee, A. H. The source and direction of causal influence in teacher-pupil relationships. *Journal of Educational Psychology*, 1968, *59*, in press.

Zeisel, H. *Say it with figures.* (Rev. ed.) New York: Harper, 1957.

Index